WAITING FOR WOLVES IN JAPAN

WAITING FOR WOLVES IN JAPAN

An Anthropological Study of People–Wildlife Relations

JOHN KNIGHT

University of Hawai'i Press

Honolulu

© 2006 University of Hawai'i Press
All rights reserved
Originally published in hardcover by Oxford University Press Inc., New York, in 2003

Printed in the United States of America

11 10 09 08 07 06   6 5 4 3 2 1

Library of Congress Cataloging-in-Publication Data

Knight, John, 1960-
    Waiting for wolves in Japan : an anthropological study of people–wildlife relations /
John Knight.
        p. cm.
    Originally published: Oxford : New York : Oxford University Press, 2003.

    ISBN-13: 978-0-8248-3096-0 (pbk. : alk. paper)
    ISBN-10: 0-8248-3096-2 (pbk. : alk. paper)

    1. Human-animal relationships—Japan. 2. Wolves—Japan. 3. Wildlife
pests—Control—Japan. 4. Human ecology—Japan. I. Title.
QL85.K65 2006
304.20952—dc22   2006045532

University of Hawai'i Press books are printed on acid-free paper and meet the guidelines
for permanence and durability of the Council on Library Resources.

Printed by Versa Press, Inc.

To Masayo

CONTENTS

ACKNOWLEDGEMENTS

This book is based on long-term ethnographic fieldwork in the mountain villages of the Kii Peninsula. Fieldwork was first carried out in a twenty-six month period between 1987 and 1989, which formed the basis of a doctoral thesis submitted in 1992 to the London School of Economics. This doctoral research was supported by grants from the Japan Foundation and the Economic and Social Research Council (ESRC) in the United Kingdom and was supervised at the LSE by Maurice Bloch and Jonathan Parry. During this stay in Japan I was affiliated to the National Museum of Ethnology in Osaka, where I received support and help from the Museum staff, especially Ishimori Shōzō, Nakamaki Hirochika, Tanabe Shigeharu, and Tanaka Masakazu (now of Kyoto University). Subsequent field research, from 1994 to the present day, on wildlife problems on the Kii Peninsula was made possible by Wadham College, Oxford, the Institute for the Culture of Travel in Tokyo, the International Institute for Asian Studies in Leiden, and Queen's University Belfast.

In preparing this book I have benefited from the assistance, guidance, and advice of many wildlife specialists in Japan. In particular, I am grateful to Hayama Shinichi, Ihobe Hiroshi, Mito Yukihisa, Nakagawa Naofumi, David Sprague, Takahata Yukio, and Watanabe Kunio for various forms of assistance and for the benefit of their primatological expertise; to Mizutani Tomo of the Environment Agency, Higashiyama Shōzō and Torii Harumi of the Nara University of Education, Watanabe Hiroyuki of Kyoto University, and Watanabe Osamu of the Sapporo Nature Research and Interpretation Office for sharing with me their expertise on the issues of bear pestilence and bear conservation; and to Takahashi Shunjō for sharing with me his expertise on the subject of the wild boar. I am also indebted to the Social Science Research Institute of Tokyo University and to the Primate Research Institute of Kyoto University for allowing me to use their libraries. I would like to thank Maruyama Naoki, Kanzaki Nobuo, and Takahashi Masao of the Japan Wolf Association (*Nihon ōkami kyōkai*) and Suzuki Atsuko of Wolf Pals (*Ōkami no nakamatachi*) for sharing with me their views and expertise on the subject of the wolf and for sending me various written materials on the issue of wolf reintroduction. I would also like to thank the following organizations and individuals for permission to reproduce photographs and other illustrations used in this book: Gifu Shinbunsha, Higashi Yoshino Town Hall, Iwate Nippō, the Japan Wolf Association, Miraisha, Shinano Mainichi Shinbunsha, Yama to Keikokusha, Zuisōsha, Azumane Chimao, Kurasawa Nanami, Maita Kazuhiko, Sutō Isao, Tagai Teiichi, Tsujioka Mikio, and Yazawa Takashi. I would especially like to thank Mr. Ryn Oshima for permission to reproduce the woodblock illustration that appears on the front cover of this book.

Assistance with fieldwork and research materials has been received from many quarters. A special debt of gratitude is owed to Tanigami Kazusada of the newspaper *Kii Minpō* for his assistance in field research and for the many stimulating conversations about wildlife issues we have had. Thanks are due to the staff of Wakayama Prefecture Offices and, especially, the staff of Hongū Town Hall for their advice and assistance over many years. I would like to thank Fuchi Hiromi, Hine Tomoko, Kurisu Chie, Matsuhata Michiyo, Matsumoto Miyako, Kumiko Mitchell, Nakamura Takao, Sakamoto Sachiho, Sakamoto Takako, Umeda Yoshimi, and Watanabe Atsuko for help in transcribing taped interviews from fieldwork. I am especially grateful to the people of Hongū-chō on the Kii Peninsula for sharing with me their knowledge and views about wildlife and related subjects in the course of my many visits since 1987. I would like to express my thanks to Hane Masajiro, Hine Kiichi, Ishiyama Haruhisa, Matsumoto Tadami, Nishide Tachie, Nishide Toshikazu, Sugiyama Eiichi, Suzuki Arahiko, and Tachimura Takamitsu for their assistance, encouragement, and friendship in the course of my many visits to the Kii Peninsula. I would like to express my deepest gratitude to Kurisu Hiromasa and his family for their support and friendship. I owe a special debt of gratitude to the late Suzuki Suehiro for his assistance, advice, and above all friendship over the years. Finally, I owe a special thanks to my wife, Masayo Ōya, for her help and support in the course of completing this book.

The writing of this book began while I was employed by the International Institute for Asian Studies in Leiden, and was completed at the School of Anthropological Studies, Queen's University Belfast. I would like to express my appreciation to colleagues and staff at both institutions. This book has benefited considerably from the constructive and insightful comments of the three readers appointed by Oxford University Press. Needless to say, I remain solely responsible for any deficiencies in the book.

J.K.

LIST OF FIGURES

A NOTE ON THE TEXT

Japanese terms mentioned in the text are italicized. Romanization of Japanese words is in accordance with the modified Hepburn system. Macrons are used for the Japanese long vowels *ō* and *ū*, to distinguish them from the short vowels *o* and *u*, but dispensed with in the case of internationally known Japanese words such as Shinto and place names such as Tokyo and Osaka. Japanese names are generally given in Japanese order, with family name first, except where an English-language publication is cited in which case the family name is given last. Where an individual is referred to a number of times in succession, rather than repeat the full name each time, just the family name is used with the suffix '-san' (the Japanese gender-neutral equivalent to 'Mr', 'Mrs', 'Miss', etc.) in accordance with Japanese convention—for example, Satō-san. The translations from Japanese to English in this book are mine, unless otherwise indicated. I have generally used metric measures when referring to landholdings, as these are widely used in Japan, both by officialdom and by villagers themselves. Thus although Japanese farmers refer variously to *tan* as well as ares (*āru*) as land measures, for convenience I refer only to ares in the text. Ten ares are equal to 0.247 acres or 1,000 square metres.

ABBREVIATIONS

The following abbreviations of newspaper names have been used in references to newspaper articles in this book:

AS	*Asahi Shinbun*
CGS	*Chūgoku Shinbun*
CNS	*Chūnichi Shinbun*
ES	*Ehime Shinbun*
IS	*Ikimono Tsūshin*
KS	*Kahoku Shinpō*
KSY	*Kahoku Shinpō Yūkan*
MS	*Mainichi Shinbun*
MNSC	*Minami Nihon Shinbun Chōkan*
NKS	*Nihon Keizai Shinbun*
NNS	*Nihon Nōgyō Shinbun*
NNSC	*Nishi Nihon Shinbun Chōkan*
SS	*Sankei Shinbun*
SSC	*Shizuoka Shinbun Chōkan*
TS	*Tokushima Shinbun*
TYS	*Tōkyō Yomiuri Shinbun*
YS	*Yomiuri Shinbun*

Introduction

Farmer conflict with wildlife is found throughout the world. Fields of cultivated crops, orchards of fruit trees, and food storehouses are highly attractive feeding grounds for wild animals. A wide range of animals feature in reports on crop-raiding, including wild boar, deer, monkeys, elephants, and kangaroos, as well as birds, rodents, and feral animals. Wildlife pestilence on farmland can take the form of regular low level crop-raiding that is barely noticed (as with birds and rodents) or single visits that devastate the whole crop (as with wild boars and elephants). Although minor damage to crops may be tolerated, when losses account for a significant proportion of the harvest wildlife damage becomes a serious matter, and farmers will take measures to try to stop it. Where it is deemed a threat to agricultural production and an impediment to rural development, wildlife pestilence can become a political issue and an area of state concern and expert interventions ('wildlife control', etc.). The problem is likely to be especially acute among people living adjacent to wildlife populations in remote areas, such as forest-edge cultivators who find themselves highly vulnerable to wildlife depredations. For many remote farmers, the task of crop protection is hardly less important than the work of crop production, and they must exercise a constant vigilance over the threat of animal forays on to their farmland. A variety of measures are employed to prevent or at least mitigate the wildlife threat to crops, including the use of fencing and field-guarding, traps and poisons, sensory repellents, and even charms and prayers.

Wildlife pestilence is a major problem in the remote areas of Japan. Japanese mountain villagers have always had to defend their crops against the wild animals of the forest. Japanese folklore tells of villages besieged by fearsome animals such as giant wild boars that terrorize farmers and threaten the harvest on which the village depends. Regional folk legends tell of heroic village founders who battled to drive out wild animals in the establishment of the settlement. On the outskirts of many a mountain village can be found the crumbling remains of stone walls built centuries earlier to keep wild animals out. In recent decades Japan's wildlife problem has worsened, against the background of widespread habitat deterioration in mountainous areas. Mountain villagers find themselves under increasing pressure from wild animals (often referred to simply as *yotsuashi* or 'four-legs') that enter village space and eat anything they can. Exasperated farmers complain of their *yonjūku* or 'four beast woes': depredations by deer in the morning, by monkeys in the afternoon, by wild boar in the evening, and by bears day and night (Maita 1998*a*: 170). This round-the-clock threat from forest wildlife causes economic loss, generates anxiety among besieged villagers, and (in the case of bears) gives rise to fears about public safety. In addition to cultivating farm crops in the village, mountain villagers cultivate timber tree crops in the expanses of forest surrounding the settlement. But forestry plantations too are subject to large-scale wildlife pestilence, this time in the form of browsing, barkstripping, and antler-rubbing that cause significant economic losses. In Japan foresters, like farmers, see themselves as victims of wildlife pests.

Much of the data that follows about people–wildlife relations in Japan will be familiar from remote rural peripheries elsewhere. Forest-edge cultivators throughout the world find themselves engaged in a daily struggle against intrusive wild animals that try to eat their crops and encroach on human space. An important difference should be noted, however. The context of many reported people–wildlife conflicts in Asia and Africa tends to be one of increasing human population and expanded human land-use at the expense of wildlife habitat (Hill 1997: 77). This common forest-edge zone scenario involves a high rate of local population growth that leads to a territorial encroachment on wildlife space as forest is cleared to become farmland and human settlements. Wildlife forays on human crops can be understood in terms of the consequent squeeze effect on wildlife habitat. In the remote areas of Japan, by contrast, the background to the recent, intensified conflict with wildlife is the contraction, rather than expansion, of the human population. Although wildlife crop raids have always been a concern for mountain villagers, with the onset of the rural exodus in the late 1950s, the character of the wildlife problem changed. Japanese mountain villages are today severely depopulated, as younger villagers migrate to the cities *en masse* to pursue superior employment prospects and career opportunities. Much of Japan's mountainous hinterland now consists of thinly populated villages of elderly people. It is largely because of this diminished human presence within them that Japan's mountain villages are no longer able to resist the pressure of forest wildlife.

Wildlife pestilence attracts much media attention in Japan. The wildlife problem is the source of an endless number of newspaper stories of animal damage, misdemeanours, and audacity or of farmer hardship, fortitude, and ingenuity. Wildlife damage has emerged as an issue in local elections, has been raised in the Japanese parliament, and has even been the cause of litigation in the Japanese courts. In Japan various idioms of conflict drawn from human society are routinely applied to the wildlife problem. A report in the newspaper *Mainichi Shinbun*, for example, described the nation's wildlife problem as the *kemonotachi no hanran* or 'rebellion of the beasts' (*MS* 3 June 1999). In the coming chapters, we shall encounter references to 'wild boar armies', 'monkey armies', monkey 'guerrillas', 'war between Man and deer', 'serow wars', and 'battles' with an animal 'enemy' that wreaks havoc on beleaguered villages, as well as to farmers who mount 'defences' against this wild threat from the forest. The idiom of war appears to express atavistic fears among mountain villagers of being overrun by forest animals, and takes on a special resonance in an age of large-scale human depopulation when villages appear weak and vulnerable. Given the trend in depopulation, which leads to a decline in the number of hunters along with the village population overall, this is a war that the village appears unable to win.

In the 1990s a new answer to Japan's wildlife problem was proposed. In 1993 a Tokyo-based pressure group called the Japan Wolf Association launched a campaign for wolves to be reintroduced to Japan, nearly a century after indigenous wolves had become extinct. The proposal promises a solution to the wildlife problem in the form of the return to the Japanese forest of its foremost natural predator to control the various animal pests. As one leading proponent put it, the reintroduced wolf would become the *kyūseishu* or 'Saviour' of the besieged farmers and foresters of regional Japan (*CNS* 7 Mar. 2000). In an era of rural depopulation, when remote villages are no longer able to control forest animals themselves, wolves could do this for them. At a time when the very future of upland communities is being called into question, wolves promise to make Japan's mountainous zone inhabitable once more.

THE RETURN OF THE WOLF?

Wolves became extinct in Japan at the beginning of the twentieth century. The Japanese archipelago represented the eastern extreme of the historic range of the grey wolf that extended across the northern hemisphere. Two subspecies of grey wolves existed on the Japanese archipelago: the Hondo or Japanese wolf (*Canis lupus hodophylax*) on the main islands of Honshu, Shikoku, and Kyushu, and the Ezo wolf (*Canis lupus hattai*) on the northern island of Hokkaido. The Hondo wolf disappeared in the early years of the twentieth century against the background of rabies and distemper epidemics, while the extinction of the Ezo wolf occurred in the late nineteenth century with the establishment of livestock ranches in Hokkaido and the enactment of a large-scale wolf-poisoning campaign. Although extinct, the legacy of the wolf continues. The Japanese language contains many words that include the Chinese character for wolf 狼, as well as expressions and sayings that refer to the wolf (while the English word 'wolf' has entered the Japanese language, as *urufu*). Japan has a rich body of regional folklore on the wolf, including tales and legends in which people enter into relations of exchange and reciprocity with wolves and wolves appear as benign protectors of people. Wolves even have religious associations in Japan. The wolf is one of the animals associated with the *yama no kami* or 'mountain spirit', a major deity in the Shinto pantheon. Across Japan there are Shinto shrines in which the wolf serves as the *otsukai* or 'messenger' of the *kami*, including a number of large wealthy shrines which issue protective charms bearing the image of the wolf to visitors.

Wolves are also prominent in the popular culture of present-day Japan. There are boxers, sumo wrestlers, and rock stars named after the wolf.[1] Wolves feature widely in the print and electronic media of Japan: in *manga* comics, in computer games, on television, in the cinema, in magazine articles, and in literature. Wolf imagery appears on t-shirts, on posters, on calendars, in magazines, and even on beer cans, while the sound of the howling wolf is available on compact discs in music stores. Although the wolf is not one of the traditional animals of the Oriental zodiac, it does feature in new zodiacs that have become popular among young people, and stands for a particular human personality type (individualistic, solitary, idiosyncratic, etc.).[2] Almost one hundred years after wolf extinction, this sudden ubiquity of wolf motifs, idioms, and images in contemporary Japan leads some commentators to refer to an *ōkami būmu* or 'wolf boom' (*SS* 27 May 1997). One interpretation offered for the 'wolf boom' is that it draws on a deep-seated national nostalgia for a now remote pre-industrial past when the Japanese people coexisted with nature and revered the wolf:

Is not the background to the wolf boom the latent longing that exists in the hearts of we [the Japanese people] who once worshipped the wolf? It expresses an intimacy with creatures to which we have been deeply connected, having lived alongside each other throughout the history of this island nation . . . (Nagaoka 1999: 12)

There is, however, an important international dimension to this renewed Japanese interest in wolves. The wolf ranks alongside the tiger, the elephant, and the whale as one of the foremost 'charismatic' animals of the modern world, as an instantly recognizable environmental symbol, and as an object of international conservationist concern. The Japanese 'wolf boom' can be understood, to a large extent, as part of this wider, international trend. But there is also a specifically American input into late twentieth-century wolf iconography that should be taken into account. In stark contrast to the earlier American antipathy to the wolf, in recent decades wolves have acquired an extraordinary appeal among the American public, becoming the foremost example of 'charismatic megafauna'. This new popularity of the wolf in America has led commentators to refer to an American 'fascination with the wolf' (DeBoer 2000: 98), to 'America's love affair with wolves' (Fischer 1995: 38), and to wolves as 'an object of adoration' among Americans (Grooms 1993: 32). Japan increasingly appears to share this American passion.

---

[1] Chiyonofuji, the champion sumo wrestler in the 1980s, was known as 'Wolf' (English loanword, *Urufu*) to his many fans and to the sports press. The featherweight boxer Tamaki Atsushi is one of the local sporting heroes of the Kii Peninsula (to where he traces his roots) and is known as 'the Kishū Wolf' (*Kishūōkami*) because of his never-say-die fighting spirit. *Love Wolf* (English words) and *Ōkami chihō* ('Wolf Region') are the names of Japanese rock bands.

[2] These new zodiacs are prominent on the internet, featuring on home pages, etc., as well as in magazines and books. Associated with fortune-telling, they offer a statement of one's own personality and are a guide to the personality of others and to their suitability (as a boyfriend/girlfriend or a marriage partner).

Much of the wolf merchandise sold in Japan is imported from America. The images of wolves that adorn the t-shirts and sweaters worn by Japanese youth, that are captured on calendars and posters in Japanese homes and offices, and that appear in the wildlife documentaries shown on Japanese television are typically those of North American wolves. The many books and films that supply much of the popular imagery of the wolf in Japan are of North American origin (*White Fang, Never Cry Wolf, Dances With Wolves*, and so on), while there is even a certain amount of Japanese tourism to the wolf-range regions of America. The wolf reintroduction proposal can be understood against this background.

In its literature, the Japan Wolf Association or *Nihon ōkami kyōkai* (hereafter JWA) presents the objective of wolf reintroduction in the following terms.

SHOULDN'T WE CALL THE WOLF BACK TO THE JAPANESE FOREST?
The wolf, along with the monkey, the hare and other wildlife, is an indispensable part of the forest ecosystem. But it will be nearly one century since the wolf disappeared in Japan. A forest where the wolf cannot be seen is not real nature. There is the daytime forest of birds singing, of deer running around, and of monkeys and bears searching for acorns. Then there is the night-time forest of foxes and raccoon-dogs prowling around—and of wolves howling . . . [The extinction of the wolf] came about because, with the growth of the human population and the development of industry, humanity invaded the territory of nature and did not consider the possibility of coexisting with the wild [environment]. Now, we human beings, as a result of the environmental destruction we ourselves have caused, fear for our own existence. We are now starting to realize that, because human beings and the Earth both depend on the ecosystem, human prosperity can only come about by living our lives as a part of nature. In recent years, there has flourished a movement to protect the nature that remains and to restore those things that have been lost . . . The movement to restore the wolf to the forest is part of this new era and part of the nature conservation movement that is bringing forth this new culture. At the same time as we are protecting many wild animals from extinction, let us also aim to restore the wild animals that have disappeared due to our past mistakes. (JWA 1994: 2)

The JWA argues that the disappearance of the wolf has created an ecological crisis in the Japanese forest. On account of the special place of the wolf in the forest ecosystem, the extinction of the wolf represents not just the loss of a single species, but also a general destabilization of the relations between the remaining animals and plants of the forest. According to the holistic language of ecology, the demise of the wolf ruptured the wider 'ecosystem' of the forest. The extinction of the wolf has come to epitomize the loss of Japan's natural heritage in the modern era and to serve as a grim testament to the excesses of Japanese industrialization in which 'humanity invaded the territory of nature'. The status of wolf extinction as a pivotal event in modern Japanese history is increasingly recognized in the form of magazine articles, books, and television documentaries devoted to the subject. The reintroduction proposal holds out the prospect of a twenty-first-century Japan to which the wolf has been restored and in which the much-discussed goal of *shizen hogo* or 'nature conservation' can be realized. If wolf extinction testified to the destructive consequences of early Japanese modernization, wolf reintroduction signals modern Japan's ability to repair this destruction and correct 'past mistakes'. If wolf extinction was one national turning-point, wolf reintroduction would be another, this time one for the better. Japan's fractured 'forest ecosystem' can be repaired and the Japanese people can learn how to coexist with the wolf.

The JWA proposal envisages grey wolves from Chinese Inner Mongolia being used to establish wolf populations in selected parts of the mountainous interior of Japan. The JWA proposal is a preliminary statement of aims and objectives rather than a detailed plan for implementation, and remains the initiative of a small metropolitan pressure group which has yet to be taken up by the Japanese government. The proposal does not, at present, appear to enjoy much popular support. In the most recent public opinion survey, carried out by the JWA in 1999, only 14 per cent of respondents agreed with the idea of reintroducing wolves to Japan.[3] The JWA's own survey data therefore indicate that most Japanese people see no need to bring wolves back to the archipelago. The JWA argues that this low level of support simply reflects the current lack of awareness of the issues, and that as its campaign develops this will change. It is too early to predict how successful the wolf reintroduction campaign in Japan will prove to be. There are signs that the campaign is gathering momentum. The wolf reintroduction proposal has attracted a great deal of media attention and aroused much public debate in Japan. But even if public support for wolf reintroduction does pick up in the years ahead, a key question concerns the attitudes to it in the remote regions of Japan where the wolf colonies would be established. The proposal's prospects for success will depend on how wolf reintroduction is viewed in these mountainous localities far away from Tokyo and other large urban centres. The JWA argues that, against the background of the wildlife problem, the wolf reintroduction proposal will hold a strong appeal among the residents of these remote regions.

The Japanese wolf reintroduction proposal is inspired by wolf conservation initiatives elsewhere. But wolf conservation initiatives have generated conflicts with local communities in North America, Europe, and other places. Wolf reintroduction in America arouses opposition among ranchers who see wolves as a dangerous threat to their livestock herds. Local opposition to wolf reintroduction in the American West is proclaimed on bumper stickers and baseball caps (Fischer 1991: 35), and opponents liken wolves to convicts, gangsters, shoplifters, child molesters, cockroaches, and deadly diseases such as Aids and cancer (Paystrup 1993: 163–77; Kellert *et al.* 1996: 979). The wolf has even been denounced as 'the Saddam Hussein of the Animal World', with protestors against reintroduced wolves likening themselves to the Kurds and the people of Kuwait (Grooms 1993: 141; Paystrup 1993: 111).

---

[3] Maruyama Naoki, personal communication. The first questionnaire survey was carried out in 1993, and showed 12.5 per cent support for wolf reintroduction (see Kanzaki *et al.* 1995). See also Koganezawa *et al.* (1997).

Hostile attitudes towards wolves are also reported in Norway, especially among old people and people familiar with livestock (Bjerke *et al.* 1998). Antipathy to wolves may well lead to active local defiance of wolf conservation measures and to violence against the wolves themselves. In Minnesota in the 1970s 'people choked Eastern timber wolves to death in snares to show their contempt for the animal's designation as an endangered species' (Lopez 1995: 139), while cattle ranchers in this same state reportedly 'shoot, shovel, and shut up' when they encounter protected wolves (DiSilvestro 1991: 105). There are also reports of Himalayan villagers destroying wolf-cubs (Mishra 1997: 340), of Saami reindeer-herders shooting wolves (Lindquist 2000: 182), and of Italian shepherds poisoning wolves or carrying out wolf-hunts (Meriggi and Lovari 1996: 1561).

In many of these examples, wolf conservation or reintroduction appears as both a threat to local livelihoods and an unwarranted national interference in local affairs. The wolf is deemed to be a danger to the rural livestock economy and to the people who depend on it, while attempts to protect or restore wolves appear as misanthropic outside assaults on the local community. In Norway wolf reintroduction is condemned as an illegitimate attempt by the central state to dominate sheep farmers: 'They know that if they can get farmers to accept and adapt to the wolf, they can get the farmers to accept *anything*!' (in Brox 2000: 391, emphasis in original). It is argued that the reason why the wolf has become such a 'divisive, political symbol' in Norway is because it resonates with 'the "centre–periphery dimension" in the country's history' (Brox 2000: 392). Typically, the charge of hypocrisy is levelled at the national forces that appear to be behind wolf reintroduction, for imposing something on the regions that would be unacceptable in the national centres themselves. This point was clearly made by the state legislature in Montana when it passed a resolution calling for wolves to be introduced to New York City, San Francisco, and Washington DC (Primm and Clark 1996: 1037), as well as at public meetings by anti-wolf protestors calling for wolves to be taken to Pennsylvania, New York, and Chicago (Paystrup 1993: 163)! The politicized identity of the wolf is further evident in the symbolic statements made by anti-wolf protestors in Scandinavia who travel from the regions to display dead wolves in the national capitals (Lindquist 2000: 170; Serpell 1996: 199). Wolf conservationism would appear to be linked with social division and political controversy wherever it is undertaken.

The Japan Wolf Association claims that the Japanese case would be different from these Western examples of socially divisive wolf conservation struggles. The JWA justifies wolf reintroduction in Japan on both idealistic and utilitarian grounds: as protection (through restoration) of the natural heritage of the nation *and* protection of local livelihoods. The new wolves of Japan would not just be *environmental* animals satisfying the demands of metropolitan conservationists; they would also be *functional* animals in the remote regions they enter. In other words, reintroduced wolves in Japan would not only satisfy the idealism of outsiders, but would also serve the interests of rural dwellers themselves. The basis of this claim is that, in contrast to Western societies, there is no major livestock industry in the Japanese regions. Japan does not have the same tradition of mixed farming, in which livestock and agriculture are combined, that existed in Europe, and historically domestic animals have had only a minor place in Japanese farming. In contrast to meat- and dairy-based Western diets, the traditional Japanese diet was grain based and supplemented with fish and vegetables. Consequently, in rural Japan the dominant human–animal relation is not the *positive* livelihood relationship between livestock farmer and domesticated herbivore, but the *negative* livelihood relationship between crop farmer (and forester) and wild herbivore. It follows that in the Japanese regions, in contrast to the American regions, wolf predation would be on the wild animals that tend to harm human livelihoods, and would therefore be in the interests of the local community rather than a threat to them. If among American ranchers the prospect of wolf predation provokes fears about its destructive consequences, among Japanese farmers and foresters it promises relief from wildlife damage to crops and timber.

BENIGN PREDATION

The argument for wolf reintroduction in Japan invokes what biologists and ecologists variously refer to as 'biological control' (Hone 1994: 72–3), and 'regulatory predation' (Newsome 1991). These terms denote the strategic use by human society of predatory relations in the natural world and are based on an underlying ecological model of predator–prey relations. A key tenet of the holistic science that is modern ecology is the idea that the natural world is a system consisting of interconnected parts and that this 'ecosystem' tends towards balance and stability. Predator–prey relations have often served as a favoured illustration of the principle of 'the balance of nature' (Graham 1973: 125; Grooms 1993: 94; Budiansky 1995: 12–13). In the literature of modern ecology, reference is frequently made to 'predator–prey systems', 'predator–prey cycles', 'herbivore–carnivore systems', 'functional responses', 'feedback loops', 'dynamic equilibrium', and so on. The basic idea is that predators moderate, regulate, or control the numbers of prey animals. Such regulatory predation occurs where the rate of predation increases or decreases in response to the population density of prey animals. The tendency of certain prey populations to proliferate is kept in check by the presence of predators that respond to the rise in prey numbers both by increased predation (the so-called 'functional response') and, in time, by increasing in number themselves (the so-called 'numerical response') (Messier 1995). It is argued that the effect of this linkage between predator and prey populations is to generate related cycles of fluctuation that in the long term make for equilibrium and stability. A more modest claim made for wolf predation is that it is a *limiting* factor: that it is a significant source of prey mortality along with other causes of prey mortality (human hunting, disease, starvation, etc.) but that the rate of predation does not vary with prey density and that it falls short of actual regulation (Boutin 1992: 125).

Wild predators are said to affect their prey benignly in another sense. In addition to reducing the excessive *quantity* of wild herbivores, it is sometimes argued that predators improve the *quality* of the remaining population because of the selection effect of their predations. By removing weak, biologically inferior animals, predation is said to have an important 'sanitation effect' on the prey population (Mech 1981: 265). This point is often made in connection with the wolf in North America.

One would expect . . . that in most species of the wolf's prey increased alertness and running speed would be the direct result of millions of years of wolf predation. The defense-formation of the musk-oxen, the size and strength of bison and moose, the fleetness of deer, and the nimbleness and agility of mountain sheep probably developed in this way. (Mech 1981: 267)

Wolves are variously characterized as 'culling', 'pruning', 'trimming', 'cropping', and 'managing' their prey populations (Mech 1966: 169–71; Fox 1980: 128; Milstein 1995: 86; Grooms 1993: 94). Many of these terms convey an image of the wolf as a kind of natural counterpart to the farmer improving his crop or the breeder improving his livestock. On account of its selective character, wolf predation is said to promote the long-term continuity of prey populations: 'wolves can eat, yet their prey populations can themselves survive and produce a crop that wolves can continue to harvest' (Mech 1977: 320). Some commentators even refer to 'prudent predators' (Robinson and Bolen 1989: 156). Other writers go further and suggest that predation is 'merciful' in character, that it is 'a kind of welfare work for the prey', and that the wild predator serves, in effect, as nature's 'welfare officer' (Graham 1973: 137–8).

The larger, ecological significance of the predator–prey relationship has to do with its effect on other trophic levels of the system. Predators at the top of the food chain are said to exercise a major controlling influence over the larger ecosystem, a special status indicated by a variety of terms, including 'top predator', 'top carnivore', 'summit predator', and 'keystone predator' (Terborgh 1988; Mills *et al.* 1993: 220).

A top predator is an animal at the apex of the food chain that connects all organisms in an ecosystem. . . . Top predators perform several functions that are essential to the maintenance of natural systems as we currently enjoy them. Top predators stimulate evolutionary adaptations in prey species, influence to varying degrees the composition and structure of ecosystems, support an interconnected chain of other species and signal the integrity of ecosystems. (Curlee and Clark 1995: 19)

Top predators exercise a 'top-down' control over the other levels of the system in what has been described as a 'trophic cascade' effect (McLaren and Peterson 1994: 1555). The natural ecosystem is often represented as a three-tiered structure

consisting of wild plants, wild herbivores that feed on the plants, and wild carnivores that feed on the herbivores. While the carnivores are directly related to the
herbivores through predation, they are also indirectly related to the plants on
which the herbivores feed. Herbivores that are 'predator limited' do not increase to
the maximum level made possible by the food supply and do not therefore deplete
their resource base (Hairston *et al.* 1960: 424). Wild carnivores contribute to the
regulation of wild herbivory, by keeping the numbers of herbivores below the
carrying capacity of the environment.

This kind of claim has been made for a variety of large predators. Wild cats such
as pumas, jaguars, and ocelots are said to act as 'top predators' which 'hold the key
to ecosystem stability' in neotropical forests by checking the populations of smaller
mammals and thereby protecting plant diversity (Terborgh 1992*a*: 207–11). Lions
and leopards are accorded an important role in depressing the populations of
wild herbivores in Africa, acting in effect as 'wildlife managers' (Schaller 1972:
396–407). Tigers in Asian rainforests are said to depress prey numbers and thereby
act as a 'keystone' species that exerts 'a strong structuring effect on the [wider
natural] community' (Seidensticker and McDougal 1993: 120–1). The lynx in the
Alps is characterized as nature's 'gamekeeper' (Lienert 1998: 132) and an 'ecological
keystone' (Breitenmoser 1998*a*: 136), while the sea otter and the leopard seal are
among the aquatic examples of 'top predators' that keep in check their prey (Estes
et al. 1993: 315–16; Boveng *et al.* 1998). But the animal most often cited in this connection is the wolf. Until recently, the usual example given of such predator–prey
systems was that of Isle Royale in Michigan where the establishment of a population of wolves on the island appeared (in the 1960s and 1970s) to have stabilized the
moose population there. The Isle Royale case study seemed to provide clear evidence of the ability of wolves to control prey numbers and therefore protect the
vegetation on which the prey animals depended (Mech 1981: 273–4). The Isle
Royale wolf came to be represented as 'an animal husbander, tending to maximize
the yield to himself from the basic plant-food base through the moose, and
[thereby have the effect of] stabilizing a large complex of organisms' (Huffaker
1973: 188). The Isle Royale example seemed to support the 'forage limitation
hypothesis' (Peterson *et al.* 1984: 1351), according to which wild carnivores balance
the relationship between the different trophic levels of the ecosystem. '[I]n the
1980s at Isle Royale, the old story that wolves protect a forest from an overabundance of feasting herbivores was borne out' (Peterson 1995: 158).

For many ecologists, this theory of predator containment of prey numbers and
predator regulation of herbivory is supported by evidence of the effects of predator
absence (Hairston *et al.* 1960: 422; Mech 1981: 274–5). There is a long history of
predator elimination in Europe and North America. The strategy of predator
elimination represents the deliberate removal of wild predators in order to increase
the numbers of wild herbivores valued as game animals (as well as the protection of
domesticated herbivores) (Worster 1977: 265–74). The key underlying assumption

of predator control is that predation is additive rather than compensatory: that wild predators interfere with the reproduction and growth of the wild herbivore population (for example, by preying on juveniles) rather than simply killing animals that would die anyway (the old and the sick), and therefore maintain the herbivores at a lower population density than would otherwise be the case (Seip 1992: 338). Ideally, the removal of predators would release prey animals from this constraint and allow them to increase to levels that ensured a plentiful supply of game for human hunters. But the very logic of predator control points to the danger of proliferating prey animals. If the presence of predators keeps down prey numbers, it would seem to follow that the absence of predators could allow prey animals to proliferate. Where hunting (human predation) occurs at a level able to offset the lack of wild predation, the prey population will remain in check. But where the pressure of human hunting falls short of this, prey animals can potentially increase to the point where they exhaust the vegetation on which they depend, leading to an eventual population crash among these animals. One of the best-known examples of this occurred at the Kaibab Plateau in Arizona where in the early part of the twentieth century wolves were exterminated and the numbers of other wild predators greatly reduced, after which the deer population proliferated to excessive levels, destroyed the food supply, and suffered a major die-off (Clapham 1973: 71).

The opposite human intervention to predator elimination is that of predator addition: the former removes predators in order to boost the numbers of prey animals deemed to be valuable, the latter encourages or reintroduces wild predators in order to contain the numbers of prey animals deemed to be harmful. In America wolf reintroduction advocates argue that 'the wolf will act as the much needed natural regulator of the out-of-control ungulate populations' (in Paystrup 1993: 64). In the Yellowstone National Park debate, wolves have been proclaimed a 'keystone species' that is necessary to contain the numbers of elk and thereby stop the destructive overgrazing caused by these animals (Leopold 1998: 41). These are the words of one of the project leaders of the Yellowstone wolf reintroduction initiative: 'We anticipate that the wolf in Yellowstone will be a keystone predator possessing impressive abilities to reshape ungulate populations, with considerable direct and indirect influences that will ripple through the ecosystem' (Phillips 1996a: 118). Arguments for wolf restoration in the eastern United States also invoke the wolf's potential for controlling the large numbers of deer that have become serious pests in many areas (Mech 2001: 21). Wolf reintroduction in America has also been justified as a form of rodent control (Bourne 1995: 15), as has wolf conservation in Spain (Rodriguez de la Fuente 1975: 108). Another claimed regulatory effect for wolves is the control of other predators. Proponents of wolf reintroduction in North America suggest that wolves would keep in check coyotes and thereby reduce one of the main predatory threats to livestock, and in this way offset any livestock damage they may cause themselves (McNamee 1994: 17;

Milstein 1995: 82; Pavlik 1999: 39). It is further suggested that wolf control of
coyotes would in turn benefit smaller carnivores such as weasels and eagles that
could play a valuable role in controlling rodent numbers (Milstein 1995: 82–4).

The idea that wild predators can control or limit the numbers of their prey, especially where the prey animal is a pest, is in fact widely found in the beliefs and practices of farmers throughout the world. Egyptian farmers encourage the nearby
presence of egrets, owls, and desert foxes (as well as domestic cats) as a means of
controlling the rodents that threaten their wheat and rice (Parrish 1995: 198).
Snakes are widely recognized as useful rodent-destroyers, including among
Sulawesi villagers who attribute any increase in rodent damage to their corn to a
decline in the number of snakes (Broch 1998: 217). Villagers in different parts of
south-east Asia reportedly 'welcome tigers to help them control the deer, pigs and
monkeys which come to forage on their hard-earned crops—just as they keep
house cats to try to control rats' (McNeely and Sochaczewski 1994: 190). Farmers
in remote parts of India have viewed the wolf as helping to control the numbers of
antelope that threaten their crops (Rangarajan 1996: 26). The human exploitation
of predator–prey relations extends beyond the reliance on actual predators to
include the manipulation of predator body parts and the use of magic and ritual.
Examples of this include the Maya villagers in Central America who use the
melted down fat of the jaguar to keep other animals away from their cornfields
(Rabinowitz 2000: 105), the tourist lodges in Kenya who keep away vervet monkey
pests by displaying leopard skins outside (Else 1991: 161), and the Filipino farmers
who bury black cats near their fields to protect their crops from rodents (Fujisaka
et al. 1989: 208).

The recognition of predator–prey relations is widely found in rural Japan.
Japanese hunters are acutely aware of predator–prey ties among forest wildlife,
especially where these relationships have implications for game animal populations. In addition to the animals they actually hunt, hunters concern themselves
with the numbers and distribution of rival animal predators—for example, the
foxes and raccoon-dogs that prey on and deplete small game such as pheasants and
hares. Where such rival predators are identified, they may well become the object
of eradication measures. But there is also a recognition that the natural world
contains benign predator–prey relations. Japanese folklorists (associated with the
school of *kankyō no minzoku* or 'environmental folklore') argue that the recognition of predator–prey relations is clearly evident in traditional Japanese culture.
Examples of this include the householder's appreciation of cat predation on mice
and the farmer's appreciation of snake predation on frogs and fieldmice (Nomoto
1994: 109). In earlier times Japanese villagers carried out ceremonies that invoked
the power of the cat to control the rats that damaged their crops (Nomoto 1994:
145), while Japanese silk producers petitioned snake spirits to protect their silk-
worms from rat damage (M. Hasegawa 1996: 148). A variety of birds are recognized
as *ekichō* or 'benign birds' because they feed on harmful insects, while others are

considered *gaichō* or 'harmful birds' because they feed on valuable crops. Japanese foresters have long valued weasels and sable as *ekijū* or 'benign beasts' because they catch the mice and hares that damage their saplings (Ue 1983: 291, 294). But the wolf is perhaps the foremost example of a 'benign beast' in Japanese folklore, as is evident in the many folktales on the theme of reciprocity between people and wolves, the folk custom of feeding wolves after they have given birth, and the existence of wolf shrines where farmers sought the protective powers of the wolf.

The JWA proposal is generally couched in ecological terms, and the arguments for wolf reintroduction in Japan appear formally similar to conservationist and reintroductionist arguments in North America. The JWA openly acknowledges the American wolf recovery campaign as its model and closely monitors developments in the American situation. Yet the JWA proposal makes reference to indigenous, as well as foreign, sources of inspiration. One of the striking features of the Japanese case is the way in which the principle of protective predation can be readily related to cultural tradition. It is claimed that, in contrast to the Western view of the wolf as the embodiment of evil, in Japan the wolf was associated with religious worship in certain Shinto shrines as a protective spirit that served human interests. It follows that part of the appeal of wolf reintroduction in Japan would lie in its promise to reactivate this traditional relationship between people and wolves. The rhetorical force of wolf reintroduction in the Japanese context lies, as we shall see, in the way it combines ecological pragmatism with an implicit cultural nationalism. Wolf reintroduction in Japan can be credibly advanced by proponents as *both* nature conservation *and* (culturally endorsed) pest control, and therefore as something that should command local as well as national support. The issue of wolf recovery may divide urban and rural America, but, according to the Japanese reintroductionists, it should, in principle, unite urban and rural Japan. One of the main aims of this book is to consider whether this would be the case by examining the context of people–wildlife relations in the Japanese mountains into which the new wolves would enter.

UTILITARIANISM AND SYMBOLISM

Much of the discussion of Japan's wildlife problem is specialized and technical in nature, to do with technologies of animal repulsion (the efficacy of different repellents and barriers), instruments of pest control (population regulation through birth control or culling), the carrying capacity and altered ecology of the forest, and so on. Similarly, the wolf reintroduction proposal is often presented as a technical solution (predator restoration) to a technical problem (out-of-control prey populations), while many of the critical responses to it raise technical objections of one sort on another. This utilitarian-technical discourse would appear to be consistent with the widely reported Japanese emphasis on using and exploiting wildlife and other natural resources. In his survey of attitudes to wildlife in different countries, Stephen Kellert found that among Japanese respondents there was 'a pragmatic perspective toward the utilization of animals and nature' (1991: 301), along with 'strong dominionistic and negativistic attitudes' (1994: 173). In relation to whaling and the ivory trade, Japan has long argued for the principle of sustainable use, in opposition to calls for complete bans on whaling and elephant 'harvesting' (Furuyashiki 1999). But in recent decades Japanese utilitarianism has become notorious in some circles, generating a variety of negative images and stereotypes to do with a perceived Japanese overexploitation of the natural world. Japanese greed is a common theme in reports of environmental issues, in the form of references to 'Japan's insatiable desire for whale meat' (Moulton and Sanderson 1997: 69) and to Japan as an 'environmental predator' (Holliman 1990: 284).

Wild animals are often viewed anthropocentrically by human societies. Wildlife is defined as a *resource* to be exploited when it can contribute to human livelihoods, and defined as a *pest* to be eradicated when it harms or interferes with human livelihoods. The anthropocentric character of the category 'pest' is evident in many of the terms applied to these animals in the English language, including 'harmful animals', 'troublesome animals', 'problem species', and so on. 'Animals become pests when they have an impact on some resource or value that humans hold dear' (Coleman 1993: 341). From a utilitarian viewpoint, the wildlife pest is a negative, harmful, and even destructive component of the wider living environment that should be controlled or neutralized in the interests of human livelihoods. Throughout the world unwanted animals are routinely 'removed' from human environments in the name of pest control. The scale and ubiquity of pest control operations testify to the power of utilitarianism as a determinant of human–animal relations. The utilitarian content of the category pest does not, however, preclude the existence of symbolism.

Anthropology has tended to focus on the symbolic and expressive dimensions of human–animal relations. Anthropologists have long opposed the exaggerated emphasis on the material side of human–animal relations, arguing that due weight should be given to the 'psychological' as well as the 'utilitarian' aspects of human relationships with animals (Hallowell 1926: 3–6); that animals offer human societies both 'sustenance' *and* 'symbols' (Shanklin 1985); and that animals are, to quote Claude Lévi-Strauss, not just 'good to eat' but also 'good to think' (Lévi-Strauss 1969: 162). Anthropologists have documented the existence of elaborate folk classifications of the flora and fauna of the natural environment that are irreducible to economic or utilitarian motivations (Lévi-Strauss 1966; Descola 1994). Many anthropological studies have examined the ways in which animals serve as a means of signification in different human cultures, showing how animals become 'symbols' and 'metaphors' of social relations (Shanklin 1985; Mullin 1999). In its materialist concern with the function of animals as a source of food and other products for human beings, utilitarianism is unable to account fully for the complexity of human–animal relations. But how would this anthropological approach to human–animal relations, with its emphasis on animal symbolism, apply to wildlife pests? What is the symbolism of the crop-raider? One possible answer might be to focus on the boundary-crossing behaviour that tends to be a feature of wildlife pestilence.

Drawing on structuralist principles, social anthropologists have long approached animal symbolism in terms of the idea of taxonomic anomaly. There is a well-known list of anomalous animals identified by anthropologists that includes the pangolin, a scaly mammal (Douglas 1957); the pig, a cloven-hoofed non-ruminant (Douglas 1966: 55); the cassowary, a human-like bird (Bulmer 1967: 17); the monkey, with its strong human resemblance (Ohnuki-Tierney 1987); the fox, which is similar to both dog and cat (Hufford 1992: 129–30); and the whale, which blurs the line between fish and mammal (Kalland and Moeran 1992: 6–7). These animals are morphologically anomalous in the sense of having physical characteristics that are at odds with taxonomic regularities. But another respect in which anthropologists depict animals as 'anomalous' has to do with environmental space. Where space is culturally divided into different spheres, each of which carries a distinctive moral evaluation, it can serve as a basic classifier of animals. Anthropologists have offered symbolic interpretations of the territorial mobility of wild animals in relation to cultural ideas of boundary transgression. One well-known example is Stanley Tambiah's study of rural Thailand in which he points out that the buffalo, the civet cat, the toad, and the otter are all marked as anomalous creatures because of their perceived boundary-crossing movements (Tambiah 1969: 450–1). Spatially anomalous animals have also been identified in Japan. The fox is known for its movements between village and forest (Nakamura 1987: 18–20; Nomoto 1996: 224), while fox possession tales tend to involve encounters with foxes at the edge of the village (Eguchi 1991: 428). The monkey too is said to straddle the domains of the forest (*yama*) and the village (*sato*) (Hirose 1993: 66–71).[4]

Anthropologists and other scholars have applied this perspective to animals deemed harmful, troublesome, or dangerous, to show that there may be a symbolic rather than simply a utilitarian basis to such negative representations. A major influence on this style of analysis has been Edmund Leach, who, in a famous essay on animal symbolism, interpreted the English notion of 'vermin' as referring to an intermediate category of animals that breach symbolically marked spatial boundaries (Leach 1964: 45). A prime example offered by Leach was the fox, an animal that exists 'on the borderline between edible field and inedible wild animals' (ibid.). Likewise, it has been argued that one of the reasons that the fox features so much in fables has to do with its conspicuous boundary-crossing behaviour between woodland and village (Howe 1995: 654–5). The special symbolic status of the tiger

---

[4] The anthropologist Emiko Ohnuki-Tierney has used a structuralist model of natural symbolism to analyse the monkey in Japanese culture—see Ohnuki-Tierney (1987, 1990).

in south east Asia has been explained in terms of the animal's tendency to come to
feed on wildlife at the 'intersection' of village and forest (Wessing 1986: 5–9). Both
foxes and tigers are potential livestock predators, but the argument can be
extended to crop pests. From this standpoint, animal crop-raiding becomes irreducible to simple economic loss, because it is also experienced as a transgression of
the village boundary and even as a kind of cultural violence that village society
must resist (Hell 1996: 207). The argument has also been applied to those wild
animals that enter domestic human space. It has been claimed that rodents are considered inedible in Britain because they are beasts of the field that invade the
human domain of the house (Fiddes 1991: 142–3). This kind of analysis can easily
be extended to account for pest control practices. Wildlife pests, as wild animals
that exist in human spaces, straddle the nature–society boundary and as a result
become ready candidates for order-restoring cultural practices.

Interestingly, some specialists in the field of wildlife pestilence have made use of
symbolic interpretation themselves. In the Introduction to a book on mammalian
pestilence (entitled *Mammals as Pests*), R. J. Putman suggests that some animal
pests 'are only pests when in inappropriate numbers or in the wrong context'
(Putman 1989: 2). Similar definitions are reproduced by other writers in the field.
'Wildlife pests, as perceived by man, are usually ecological dislocates, i.e. undesirable in that place at that time . . .' (Howard and Dutta 1995: 423). In this way, the
pest can be defined apart from any economic damage it causes. Although these
writers on pestilence do not actually refer to the writings of Edmund Leach and
Mary Douglas on the theme of boundary-crossing and symbolic disorder, the similarity in reasoning is clear enough. It follows from this cultural definition of pests
that pest control becomes more than simply the technical removal of harmful
animals. '[T]he enthusiasm of some people for pest control may be related to some
dark overtones in history reflected in the origin of the word "pest" from the Latin
word "pestis" meaning plague or contagious disease' (Hone 1994: 2). It has been
suggested that the language of pestilence is used to make certain animal species
into 'scapegoats' (Anderson *et al.* 1989: 252; Dunstone and Ireland 1989). Some
'pest problems', in other words, prove to be 'illusory' (Putman 1989: 9). The label
pest serves to simplify a complex situation by projecting blame on to certain
animals, thereby obscuring the wider context of causation from which the 'pestilence' problem has arisen.

As with wildlife pestilence, wildlife conservation attracts utilitarian explana-
tions. Much wildlife conservation is justified as *resource* conservation: the hus-
banding of a resource for the long term rather than squandering it in the short
term. This form of conservation stands for the sustainable exploitation of a
resource, and is characterized by an ethos of rational, efficient management
directed to the goal of maximizing the productivity of the natural world, recalling
similar economic rationalist arguments applied to other kinds of 'natural resources'
(Worster 1977; Oelschlaeger 1991: 281–9). This classical form of utilitarian conser-

vationism has seen something of a resurgence in recent years in the guise of the 'participatory conservation' orthodoxy where the emphasis is placed on involving the local community in wildlife conservation initiatives by allowing a degree of exploitation of wild animal populations as a condition of effective conservation (Heinen 1996). The underlying logic here is that wildlife will be conserved by local people where it is useful to them. But this is not the only way in which utilitarianism can predicate conservationist discourse. As we have seen above, certain forms of wildlife conservation are justified in terms of the control of wildlife pests rather than exploitation of wildlife resources. In accordance with the doctrine of regulatory predation, wild predators such as the wolf are said to serve as benign agents of pest control. Although it may not be directly exploited itself as a resource, the wild predator is indirectly useful to human society.

However, there is another strand of conservation, sometimes referred to as preservationism, that does not rely on such utilitarian justifications, but seeks to protect or preserve nature as an end in itself. Wildlife is protected not as a valuable resource, but as a component of a (culturally important) natural heritage or biodiversity. Such preservationism may well be based on a dualistic view of nature and culture, according to which nature is a sphere which should be free from human resource appropriation. Wildlife conservation informed by this perspective can be understood as a kind of symbolic practice, one which attempts to protect or maintain the threatened boundary between nature and culture. This symbolic dimension of conservationist discourse is highlighted by Kay Milton in her study of wildfowl conservationism in the United Kingdom, where she invokes the ideas of Mary Douglas.

Nature is . . . seen as separate from humanity; the boundary between human and non-human processes defines the natural. The conservation of nature, as conservationists understand it, thus requires the preservation both of the separate things that constitute nature (the species, sub-species and ecosystems) and of the quality that makes them natural (their independence from human influence) . . . This makes conservation, inevitably, a boundary maintaining exercise. In order to conserve the things that constitute nature, the boundaries that separate them must be maintained, and in order to conserve nature's 'naturalness', the boundary between the human and the non-human must be preserved. So it is not surprising if conservationists sometimes appear, when viewed through the filter of Douglas' model of symbolic classification, to be acting like nature's housekeepers, obsessively restoring order by putting things where they belong . . . (Milton 2000: 242)

While the symbolism of wildlife pestilence has to do with nature's threat to culture, the symbolism of wildlife conservation is based on culture's threat to nature.

This form of symbolic analysis none the less presents certain problems. The emphasis given to anomaly in anthropological analyses of natural symbolism has been criticized on the grounds that it reflects the structuralist logic employed by anthropologists rather than 'the informal logics of folk systems' (Ellen 1993: 183). One major challenge to the structuralist tradition of animal symbolism studies has come from anthropologists working on hunter-gatherer societies. It is argued that hunter-gatherers do not share the preoccupation with human–animal contrast and discontinuity on which anthropological animal symbolism is based, but tend to have a much more inclusive disposition to the non-human animals around them. Indigenous hunters are said to attribute will, agency, and other aspects of person-hood to the animals they hunt, and to understand these animals as part of a common domain of sociality marked by egalitarianism, mutualism, and trust (Ingold 1994; Bird-David 1993; Howell 1996). From this perspective, *dualistic* interpretations of animal symbolism that draw on the notions of 'metaphor' and 'analogy' become inapplicable to *monistic* hunter-gatherers. As Ingold puts it, 'to claim that what is literally true of relations among humans (for example, that they share), is only figuratively true of relations with animals, is to reproduce the very dichotomy between animals and society that the indigenous view purports to reject' (Ingold 1994: 19). Attempts to understand such societies in terms of a culture-bound theory of natural symbolism only end up obscuring the reality of human–animal relations that symbolic analysis is supposed to reveal. Herein lies the challenge for an anthropological theory of animal symbolism: to be flexible enough to represent the diverse and complex ways in which human beings experience the non-human animals that share their living environment.

One could be forgiven for thinking that the relationship of 'sharing' and 'trust' between the indigenous hunter and his prey has little in common with the relationship between the farmer and the wildlife pest, given the obvious antagonism that marks the latter. Such a conclusion would, after all, seem to follow from the tendency among many scholars to dichotomize human–animal relations in terms of the principle of domestication which is held to redefine radically the human relationship to the natural world. Here domestication represents not just the narrow cultivation of crops or the raising of animals, but a wider transformation of human society's perception of nature in what amounts to 'a whole system of domestication' (Knobloch 1996: 3) that entails a general 'subjugation of nature' and 'domination and manipulation of living creatures' (Serpell 1996: 218) and therefore the extension of 'object' status beyond domestic animals to include 'all animals, wild and not wild' (Kent 1989: 15). According to this framework, the Japanese mountain villagers featured in this book appear on the side of domestication and would therefore present a clear contrast to monistic hunter-gatherers. However, in the following pages we shall see that the representations of animals in Japan are rather more complex than this suggests. Although the relations between Japanese mountain villagers and forest wildlife are marked by anthropocentric orientations, utilitarian assumptions, and considerable antagonism, wild mammals can also attract human concern, affection, and even identification. The wildlife 'pests' and 'resources' featured in this book are not therefore reducible to a simple 'object' status and human behaviour towards these animals is not insulated from the considerations of morality that apply to human society itself. People–wildlife relations in Japan are marked by perceptions of commonality that tend to divide the village in its war with the 'enemy' from the forest.

The book is organized as follows. Chapter 1 introduces the social context of Japan's wildlife problem by outlining the economy, society, and recent history of Japanese mountain villages. It describes the various industries on which local livelihoods depend and identifies the different groups of people that interface with wildlife—farmers, foresters, and hunters. Chapters 2–5 examine human–wildlife relations in Japan, with particular emphasis on the problem of wildlife pestilence, focusing respectively on wild boar, monkeys, deer and serow, and bears. These chapters highlight the different relationships to these animals on the part of farmers, foresters, hunters, and other categories of stakeholder such as conservationists and tourists, against the background of the symbolism of the animals in question. In Chapter 6, we return to the subject of wolves and the proposal to reintroduce them to Japan, and look at the reactions to the proposal to date. The ethnographic focus of the book is on the mountain villages of the southern Kii Peninsula in western Japan. Anthropological research has been carried out in the peninsular municipality of Hongū-chō and surrounding areas since the 1980s, beginning with a two-year spell of fieldwork from 1987 to 1989, followed by regular annual visits (of between two and ten weeks' duration) from 1994 to 2001. This book also draws on a variety of Japanese-language written sources, including books and articles by folklorists, zoologists, wildlife conservationists, and other scholars, as well as hunting magazines and newspaper databases.[5]

---

[5] News items, articles, and commentaries on the theme of hunting and wildlife published between 1984 and 2000 were surveyed. The databases used were those of the *Asahi Shinbun* and *Nikkei Telecon*.

1
Mountain Villages

Hongū-chō is a mountainous municipality located on the Kii Peninsula in western Japan. It lies in the south-east corner of Wakayama Prefecture, bordering Nara Prefecture to the north, and forms part of the Kansai region. Lying on the Pacific side of the main island of Honshu, the climate of Hongū is generally warm, with a high annual rate of precipitation. The municipality of Hongū-chō covers an area of 2,040 square kilometres, most of which (93 per cent) is forest land. The landscape consists of steep hills and low mountains, along with a number of high mountain peaks: the highest peak (Ōtōzan) is over 1,100 metres, and there are seven other peaks of around 1,000 metres. Topographically, the terrain can be considered as 'low mountains', an intermediate status between hills and high mountains (cf. Guzzetti and Reichenbach 1994: 69–71), and only in the neighbouring municipality of Totsukawa-mura to the north does a truly 'highland' topography emerge, with mountain peaks of up to 1,800 metres. Hongū-chō consists of around fifty villages, generally located on low altitude slopes of below 500 metres, that range from concentrated downstream settlements with hundreds of households to sparsely populated upstream settlements of only a few. In Japan such hilly settlements are formally designated *sanson* or 'mountain villages'—a term that includes both low-lying hill settlements and more elevated settlements, and that is usually contrasted with *nōson* or 'farming villages'. Mountain villages are estimated to account for less than 5 per cent of the national population.[1]

As a result of post-war urban economic growth, Japan's mountain villages have lost much of their population through outmigration to the cities. In 1970, in response to this trend, the Japanese government passed what is generally known as the *Kasohō* or 'Depopulation Act', a piece of legislation that addressed the problem of population decline by providing extra government resources for designated *kaso chiiki* or 'depopulated areas'. Depopulated municipalities account for one-third of all Japanese municipalities, cover one-half of the national land area, and make up around 6.5 per cent of the national population (KKTK 1994: 2–12). They have a particular kind of population structure, with few younger people of reproductive age and large numbers of older people. These trends are fully reflected in Hongū-chō, one of the sixteen depopulated municipalities of Wakayama Prefecture. In the

---

[1] It is because of their relatively low elevation that in this book I sometimes refer to Hongū settlements as 'upland' settlements or villages, even though it might be expected that the adjective 'highland' would normally be applied to 'mountain villages'.

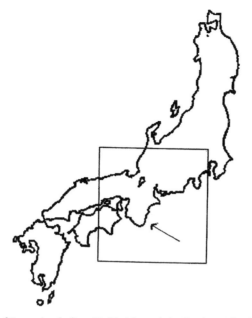

FIG. 1.1. A map of Japan (excluding Hokkaido and the Ryukyu Islands) showing the Kii Peninsula

post-war period, Hongū experienced large-scale urban outmigration: between 1955 and 1995, the population of Hongū fell by nearly 60 per cent, from 10,276 to 4,310 people, and is projected to fall further to 3,342 people by 2005 (Hongū-chō 1996: 21). While the individual population of Hongū fell by over half, the decline in the number of households was around 20 per cent, indicating that depopulation has been due largely to the outmigration of younger family members rather than of whole families. The migration of younger people to the cities has led to rapid population ageing in the villages of the Kii Peninsula. In 1960 people aged 60 and over accounted for 11 per cent of the Hongū population, but by 1995 they made up 44 per cent. Remoter, upstream villages tend to be more depopulated and more aged than downstream settlements. This is of particular significance, as we shall see, in relation to the wildlife problem, which tends to affect disproportionately these remoter villages.

FARMERS

There is a long agrarianist tradition in Japan according to which farming is viewed as the core of Japanese society and the basis of Japanese civilization (Havens 1974; Ogura 1979: ch. 1; Ohnuki-Tierney 1993: ch. 6). Japanese farmers have long grown a variety of crops, including dry-field crops such as wheat, barley, and millet, as well

FIG. I.2. The rice harvest in Hongū

as the wet-field crop of rice. Rice occupies a key place in Japan's agrarian tradition and rice farmers are often portrayed as intensely patriotic producers: 'No crop had been more valued than rice, and a farmer could perform no greater service for his country than to grow rice' (Niide 1994: 18). Rice cultivation transforms the village landscape over the summer months, with the lush green paddyfields of the early summer giving way to the golden yellow ricefields of the late summer that present a stark contrast with the dark green forest that surrounds them. Japan's monsoon climate, with its high levels of early summer-time precipitation, readily facilitates the practice of wet-field rice farming. Due to the restorative effects on the soil of the annual flooding of their fields, Japanese farmers are able to carry out continuous rice cropping, from one year to the next, without having to resort to regular fallowing periods. In the past farmland was cultivated throughout the year, with the production of rice in the summer succeeded by the production of wheat and barley

FIG. 1.3. This photograph of the rice harvest shows how the field is surrounded by plantation forest

in the winter. In contrast to European mixed farming, livestock has occupied only a minor place in Japanese farming.

In Japanese the word for rice, *gohan*, is synonymous with food (as with bread in English). Rice is the staple of the traditional Japanese diet, normally eaten three times a day, with fish and vegetables (including soya beans) as supplements. Rice is present in the snacks between meals and rice, of course, is what sake is made from. In Japan rice is associated with physical strength. At breakfast and lunch, men with manual labour tasks to perform will tend to have more than one bowl of rice with their meals. This belief in the strength-giving property of rice is evident in the following custom recounted by Hongū people: when a forester is overcome by a sudden fatigue in the forest, he can revive himself by eating one or two grains of rice from his lunchbox (that have been deliberately saved for such a situation) or, failing this, by writing the Chinese character for rice (米) on the palm of his hand. As well as being a daily food, rice is a food that is served on special occasions. It is offered to the Shinto *kami* at shrines in the form of glutinous rice cakes known as *mochi*, and in the form of sake ritually drunk by the bride and the groom at Japanese weddings. Rice is also an offering made to the family dead: cooked rice is offered twice a day to the ancestors at the ancestral altar (known as the *butsudan*) and uncooked rice is offered on the periodic visits to the family graves. Because of its central place in human livelihoods, rice has traditionally been treated with the utmost respect in

Japan. The honorific prefix '*o*' is applied to rice (*o-kome*) and used when referring to rice transplanting (*o-taue*). Above all, rice should never be wasted. Japanese children are warned that they will go blind if they do not eat up all the rice in their rice bowl, while rice harvesters are careful to gather in all the rice stalks (even, in some cases, going around at the end of the harvest to pick up individual grains that have fallen to the ground).

Farming has long been associated with regional and national development in Japan. In the mountainous country of Japan the mountains themselves have tended to be considered as inferior, unproductive land, and a premium has been placed on the existence of flat land suitable for the cultivation of crops. Japanese history contains many examples of major land reclamation initiatives directed at extending the area of arable land and increasing the scale of farm production. Special emphasis has been placed on rice production.

Until 1955 the unit of measure for rice volume was the *koku*, a unit based on the minimum amount of rice required for one man to live on for one year (Yuize 1978: 264). One *koku* approximates to 150 kilogrammes that in turn amounts to 1,400 calories, a figure that corresponds to the minimum diet (when combined with vegetables and fish) for one person. A one million *koku* domain was a territory able to support a population of one million people. In this way the population potential of an area of land could be abstractly calculated, with the *koku* capacity of a territory representing a sort of census. Rural poverty was attributed to population surplus and land scarcity. This sensibility is especially pronounced in mountainous areas, which have traditionally been deemed land-poor places with a limited arable basis for settlement. An indication of the relative poverty of areas such as Hongū is that white rice was rarely eaten before the modern period; instead, rice would be mixed with millet and potatoes and eaten in the form of a gruel known as *kayu* (a custom that continues, to some extent, today). Similarly, *mochi* or rice cakes would be combined with millet (*awamochi* or 'millet rice cake') rather than made solely with rice. Nowadays, however, the norm is to eat pure white rice and pure rice cakes.

This situation of land scarcity in mountainous areas required that attention be given to population control. Population limitation measures such as abortion and infanticide, known colloquially as *kuchiberashi* or 'mouth reduction', have long been carried out in Japan. Thomas Smith points out that in the eighteenth century the use of infanticide to limit family size was a common feature of Japanese villages 'where the family and farming unit were indistinguishable, where decisions concerning one required decisions about the other, and where farming was intensely competitive and perpetuation of the family a religious duty' (Smith 1977: 147–8). The connection between rice and people, farming and family life, is fully evident in the Japanese word *mabiki*. Containing the Chinese characters for 'space' (*ma*) and 'pull' (*hiku*), *mabiki* has its origin in farming—the selective thinning of the ricefield.

[C]ommon people saw *mabiki* as rational. It was what left 'space' for siblings—and by extension the population as a whole—for living and growing . . . For those who recognized that another pregnancy would deplete the body and energies of a mother, such spacing would indeed be like that in the rice fields where culling weaker shoots means more nutrients for the stronger ones. In a world where nutrients and energies reach natural limits, harvesting human resources to make a population strong and healthy seemed as justified as the operations of a farmer on his fields. (LaFleur 1992: 179)

Given the scarcity of arable land, one would expect population restriction to have been of particular importance in mountainous areas. The folklore on the Kii Peninsula makes reference to both infanticide and geronticide.[2]

In the course of the twentieth century, Japan has changed from a predominantly farming society to an urban-industrial society. In 1900, over two-thirds of the Japanese working population was employed in primary industries, centring on agriculture, but this has fallen to around 5 per cent.[3] Agrarian decline has been especially marked in recent decades. In 1970 there were 5.4 million farm households in Japan, but by 1995 the number had fallen to 3.4 million. At the same time, the character of Japanese farming has changed from a labour intensive activity into a mechanized, technologically advanced one. Most rice-growing households today own farm machines (tractors, transplanters, harvesters, etc.), use synthetic fertilizers, insecticides, and herbicides on their fields, and grow one or more of a limited number of standardized rice varieties. These new technological inputs have greatly reduced the physical drudgery of farming tasks such as seedling transplanting, weeding, harvesting, and threshing. In addition, during the twentieth century Japanese farming changed from being a full-time occupation to a part-time one. The great majority of Japan's farming households farm on a part-time basis, deriving income from non-farming, as well as farming, activities. According to official census findings, in 1995 around 2.9 million of Japan's 3.4 million farming households (84 per cent) were part-time farming households. In Japan the category of part-time farming divides into two types: Type I part-time farming households, that derive more of their income from the farm than outside work, and Type II households, that earn a greater proportion of their income from outside work than from the farm. Despite their designation as 'part-time' in contrast to specialized or full-time farming households, Type I part-time households have been characterized as 'predominantly agricultural households' sufficiently similar to full-time households to allow them to be usefully considered together and in contrast to the Type II households (Jussaume 1991: 49–50). Taking the full-time and Type I

---

[2] A book on Hongū folklore published in 1985, and based on interviews with elderly local people in the early 1980s, contains a number of references to infanticide (KMG 1985: 155). The Kii Peninsula, like other Japanese regions, has its share of geronticide lore, including tales of old women abandoned in the forest (HYMKI 1992: 313–23).

[3] Unless otherwise indicated, the following national and local statistics on farming are taken from the official Agricultural Census figures of the Ministry of Agriculture (Nōrinsuisanshō n.d.).

households together, we find that, in 1960, they made up 68 per cent of the total, but that by 1995 only 31 per cent. In other words, it is the Type II farming households that have come statistically to dominate the Japanese farming sector.

Hongū is not a major agricultural area and farming makes only a minor contribution to local incomes. Local farmland is used to grow a range of crops, including rice, potatoes, soya beans, cabbage, spinach, radishes, and onions, along with a range of fruits. There are a great many small fields, often in the form of hillside 'terraces', rather than large expanses of flat farmland. In 1995 there were only 179 hectares of farmland, out of the total Hongū land area of 20,406 hectares—less than 1 per cent. When compared with the 1960 figure of 508 hectares, this figure of 179 hectares represents a decline in the farmland area of nearly two-thirds in thirty-five years. At the same time, the number of farming households has fallen by three-quarters: in 1960 1,307 households were classified as farming households, making up 57 per cent of local households, but in 1995 there were only 312 farming households (out of a total of 1,829 households)—just 17 per cent. These figures do not actually reflect the ubiquity of cultivation in Hongū, because they exclude small-scale growing of garden fruit and vegetables next to the house. Yet they do serve to show the decline of farming as a livelihood activity. This minor status of farming in Hongū is further evident in the relatively small number of commercial farmers (i.e., those who sell a proportion of their produce to the market): while nationally more than three-quarters of farming households in Japan are *hanbai nōka* or 'commercial farmers', in Hongū such households account for less than half (45.5 per cent) of farming households. These official figures should be treated with a certain amount of caution; they refer to registered sales and not to the informal transactions that take place between households. At a time when most Hongū households do not grow rice, some purchasing households buy rice from other local households with surpluses, rather than rice from the Agricultural Co-operative (the quality or safety of which may not be trusted). None the less, compared to both prefectural and national averages, a high proportion of farming households in Hongū farm for self-consumption.

Rice-growing is the primary form of arable cultivation in Hongū: 266 households cultivate rice, 85 per cent of all farming households. There are 126 hectares of ricefields, accounting for around 70 per cent of the total area of farmland in Hongū. This riceland varies in form, from irregular hillside plots that are found in remoter villages to the large, evenly shaped, low-lying fields that have been reclaimed through the draining of marshland in modern times. The village of Kotsuga (from which many of the examples of crop damage in the following chapters are taken) is one of the main local farming settlements: 16 out of the 27 households in the village grow rice, around 60 per cent. Kotsuga contains an expanse of flat, low-lying farmland, comprising some 626 ares of active ricefields. The average area of ricefield farmed by Kotsuga households is therefore around 40 ares, but this figure conceals a wide range of landholdings, from 16 ares to 95 ares. In the case of larger landowners, ricefield landholdings may well be fragmented in a number of

FIG. 1.4. A fallowed ricefield surrounded by forest on three sides. This kind of field is highly vulnerable to wildlife forays from the forest

separate sites, reflecting the recent history of piecemeal acquisition of land. In recent decades, as a result of rural depopulation, the fragmentation of landhold-ings has been exacerbated as migrant households sell their riceland to other house-holds in the village. The fragmented character of local landholdings is a source of inconvenience for cultivators who in the growing season have to move between the different sites that may lie on opposite sides of the village. Fragmented landhold-ings are also a problem in relation to the task of protecting fields from wildlife pests. But set against this inconvenience, the fragmented pattern of landholdings can offer the farmer a degree of security against field damage by wildlife, as well as other kinds of natural disasters.

Rice-growing in Hongū is in decline. Many local ricefields lie fallow: only 91 of the 126 hectares of riceland are actually cultivated, the other 35 hectares being set aside. In recent decades the amount of rice grown in Hongū has steadily declined: 507 tonnes of rice were harvested in 1960, but the rice harvest fell to 304 tonnes by 1995. The decline in rice farming was particularly pronounced in the 1980s and 1990s, as the Japanese government set out to control surplus production nationally and encouraged acreage reduction through set-aside and conversion. Population decline has also contributed to the decline in rice-growing. Rice cultivation is a highly labour intensive activity, and requires concentrated inputs of labour at dif-ferent points in the production cycle (i.e. transplanting and harvesting), but in depopulated villages there may no longer be enough people to supply the requisite labour at these times, or indeed to undertake the various other laborious tasks associated with rice-growing (weeding, the applications of fertilizers and other chemical inputs, the maintenance of irrigation and drainage channels, and so on). However, while the area of rice cultivation in Hongū has declined, the productivity of the remaining ricefields has increased: in 1960 1.95 tonnes of rice were yielded for each hectare of riceland, while by 1995 this increased to 3.3 tonnes. In addition to improvements in seed quality and the use of fertilizers and pesticides, one main reason for this change is the withdrawal from production (and conversion to other uses) of smaller, inferior upland ricefields, leaving a higher proportion of superior fields. None the less, overall rice-farming in Hongū is in decline, especially in remoter parts of the municipality.

Two-thirds of the farming households in Hongū are part-time—207 out of 312 households. Around 93 per cent of these part-time households are in the Type II category, earning most of their income from off-farm work. Typically, it is the head of the household who works off-farm, whether through regular salaried employment (the Town Hall, Agricultural Co-operative, the tourist sector, and so on) or casual employment (in construction, forestry, and tourism sectors). Most Hongū farmers (93 per cent) do fewer than 150 days of on-farm work a year. Only 44 people work more than 150 days a year on the farm—around 7 per cent of Hongū farmers, compared with a national figure of 22 per cent. As most farming in Japan is part-time farming, it tends to be undertaken by the elderly and by women. Japanese farming is often characterized as *sanchan nōgyō*—'three *chan* agriculture', the 'chans' (*chan* is an affectionate suffix used in addressing and referring to intimates) being *Okāchan* (Mother), *Ojīchan* (Grandfather), and *Obāchan* (Grandmother). Over 3.7 million of Japan's 9 million farmers, or around 41 per cent, are aged 60 and over. In Hongū the proportion of older farmers is even greater: 391 of the 630-strong farming workforce, or around 62 per cent of farmers. The rapid ageing of the farming population is viewed as signalling the end of farming in Japan. 'Without an increase in young people coming in and taking over, Japanese rice production, and indeed all of Japanese agriculture, is headed for oblivion' (Kubō 1994: 6). Few young people take up farming. In addition to the poor prospects of farming as an industry, farming has a serious image problem among rural youth, especially young women from whom the farmers' wives of the future must be drawn.

National, prefectural, and municipal governments have responded to the farming crisis in a variety of ways. Regional authorities have launched advertising campaigns (posters in the Tokyo subway, print adverts, television commercials, etc.) exhorting migrants from the regions to return to their rural hometowns, while some rural municipalities offer monetary incentives to encourage return migration. In addition to migrants, unrelated outsiders willing to take up farming have been actively recruited by remote municipalities. Some prefectures have established offices in metropolitan areas to field enquiries from would-be rural settlers and have set up assistance and training programmes to attract *shinnōmin* or 'new farmers' to their rural areas. Wakayama Prefecture has attracted its fair share of 'new farmers'. Since the late 1970s more than sixty new families have come to settle on the southern part of the Kii Peninsula, some two-thirds of which are clustered on the coast, while the remaining third have settled in the mountainous interior, including in Hongū. The Hongū newcomers are typically young (in their twenties and thirties) and university educated. Most practise organic farming, and rent farmland on which they grow rice and a variety of vegetables and fruits. Some of the newcomers pursue a lifestyle of near self-sufficiency in which they cultivate a wide range of crops to support themselves and minimize their use of money. In addition to farming, some of them pursue some artistic activities such as painting, writing, and music. The newcomers tend to inhabit remote properties, both out of choice (as a positive preference for out-of-the-way locations) and due to availability (as remote villages have high rates of depopulation and abandonment). But the proximity of their fields to the forest can make these new families especially vulnerable to wildlife damage.

FORESTERS

Japanese mountain villages are surrounded by forest. There are more than 25 million hectares of forest and woodland in Japan, making up around two-thirds of the national land area. The verdant character of the national landscape is captured in a variety of Japanese expressions such as *midori no rettō* or 'green archipelago' and *shinrinkoku* or 'forest country'. The word generally used for forest in Japanese is *yama*—a word that refers to both mountains and forest. The Japanese *yama* comprises two main kinds of indigenous forest, known as *bunarin* and *shōyōjurin*. *Bunarin* or beech forest is a cool temperate deciduous forest that is widely found in eastern Japan and at higher elevations (700–1,500 metres), while *shōyōjurin* or Lucidophyllous forest is a warm temperate forest that is common in western Japan and at lower elevations (below 500 metres) and also found in the wider East Asian area. The Kii Peninsula is part of the Lucidophyllous forest zone of western Japan, and it was mostly this vegetation that, until the modern era, surrounded human settlements in the interior. However, in the highland interior of the peninsula a large area of beech forest is also to be found. The vegetative diversity of the southern Kii Peninsula has led some local writers to declare that the region has a special, unique status as the site where Japan's 'two ecologies' meet (Ue 1994: 4–6).

Around 14 million hectares of the Japanese forest (56 per cent) is 'natural forest' (known variously as *tennenrin* or *shizenrin*), a category that includes primary and secondary forest. Much of Japan's primary forest has been lost, and *tennenrin* is commonly estimated to make up only around 5 per cent of the total forest area in Japan. Much of the *tennenrin* on the Kii Peninsula has disappeared in recent decades. Between 1960 and 1980, more than a quarter of the Hongū *tennenrin* was felled. By the year 2000, the *tennenrin* area had fallen to 6,350 hectares, almost one-third of the whole forest area (Hongū-chō 2000*a*: 4). Around 18 per cent of the Hongū forest area is nationally owned, and over half of this national forest area is *tennenrin* (including protected watershed forest). But, in response to financial pressures, the national Forest Agency has carried out large-scale logging of the interior forest in recent decades in an attempt to boost revenue from log sales. This logging has led to great wildlife habitat loss, with far-reaching consequences, as we shall see. However, much of Japan's 'natural forest' is in fact pine forest that has been created by human disturbances of the evergreen oak forest such as logging for timber or clearing for swidden farming (Nakagoshi 1995: 91). The red pine tree *Pinus densiflora* has long been exploited in Japan (and other parts of East Asia) for, among other things, timber, firewood, and pine resin. This secondary pine forest has been maintained under conditions of intensive forest use; it includes deciduous oak trees that grow under the pine canopy and are cut for charcoal on a twenty-year cycle (Kamada and Nakagoshi 1996: 20). The pine forest was maintained by regular human disturbance activity within it which had the effect of clearing the forest floor and allowing pine seedlings to establish. As a result of the human withdrawal from the pine forest, this activity is reduced and pine succession inhibited, and the deciduous oaks beneath the pine canopy eventually succeed the old pine stands.

For the majority of the Japanese population, the *yama* appears a distant place, essentially beyond the sphere of human habitation. But the people who actually live in upland areas see the mountain forest in a more differentiated way. The primary distinction made is that between the nearby *satoyama* or 'village forest' and the faraway *okuyama* or 'inner forest'. The two spheres are associated with different sorts of vegetation and with different purposes and activities. The *satoyama* (known in the Hongū area as *jigeyama*) is that area of forest surrounding the village and traditionally represented as an intermediate zone between the village and the real forest of the interior. Being part-woodland, part-grassland, and part-farmland, the *satoyama* was a semi-domesticated space that was important to village livelihoods. In the post-war period, the *satoyama* has declined and its character has changed. Oil and gas replaced the *satoyama* fuels, chemical fertilizer replaced *satoyama* fertilizer, and machines replaced farm animals, particularly cows, which meant that the *satoyama* was no longer grazed or used as a source of fodder. Instead, the space of the *satoyama* has been largely reforested, to become an extension of the timber forest (see below). Consequently, the graduated separation of village and forest has given way to a sharp interface, with villages now surrounded by tall dark conifer forest. Upland Japan is today marked by sharp boundaries between village clearings and dense forest. Old photographs show villages surrounded by treeless mountains—that were known as *hageyama* or 'bald mountains'—but these nearby mountains are now covered with tall tree growth. It is as though the forest has crept down into, or to the very edge of, the village. This is a change that has important implications for the problem of wildlife pestilence.

The *okuyama* is the remote, unfamiliar part of the mountains. It is a rugged and inaccessible place that has been only partly penetrated by roads and the forestry industry. The *okuyama* is a quintessentially wild space that retains much primary and secondary forest (and relatively few timber plantations) and is associated with wild animals (as well as ghosts and demons). It is viewed as a dangerous and frightening place where people can easily get lost. Japanese mountains typically consist of a great number of peaks and valleys; according to one local characterization of the mountains of the Kii Peninsula, they are like the ribbed underside of a *shiitake* mushroom. Travellers can easily take a wrong turning, especially after dark, and the rescue of those who go missing is difficult. However, there is no clear boundary between *satoyama* and *okuyama*; it is generally considered to take more than an hour or so to reach the *okuyama* from the village on foot, although nowadays new forest roads allow some parts of it to be reached within half an hour. There is a sense that, as forest roads increase in length and number and the *yama* is opened up, the *hontō no okuyama* or 'true *okuyama*' recedes and comes to be located that much further away. Some people even suggest that there no longer is a 'true *okuyama*' on the peninsula because of forest roads and the activities of foresters. Knowledge of the *okuyama*—the network of paths that run through it, the animal and plant life in it, the dangerous places to be avoided—tends to be confined to those people, such as foresters and hunters, who regularly set foot in it.

Forestry is the dominant industry in the mountainous areas of Japan. Japanese forests have long been manipulated to supply fuelwood and timber, with the preferred pattern of growth varying from one period to another. In the early Tokugawa era, for example, a fuelwood forest was encouraged by 'rulers who were more concerned to assure food and fuel supplies than timber stands', but later on priorities changed and, with timber scarce, 'rulers more consistently promoted conifer growth' (Totman 1989: 247 n.). Since the 1950s, when charcoal and fuelwood were replaced by modern forms of energy such as electricity, oil, and gas, forestry production has switched from hardwood trees for charcoal to softwood timber species to supply housing, construction, and civil engineering markets. Timber plantations today make up more than four-tenths of Japan's forest area and over a quarter of Japan's total land area. These plantations are dominated by two main tree species, Japanese cypress (*Chamaecyparis obtusa*, in Japanese *hinoki*) and Japanese cedar (*Cryptomeria japonica*, in Japanese *sugi*), that are favoured on account of their fast growth and adaptability to a range of different environments. These geometrical blocks of plantation forest, consisting of neat lines of standardized, same-aged trees, dominate the visible landscape of upland Japan. In the mountainous interior of the Kii Peninsula, timber plantations make up an even higher proportion of the forest. The area of timber plantations in Hongū is 12,314 hectares, accounting for two-thirds of the municipality's forest area (Hongū-chō 2000*a*: 4). Cypresses make up six-tenths and cedars nearly four-tenths of the Hongū plantations (pines accounts for less than 2 per cent).

The background to the present-day ubiquity of timber plantations is the large-scale logging that took place in Japan during the pre-war and wartime periods, which resulted in a national landscape of bare mountainsides. This overfelling had major environmental consequences in the form of landslides and extensive flooding in many downstream districts of Japan. One of the main government priorities of the post-war years was to restore tree cover to the bare mountains. A nationwide reforestation movement was launched after the war, with the Emperor as its figurehead, in which tree-planting events and ceremonies were held throughout the country. In the following four decades an estimated 10 million hectares of new timber forest were planted, restoring the national landscape of green mountains. The post-war reforestation of the mountains has been proclaimed a great patriotic achievement on the part of the Japanese people, and is a source of considerable pride within the Japanese forestry industry. In restoring the trees to the mountains, reforestation replenished the nation's wood stocks and contributed to the recovery of national resource security. As a result of this trend, Japan's forest area has actually increased over the twentieth century as a whole, from around 22.5 million hectares in 1900 to the present level of more than 25 million hectares (Umebayashi and Oya 1993: 203). During this same period, the plantation forest area has increased tenfold to its current level of 10 million hectares—from less than 5 per cent of the total forest area in 1900 to more than 40 per cent in the present day (ibid.).

Plantation forestry on the Kii Peninsula can be traced back to the seventeenth century and the Yoshino tradition. Yoshino forestry is known for its highly intensive methods that include close planting of saplings, frequent thinning of the growing trees, and long rotations to produce high-grade narrow-ringed timber. However, post-war plantation forestry differs from pre-war plantation forestry in important ways. Before the Second World War, timber plantations were largely confined to north-facing mountainsides. *Yama wa kitamuki* or 'the forest faces north' is a traditional saying that expressed the idea that conifers such as cedars grow better on the colder, less exposed north side of the mountain where the soil retains more moisture. The south side of the mountain consisted of a mixed forest, particularly trees used for charcoal such as evergreen oaks and live oaks that were believed to be made harder by the sun (Nomoto 1990: 25). Another feature of earlier plantation forestry was that a belt of mixed forest was left at the top of the mountainside near the ridge, while on high peaks a timberline of 800 metres was generally observed. All this changed in the post-war period as a result of the reforestation programme. Cypress and cedar plantations were established on both sides of the mountains, south as well as north, while the new timber plantations often

FIG. 1.5. The mountains of the Kii Peninsula showing the effects of plantation forestry

extend up to the ridge of the mountain and in some cases even above 800 metres. In short, the environmental impact of plantation forestry in the post-war period has been of a different order.

There are two main forms of forest ownership in Japan: *kokuyūrin* or nationally owned forest that makes up 31 per cent of the forest area, and *shiyūrin* or privately owned forest that makes up 59 per cent. There are around 2.9 million private forest owners, and some 2.5 million of these are individual forest owners (families), the rest being companies, municipalities, and other public bodies (JOFCA 1996: 12). Individual forest owners 'typically manage small-scale operations covering less than 5 hectares' (ibid.). In Hongū the proportion of privately owned forest land is higher than is the case with the nation as a whole: three-quarters of Hongū forest land is privately owned and only 18 per cent nationally owned (the remaining forest is owned municipally and by wards). The distribution of private forest land in Japan is highly unequal, as the post-war land reform, which redistributed farm-land, did not affect forest landholdings. In Hongū (according to 1980 figures), 778 (out of 1,881) households owned forest land—41 per cent of households. Most forest landholdings in Hongū are small: 85 per cent of forest-owning households own 5 hectares or less; 12 per cent own between 5 and 20 hectares; 2 per cent own between 20 and 50 hectares; and the remaining 1 per cent own 50 hectares or more. This top category contains some extremely large forest landholdings, including forest landowners with holdings of up to 500 hectares.

Forestry labour consists of both wage labour and family labour. On the large forest estates forestry is a permanent occupation, and there are even instances of second generation forest labourers who work on estates that their fathers worked on before them. Although both men and women work as forest labourers, almost all full-time forest labourers (i.e. those who work over 150 days a year) are men, while women generally work fewer than half this number of days. Women are employed to plant saplings in the spring and to weed young plantations in the summer. Private foresters band together in the management of their forests, forming *shinrin kumiai* or 'Forestry Co-operatives' that employ forest labourers on which the Co-operative members can draw for specific forestry tasks. In recent decades there has been a sharp decline in the number of people working in the forestry industry in Japan. In 1960 there were 440,000 forest labourers in Japan, but by 1995 this fell to just 80,000, a decline of over four-fifths (JOFCA 1996: 13). In Hongū in 1965 there were 861 forest labourers, but by 1994 this figure had fallen to around 150. The existing forestry workforce is an aged one, and younger men tend to opt for the better-paid construction jobs instead of forestry jobs. The consequence of this forest labour shortage, on top of the trend towards absentee forest ownership, is a greatly diminished level of silvicultural maintenance of timber plantations.

There remains a strong tradition of family forestry in Japan. The Japanese stem family, known as the *ie*, is an intergenerational structure that ideally outlasts its individual members. In broad terms, the *ie* consists both of extant family members and of past generations of family members in the form of the ancestors ritually memorialized in the *butsudan* altar. Although actual families may vary considerably, the ideal of the *ie* as a longitudinal entity that is perpetuated over time remains influential. In upland Japan, forest landholdings have been an important prop to the stem family, providing an economic stake that helps to ensure family continuity through succession. But this means keeping intact and passing on the forest land. Part of the reason for the ideal of retaining forest land is that families become intimately connected with the forests they own. The fruits of the labour of the earlier and present generations should be passed down to following generations in the form of good, robust trees that have accrued a high value. It is because of this ancestral labour input into them, along with the long timespan involved in timber growth, that trees come to serve as an important medium for intergenerational family relationships. Foresters commonly point out that it takes three generations to grow good timber: the first generation does the planting, the second generation carries out the main silvicultural tasks that ensure straight and sturdy growth, while the third generation does the felling. If it is the third (harvesting) generation that gets the benefit from the efforts of the earlier two generations, it is incumbent on the present-day beneficiaries, in turn, to raise seedlings, plant saplings, and look after maturing stocks that will benefit *their* descendants in the future. But in an era of large-scale depopulation, most forest-owning families on the Kii Peninsula harbour fears about family succession and many express apprehension about the prospects for the family forest in the absence of one of their sons returning from the city to take over its management.

Recent decades have seen a deterioration of the timber plantations in connection with the trend of outmigration. It was estimated in 1995 that some 70 per cent of Japan's timber plantations were under thirty-five years old and therefore in need of silvicultural attention (JOFCA 1996: 3). However, owing to the costs and scarcity of forestry labour, basic silvicultural tasks such as pruning and thinning have not been carried out in many of these plantations. The effect of not thinning these plantations is to slow the rate of growth of the individual trees and, therefore, to extend the rotation time, as well as to change the appearance of the plantations. Villagers find neglected plantations a depressing sight to look at, and refer to them variously as *moyashiyama* or 'beansprout forest', a forest resembling so many sprouts of a germinating bean. Mountain villagers tend to blame the government for this all-too-visible deterioration in the timber plantations that surround them. They believe that the Japanese government, which encouraged foresters to plant their mountains over with timber conifers in the 1950s and 1960s, has a moral responsibility to support the sons and grandsons of the tree-planters today—but one which it has failed to honour. For many foresters, the primary expression of this betrayal of the domestic forestry industry is the high level of Japan's wood imports. In the course of its post-war recovery, Japan experienced a shortage of usable wood products, and from the 1960s began importing large quantities of wood from south-east Asia and other parts of the world. In subsequent decades the scale of Japanese wood imports has increased enormously: in 1965 imported timber accounted for only 13.3 per cent of timber consumed in Japan, but by 1994 timber imports amounted to over three-quarters (JOFCA 1996: 8). The effect of timber imports is to displace home-grown timber from the market and accentuate the neglect and abandonment of domestic timber plantations.

Japanese forestry is criticized on environmental and conservationist grounds. Large-scale logging disrupts the traditional pattern of rainfall water-flow (something of particular importance on the Kii Peninsula on account of the high rate of precipitation), and can lead to downstream floods, landslides, and river silting. With the replanting of the logged areas and the subsequent restoration of tree cover, the worst effects of forest clearance will be short-lived; indeed, the forestry industry has argued strongly that the new timber plantations play an important environmental role as 'sponges' that retain water and control the flow of rainwater. Another common environmental objection to forestry plantations is that they are based on the inhibition of other forms of life: the growth of grass and undergrowth more generally, and by extension the animals which live off these plants. On account of the tradition of dense planting (along with the neglect of thinning), plantations on the Kii Peninsula are typically dark places that have little or no vegetative understorey. As a result of the replacement of the earlier forest vegetation by conifer plantations, much wildlife habitat has been lost. On top of this, timber forestry destabilizes the habitat conditions of forest fauna. The effect of the sequence of clearfelling the original forest and then establishing a plantation is, first, to increase greatly the food supply for forest herbivores, and then, some years later, to suddenly decrease this food supply when the plantation canopy forms and the undergrowth below is shaded out. As a result, wild herbivore numbers multiply in the earlier phase, but face a severe food shortage in the later phase. The surplus animals respond by feeding elsewhere, whether in other, younger plantations or on village farmland.

Road-building is another main source of criticism of forestry. As part of the post-war reforestation vision, a network of forest roads was established to support and improve access to the new timber plantations. In Japan the steep inclines of forested land have proved a formidable obstacle to extracting timber and transporting it to market. Forest roads greatly improve access, both for initial logging and the later phase of plantation forestry, and forest landowners naturally support their construction, arguing that they are an integral part of the *kaihatsu* or 'development' of the mountains. More generally, there is a widespread view in mountainous areas that all roads are a good thing in so far as they improve integration and reduce isolation. Local politicians routinely call for new roads and for the improvement of existing roads, and the issue often figures in municipal and prefectural elections. As a result of this persistent local demand for roads, forest roads have been established throughout the mountainous interior of Japan. Since 1970 the amount (that is, length) of forest roads in Hongū has more than doubled. But while these roads improve human mobility in the mountains, they can adversely affect the mobility of wild animals. Forest roads often cut through animal paths and trails, the effect of which is to disrupt the movements and feeding patterns of forest wildlife and to isolate animal subpopulations from one another. This expansion of forest roads seems to have made animal mobility more unpredictable and animals more difficult to hunt or trap, while another consequence is the high frequency of wildlife road-kill incidents. The fragmentation effect of forest roads on wildlife habitat is sometimes cited as a contributory factor in the rise of wildlife pestilence.

Another negative environmental impact of plantation forestry arises from the productive reassignment of farmland to forestry. Across Japan arable land has been planted over with conifers to become timber plantations and thus converted, in effect, to forest. Between 1984 and 1988, for example, 632 ares of Hongū farmland were converted to timber forest. The reason for converting abandoned farmland to plantation forest is because the latter requires a far lower input of labour, allowing people to leave the village to live and work outside, while continuing to put their land to a productive use. As a result of this trend, the forest area has expanded; in Hongū the forest has increased from 90.7 per cent of the municipal area in 1970 to 92.7 per cent in 1995. Many local people find this trend a disturbing one. First, farmland is referred to as *senzo daidai no tochi* or 'ancestral land', and to sell off, abandon, or afforest arable land can appear as a breach of this intergenerational contract with forebears. Secondly, even though the increase in the forest area is proportionately small (in the case of Hongū, only 2 per cent), this extra forest has a considerable visual impact. Coming in the wake of the conversion of the *satoyama* into conifer plantations, this afforestation of peripheral farmland further reinforces the sense of forest encroachment on the village, which comes to feel a dark and *sabishii* or 'lonely' place. This, in turn, adversely affects the remaining farmland on the forest-edge by reducing the sunlight it receives and by making visits from wildlife pests that much easier.

In the remote regions of Japan hunting has been an important livelihood activity that procured a range of valuable resources, including meat, medicines, and hides, and yielded significant seasonal income. In remote mountainous parts of northern Honshu are found the famous *matagi* hunting villages, the customs of which have been extensively documented by Japanese folklorists. However, for the great majority of the quarter of a million registered hunters in Japan, including those on the Kii Peninsula, hunting is an expensive recreational pastime rather than an income-yielding occupation. Hunting in Japan is usually differentiated into two categories: *ōgataryō* or 'large-scale hunting' that is directed at wild boar and deer and *kogataryō* or 'small-scale hunting' that is directed at birds and small game animals. Japanese hunters are allowed to hunt twenty-nine species of bird, including pheasants, crows, sparrows, and ducks, and seventeen species of animals, including wild boar, deer (stags), bears, hares, foxes, raccoon dogs, weasels, and squirrels (Environment Agency 1997: 438). In 1992 around 3 million birds were captured or killed through hunting (over a quarter of which were sparrows), while 330,000 animals were hunted (over half of which were hares) (ibid.). Most Japanese hunting takes the form of chase or pursuit hunting involving armed men with dogs, but trapping is also practised. In 1995 there were over 200,000 registered shotgun and rifle users, making up 85 per cent of all registered hunters in Japan, while the number of trappers stood at around 20,000, less than one-tenth of the total number of hunters (the remaining 6 per cent were airgun users) (Kankyō Chō 2000*a*). In Hongū there are 76 registered hunters—63 registered shotgun or rifle holders and 13 registered trappers.

In Japan hunters must join a local branch of the Hunting Association known as the *ryōyūkai* (literally 'hunting friends society'). The local *ryōyūkai* disseminates information on hunting, holds regular meetings, and elects officials who link with prefectural and national levels of the *ryōyūkai* and who liaise with municipal, prefectural, and police authorities. Hunting in Japan is a tightly regulated activity. In order to obtain a hunting licence, hunters must pass an examination in which they are tested on their ability to identify instantly game species and on their knowledge of safety procedures. All applications for shotgun ownership are reviewed by the police, and applicants must attend a course of instruction on gun ownership; even after the hunter is licensed, his status will be reviewed at regular intervals thereafter. Once he has his licence, the hunter must pay registration and hunting fees to the governments of the prefectures in which he intends to hunt. There is a specified winter hunting season (that varies, to some extent, with the game species) and there are areas in the forest where hunting is prohibited. There are restrictions on methods and devices used in hunting, and on the number of game animals that can be caught per day and per season. Many hunters complain about these restrictions, and fear that they are likely to become even tighter in the future. One of the reasons for this ever-greater regulation of Japanese hunting is the much-publicized annual toll of hunting accidents: for example, 115 incidents in 1995, including 13 fatalities (Kankyō Chō 2000*b*). It is in order to keep these incidents to a minimum that Japanese hunters are subject to recurrent safety campaigns, along with the legal restrictions.

Hunting in Japan appears a highly Westernized activity. Japanese hunters make use of Western dog breeds, wear camouflage fatigues and peaked caps, and read hunting magazines that advertise foreign-made hunting accessories and carry articles about hunting in foreign countries. The Westernized image of Japanese hunting is reinforced by the widespread use of the English word 'hunter' (*hantā* in its Japanese pronunciation) among hunters to refer to themselves. Japanese hunters use shotguns, rifles, two-way radios, radio-collars for hounds, and heat sensors to detect wounded game, and most of this hunting technology is imported from Western countries. As a recreational activity that usually takes place at weekends, hunting is variously characterized by hunters as *supōtsu* or 'sport', as *asobi* or 'play', as *undō* or 'exercise', and as a *shumi* or 'hobby'. For many hunters in Hongū, hunting is an all-consuming passion, one that occupies them even outside the winter hunting season—through the year-round care of hounds, through reading hunting magazines and books and watching videos (of hound trials, etc.) in their spare time, and through routine discussion and conversation about hunting matters with fellow hunters. Much Japanese hunting, especially of larger animals such as the wild boar and the deer, takes place in groups. Hunting groups attach great importance to 'teamwork' or 'teamplay' (English loanwords used) and sporting analogies (typically from baseball) are often employed to talk about hunting, with the leader of the group likened to a *kantoku* ('manager') of the rest of the *chīmu* ('team').

Although Westernized in form, there are aspects of Japanese hunting that are not found in Europe and North America. One of these is the strong moral disapproval of hunting from the perspective of Buddhism. *Fusesshōkai*, 'the precept of non-lifetaking', is the first of the five Buddhist precepts, and instructs the Buddhist to respect the life of other living beings ('We pledge not to kill living things'). The

FIG. 1.6. A group of hunters in Hongū

precept refers to hunting along with other kinds of killing such as the slaughter of domesticated animals and the taking of human life. Many Buddhist texts condemn hunting and meat-eating as wrongful conduct, warning of the terrible consequences of such actions. In Japan, the sinful character of hunting is explicitly recognized in the terminology traditionally applied to it, with hunting referred to as *sesshō* or 'lifetaking' and the hunter known as a *sesshōnin* or 'lifetaker'. A further expression of this moral concern that surrounds hunting in Japan is the annual memorial, known as *kuyō*, for the spirits of dead game animals held by each *ryōyūkai*.[4] At a special memorial stone, offerings of food (fruit, vegetables, and ricecakes) and sake are made, and hunters console and express gratitude to the spirits of the animals killed over the past hunting season. Hunters state that the short, simple ceremony is a way of expressing regret—of saying *mōshiwakenai* (literally, 'there is no excuse')—to their prey. The formal purpose of the rite is to expedite the posthumous wellbeing of the animal spirits and their attainment of buddha status (known as *jōbutsu*). But the rite is also understood as a pacification measure that transforms the animal's spirit from a state of restless suffering, highly dangerous to those people (the hunters) responsible for causing it, to a state of repose. From this religious perspective, hunting in Japan is a morally dubious

---

[4] In some cases, a similar rite, known as an *ireisai*, is carried out by a Shinto priest.

activity that opens up its practitioners to the danger of spirit revenge (known as *tatari*).

For most hunters in Japan, hunting is not a significant livelihood activity. Even in mountainous areas, the primary occupations have been farming and forestry. In Hongū there are hardly any occupational hunters left (that is, men who rely on hunting as their sole or main source of income); the *ryōyūkai* is almost entirely made up of recreational hunters who tend to be farmers, forestry workers, construction workers, and so on. The categories of forester and farmer on the one hand, and hunter on the other, are, to a large extent, overlapping ones. In general, therefore, the terms 'hunter' and 'farmer' used in this book refer to *a difference among farmers and foresters*—that is, between most farmers and foresters who do not hunt and the minority who do hunt. Yet the distinction between hunters and non-hunters in upland Japan remains a meaningful one. Hunters do stand out; in the villages of Hongū, everybody knows who hunts and who does not. There is a tendency for hunting to run in the family, and it is a little unusual in a family where there is no history of hunting for someone to start hunting. There is also a tendency to classify villages according to the presence of hunters within them: references are sometimes made to *ryōshi no mura* or 'hunter villages' and *ryōshi no nai mura* or 'villages without hunters', with the former tending to be the remoter, more upstream villages, and the latter the more downstream villages.

Despite its 'recreational' character, hunters readily attribute to the hunt a serious purpose and give the impression that, while it may not strictly speaking be a job, it is a labour of sorts. Hunters may well characterize their hunting as a form of public service, using the term *hōshi* or 'service' (consisting of the characters for 'obey' and 'serve'). This is because of the widely held view that the more animals that are hunted by hunters in the winter hunting season, the fewer animals there will be in summer to cause damage to village farms. The folklorist Hagihara Sahito makes this point when he points out that hunting in Japan has largely been *bōgyoteki shuryō* or 'defensive hunting' in which farmers hunt to protect their crops from wild animals, rather than *kōgekiteki shuryō* or 'offensive hunting' in which they hunt to obtain animal products (Hagihara 1996: 196). The link between hunting and pest control is enshrined in Japanese hunting law. According to the 1918 Wildlife Protection and Hunting Law, hunting is allowed for 'special purposes' which 'contribute to ". . . the improvement of the human living environment", and ". . . the promotion of agriculture, forestry, and fisheries"' (Mano and Moll 1999: 128). 'It can be considered that pest control . . . has been the dominant concept guiding wildlife administration systems this century' (Hazumi 1999: 210). The idea of hunting as a kind of public service also refers to the role of culling that some hunters undertake. Throughout the year rural town halls call on local hunters to catch and kill problem animals. In Japan large numbers of birds and animals are killed in this way each year. In 1992, for example, 1.28 million birds and 100,000 animals were captured in the course of such pest control operations

(Environment Agency 1997: 438). Thus, Japanese hunters in effect hunt in two different ways: qua (recreational) hunter in the winter hunting season and qua (employed) culler throughout the year. But for many hunters, there is little real difference between hunting and culling because winter season hunting, like culling, reduces the number of wildlife and therefore benefits the wider community. In other words, the rationale of Japanese hunting is protective rather than productive.

There is another respect in which hunting is viewed as a kind of public service. Hunters provide village security in relation to the forest. When a forest animal (a deer, a feral dog, or even a bear) is sighted in and around the village, somebody will contact the hunter's household to ask him to deal with the animal (some hunters are even asked to help dispose of wild animals killed on the road). But it is in the mountainous space beyond the village where human society is likely to call on the hunter's help. The police are occasionally called out to deal with wildlife incidents, such as a bear encounter, an attack by a wounded wild boar, or the sighting of a pack of stray dogs, and at such times they normally contact the *ryōyūkai* for advice and assistance. When somebody is lost in the remote mountains, the police may well contact the *ryōyūkai* to ask for volunteers to assist or even lead the search—i.e. those hunters familiar with the area of forest in question. When the Town Hall wants to know about wildlife stocks, or when a wildlife researcher visits, hunters (again through the *ryōyūkai*) may well be asked to help out and take visitors into the forest and guide them around. A further example of the security role of hunters occurred during the visit of the Emperor to the Kii Peninsula in 1977 for a large forestry festival (the 'National Tree Planting Festival' known as the *shokujusai*). For the duration of the festival, local hunters joined the police in patrolling the forest around the ritual venue. In their capacity to switch, in these ways, to the status of unofficial public servants, hunters differ from other categories of forest recreationist. In Japan hunting is not just one recreational pastime among others.

Hunters sometimes invoke tradition to valorize hunting and mark it out from other occupations. One way in which hunters express the fundamental importance of hunting is to represent the 'Japanese people' as a *shuryō minzoku* or 'hunting people'.[5] This claim may seem a little strange at first, even to Japanese ears; it is much more common for the Japanese to represent themselves as a *nōkō minzoku* or 'farming people' in line with the agrarianist (and more specifically, rice-centred) notions of national identity mentioned above. None the less, I have heard Hongū hunters use such language; indeed, some of them explicitly invoke the Jōmon era to ground their claim to be heirs to an ancient cultural tradition.[6] In

---

[5] This national self-characterization is occasionally made in Japan by Japanese folklore scholars and other writers (e.g. Saitō 1983: 20).

[6] The Jōmon period, named after its distinctive style of pottery, is the foraging period usually dated 10,000 BCE–300 BCE. One reason why some Hongū hunters have embraced this Jōmon identity would seem to lie in the discovery in the early 1990s of Jōmon-era stone implements (stone axes, stone hide-cutters and pounding stones) within the municipal area. According to *Kōhō Hongū*, the Town Hall newsletter, the discovery indicates the location of an ancient hunting camp (Hongū-chō 1992: 5).

addition to invoking the past to support hunting, Japanese hunters also rhetorically point to the future. Although hunting accounts for only a very small proportion of the meat consumed in present-day mountain villages, hunters sometimes refer to food-getting when discussing the importance of hunting. An example of this was the prediction by one Hongū hunter that, as the decline in Japanese farming continues and Japan finds itself ever more dependent on food imports from abroad, hunting will become much more important to the nation because, in the event of another world war, the Japanese people would no longer be able to feed themselves. At this time of crisis, they would realize the importance of hunting and other means of food-getting from the forest. It was important for this man that his son and his grandsons continue the hunting tradition in order to ensure that they will be able to feed themselves in the unsettled times that lie ahead. Hunting may not be practised for livelihood, but it retains the status of a potentially vital livelihood activity in times of adversity.

Although hunters themselves emphasize their larger importance to local society, there exists an altogether more negative view of hunting. There is a tendency among non-hunters in Hongū to stereotype hunters as people who lack the virtues of diligence and frugality and even as reckless and anti-social people. This is attested to by certain local sayings, in which hunting is likened to gambling, such as *jirijiri teppō ni dosa bakuchi* or 'little by little with the gun, all at once by gambling'. The saying succinctly states that, while the hunter loses gradually and the gambler loses in one go, in the end they both lose. From this perspective, hunting appears as a kind of anti-occupation, which distorts a man's life because of the demands it makes on his time and money. The hunter may well be viewed as a man who is likely to waste money on dogs, guns, and hunting gear, to waste weekends in the mountains that he might otherwise spend with his family, and to run an unacceptably high risk of injury or worse in the course of the hunt. From this critical point of view, risking injury for one's job (forestry or construction) is one thing, but risking injury in the course of a pastime is quite another. Hunting is at odds with the norm of frugal household economy. Non-hunters often condemn hunting as time-wasting. I have heard hunters referred to as *himajin* or 'idlers' because of the time they spend in the mountains. On top of these doubts about the character of hunters, there are widespread fears about the threat posed by hunters to public safety. Tensions arise between hunters and the wider society over wounded game animals, hounds, and stray gunfire. Hunting weapons are a particular point of contention; in the largely gun-free society of present-day Japan there is a fear that hunting weapons could be obtained and used by criminals (Satō 1979: 111).

Hunting is in decline in Japan. The total number of hunters has fallen by more than half since the mid-1970s: in 1976 there were more than 530,000 registered hunters, compared to the quarter of a million in the present day. As the number of hunters decreases, the average age of the hunters in Japan steadily increases (to around 60 years old today, according to one much-quoted figure), while in many *ryōyūkai* there are hardly any hunters below the age of 30. Hunters themselves point out that the causes of this decline include the ever-stricter regulation of hunting in Japan and the negative image of hunting in Japanese society. But clearly the decline in the numbers of hunters is also due to the overall trend of rural depopulation. As sons migrate to work and live in the city, few young men remain in the village to follow their fathers and take up hunting. As we shall see in the following chapters, this decline in the number of hunters in mountain villages appears to have had a significant effect on people–wildlife relations and is one of the main reasons advanced by the Japan Wolf Association in support of its proposal to reintroduce wolves to Japan.

ANIMALS

It is not only human beings who occupy the space of upland Japan. The presence of birds and animals is a ubiquitous one in the mountain villages of the Kii Peninsula. In the past an assortment of creatures were commonly found in and around old houses, such as flies and mosquitoes, swallows nesting up on the roof beams and snakes living beneath the floorboards. Everybody is familiar with the early morning chattering of crows ('*kaakaakaa*') in and around the village garbage dumps, the graceful movements of the kite gliding high in the sky above the river, and the sight of the raccoon-dog scampering along the road at night as it is illuminated by car headlights. There is much local animal omen lore: the woodpecker is a weather-forecaster, the pheasant predicts earthquakes, and the crow foretells a human death. Monkeys encountered in the morning were highly inauspicious, enough to make a forester turn back to the village and forgo his work that day, while wolf howls were warnings of disaster. Some Hongū families have shrines for snakes (believed to live under the house or homestead) to which daily offerings are made in return for benign protection of family members. A figurine of the fox is installed in the village shrine as the benevolent messenger of Inari, the rice spirit, while foxes are also seen as inauspicious animals (as in stories—including recent ones—of fox spirit possession). Many people claim to have been tricked by the raccoon-dog in the mountains: the victims of *tanuki no waza*, 'the raccoon-dog's tricks', include the hunter in pursuit of what he thinks is a wild boar or a deer but which turns out to be another (inferior) animal, the forester who hears the sound of falling trees in the distance but on investigation discovers that no trees are down, and villagers returning from the forest at night who follow lights that they see ahead of them but end up getting themselves lost as a result.

Japanese mountain villagers commonly anthropomorphize wild animals. The birds and mammals of the forest are routinely ascribed a wide range of human characteristics. They are seen variously as greedy, clever, crafty, deceptive, stupid, cautious, curious, angry, vengeful, loving, cute, childlike, friendly, brave, manly, cowardly, gregarious, and lonely. They behave in seemingly human-like ways, such as taking a bath (the wallowing wild boar) and playing (monkey troops). In Japan wild animals are believed to have a *tamashii* (soul or spirit), just as human beings do; consequently, the killing of an animal, like the killing of a human being, opens up the person responsible to the risk of spirit vengeance (hence the hunter's memorial service for dead game animals mentioned above). Another aspect of this popular animal-directed anthropomorphism is the attribution to animals of human-like relationships such as conjugality. When foxes kill chickens in the village it is said that *fūfu* or 'husband and wife' foxes are involved; when a crow is shot (by cullers) its *tsure* or 'spouse' cries out angrily; and when stags make their 'sad' cry in the autumn mating season they are said to be *yome o sagashiteiru* or 'looking for wives'. The meanings projected on to wild animals in turn make them powerful natural symbols of human attributes and qualities. Pheasants, monkeys, and bears are associated with maternal love, while wild boars, deer (i.e. stags), and bears are all symbols of masculinity. As we shall see in the following chapters, pestilence behaviour encourages a range of other anthropomorphic projections, albeit of a more negative kind in which the animals are likened to war enemies and criminals.

People also have or develop particular or personalized relationships with animals. Villagers born in the year of a zodiac animal, such as the wild boar, the monkey, or the rat, may find themselves likened to the personality of these animals (impulsive, intelligent, and resourceful, respectively). In the past one explanation among villagers on the Kii Peninsula for their fear of certain animals (such as snakes) had to do with the custom of burying the newborn baby's placenta in the forest: the first animal to disturb the mound would be the animal which that person (whose placenta it is) most fears throughout his or her life (Ue 1987: 265). Wild animals are occasionally kept as pets by villagers—for example, hares, weasels, wild boar, monkeys, deer, and flying squirrels (many of which are obtained by hunters as the young of animals shot or trapped). Many Hongū families keep songbirds (especially the popular *mejiro* or Japanese white-eye) that they have caught in the forest, and some enter their songbirds in regional competitions held in the coastal city of Shingū. The feeding of wildlife is a common practice; crows, kites, tits, sparrows, pigeons, raccoon-dogs, foxes, martens, monkeys, stray cats, and stray dogs are all occasionally (sometimes regularly) fed by villagers in Hongū. Examples of regular animal-feeders I have come across are the old man in Kirihata who feeds sweetfish to kites in the summer and who has learnt to imitate the kite's '*pipipi*' cry to attract them; the old widow in Shitsukawa who puts out leftover food for a pair of crows every morning at around 9 o'clock; and the old man in Kotsuga who takes home-grown peas and beans to the railway station in the coastal city of Shingū where he feeds them to the large flocks of pigeons that congregate there. Some of these voluntary feeders of animals are guided by religious teachings (such as the Buddhist idea that compassion towards animals is a virtue, and one that is likely to be rewarded). One man I knew was also in the habit of stopping his car upon spotting animal victims of road kill, picking up the animal's remains, and burying them in the nearby forest. He believed that were the animal to be left on the side of the road where it died, it might itself become the cause (through spirit vengeance) of further road accidents.

The wild animal population in the forest has long been viewed as a kind of demographic rival of the mountain village population. The *yotsuashi* or 'four-legs' of the forest are known to compete with villagers for the same forest foods such as nuts and berries, as well as for village crops. This sense of trophic rivalry is well summed by the words of an old woman in a mountain village in Yamagata Prefecture about the forest animals that bother her: *kuchi no aru mono wa minna kirai*, 'I hate everything with a mouth' (Umeda Yoshimi, personal communication). Forest animals are a problem because they have equivalent mouths to human mouths: mouths that are drawn to the same food as are human mouths. Space in the remote mountainous areas of Japan is, in a sense, defined in terms of both human and wild animal populations, such that human-occupied land in the village implicitly represents wildlife-removed land, while wildlife is always *potentially* present in this human space. Consequently, human dwelling must have an active, energetic, and (viewed from the forest) repulsive character, with people simultaneously inhabiting land *and* preventing rival (animal) habitation of it. The active character of this human settlement of land takes the form of customary village routines such as the morning walk around the fields, specially designated days for collective weed and brush clearing along the forest-edge, and the regular repair and maintenance of fences and traps. Another aspect of this demographic rivalry is the local view of forest animals as prone to increase beyond the ability of the land to support them, as was the case with the human population in the village in the past. This equivalence is further expressed by the term *mabiki* that, as we have seen, originally referred to the removal of inferior ricestalks from the paddyfield, but was extended to cover the act of infanticide. Interestingly, this term is also applied to the hunting of forest animals. In both cases, human society must make efforts to contain populations—whether human or animal—that threaten to increase out of control.

In this book the focus is on present-day wildlife pestilence—i.e. pestilence in the 1980s and 1990s, in the era of large-scale depopulation. Most Hongū households have experienced it in some form or other and most Hongū settlements make efforts to resist wildlife pests, including through the use of scarecrows, repellents, traps, poisons, and dogs, while some farmers resort to field-guarding. In Hongū wildlife damage is the subject of frequent comment and complaint, and most people have strong views on the subject. The primary concern is with the rice crop. According to figures from the Agricultural Cooperative for 1997, 41 Hongū households reported damage to their rice crop, altogether affecting 425 ares of ricefields. Half of this damage and loss is attributed to *jūgai* or 'wildlife pestilence', while the rest is caused by insects, typhoons, and so on. Over 80 per cent of rice producers in Hongū insure themselves (through the Agricultural Co-operative) against wildlife

TABLE 1.1. *Town-hall reports of wildlife pestilence in Hongū, 1995–2000*

Product	Wild Boar	Monkeys	Deer	Hares	Crows	Others	TOTAL
Rice	32	1	38		6	1	78
'Vegetables'	3	12	5		6	3	29
Potatoes	7	4			1		12
Radishes		4		1			5
Soya beans			1	1			2
Corn					1		1
Onions		1					1
Cabbages		3					3
Scallion		1					1
Arum root	2						2
Ginger	1						1
Tea	5		1				6
Persimmons		7					7
Chestnuts		7				1	7
Feed					6	1	7
Pasture		1					1
Mushrooms		5					5
Bamboo-shoots	22						22
Conifers	2		21	2			25
Other trees	2		1				3
Star anise	1						1
Sweetfish						3	3
Pigs					1		1

Note: The category 'other' includes foxes, sparrows, pigeons, and cormorants.
Source: Adapted from Hongū-chō 2000*c*.

damage. Another source of information on crop damage is the municipal government. Table 1.1 summarizes the reports of wildlife pestilence received by the Hongū Town Hall for the six-year period, 1995–2000. It lists the wide variety of farm and forestry crops damaged and the category of bird or animal deemed responsible for the damage. The reason for reporting damage to the Town Hall is to have the animals responsible culled. In response to a reported incident, the Town Hall dispatches an official to visit the site and verify the damage caused, often taking photographs as evidence of the damage. The official will make an estimate of the cost of the damage, even though the Town Hall offers no compensation to farmers. In the absence of compensation, many farmers and foresters do not bother to report wildlife damage, especially where it is small in scale. Thus, while it provides an indication of the range of wildlife damage, the table does *not* represent the total amount of wildlife damage that actually occurs.[7]

[7] However, in response to this trend, the Hongū Town Council passed a new ordinance in 1997 that established a special fund to subsidize protection measures against wildlife damage. This municipal support for farm protection remains small scale and limited. Up to half the cost of the protection measures can be covered, and the upper limit of the subsidy is ¥100,000.

The following chapters look in detail at a number of the wildlife pests mentioned in Table 1.1, such as the wild boar, the monkey, and the deer, as well as other animals, such as the bear, not mentioned in the table. Chapters 2 to 5 describe the conflict between these animals and human society, including the damage done to farming and forestry and the various efforts made to stop it. These chapters also document other aspects of the human relationship with wildlife, especially hunting, tourism, and conservationism. People–wildlife relations are shown to have a symbolic as well as material dimension, such that these animals invite human identifications even as they affect human livelihoods. We shall see that the Japanese forest-edge is the site not just of so many material relationships with wild animals, but also of manifold and often complex symbolic representations of them.

2

Wild Boar

In the foyer of the Mountain Village Development Centre in Hongū, the head of a male wild boar has been mounted on one of the central pillars, near to a display of old farming and forestry tools and other traditional artefacts. The Centre is where the Education Section of the local government is located, and one of the tasks of this section is to encourage Hongū citizens to learn about the cultural traditions and natural heritage of their town. Publications produced under the auspices of the Education Section show that the wild boar figures prominently in the animal folklore of the Hongū area. One well-known local legend tells of the wounded wild boar that disguises itself as a human being in order to enter the village of Yunomine and bathe in the hot springs there (to cure its wounds from the hunt). Another legend tells of human children abandoned in the forest who are raised by wild boar and grow up to be forest giants. In the past when walking through the forest villagers protected themselves from snakes by invoking the name of the wild boar (*yamada no hime*, 'the Princess of the mountain fields'), as it is an animal that is known to prey on snakes. But for many of the local people that visit the Centre, the sight of the wild boar is likely to recall more immediate concerns and experiences. For farmers, the wild boar is one of the most serious farm pests, one that can destroy a whole crop in a single night. For hunters, the wild boar is a potential reminder of many a hunting adventure in the forest, including incidents in which fellow hunters were injured or beloved hounds killed. This chapter examines these different local perceptions of, and relationships with, the wild boar. The first part of the chapter looks at the problem of wild boar pestilence, while the second part focuses on the hunter's view of the wild boar, and the way it overlaps with, but diverges from, that of the farmer.

The Japanese wild boar (*Sus scrofa Linnaeus*) is a highly adaptable animal that occurs in a variety of habitats in Japan, from the mild south-west to parts of northern Japan, but does not occur in the north-east of Honshu or in Hokkaido. In the Ryukyu Islands a different subspecies of wild boar, *Sus scrofa riukiuanus* (*ryūkyū inoshishi*), is found.[1] The Japanese wild boar[2] is one of the seventeen subspecies of

---

[1] *Sus scrofa riukiuanus* was recently included in the IUCN Red List as having a 'vulnerable' status (Oliver *et al.* 1993: 112).

[2] Here, notwithstanding the tendency among zoologists to refer to *Sus scrofa leucomystax* as the Eurasian wild *pig*, I refer to the subspecies in Japan as the wild *boar* rather than the wild pig, as this tends to be the convention in English language references to the animal in Japan.

the widely distributed Eurasian wild pig (*Sus scrofa leucomystax*). The Eurasian wild pig is a gregarious animal that forms herds (or 'sounders') of six to twenty individuals, centred on one or more females and their litters, with sub-adults from previous litters on the fringe of the herd, along with adult males during the mating season (Oliver *et al.* 1993: 114). Wild boar are known for their high rates of reproduction (giving birth to up to seven piglets at one time), but population numbers fluctuate from year to year, in connection with food availability and disease. In human-altered environments the wild boar is a largely nocturnal animal that can travel up to 15 kilometres during the night, while over a two-to-three month period the home range of adult boars has been estimated at between 500 and 2,000 hectares (ibid.). The diet of the wild boar is predominantly herbivorous, consisting of roots, tubers, seeds, and fruits, but it also feeds on earthworms, frogs, and insects. Hongū hunters characterize the wild boar as *yama no sōjiya* or 'the cleaner of the forest' because of the way it seems to eat everything in its path. According to one estimate, each day an individual adult wild boar needs to ingest around 50 grammes of vegetable matter for each kilogramme of bodyweight (Howells and Edwards-Jones 1997: 78). In agricultural areas, as we shall see, it tends to feed on a range of cultivated crops, bringing it into conflict with farmers.

IMAGES OF THE BOAR

The Japanese name for the wild boar is *inoshishi*, but in rural areas it is commonly referred to simply as *shishi*, a name that originally applied to all hunted animals (i.e. including the deer, serow, and bear). Japanese folklorists offer a number of different accounts of the etymology of the word *inoshishi*. According to one theory, the wild boar was known as *unoshishi* because of the '*ui ui*' cry it makes, but that over time the word *unoshishi* came to be pronounced as *inoshishi* (Tabuchi 1992: 67). According to another theory, the '*i*' of the word *inoshishi* was written with the Chinese character for 'angry' to give the meaning of 'angry beast' (Nakamura 1981: 49). This association of the wild boar with anger is widely found among Japanese hunters, for whom it is an animal known for its tendency to charge and injure men and dogs in the course of the hunt, especially when wounded or cornered. Another reason for the animal's association with anger is that, when confronted by a human being, the fur on the wild boar's back is known to bristle, becoming a physical sign of its state of rage (ibid.). The angry temperament of the wild boar makes it appear a reckless animal. There are a number of words or expressions in Japanese that refer to this characteristic of the wild boar: *chototsu* (a word that includes the Chinese character for wild boar) or 'recklessness'; *inoshishi no teoi* or 'the wounded wild boar', a metaphor for a dangerous situation; and *inoshishi musha* or 'wild boar warrior' that refers to 'somebody who behaves heedless of the consequences' (Takahashi 1997: 33–4). The wild boar is the last of the twelve animals in the

FIG. 2.1. An *ema* (votive plaque) for people born in the year of the wild boar from the shrine of Mitsumine. One writes one's name, address, and request (good health, prosperity, exam success, etc.) on the back and places it on a special rack in the shrine grounds

Oriental zodiac, and people born in the year of the boar (1947, 1959, 1971, etc.) are said to have the boar-like characteristics of determination and impetuosity (but also sincerity).[3]

Other features of the wild boar include its fecundity and its physical power. The wild boar is known as a rapid breeder. Accordingly, references to the animal tend to be made in connection with human reproduction and childbirth. In some parts of Japan there was a belief that the wild boar is a pest that opts for the fields of those families in which there is a pregnant woman (Sutō 1991: 263). Similarly, the hunter with a pregnant wife is said to have a greater chance of success in the boarhunt because the wild boar is drawn towards him (Suzuki 1982: 63). The wild boar may well be associated with plenty and multiplicity, more generally. When one wild boar is caught, there are always others to take its place. Wild boar abundance is captured in a number of expressions applied to the animal, such as *yama no shirami* or 'mountain lice' and *konoha to onaji* or 'like the leaves on a tree' (Sutō 1991: 218). The wild boar sometimes serves as a symbol of increase and prosperity. In Hiroshima, there was a belief that a man could become wealthy by keeping a clump of wild

[3]　One public figure born in the year of the wild boar and known for his boar-like personality is the comedian and actor Beat Takeshi (whose real name is Kitano Takeshi), a man who managed to resume his career after a life-threatening road accident left him with a serious speech impairment.

FIG. 2.2. Stamps bearing the wild boar's image are issued in the year of the wild boar, every twelve years

boar fur in his purse (Suzuki 1982: 65), while in the Meiji era the image of the wild boar appeared on ¥10 notes. Another impressive feature of the wild boar is its size and power. The eighth century *Kojiki* famously refers to a wild boar that was 'as big as a cow' (Yoshino 1989: 16), while the wild boar was also referred to as *yamakujira* or 'mountain whale' (Tabuchi 1992: 65). The wild boar is known to be able to overturn rocks when rummaging for food (Kobayashi 1989: 140). Throughout regional Japan there are tales of *ōjishi* or 'giant boars' that refer to animals of 100, 200 and even 300 kilogrammes in weight.[4] Newspaper reports of wild boars killed after crop-raiding or attacking people invariably refer to the animal's weight, such as the story about a boar caught in Yoshino (to the north of the Kii Peninsula) that reportedly weighed 148 kilogrammes and had enough meat on it to feed over 700 people (*AS* 19 Jan. 1996)![5]

FARMERS AND BOARS

Pestilence

Wherever it occurs, the wild pig or wild boar is a serious crop pest. Human conflict with wild pigs is found throughout the world. Warthogs, bush pigs, and forest hogs raid crops in Africa, wild peccaries damage crops in Central and South America, and wild boar/wild pigs are a major farm pest in Europe and Asia.[6] Smaller animals may be responsible for more actual damage, but wild pig raids, while less frequent, can be devastating in their effect, destroying the crop in one visit, and have even at times been a cause of rural famine (Sunseri 1997). It is this destructive potential, as much as the actual damage caused, that leads farmers to focus disproportionately

[4] See Hayakawa (1982: 64–5), Iino (1989*a*: 83, 84), and Sutō (1991: 135).
[5] See also *AS* 18 Nov. 1991 and *AS* 7 Oct. 1993.
[6] For assorted wild pig damage in Africa, see Vercammen *et al.* (1993: 97), d'Huart (1993: 89–90), and Naughton-Treves (1998). For wild boar damage in Europe, see Merrigi and Saachi (1992) and Andrzejewski and Jezierski (1978). For wild boar or wild pig damage in Asia, see Brooks *et al.* (1989), Sekhar (1998), Oliver *et al.* (1993: 115–17), and Rye (2000).

on wild pigs as a crop-raiding threat. Farmer hatred of wild pigs is widespread and wild pigs have often been the object of eradication efforts. In Japan too, the wild boar is viewed as a harmful animal, one that can condemn rural populations to poverty and hunger. In 1749, for example, 3,000 people died of starvation in what has come to be known as the *inoshishi kikin* or 'wild boar famine' (Kanzaki 2001: 259). Japanese regions suffering from wild boar damage have tended to be viewed as poor, backward places that are undesirable to live in, a view expressed in the following saying (addressed to young women in rural areas): 'When you get married, choose a place where there are no wild boar' (in Nakatani 2001: 219). A further indication of its status as the primary animal threat to human livelihoods is the reference to the wild boar as the *gaijū no ōja* or 'King of pests' (Nomoto 1994: 170; *MS* 29 July 1990).

As we shall see at length below, the wild boar is deemed a threat to the farmer rather than the forester. But the wild boar is still responsible for a certain amount of forestry damage. The other forestry pests we shall look at in this book, such as the deer, serow, and bear, are drawn to the foliage or the stems of plantation trees. The wild boar has little interest in the trees themselves, but is attentive to the foraging opportunities offered by the soil around them. Through its rooting activity in search of wild tubers, the wild boar creates large holes at the foot of the plantation tree. One of the basic rules in plantation forestry is that conifer saplings should be planted in a way that ensures they are firmly rooted in the soil as a condition for straight, consistent growth thereafter, but the actions of the wild boar can have the effect of destabilizing young trees. As a result of wild boar rooting around them, plantation trees may tilt to one side and even topple over. The after-effects of wild boar visits to a timber plantation will, in time, become readily noticeable in the uneven appearance of the trees, as trees that were planted together come to stand at varying heights. The forester can minimize such damage by regularly weeding the plantation in order to obstruct the growth of the subterranean tubers that attract the wild boar. As a rule, it is neglected plantations, in which a certain amount of undergrowth has emerged, that are the most vulnerable, while the plantations that have been conscientiously cared for (their weedy undergrowth cut and cleared) are assumed to be safe. This association between the industry of the forester and the security of the plantation finds expression in the forester's proverb: *shishi o kama de oe*, 'drive away the wild boar with your sickle' (Kusaka 1965: 117).

The wild boar is, above all, a farm pest. This has long been the case in Japan. The Japanese farmer's struggle to protect fields against the wild boar is mentioned in the eighth century *Manyōshū* (an anthology of poetry), while large-scale wild boar damage in some regions during the eighteenth and nineteenth centuries is well documented. Reports of *nojishi shutsubotsu* or 'wild boar forays' in what is now the Hongū area appear in historical documents from the nineteenth century, and in some cases such wild boar damage to farmland appears to have been very serious. In the summer of 1896, for example, considerable boar damage occurred in the village of Mikoshi, as a result of which large numbers of wild boars were shot. A contemporary record refers to the Mikoshi boar damage and the appropriate response to it as follows:

The wild boar comes out into the fields at night to damage the stems of the wheat and to dig up and eat the potatoes just at the time they are sprouting shoots. By nature, the wild boar is a fierce animal which eats crops, and then during the day hides away in the deep forest. As it does not feed at midday, during the midday hours dogs should be used to chase out the wild boar [from the forest into the open] to be shot to ensure protection [of the village]. (in Hongū-chō 2000*b*: 44)

A wide range of crops are damaged by the wild boar in Japan, including rice, potatoes, bamboo-shoots, cabbages, corn, soya beans, and mushrooms, and many kinds of fruit such as persimmons, *mikan* oranges, and chestnuts. Rice and potatoes are particularly vulnerable. Surveys from western Japan in the 1960s and 1970s show that in some areas up to 40 per cent of rice-farming households were affected by wild boar damage, and that on average these affected households saw their rice harvests halved as a result (Takahashi 1995: 39). In parts of Nagano Prefecture in the 1960s, wild boar damage accounted for as much as one-third of agricultural incomes (SMS 1969: 24). According to a 1980 Ministry of Agriculture survey, wild boar caused more than ¥1.6 billion (~ $8 million) in crop damage, far more than the damage caused by all other animal pests put together (Sutō 1991: 122–3). It has been estimated that a single animal can account for up to 30 kilogrammes of potatoes in one night (through feeding and trampling) (Miyamoto *et al.* 1995: 398). In the 1960s wild boar damage led many Nagano farmers to give up cultivating potatoes and other tubers in favour of different crops (such as honey) that would be safe from the boar's attentions (SMS 1969: 24). The wild boar problem is particularly marked in the interior of the Kii Peninsula. Surveys show the peninsular prefectures of Wakayama and Mie to be among those most seriously affected by wild boar damage (Sutō 1991: 172–4). In Hongū, according to the wildlife pestilence data shown in Table 1.1 (in Chapter 1), 77 wild boar incidents were reported for the period 1995–2000, including 32 incidents affecting rice, 22 incidents affecting bamboo-shoots, and 7 affecting potatoes. However, when shown these figures, some local people suggest that the number of actual boar incidents is much higher because many farmers do not bother to report small amounts of damage to the Town Hall (as there is no compensation available anyway).

Nojima Akio and his wife Kanemi, both in their early seventies, are forest labourers in the Hongū village of Hoshinbo. During the summer (a slack season for foresters), they cultivate around thirty ares of riceland, made up of nine fields. They have two children living nearby who with their families come to help at the busy times (rice-transplanting and harvesting) and normally receive part of the harvest in return. However, the Nojimas' ricefields are close to the forest and face a constant threat from wildlife.

First, there are deer, which come after we plant the rice saplings in May . . . Sometimes we have to re-plant the ricefield because of the deer . . . But when the rice plant grows taller and gets rough and bushy the deer stop coming, and the wild boars come. They come in July, just when the rice grain is still hard, and chew it to get the juice and then spit out all the rubbish [in the field] . . . They come even though the grain hasn't yet ripened, and in one night they can do a lot [of damage], and this can go on day after day . . . They knock over the rice-stalks and roll over in the field to cover themselves with mud . . . When this happens, you can't harvest it and it's all ruined . . . In one day they can destroy rice that the two of us could live off for a month! . . . There is also damage to the [dry]fields, as they come to eat the sweet potatoes . . .

In September 2000 the Nojimas lost two-thirds of their rice harvest through wild boar damage. As a result, the following year they had only enough rice for their own household, and for the first time they were unable to give home-grown rice to their children's families who had to purchase rice from the Agricultural Co-operative instead. As their ricefields were not insured, the Nojimas received no compensation for the damage they suffered, and as a result of this experience they no longer believe that there is much point in continuing to grow rice. In the summer of 2001 they greatly reduced the scale of their rice-farming, cultivating only three of their nine ricefields.

Shinya Takehisa is a 71-year-old retired carpenter in the Hongū village of Kirihata. His house is in the upper part of the village and his fields lie at the very edge of the forest. In 1998 he grew 33 ares of rice, and estimates his annual harvest to be around 1,350 kilogrammes of rice. He usually sells around half of this; the other half of the harvest is distributed between his own household and the households of his eldest and second sons (living in Kobe and Osaka respectively), while a little is given away to friends and other relatives as gifts. Both sons and their families come to help out with the rice-growing, especially at harvest time. But in recent years the family ricefields have been damaged repeatedly by forest wildlife. He mentions, with a half-smile, the raids on one of his ricefields that is surrounded by forest: while monkeys enter this field by day from one side, wild boars enter this same field at night from the opposite side. Although boar raids are far less common than monkey raids, and the boar group far smaller (three to five boars compared to thirty-odd monkeys), the boar raids cause much greater damage. In 1998 half of the rice harvest was lost through boar damage. Shinya-san was insured and received a payment of ¥38,000 (~$335), but says that this did not cover his actual loss which was more than ¥100,000 (~$880). As a result of persistent boar damage, each year he has reduced the amount of riceland he farms, so that by 2001 he cultivated only 20 ares. Even among neighbouring households where (unlike his own) a son has returned from the city to settle locally, Shinya-san sees little future for farming because the wild animals of the forest now feel free to run amok in the village.

Kurisu Shōzō is the 50-year-old owner of one of the handful of petrol stations in Hongū, and is also one of the youngest town councillors. With his wife, he cultivates 10 ares of riceland, consisting of four fields. In 2000, during one late summer night three of his four fields were completely destroyed by wild boar. As he was only farming a small area of land he did not insure the crop, and estimates his losses at around ¥100,000 (~$875).

There are three of us [households] farming over there and I planted two weeks after the other two. As I was two weeks late in planting, I was aiming to harvest about two weeks later than them, but in the end I was three weeks late [with the harvest] as I was busy [with the petrol station] . . . Apparently, some time earlier a wild boar had already been seen in a ricefield nearby and neighbours warned me then that I should harvest my fields soon, but I just didn't have the time to do it. In the end, that's why 75 per cent of the harvest was damaged. . . . [Beforehand] I was thinking that I had done a good job [growing the rice] and so it was really upsetting when it happened . . . I was so angry that if I had had a gun in my hands I would have shot them there and then . . . I'm sure that there was more than one boar, probably a mother and her young . . . There was an electric fence around the ricefields, but on one side there were only metal sheets and they seem to have dug underneath them using their noses and feet, like moles.

As he himself admits, because of the circumstances in which the damage occurred he received little sympathy from neighbouring farmers and other villagers. Although he took measures to protect the fields, such as putting in the electric fence, he foolishly took an enormous risk by harvesting so late. In general, villagers tend to co-ordinate and synchronize their rice-growing. One reason for this is that farmers pool their labour at the peak periods of rice-transplanting and harvesting, but another reason is that they can share the risk of wildlife damage and avoid the great increase in risk involved in harvesting later than others. In other words, in addition to the pooling of labour, synchronized farming allows for the pooling of risk. But so busy was he running his petrol station, Kurisu-san was unable to keep to the schedule of the other two farmers, and delayed his rice-growing not once but twice—first, by transplanting late and then by harvesting even later, such that his harvest finally took place three weeks after the others. As a result of this experience, he has decided to give up growing rice. One gets the impression from speaking to him that, above all, his pride has been hurt by the incident, as he was aware that, at a time of year when farmers tend to be complimenting each other on their rice harvest, news of his own disaster had circulated widely in the town and beyond, showing him to be either arrogant or incompetent. This example also highlights one of the problems that arises with part-time farming (especially Type II part-time farming): that co-operation between farmers can become much more difficult because of the off-farm occupational demands on their time.

Although one common image of the wild boar is of an animal that devours and destroys anything in its path, it can also appear as a discerning feeder. Suzuki Tokuzō is the largest rice farmer in the Hongū village of Kotsuga, with 110 ares of riceland which he farms with his wife, his son, and his son's wife. Their ricefields have suffered much damage from boar raids, and he described to me the wild boar's feeding behaviour in the following way.

It is only after they have filled their stomachs that they play around [wallow] . . . They probably know in their heads that it [the rice] is something grown by human beings and that they could be caught at any time—that's why they eat first of all . . . And once they have tasted food produced by human beings they discover that the taste is completely different from all the natural stuff in the forest . . . That stuff in the forest, after all, is not tasty at all—those nuts and acorns taste completely different [from crops] . . . They know full well the taste [of the rice]. Wild boars are no different from us—we too prefer to eat tasty things, don't we? Once they remember that taste, they are sure to come back the next year.

This farmer goes on to suggest that the wild boar's enjoyment of 'tasty' food extends to a preference for some varieties of rice over others. He believes that wild boar prefer the popular *koshihikari* ('Streaming Light') variety of rice because it is tastier than other varieties (he himself grows *koshihikari* precisely because of its superior taste). But I have also heard that wild boar prefer ricefields that grow *mochigome* or glutinous varieties of rice rather than ordinary, non-glutinous varieties. This same belief that wild boar are discriminating rice-eaters appears evident in claims that they do not bother with the organic ricefields of recent settlers (from the city) because of the poor taste of this rice.[7]

The wild boar's crop-raiding behaviour is facilitated by its highly developed sense of smell. The animal is said to have a *senribana* or 'thousand-league snout' (Hida 1967: 145) that enables it to smell the presence of crops from faraway. In the Hongū village of Komori, Mori Shigeru, who has suffered many boar raids on his potato fields (but also hunts the animal in the winter), explained to me the wild boar's extraordinary sense of smell in the following terms.

Its sense of smell is much greater than a human's and much greater than a dog's. It is written in books that it is twenty-five times or fifty times more powerful [than a dog's]. And so, if there is a river here, and the wild boar is passing along on a path on the other side of the river over there, and over here I am growing sweet potatoes, it can smell them in the wind and will come over and dig up the sweet potatoes.

---

[7] This last claim should be largely understood as a kind of joke at the expense of the newcomers who grow unusual varieties of rice that, while suited to their distinctive form of farming, are widely believed by local people to have an inferior taste. Thus, for the wild boar not to eat the newcomers' rice is a statement less about the discerning palate of the wild boar than the poor taste of organic rice *that even wild animals reject!*

Nojima Akio of Hoshinbo also referred to the boar's powerful sense of smell when he talked about boar damage to his bamboo shoots:

Its nose is really clever. The proof of this is that it eats up all the bamboo shoots even before they have emerged from the soil and before they become visible . . . It can dig fifty centimetres down [into the soil] . . . Its sense of smell is amazing.

As these comments suggest, in addition to its ability to locate food deep in the soil, the wild boar is well able to get at this food. The animal is known for the sheer power of its rooting activity, which enables it to 'dig' down into the hardest of soils (Ue 1983: 30). The tusks of the wild boar are commonly likened to a variety of farming and digging tools, including a spade or a hoe (Tabuchi 1992: 61), a plough (SMS 1969: 24), and even a power shovel (Mainichi Shinbunsha 1965: 27). This human admiration for the wild boar's digging abilities is evident in a well-known Japanese folk tale, *Inoshishi mukoiri* or 'Wild Boar Bridegroom', in which a poor farmer promises to give his daughter away in marriage to a wild boar in return for the animal helping him out with his farmwork by using its tusks as a hoe (Fukuda 1994: 74–5). This folk tale would seem to give expression to a wistful thought entertained by many a farmer: if only the wild boar's digging power could be turned away from crop destruction and used instead for crop production. But the rummaging ability of the boar consists of skill as well as power. The wild boar's *takumi* or 'ingenuity' at feeding on crops is manifested when it raids a field of sweet potatoes by eating the potatoes while leaving the visible stem intact, so that in the morning when the farmer sees the standing stems he believes that everything is normal, and it is only later on in the afternoon that he notices that the leaves have withered and that something is wrong with his fields (Sutō 1991: 139).

Crop damage by the wild boar is caused not simply by feeding, but also by trampling and wallowing. Trampling occurs because the movement of wild boar across farmland has a flattening, steamroller effect on everything in its path, and therefore represents a cause of crop damage on top of actual crop-foraging. Wallowing can then compound such damage. The wild boar is believed to find relief from lice and fleas through wallowing. According to a common local explanation, after the wallow when the mud dries hard on its body, the boar rubs itself against a tree or a rock to kill these annoying parasites. Wallowing behaviour is sometimes referred to by villagers as the boar's *ofurohairi* or 'bath-taking', not without a certain irony (as the animal ends up visibly dirtier than before). There are special muddy sites in the forest known as *nutaba* where boars wallow and where in the past hunters would stalk wild boar at night. But human settlements also offer the wild boar attractive wallowing opportunities. As referred to above by Nojima Akio, one obvious wallowing ground in the village is the summertime paddyfield where the boar can roll around in the cool mud, levelling a large area of growing ricestalks in the process. When the farmer visits the field the next morning, he discovers the shocking sight of flattened crops, a scene of such destruction that it appears as though a *rōzeki* or 'riot' had taken place there during the night (Hayakawa 1982: 32; Ue 1983: 14).

For many of Japan's upland farmers, the wild boar is a hated animal. In Miyazaki Prefecture farmers who repeatedly suffer damage to their fields come to view the wild boar as a *nikuki abaremono* or 'hateful rowdy' (Sutō 1991: 119). The following comments of a farmer in Ehime Prefecture, in a letter to a local newspaper, indicate the intensity of feeling that the wild boar can arouse.

In the *Ehime Shinbun* of the 26th of November, I read an article in which it was reported that the police had captured a wounded wild boar, but then, because it was captured in a non-hunting area, later released it after having its wounds treated. From the point of view of wildlife protection or animal-loving sentiments, this might be seen as worthy conduct, but I would like us to think again about the kind of animal involved. It [this incident] made me realize that if you have never actually suffered wild boar damage yourself, you cannot really understand its impact. I would like people to understand even a fraction of the feelings of the farmer who, over the year, puts everything into growing his crop, only then to have it eaten up and destroyed, so that he is left standing, shocked and paralysed in front of fields he can no longer harvest. Even though mountain village farmers put up nets and fences around their fields, and try all sorts of other ways [to protect their crops], they still suffer wild boar damage. From time immemorial they have been overwhelmed [by the wild boar] so that at times they were practically unable to farm at all or their land became worthless. Given this situation [in the past], you can realize how bottomless is their hatred for the wild boar. If it was a human being who had become such a serious criminal, he would be arrested, and he would hardly be allowed to escape just because he was caught in the wrong area. The wild boar that was released may well multiply to become ten or twenty animals by next year, and then come and [again] destroy our fields in the spring . . . (Farmer, aged 73, *ES* 6 Dec. 1997)

In this letter, the wild boar is likened to a criminal or a deviant, an idiom often applied to it, as well as to other forest animals. But in addition to the language of criminality, the crop-raiding behaviour of the wild boar tends to attract the idiom of war. The language of war pervades many reports of boar damage to farms. 'Since long ago there has been a desperate war between wild boar and peasants' (Mainichi Shinbunsha 1965: 27); 'the wild boar was [for the village farmer] the same as an enemy soldier', while the farmers who guarded the fields at night from the boar were 'soldiers' (Hayakawa 1982: 239; cf Sutō 1991: 163); and the wild boar are said to 'invade' village farmland (Iino 1989*a*: 80; Sutō 1991: 152). The farmer's conflict with the wild boar is a *tatakai* or 'battle' (Nomoto 1990: 62; Tabuchi 1992: 63), the animals themselves form a threatening *inoshishi gundan* or 'wild boar army' (Hidaka 1996: 53–4), and the measures and tools deployed against the wild boar are so many *heiki* or 'weapons' in the war (*AS* 13 Apr. 1994). The wild boar has even been 'adjudged the victor' (*gunpai ga agari*) in this 'war' with farmers (SMS 1969: 24). A recent representation of the militaristic character of the wild boar appeared in the 1997 animation film *Mononoke hime* (*The Mononoke Princess*), which showed the wild boar of the forest forming a large army to wage war with human society.[8]

The wild boar 'war' appears to have worsened in conjunction with village decline. Rural depopulation and agrarian abandonment provide conditions under which the wild boar can thrive. As a result of the human abandonment of the *satoyama* area surrounding the village, this space becomes good wild boar habitat. As a farmer in Hiroshima Prefecture puts it, 'when people don't enter it [anymore], the forest becomes heaven for the wild boar' (*CGS* 30 Jan. 2000). Another feature of depopulated villages is an increase in abandoned farmland, which, as it becomes overgrown with wild vegetation, provides convenient cover for the wild boar as it raids adjacent fields (Eguchi 2001: 196). A further reason that depopulated villages become easier for the wild boar to raid has to do with the decline in human numbers, especially of young people, because this tends to diminish human resistance to boar encroachment. The folklorist Sutō Isao cites a 1969 newspaper report from Nagano Prefecture that describes the effect of depopulation as having reduced the number of village 'soldiers resisting the wild boar' (Sutō 1991: 163). Seemingly aware of this change, wild boars have become more open and brazen in their raiding: 'as if foreseeing this [population decline], wild boars now calmly emerge, even when there is somebody around, and proceed to raid the field without any hesitation' (ibid.). This new boldness is reflected in the headline of the newspaper article that reads 'Arrogant Wild Boars—Beasts Rule' (ibid.). Yet if wild boar damage is exacerbated by depopulation, it can also contribute to rural depopulation. Surveys of depopulated villages have shown that wild boar damage is one of the main reasons given by families for migrating to the city (Takahashi 1995: 38). Other reports from western Japan further indicate that wild boars, through their recurrent raiding of farms, accelerate the depopulation and abandonment of remote hamlets (Sutō 1991: 163–4; cf. Palmer 1983: 332). One writer even suggests that wild boar pestilence is 'the final blow to mountainous regions [of Japan] suffering from depopulation and agrarian abandonment' (Tokida 2001: 244–5).

Responses

Wild boar damage to fields is not passively accepted by farmers. Farmers attempt to protect their crops by making the village an unappealing, difficult, and dangerous place for the wild boar to visit. Fields are protected from wild boars by the use of light, smell, noise, physical barriers, and human (or canine) guards. Olfactory deterrence is one of the main strategies of farmland defence because of the wild boar's renowned sense of smell. As the wild boar is known to be wary

---

[8] The theme of the film is that of the conflict between human society and forest animals in general, but it is significant that the wild boar is picked out as offering the most robust and spirited defence of the forest against the technologically superior human society.

of human smells, old clothes and human hair (in net-bags) are placed in and
around the fields. To this end, one of the duties of the farmer's wife was to collect
the hair of family members (beginning with her own) from combs and brushes,
while other sources of human hair were the village barber shop and hairdressing
salon. In some areas, a putrid substance made from human urine (ideally, a man's)
was smeared over posts placed around the edge of the field to be protected
(Miyamoto *et al.* 1995: 391–2). Other strong-smelling substances used to keep the
wild boar away include burnt human hair, charred bird feathers, fish entrails, and
the bones, fat, or rotten flesh of the wild boar itself (obtained from a hunter).[9]
Obnoxious-smelling chemicals are also used. A farmer in the Hongū village of
Bujū, for example, told me how he sprinkles around the borders of his ricefields the
highly pungent chemical preservative he uses for his house roof tiles. In this way,
farmers attempt to use the wild boar's great weapon in the crop-raiding 'war'—its
sense of smell—against it.

Noise is another important source of deterrence on account of the boar's acute
sense of hearing. Assorted noise devices, known as *shishiodoshi* or 'boar-scarers', are
employed. In many Japanese mountain villages the river tends to form a natural
boundary with the forest at the lower end of the settlement, and serves as one of
the main sites where systems of noise deterrence are established. One common
'hydraulic' device consists of a long pole suspended across the river and from which
hang wooden sticks that dangle on the surface of the water in close proximity to
protruding rocks. The river current carries the sticks a short way downstream
before they then swing back to smack against the rocks, creating a pattern of noise
that deters boars in the forest from approaching the river that they must cross to get
to the village. Another water-powered noisemaker is the *shōzu* or 'water-collector'
that consists of a section of bamboo stem balanced on a fulcrum in see-saw fashion,
which intermittently fills with water (from an adjacent water supply, usually a
hose) before tilting over under the weight of the water, hitting with a loud bang a
sheet of corrugated iron placed below (see Nomoto 1990: 60–1). Wind-powered
noisemakers are also used, such as rows of light bulbs suspended from a rope-line
to make an intermittent, clinking noise in the breeze, which are established
adjacent to fields. Nowadays, battery-powered sources of noise are used as well,
such as radios or alarm clocks left near the fields. For example, in an effort to
protect its bamboo-shoot harvest from the wild boar, one Kyoto temple placed
near its bamboo groves a batch of alarm clocks set to go off at different times during
the night (Mainichi Shinbunsha 1965: 29).

Finally, in addition to these other devices, there are human-activated noisemakers known as *odoshi* or *naruko*. These are metal clangers and clappers that are used
to frighten away a variety of crop pests from the fields, including sparrows, crows,
and monkeys. Usually placed adjacent to the fields, the contraption is connected

[9] See Sutō (1991: 158–9), Nomoto (1990: 60), and Tabuchi (1992: 63).

to the house by a wire, which can be tugged at regular intervals to disturb any incipient crop-raiding. One family that uses such noisemakers to defend fields against the wild boar is that of the forest labourer Ōjino Tōru in the Hongū village of Bujū. Located at the upper end of one of the remotest settlements in the municipality, the Ōjino ricefields are surrounded by forest on three sides and are therefore highly susceptible to boar raids. As a result of repeated losses to the wild boar in recent years, the Ōjinos have devoted considerable thought and effort to protecting their vulnerable rice crop. To this end, the Ōjinos place a particular reliance on their *naruko* clanger—a home-made tin-can contraption that is suspended from a tree in a bamboo grove next to the ricefields and connected by a long wire to their house. During the summer months, the couple take turns waking up at different times in the night to pull the wire and set off the clanging of the tin cans over in the fields. Although their ricefields are at risk throughout the night, the critical time is between 11 p.m. and 1 a.m., during which a special effort is made to activate the *naruko*.[10]

The best means of discouraging a wild boar from visiting a field is to establish a continuous human presence there. Until recently, it was common for family members physically to guard the ricefields through the night, especially in the late summer and autumn in the run-up to the rice harvest. The field guard had the duty of making deterrent noises, by shouting out ('*hoooi hoooi*'), by beating drums, or by tugging clapper devices, often from inside a small field-side hut known as the *yaraigoya* or 'drive away hut' (Ue 1983: 12). In some areas of Japan farmers traditionally guarded their fields for up to forty nights over the rice-growing season (Miyamoto *et al.* 1995: 392). The word normally used for field-guarding is *ban*, as in *tanbōnoban* ('ricefield-guarding'), *hatakenoban* ('dry-field-guarding'), *shishinoban* ('wild boar-guarding'), and (see next chapter) *sarunoban* ('monkey guarding'). Night-time field-guarding is one of the most unpleasant duties to perform. It disrupts a person's normal diurnal rhythm, making him or her tired during the daytime when they should be at their most productive. It is also a somewhat scary job to carry out because of the fear of the wild boar itself, the fear of other animals such as snakes, and the general unease at being so close to the forest at night. There are tales of field-guards who see or hear strange things in the night (odd animal sounds, lights in the mountains, ghosts, etc.). Sometimes *shishinoban* is undertaken by two people, as the presence of a second person both helps to ensure that the first guard does not fall asleep and offers a psychological comfort in the night darkness. The theme of night-time field-guarding is one that can occasion joking and banter. Many tales are told of

[10] It is an interesting coincidence that, according to the Oriental animal zodiac, the period between 9 and 11 o'clock at night are the hours of the boar—as the 24 hours of the day are divided into twelve according to the animal series and the boar is the last animal in the series. Consequently, boar raids may well take place in or around the hours of the boar. None of the farmers interviewed, however, actually pointed this out to me.

field-guards who fall asleep on duty or field-guards who drink sake to pass the time but end up getting drunk—in both cases leaving the field dangerously unprotected despite their physical presence.

Hōjō Takahiro farms 34 ares of ricefields in the Hongū village of Kirihata. Hōjō-san worked for the local branch of the Agricultural Co-operative, retiring some years ago. As his ricefields lie in the upper part of the village next to the forest, they are highly vulnerable to the wild boar. In the past, the ricefields in this part of the village were often raided by the wild boar in autumn, and some Kirihata villagers recall that night-time field-guarding in autumn was common in their youth. Until recently, members of the Hōjō family too guarded the family ricefields at night to protect the rice crop. Hōjō-san stresses that field-guarding was a very physically demanding duty, one that he is no longer able to do and that younger members of the family would not consider doing. *Shishinoban* was also difficult to carry out effectively because the family's ten ricefields are not all in the same place but scattered in a number of sites; he would therefore have to patrol from one site to another rather than simply take guard in one place. However, this constant moving around from one site to another did mean that he was assured of staying awake, whereas it was not unheard-of in his village for stationary field-guards to doze off and allow wild boars into the fields. He would not patrol the whole night long, but up until around 1 o'clock in the morning, because after this time the risk of a boar raid greatly diminishes. If a wild boar made an appearance before midnight, he would then feel confident that the boar would not return again that night and would take the opportunity to return home early.

Even this physical human presence does not deter the wild boar completely. Farmers who patrolled fields in different sites (such as Hōjō Takahiro) recall that at any given time during their watches up to half the fields were unprotected and at risk. But even the stationary field-guard, continuously present beside the field, is not always effective. It is said that, on discovering a human field-guard, the wild boar bides its time in the nearby forest, waiting for the opportunity to mount its raid. The animal is said to refrain from raiding under a bright moon, preferring to seize its chance when the moon wanes and the field darkens (Miyamoto *et al.* 1995: 398–9). Repeated attempts at raiding in the course of a single night are not unusual. Noshita Sadao in the Hongū village of Hoshinbo recounts the following incident (recorded in a published survey of Hongū folklore).

One night when I was on guard, a wild boar appeared at around 9 o'clock, making a noise like rainfall, '*shashashasha*'. I quickly went into the hut and from there I shouted out in a really loud voice. The wild boar then jumped out [of the field] and went back [to the forest]. Thinking it had gone, I decided to lie down for a while, but then I realized that it had returned. This pattern was repeated about four times. The next thing was when, in the morning at about the time the sky was getting white, the wild boar came and got underneath the hut. It seemed to be trying to pull away the floorboards with its feet! I was startled but did not have a gun with me, so I picked up the metal rice-husker and suddenly started hitting it with that . . . The startled wild boar [finally] ran away . . . (WKMK 1981: 80)

As this incident suggests, the wild boar seems to know the state of alertness of the field-guard, and is believed to take advantage of those times during the night when the field-guard starts to doze. A housewife in the Hongū village of Komori describes the annual *takakai* or 'battle' with the wild boar that she and her husband engage in.

[T]here is [around here] an unending battle with the wild boar, which gets worse each time . . . [E]very year, three or four weeks before harvest, we physically guard the fields at night by patrolling them and beating drums. But then, becoming more and more tired, we eventually let our guard down for a few moments—and discover that the wild boar has entered the ricefield.[11]

Farmers in Miyazaki Prefecture make similar claims, adding that after the wild boar has filled its stomach it makes a loud noise to wake up the sleeping guard before making its escape (Sutō 1991: 139). The animals do not just raid the farmer's fields, but seem to exult in overcoming human attempts to stop them. But another problem with field-guarding was that it tended to move the problem along, rather than solve it. This was because the wild boar might well respond to the presence of a field-guard in one place by simply moving to another field where guards are absent and feed itself there instead (SMS 1969: 24). Thus, when one family starts guarding its fields, this tends to pressurize adjacent farmers to do likewise.

Sometimes the burden of nocturnal field-guarding was shared by neighbouring households whose fields were near to one another. In Japan, as noted earlier, it is common for village farmers to pool their labour in the process of rice production, especially for the intensive tasks of transplanting and harvesting. Often this inter-household co-operation was extended from farming the fields during the day to guarding them by night, in this way lightening the burden of field protection. Collective field defence could also be organized on a village-wide rota basis with each farming household taking turns. In some cases, village farmers formally establish an *inoshishi kumiai* or 'Wild Boar Association' to organize the protection of their fields through rota systems for field-guarding or collective investment in, and maintenance of, electric fences (e.g. *CGS* 30 Jan. 2000). None the less, night-time field-guarding remains rare and exceptional in present-day mountain villages; there may be a growing need for it, but most people today are not prepared to carry out such a tiring, disruptive undertaking. Where serious wild boar damage occurs and fields have to be actively defended, it is more likely that the farmer will delegate the task to a dog tethered to posts near the fields in question. Sometimes the farmer and his dog guard the crop together, with the farmer resting in a van, while

[11] This description is taken from a local newsletter, *Hidamari*, where it first appeared.

his dog keeps watch on the fields outside. One such farmer I met employed the local Kishū breed of dog for *shishinoban*, a breed traditionally used for hunting; he told me that the Kishū hound was an especially effective field-guard because it had been bred to hunt boars. The protective role played by the Kishū hound is also emphasized by breed experts who claim that its 'great mission' has been that of *yama no gaijū kujo* or the 'culling [of] forest pests' (Kawada 1971: 27).

Other countermeasures include barriers and traps. In the past many villages physically separated themselves from the forest by erecting around them walls or fences known as *shishigaki* or 'boar walls', while others created dikes around the village perimeter to block the wild boar's entry. Made of wooden posts, stones, or dried mud, the *shishigaki* were sometimes referred to as *chōjō no omomuki* or 'castle walls' that could make the village resemble a *toride* or 'fort' (Ue 1983: 23). So impressive were these structures that some of them were even likened to the famous Great Wall of China (Yagasaki 2001: 130). Well-known examples of *shishigaki* include the Azukijima wall (in present-day Kagawa Prefecture) built in the mid-eighteenth century that was one and a half metres high and more than a 100 kilometres long, or the Neo wall (in present-day Gifu Prefecture) built in the early nineteenth century that was two metres high and 80 kilometres long (Hanai 1995: 59–60). In 1770 a large *shishigaki* was built in the Kumano area of the Kii Peninsula, and peninsular villagers carried out regular maintenance of the wall on especially designated *kakibushin no hi* or 'Wall Repair Days' each year (Yagasaki 2001: 145). Boar walls such as these required an enormous amount of village labour both to build them (up to ten years in one case) and to maintain them afterwards. These extensive structures are seen both as 'proof of the enmity [*ikan*] felt towards the wild boar' on the part of generations of farmers, and (given the amount of labour put into them) as a testament to the scale of village co-operation and to 'the unity of local society' in the past (Chiba Tokuji, in Sutō 1991: 154). Most of these structures now lie in ruins, often buried in the forest surrounding the village, and no longer play a role in protecting village farmland. But for present-day villagers, the nearby presence of the boar walls can still serve as a moving reminder of the spirit of self-sacrifice of past generations. 'They seem to be something built with a readiness to shed blood for the sake of descendants. There were even people who collapsed through overwork and cut short their lives in the building of the boar wall' (in Sutō 1991: 156).

The modern equivalent of the *shishigaki* is the iron-mesh fencing that surrounds many mountain villages today. Villagers coming back from the forest at the end of the day pass through a gate that they must close after them. The boar gate might be located at the foot of the mountain or, where there are dwellings higher up on the mountainside, at the divide between field and forest. Since the 1960s electric fences have been introduced to protect crops from the wild boar, and have even been hailed as a *kindai heiki* or 'modern weapon' in the 'war' with the boar (SMS 1969: 24). Much of the settlement area of upland Japan has now been sealed off from the forest with such fencing. Drawing on the analogy with medieval warfare, media reports refer to the spread of this conspicuous perimeter fencing as an expression of a *chōjō sakusen* or 'castle wall strategy' in the human struggle with the wild boar (*CGS* 9 Jan. 2000). The extent to which rural dwellers rely on these physical barriers is indicated by references to the new fencing as the *mamorigami* or 'protector god' of the village (*CGS* 9 Jan. 2000). Indeed, villages without fencing tend to look on enviously at neighbouring villages that have it, and may well follow suit eventually. An example of this in Hongū emerged in an interview with the town councillor Sugiyama Eiichi, who lives in the village of Kirihata, which used to be protected by a stone boar wall (the crumbling remains of which still exist, but now concealed by the forest). In the course of referring to the new electric fences put up in other villages, and how valuable they have proved, the councillor stated to me outright that his own village now found itself in a situation where it should follow suit and 'put up a boar wall like we had in the past'. In addition to these village barriers, individual field plots are protected with corrugated-iron fencing. These metal sheets are said to be effective because the wild boar is startled by the clanging sound made by the metal sheets when it touches or hits them.

Traps are another village defence against the wild boar. While barriers are meant to prevent the wild boar from reaching the fields, the purpose of traps is to ensure that the numbers of wild boar are reduced, as well as to provide a supply of meat in the process (and therefore a degree of compensation to villagers who have suffered earlier boar raids). One kind of trap used in the past was the pitfall, known as the *shishiana* (literally 'boar hole'), which was located along boar-paths in the forest beyond the village or along the outside of the *shishigaki*, and which often contained sharpened bamboo staves on which the falling boar would become impaled (Yagasaki 2001: 129–30). In recent years steelwire spring traps, known as *kukuri-wana* or 'binding traps', have become common. In this trap the leg or head of the wild boar is caught in a wire noose that tightens as the animal struggles. Another kind of trap is the baited enclosure, known as the *hakowana* or 'box-trap'. On entering the enclosure trap to feed off the bait, the boar trips a wire that releases the suspended door to seal the entrance. Successful trappers can become heroes in their local communities. When a boar-trapper in Aichi Prefecture captured seven boars at once in a home-made enclosure trap, a large crowd of villagers gathered around the trap to applaud him as he dispatched the animals (Sutō 1991: 192–9). Another example of a boar-trapper becoming a local hero is reported for Tochigi Prefecture: when a man who had caught some twenty wild boars with a home-made trap was arrested by the police for trapping without a hunting licence, local farmers, who had suffered frequent bouts of boar damage, got together and protested against the arrest, collecting some 750 signatures to petition for him to be released. As one of the protesters put it, 'in this community he is a hero who was protecting the local way of life' (Anon. 1998: 65).

The farmer's struggle with the wild boar is a protracted one. The animals can be kept at bay for long periods of time, but then suddenly seize the opportunity to carry out their raids, often with devastating consequences. The farmer knows that a single lapse is enough for his crop, so painstakingly cultivated over the hot summer, to disappear in a cool autumn night. Farmers are all too well aware of the wild boar's determination and persistence. Wild boar seem to have the ability to overcome most of the obstacles put in their way. The sense that boar raids are ultimately unstoppable is indicated by some of the imagery attached to them. The night-time boar raid has been likened to a 'wind' that blows into the village from the forest (Hayakawa 1982: 38). It is because of its remarkable ability under the cover of night to penetrate the most elaborate of village defences and infiltrate the best-protected farmland that the wild boar is sometimes likened to a *ninja*—the famous assassins of the medieval past renowned for their stealth and indetectability. For example, the crop-raiding boar is said to approach the farmer's fields 'on tiptoe like a *ninja*' (Sutō 1991: 138–9; cf Bekki 1979: 106). The term *taiji*, denoting 'conquest' or 'campaign', is often used in relation to the wild boar, especially in the case of a very large animal.[12] More than simply the culling of a pest, the term *taiji* connotes the overcoming of a menacing threat, even an evil monster. It is perhaps this aspect of the wild boar threat that helps to account for the employment of supernatural means to resist it.

Japanese religion is known for its diversity and variety, comprising a number of different, if intertwined traditions, including Buddhism, Shinto, and ancestor worship. Buddhas, *kami* spirits, and ancestors all play their part in the defence of village farmland. In some regions of Japan, an amulet or charm of the bodhisattva Jizō was buried in the field to protect it from the invasions of forest animals (Kawaoka 1994: 720). In Kitayama (to the east of Hongū on the Kii Peninsula), sprigs of *sakaki* or *Cleyera japonica* (a plant associated with Shinto *kami*) were offered to the *kami* at village festivals and afterwards buried in fields to stop wild boar damage (*MS* 23 Sept. 1990). In the Kyūshū village of Suye-mura, studied by the American anthropologist John Embree in the 1930s, bamboo stalks cut for the Tanabata festivity, that are associated with the return of the ancestors around the time of *bon* (the midsummer ancestral festival), were used by farmers to protect their fields from wild animals such as the wild boar (Embree 1939: 287). As we shall see in Chapter 6, another source of supernatural protection of farmland from wild boar was provided by wolf shrines such as Mitsumine Jinja, through which farmers could tap the power of the wolf to defend their crops. After making a pilgrimage to the shrine to obtain the *mamorifuda* or 'protective charm', the farmer would affix it to a wooden post placed at the edge of the field to be protected (Yagasaki 2001: 132). According to some reports, the *mamorifuda* really did prove to be an effective defence against crop-raiding boars, to the point where it has been suggested that

---

[12] See Kinoshita (1979: 74), Hayakawa (1982: 240), and Sutō (1991: 183, 274).

the white paper charm, on account of its conspicuous appearance and smell, might inadvertently have had a scarecrow effect (ibid.).

Some Japanese scholars emphasize the difference between, on the one hand, the relatively non-violent Japanese response to the wild boar problem (as epitomized by the reliance on the *shishigaki*), and, on the other, the more violent Western response to wild boar pestilence, seeing in this difference a *cultural* contrast between a Japanese world-view based on human–animal continuity and a dualistic Western world-view (see Takahashi 2001: 369–70). Yet violence clearly has been a part of the human–boar relationship in Japan. The gun has occupied an important place in the Japanese farmer's struggle with the wild boar. During the Edo period (1603–1868), gun possession was carefully restricted by the public authorities, wary of the possibility of guns being used in civil disturbances or rebellions. Moreover, in 1685 the fifth *shōgun* Tokugawa Tsunayoshi passed an edict prohibiting the killing of animals, domestic or wild. Known as the *seirui awaremi rei* or Compassion for Living Things Edict, this edict is believed to have been inspired by Tsunayoshi's Buddhist beliefs. But the measure has also been viewed as an attempt to secure social and political pacification (the banning of gun possession) (Maruyama *et al.* 1996: 199). Special dispensations for peasant gun-holding were sometimes issued where serious wildlife damage to farms occurred, and in some areas the rate of gun possession seems to have been quite high. Written records show that for some remote regions in the late eighteenth and early nineteenth centuries there were as many as twenty-five guns per village—that is, a gun for every second household (Hanai 1995: 57). More generally, it has been suggested that in the late nineteenth and early twentieth centuries guns were regarded by mountain villagers threatened by wild boar farm raids as, in effect, a *nōgu* or 'farming tool' that was barely less important to successful cultivation than the peasant's hoe and sickle (Sutō 1991: 50; Hanai 1995: 56).

Although some Japanese farmers used guns themselves, others have been dependent on hunters to dispatch wild boars for them. Japanese folklore contains many tales of brave hunters who save the village from the ravages of giant wild boar. In one village on the Kii Peninsula, a great boar-hunter of the past is deified as Kariba Myōjin, 'Bright Spirit of the Hunting Grounds'. According to legend, the village was besieged by a giant boar, which repeatedly raided village fields, leaving the villagers poor and hungry. But with the help of an outside hunter, the rampaging boar was finally conquered, and the heroic hunter was enshrined as a result (Ibaraki 1993: 120–1). Similarly, an annual festival is held in the Chichibu area to give thanks to Yamato Takeru no Mikoto for vanquishing a giant boar running amok in the village (Iino 1989*a*: 78). In the past, in many areas of Japan the authorities offered bounties (in rice) to hunters for the killing of wild boar during the rice-growing season.[13] But there are also examples in Japan where local wild boar populations

---

[13] See Sutō (1991: 156), Hayakawa (1982: 32), *MS* (19 Feb. 1989), and Mukōyama (1993: 33).

have been deliberately exterminated. In the Hokuriku region in the 1720s, in response to large-scale wildlife damage to farms (caused by heavy snowfall which deprived the animals of access to forest feeding grounds), all male villagers between the ages of 15 and 60 were called up and equipped with spears to eradicate wild boar and deer (Chiba 1995*a*: 120–2). Another well-known example of wild boar eradication took place on the island of Tsushima at the beginning of the eighteenth century. 'On this island there were at one time very many wild boars—so much so that it could have been called "Wild Boar Island"—which were a cause of continuous hardship for local people' (Tabuchi 1992: 64). Battue-style hunts involving large numbers of people were carried out in which the wild boar were driven out into the open and killed, the effect of which was to erase almost the entire wild boar population from the island (Sutō 1991: 190).

These exterminist sentiments towards the wild boar are further evident in attempts to control wild boar in modern times. Local governments administer wild boar bounty systems which involve fixed payments to hunters for each boar killed, conditional on the hunter presenting to the Town Hall proof of the kill (such as the tail or the limbs of the animal). In the present day, hunters are mobilized to defend the village from wild boars through participation in *kujotai* or 'culling squads'. Municipalities in Nagano, Hyōgo, and other prefectures have established *bokumetsutai* or 'extermination squads' and waged *bokumetsu sakusen* or 'extermination campaigns' against the wild boar (SMS 1969: 24; Sutō 1991: 180), while in Okinawa calls have been made for the *zenmetsu* or 'annihilation' of the wild boar because of its damage to pineapple plantations (Sutō 1991: 184). It is not at all unusual for farmers who have suffered repeated boar depredations to voice such exterminist sentiments. As one farmer in Ehime Prefecture put it by way of encouraging a boartrapper: 'Please catch all of the wild boars. It would be better if there were not one of those things around. Where they exist, they just cause problems' (in Kurita 1999: 88). Such comments might suggest that the hunter is the natural ally of the farmer in the 'war' with the wild boar. Hunters hunt the wild boar in the winter hunting season, and are called on to cull the boar throughout the year. Hunters, like farmers, readily invoke the language of 'war' in relation to the wild boar. However, as we shall see, the hunter's perspective on this 'war' differs in important ways from that of the farmer.

HUNTERS AND BOARS

The Boar Hunt

The wild boar is a favourite game animal among Japanese hunters. In the 1970s and 1980s on average around 60,000 wild boars were annually killed through hunting and trapping in Japan (Oliver *et al.* 1993: 116). In the 1990s the numbers of wild boar killed increased sharply, reaching an annual figure of more than 100,000 animals by the late 1990s, the highest recorded figure in modern times (Tokida 2001: 250). Over 80 per cent of these animals are killed as game animals, while the rest are killed as pests. The *shishi* (as hunters normally refer to it) is widely viewed as the foremost game animal—the *shuryōjū no hanagata* or 'star among game animals' (Ue 1990: 162). Hongū hunters point out that the boar hunt is a special experience, and refer to its *daigomi* or 'sweet taste', its *tegotae* or 'pull', and its *suriru* or 'thrill'. Along with the experience of the hunt itself, the appeal of boar-hunting has to do with the highly valued taste of boar meat. The tastiness of boar meat is explicitly connected to the boar's diet and to the amount of fat on the animal. Hongū hunters distinguish between tasty *okajishi* or 'hill boars' and less tasty *sakojishi* or 'valley boars' on the basis that the former feed on chestnuts and other nuts and berries of the forest, while the latter feed on assorted detritus along the river valley. In some northern parts of Japan the meat of the wild boar is said to be at its tastiest—'even tastier than beef'—in the last third of December and the first third of January because of the rich fat deposits on the animal at this time of year (Nishiura 1989: 174–5). Another valuable part of the wild boar in the past was the gall bladder, which, like that of the bear, is considered an all-purpose tonic in Japan.

Two basic methods of hunting wild boar can be distinguished. One is *neyadome* or 'lair-stopping' (also known as *hoedome* or 'bark-stopping'), in which the boar is stopped at or near its lair by the barking hound. *Neyadome* tends to be synonymous with *tandokuryō* or 'solo hunting' that involves just a single hunter and his hound. The more common method of boar-hunting is known as *machibauchi* ('waiting-spot-shooting') or *makigari* ('circle-hunting') in which the wild boar is driven towards concealed shooters who dispatch it. In *machibauchi* the hunting group (which may well consist of ten or more men) is marked by a division of labour between two principal roles: the *seko* chaser and his hound who flushes out the boar from its lair and drives it down the mountains, and the *machi* shooters who wait in set positions along its likely escape routes. The *seko* takes his hounds into the mountains, along the animal paths of the forest, following the scent of the boar. As one who runs with the hounds along low, narrow animal corridors in the forest, the *seko* must have a special fitness. It is a physically demanding role that only some hunters are able to carry out. The *machi*'s role is to wait at particular spots around the mountain, which should accord with the escape routes of the hunted animals. The *machiba* or 'waiting spot' should be a concealed place along one of these routes that affords a good aim at any fleeing animal. Typically, there will be one or two *seko* and anything from one to ten *machi* strategically placed around the mountain. In principle, the larger the hunting group, the greater the chances of success. The *seko* is the key player, the one on whom the others depend to track down the wild boar and drive it in their direction. The *machi* is expected to consummate the work of the *seko* by shooting accurately when he gets the chance.

Despite their size and number, wild boar are generally recognized to be *torini-kui* or 'difficult to catch'. Just as the wild boar is adept at breaching human farm defences, so it has a legendary capacity for evading the hunter and his dogs. Locating a wild boar in the forest is one thing, catching and dispatching a fleeing animal quite another. One reason for the difficulty of boar-hunting is that, in addition to its highly developed senses of smell and hearing, the wild boar has what is known as *tennen no chie* or 'natural wisdom'. I first heard this expression when it was mentioned by the Komori hunter, Mori Shigeru, in the course of an interview in 1994.

They [wild boar] have what you might call natural wisdom. They have something that we human beings don't understand. Old people in the past used to say, 'it's not good to talk over tomorrow's [hunting] operations this evening . . . because the mice will go and tell [the wild boar]'. We say to ourselves, 'tomorrow, we will go here and we will go there, so and so will go over there'—but really it's bad to talk over the operations like this because the next day you find that when you go [to that place in the mountains], the wild boars will not be there, even though they normally come to feed at that place every night . . . That's a real mystery.

Hunters in other regions characterize hunting as 'pitting your wits against the wild boar' (in Imai 1979: 68).

Hunters view the wild boar as an extremely elusive animal. This is most evident during the chase itself. Hongū hunters suggest that the wild boar deliberately leads the hunting party into difficult, challenging terrain, as though it were testing the physical abilities of hunters and dogs to their limits. According to Mori Shigeru, a fleeing boar rarely allows itself to be cornered; even where it seems to be in danger, it manages to pull off unlikely escapes time after time. Hunters say that one of the *shishi*'s tactics is to move to the very edge of its territory and then discreetly reverse back to bypass its pursuers who forlornly continue the chase into the remote mountainous interior. Another *shishi* trick is to move in a figure of eight, to the great confusion and frustration of hunters and hounds. Young hounds are especially likely to end up being outwitted by the wild boar. Hunters in Kyushu say that, when chased, the boar runs around in a wide circle and then suddenly moves out of it to escape, leaving the hapless dog still running round and round, unaware that it has been tricked (Sutō 1991: 138). But the wild boar is also said to fool the hunter by disguising its tracks—by *tsumasakidachi* or 'walking on tiptoe', by walking over ground frost, or by deliberately messing up its tracks (*ashimotoarai*, literally 'rough feet'), especially in the vicinity of the lair. It is because of this well-known resourcefulness of the *shishi* that hunters routinely refer to the animal as an *aite* or 'opponent' which, above all other animals in the forest, offers the hunting group a *chōsen* or 'challenge'.

Japanese hunters draw on a variety of information sources and tools in their pursuit of the wild boar. They use their own knowledge of the landscape to locate the likely whereabouts of a wild boar (i.e. south-facing mountainsides with pasania [*shiinoki*, Castanopsis spp.] forest vegetation) and their own tracking skills to detect signs of the boar (such as boar tracks, disturbed piles of earth, mud marks, etc.). In the course of tracking, in addition to their own senses, they use the senses of their hounds. Hunters also make use of technological gadgetry, including two-way radios, heat sensors, radio-collars for hounds, etc., while second-hand intelligence (tip-offs from foresters or plant collectors) can prove valuable too. But another aid which Japanese boar-hunters draw on to help them catch their elusive prey is the *koyomi* or calendar almanac. The *koyomi* is an astrologically based annual register of the days and months of the year classified according to their auspiciousness, which is widely consulted in Japan for the planning of weddings, funerals, distant journeys, and other special events, especially where these involve an element of uncertainty or danger. Earlier generations of hunters on the Kii Peninsula are said to have decided the day of the hunt with reference to the almanac. Although rarer today, almanacs continue to be used by hunters. In a boar hunt in January 1999, I observed a group of hunters from the Hongū village of Kotsuga consult a printed almanac (produced and sold by a large Shinto shrine in the region) to determine which direction to approach a certain mountain known to be boar habitat. Although in this case the direction chosen did not lead to success, the incident indicated that boar-hunting continues to be understood, in part at least, in terms of the influence of the unseen forces of the (super-)natural world.

In Hongū adjectives such as *kashikoi* or 'smart', *rikō* or 'clever', and *zurui* or 'crafty' are routinely applied to the wild boar. These characterizations are often made by the farmer in connection with the boar's skill at accessing protected fields in which it shows cunning and patience (as we have seen above). But hunters too refer to the wild boar's amazing capacity for knowing or anticipating human actions and intentions. Some hunters in Hongū attribute a kind of calendrical awareness to the wild boar. One of the most frustrating times for Japanese boar-hunters is in the autumn when they hear about one boar raid after another on local ricefields, but are unable to do anything about it themselves until the start of the hunting season in November (even if culling licences are promptly issued in response, it may well be other hunters who are the ones called on to undertake the cull). The raiding boar often leaves a clear set of mud-tracks leading to a boar-path in the forest, almost inviting the hunter to follow. Some hunters will in fact make a note of such events and even trace the direction of the tracks in the forest, in the hope of putting this information to use later on in the hunting season. However, it is said that when the hunting season finally begins on 15 November, the boar raids suddenly stop and wild boars disappear, leading many a hunter to speculate that the animals somehow know that it is no longer safe for them to leave the forest. Hunters in other parts of Japan make similar claims—for example, that with the onset of the hunting season the wild boar not only stays in the forest but moves within the forest to protected (non-hunting) areas for safety (Sutō 1991: 135). It is as though the wild boar has a knowledge of dangerous times and dangerous places.

The *shishi* is viewed, above all, as a fighter. It is known as an animal that 'has confidence in its fighting ability' (Ue 1983: 37) and is sometimes referred to as a *mōjū* or 'fierce beast' (as in the Hongū document of 1896 about boar damage cited above), a term normally applied to wild predators such as the bear and the wolf. Japanese hunters point out that the wild boar can kill any animal that confronts it, and that wild boar have been known to kill tigers on the Korean Peninsula (Furuya 1999*b*: 81). The wild boar's clash with the hounds, when the boar engages one or more hounds, is one of the most thrilling moments of the hunt. 'When it fights, it fights all-out. In its head the war strategy of protracted struggle does not exist . . . When it is surrounded by dogs, for some ten minutes it frantically resists' (Kitagawa 1979: 55). But the wild boar also takes on the hunter himself. Ishikawa Takeichi, a hunter from Mie Prefecture, recalls the following experience.

I lifted my gun and aimed at the head of the wild boar, and moved towards it. Even though the wild boar was fighting the dog, when it discovered a human being nearby, it suddenly shook off the dog and charged. It all happened in an instant. In no time at all, it was coming at me. However small a wild boar is, its movements are fast and its bite frightening. I felled it as it was barely two metres away from me'. (Ishikawa 1979: 39)

The wounded wild boar, hit by the hunter's fire, does not give in, but becomes all the more dangerous. The danger posed by the wounded boar is a major preoccupation among boar-hunters. The veteran Hongū hunter and trapper Inui Mitsunori referred to this danger in the following terms.

When the wild boar is cornered, by men and dogs, and when it thinks, 'I can't get away', then it will come for you. While it can escape it will escape, but when it no longer can escape it will come at you . . . especially a boar that is wounded. They are the most frightening ones, the ones that have been shot or have been caught in traps before, the ones that have had all sorts of serious injuries.

The wounded boar is difficult and dangerous to catch because of its frantic disposition and erratic movements—the seriously wounded boar is sometimes said to be in a *shinimonogurui* or 'dying rage'. There are endless hunting tales of wild boar spirit and valour, usually involving wounded animals: the wounded boar that is surrounded by five or six dogs but still manages to escape; the boar that escapes despite being shot three or four times by the hunter; the boar that is shot in the head or in the heart but still finds the strength to run in a vain attempt to flee; and the dying boar that uses its last reserves of energy to knock the hunter over. The sheer indomitability of the *shishi* sometimes seems to transcend death itself. A hunter in Kōchi Prefecture recalled how he once came across 'a dead wild boar standing on all fours with its feet buried in the ground, as though it were making a last stand' (in Katsuki 1995: 328). Trapped boars too refuse to die quietly. An example of this was the wild boar caught waist-high in a wire trap outside one peninsular village: despite being assailed by farmers with hoes and clubs and by village dogs, the desperate boar saw off its attackers and escaped to freedom (Ue 1983: 34–5).

Along with its fighting spirit, the wild boar is endowed with a fighting physique. All adult boars are dangerous because of their sheer size and physical power when charging and because of their ability to bite. According to one description, the charging boar moves swiftly, smoothly, and unstoppably as though it were 'a drumcan on a rollercoaster' (*AS* 22 Nov. 1992). The male boar has an additional, fearsome weapon in the form of its sharp, lacerating tusks. Hunters sometimes liken the boar's tusks to *katana* or 'swords' and *kamisori* or 'razor blades' which they know are able to wound and kill them and their dogs. But, as the tales of wounded boar resistance above indicate, the wild boar can also resist the powerful human weapons used against it. The *shishi* is known as an almost armour-plated adversary because of its habit of coating its fur with pine resin. It does this by rubbing its back against pine trees in the forest, transforming its body exterior into a virtual carapace (the word *teppan* or 'iron plate' is used) that the hunter's shotgun can barely penetrate (Sutō 1991: 141). Among male boars during the mating season, 'the fat under the skin hardens to become like a plank of wood, which is known as [the boar] "wearing armour" [*yoroi o kiru*]' (Shinoda 1995: 51). This physical change equips male boars to fight one another, but also makes them a more formidable enemy for human hunters.

The qualities of courage and defiance that are associated with the wild boar make it an object of admiration and even identification among Japanese hunters. In Japan boys are sometimes named after the wild boar, by being given the character for wild boar 猪 in their personal names—such as Inosuke, Inokichi, and Iichirō. There are many examples of this in the mountainous areas of Japan (e.g. Hayakawa 1982: 240). The wild boar epitomizes the masculine traits of boldness and determination; one contributor to the *Shuryōkai* hunting magazine even praises the wild boar as a *danseiteki de daitan na dōbutsu* or 'manly fearless animal' (Satō 1979: 111). The wild boar is particularly associated with the qualities of courage and boldness. In Japanese there is an expression, *choyū* or 'boar courage', that refers to 'courage without looking ahead' (Akatsuka *et al.* 1993: 682). Sometimes the manly qualities of the wild boar are believed to extend to a capacity for chivalry. The writer Hida Inosuke, who has written about hunters in different regions of Japan (and whose personal name, incidentally, contains the wild boar character), states that the male wild boar is a *yūkan* or 'courageous' animal which, when hunted, acts as a decoy by encouraging the hounds to pursue it, thereby enabling the female and young boars to escape to safety (Hida 1967: 155). A similar point is made by a hunter in Tanzawa who recalls that when he was pointing his gun at a female boar and just about to shoot, a male boar suddenly charged him from behind to protect her (*AS* 22 Nov. 1992).

If the 'courageous' boar attracts admiration from the men who hunt it, it also presents these men with practical tests of their own courage. Inui Mitsunori suggests that the charging boar reveals the weakness of many of his fellow hunters.

If you make a mistake at that moment, it could be the end. Because it could be devastating, people just run away. They run away as soon as they see it [the boar]—those kinds of people. The worst ones even leave their guns behind—they just chuck them away in the forest [and flee]. Later, they will come back looking for their guns [but don't find them]. And then, after three or four years have passed, some forest labourer will find it. That's what happens. They just do not have the strength to hunt. Those kinds of people really exist. From out of their mouths they talk about the great things they have done, but they are really no good for anything and they never catch a thing . . .

Inui-san illustrated the point by referring to a local man who was gored to death by a boar in a recent boarhunt.

That person fired his gun at a boar that was charging up the slope at him but he didn't hit it. He did not really have courage. If only he had had courage . . . You have to wait until the boar comes up close. Then you wait until the end of the gun nearly touches its [the boar's] head [and then fire] . . . But he wasn't somebody who had such courage . . . You don't want to take that that kind of person along [hunting with you] . . .

The preoccupation with fear is found among hunters more generally. Frightened hunters are doomed to failure. 'If you think that the animal is frightening, then you cannot confront it. If you think it's scary to hunt alone deep in the forest, then you've already lost' (Ishikawa 1979: 40). One main reason for this is that the wild boar is believed to be aware of such human weakness and all too likely to exploit it at a crucial moment. This point is made by hunters in Mie Prefecture who say that in choosing its escape route during the chase 'the wild boar goes in the direction of the weak-hearted man [in the group]' (Kimura 1979a: 65). The *machi* shooter who gives in to fear and shows himself to be a *ki no yowai hito* or 'faint-hearted person' becomes the weak link in the chain. Conversely, the successful *machi* are those men who are mentally prepared for the boar hunt and able to stay calm in the face of danger. In describing the requisite qualities of a good *machi*, Inui Mitsunori likewise stresses the overriding importance of courage.

If you hit the right spot, then one shot is enough . . . You get yourself calm, look at the boar's movements, then you aim for the area of the heart, the head, or the spine . . . But if you aim here and then aim there, and are unsure, and then suddenly fire, you won't hit a good place . . . You must confirm to yourself where you are going to hit . . . Remember one thing. When you shoot a wild boar you shoot it with courage [*shishi wa utsu no wa dokyō de ute*]. With courage. You shoot it with the gun, but you [really] shoot it with courage. If you don't have that, you won't catch anything . . .

The encounter with a wild boar reveals something fundamental about a man. Men change when they hunt because, once they are out in the forest with their dogs and with their fellow hunters, they start to feel the *ryōyoku* or 'hunting desire'

FIG. 2.3. A hunter in Miyazaki Prefecture carrying a wild boar hunted in the forest back to the village

within them. The cold winter weather helps to bring about this change in men. As Mori Yukimitsu of Komori put it, explaining to me the pleasure of the boar hunt on a really cold day, 'if it's not cold, there is no hunting desire and human beings don't boil [*ningen wa waite konai*]'. Hunters elsewhere make the same point, such as the following contributor to the *Shuryōkai* magazine:

There is a phrase that I like: 'Whatever it is, do it with spirit'. As man and dog become one [in the hunt], you go out and do your best. This is where a man's adventure is born. Forgetting all worldly thoughts, a joy emerges that only the hunter can taste'. (Matsuoka 1979: 62)

Identification with the wild boar generally takes the form of a desire to be victorious over it in the hunt. If a man is to be a successful boar-hunter, he must himself possess some of the spirit of the animal he is chasing. Hunters take pride in the number of wild boars they have killed. In some cases, hunters have their wild boar victims—usually the larger and more impressive animals—stuffed and mounted as trophies, or preserve the memory of the kill with a photograph in which they pose next to the dead animal.

The wild boar's association with masculinity is further evident in the fact that, for boar-hunters, the archetypical *shishi*—the supreme 'enemy'—is the male boar in mating season. The hunting season coincides with the mating season of the wild boar (in the middle of winter), the time of year when it is at its most aggressive. As Inui Mitsunori puts it, 'when another boar comes along to your own [i.e. a boar's] territory, then there will be a battle [*kassen*] to drive it away'. At this time, male boars fight each other for females, fights that can lead to the death of the defeated animal. These truculent males, known as *gari* or *garippo*, pose a special danger to hunters and hounds; some hunters even characterize them as potential *inugoroshi* or 'dog-killers' because of the exceptional ferocity they show towards the hounds. Even accomplished hunters may find themselves overawed in the presence of the *garippo*. But the hunter who is ready to match such boars in spirit will be successful. 'For somebody who has a bold spirit [*takumashii seishin*] and is ready to deal with the behaviour of the animal to be confronted, the *garippo* will appear as no more than a weakened wild boar' (Ishikawa 1979: 40). If wild boars in general set a test for the men who confront them, the *garippo* pose a further, extra-special challenge which sorts out the superior hunters from the rest. This perception of the extraordinary power of the male boar is further evident in the custom (reported among older hunters on the Kii Peninsula) of consuming the testicles of the wild boar to enhance a man's *seiryoku* or 'vitality' (WKRNS 1979: 61).

Boar Wars

Like the farmer, the hunter applies the language of war to the wild boar. As an occasion for men to display courage, strength, and teamwork, the boar hunt is routinely likened to warfare, and there exists an extensive lexicon of militaristic terminology employed by hunters. Boar-hunters refer to the group of hunters as the *ryōtai* or 'hunt squad', to the hunt as a *tatakai* or 'battle', to the hunting ground as a *senjō* or 'battlefield', to hunting plans as *senpō* or 'battle tactics', to a pause or stand-off in the hunt as a *kyūsen* or 'armistice', to hunting success as *senka* or 'war gains', to past hunting experience as a *senreki* or 'war record', and so on.[14] Boar-hunters sometimes apply military nomenclature to themselves: the lead hunter in a Hongū hunting group is the *kyaputen* or 'captain', while elsewhere overbearing hunters, who always think they know best, are *yama no taishō* or 'mountain generals' (Yamamoto 1995: 64). The war idiom readily extends to the wild boar itself, with hunters referring to the boar as the *yama no mosa* or 'mountain war veteran', to the

[14] See Mainichi Shinbunsha (1965: 24), Fukuya (1979: 74), Miyoshi (1979: 53), Shibahara (1995*a*: 39), Shibahara (1995*b*), *AS* (22 Nov. 1992), Sutō (1991: 119), and Fujiwara (1999).

FIG. 2.4. A dead wild boar after the hunt

boar's tusks as *buki* or 'weapons', and to trophies from the boar hunt as *rekisen no torofii* or 'war trophies'. One hunter on the Kii Peninsula recalls that it was his grandfather's tales of the boar hunt, conjuring up images of 'a young warrior [*wakamusha*] heroically fighting the enemy', that inspired him to become a boarhunter himself (Seko 1988: 10).

The hunter's boar war has its human casualties. Through their encounters with charging boars, hunters suffer serious injuries and incur long-term disabilities (in some cases, becoming crippled). Many a boar-hunter has scars to show from past battles, usually on one of his legs; some even have permanent metal plates in their limbs to support bones that were fractured in past hunts. Although such incidents seldom occur, every boar-hunter knows that the *shishi* is a potential mankiller. As one boar-hunter put it, fatal boar attacks on the hunter occur 'once in a hundred times, but 99 per cent of the time it will be victory for Man'. But when such human fatalities do occur, they come as a major shock that everyone talks about for weeks and months afterwards. In January 1997 a hunter from the

Takada area of the Kii Peninsula was killed by a wild boar in the course of a hunt. In the following days the incident became the dominant talking-point among Hongū hunters. I recorded the following account of the fateful hunt from a Hongū hunter.

Five people went out boar-hunting, and one of them shot the *shishi*. The [wounded] *shishi* headed for this man's spot. While the *shishi* was coming up to the top of the mountain, it was hit [a further] three times, but the *shishi* was still on its feet, and headed for the mountain peak where that man was. That man then thought things were hopeless, and tried to escape but fell. The *shishi* then descended to where he fell and gored him. The *shishi* stood there like a Deva King [*niōdachi*], dripping with blood, and then left. The other four hunters vowed to wage a war of revenge over the hunter's death and went after the *shishi*, but they didn't catch it.

Direct human deaths in the boar hunt are rare. The more common victims of the wild boar are the hounds used by the hunters. In general, Japanese hunters fight the wild boar vicariously through their hounds rather than directly themselves, and it is the hounds that are exposed to the greatest danger. Brave dogs are vulnerable to being cut and gored by the boar's tusks, and boar-hunters often carry a needle and thread with them in case they have to perform emergency surgery on their dogs. It has long been said by peninsular hunters that *yoi inu wa nagaiki sen* or 'a good dog does not live long'. Given their position on the front line, the idiom of warfare is naturally extended to the hounds. Hounds are referred to as *heishi* or 'soldiers' and *taishōken* or 'dog generals' (see Chiba 1977: 106); they are given warrior names, such as *Wakamusha no Tora* or 'Tiger the Young Warrior' (Takashita 1995: 47); their hunting injuries are prestigious *kunshō* or 'medals' that display past bravery in battle (Kimura 1979*b*: 53); and hound deaths caused by the *shishi* are poignant *senshi* or 'war deaths' that, like the death of a hunter, should be avenged (Urayama 1995: 97). In one example of such a 'war of revenge' against the wild boar over the death of a hound (reported in the *Shuryōkai* hunting magazine), a group of hunters from Kagoshima Prefecture pursued the *inukiri* or 'dog-killer' for three years before finally exacting full revenge (Shibahara 1995*a*; 1995*b*). On completing the kill, the hunters visited the grave of the dead hound, reported to it the day's momentous events, and placed at the grave a clump of fur from the slain boar as an offering (Shibahara 1995*b*: 44).

There is a further dimension to the antagonistic relationship between human beings and wild boar in Japan. The hunter has long been deemed to be vulnerable to the *tatari* or curse of the wild boar. One such folk tale of the wild boar's *tatari* tells of the greedy hunter who hunts wild boar excessively until one day, when out hunting in the forest, he mistakes his own mother for a wild boar and kills her (Chiba 1995*a*: 141–2)! But the theme also appears in reports of present-day hunting, such as a 1995 article in the *Asahi Shinbun* newspaper, entitled 'Memories of the Late Leo', that tells of a hunting accident in which an injured boar-hunter was saved by his hound. In the article the old hunter tells of how he had slipped on the wet mountainside and tumbled down into the valley below, dislocating a shoulder and breaking a leg. Although in the end the old man was saved, he recalls that in his darkest moments of despair alone in the *yama* he found himself wondering if he had been cursed by all the wild boar that he had killed over the years (*AS* 9 Apr. 1995). Hunters respond to this spirit danger in a number of ways. One response is to practise moderation in hunting, while another is to give up hunting altogether. Chiba Tokuji reports that the mountainous interior of the Kii Peninsula is one of the places where a hunter stopped hunting after a thousand kills; the possible consequences of not doing so include the hunter encountering a *kaii* or 'monster' in the forest, or even that the hunter's dog would turn on the hunter himself (Chiba 1975: 248). Another response is to pacify the spirit of the wild boar through some form of ritual. Hunters in western Japan erected special memorial stones, known as *senpikizuka* or 'one thousand head mounds', for the spirits of their wild boar victims (Kaneko *et al.* 1992: 53; Chiba 1975: 245–53). According to hunters in Miyazaki, 'if you catch one hundred wild boars and do not set up a wild boar mound, you will be cursed by the mountain spirit' (Suzuki 1982: 63). Some hunters have gone even further and, in addition to giving up hunting, became Buddhist monks in an attempt to atone for their hunting past (Nagamatsu 1993: 28–32).

Culling too raises fears of wild boar *tatari*. This is especially the case with large-scale culling, as in the example, mentioned above, of the wild boar eradication campaign on the island of Tsushima in the eighteenth century. In order to protect the island's cullers from spirit revenge, Shinto priests were called to make a ritual request for forgiveness and to pacify the spirits of the animals slain (Sutō 1991: 191), while young boars were captured alive and taken to the nearby Korean island of Makishima where they were released (Tanigawa 1980: 293–4). But even present-day cullers of wild boar recognize a certain spirit danger. The *Shuryōkai* hunting magazine occasionally mentions examples of present-day hunters and cullers carrying out *kuyō* memorials for specific animals they have killed. One such report from 1979 describes the cull of a 'giant wild boar' in Kagoshima by a group of hunters. After finally succeeding in killing the animal following a number of failed attempts, including one in which they lost a boarhound to the wild boar, the group held a celebration party afterwards in which the hunters offered the heart of the wild boar to the mountain spirit, but also undertook to 'pacify the spirit of the wild boar' (Kinoshita 1979: 77).

FARMERS, HUNTERS, AND BOARS

The wild boar is a pest for the farmer and a resource for the hunter. There have been efforts to enhance the wild boar's status as a resource beyond the sphere of hunting. Since the 1970s, wild boar have been farmed in Japan, in response to the growing popularity of wild boar meat which is marketed as *yasei no aji* or 'the taste of the wild' (Takahashi 1995: 41). Demand for wild boar meat has increased with the growth of rural tourism and its constituent guesthouses and roadside eating houses. Some commentators see the trend towards boar-farming as a promising one for remote areas, even suggesting that the wild boar, which is blamed for rural depopulation, could, through the farming of boars for their meat, help support local communities instead (Takahashi 1995: 55). The wild boar, hitherto the farmer's enemy, the age-old threat to village farms, may yet become the future source of the farmer's livelihood. Where, once, Japanese villagers routinely built 'boar walls' to keep the wild boar out, they may soon be erecting fences to keep them *in*—as valuable livestock. Another way in which the wild boar is exploited as a resource outside of hunting is in connection with tourism. Although the wild boar does not feature in wildlife tourism in Japan as much as other animals such as the monkey and the deer, there are examples of wild boar tourist attractions. Perhaps the best known example is Inoshishi Mura or Wild Boar Village in Shizuoka Prefecture (see Fig. 2.6) that attracts up to 300,000 visitors a year and puts on circus-type shows in which trained boars jump through hoops, balance on large balls, and even compete in races (*SSC* 28 July 1998). However, these new forms of exploitation of the wild boar are small in scale. For most of the non-hunting population of remote rural Japan, the wild boar remains above all a serious farm pest.

In this chapter we have seen that farmers and hunters in Japan are each fighting a 'war' with the wild boar. To a certain extent, this can be seen as a common war. Most hunters farm, and some are victims of boar crop raids themselves, and, even where they are not directly affected, hunters share the sense of transgression of their neighbours following a boar raid on the village. Moreover, farmers turn to hunters for protection from the wild boar through hunting and culling, and when hunters catch a boar, farmers too will celebrate their success, seeing in it one less boar to threaten their fields. Yet this apparent unity of farmer and hunter is ultimately mis-leading. The language of 'war' may be shared, but this obscures different under-standings of its significance and purpose. This division centres on the issue of culling—which, as we have seen, is commonly known as *mabiki* or 'thinning'. In relation to forest wildlife, *mabiki* connotes a natural population always tending to increase in number and overwhelm villagers. The term *mabiki* is readily applied to the fast-breeding wild boar, as is evident in the following comments of a Hongū resident.

When the wild boar comes to the village and ruins the fields, you have to kill it . . . People [sometimes] say that its wrong to catch wild boar, that it's wrong to catch deer, that we have to protect them, and that it's cruel [to catch them]. If everybody felt like that, then the wild boars would increase and humans beings [in upland areas] would not be able to live their lives.

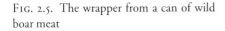

FIG. 2.5. The wrapper from a can of wild boar meat

FIG. 2.6. An advertisement for the Wild Boar Village visitor attraction in Shizuoka Prefecture

The term *mabiki* gives clear expression to the farmer's view that the purpose of hunting should be to remove harmful animals like the wild boar. As we have seen, many a farmer would like to see the crop-raiding wild boar exterminated.

Despite this, hunters tend to have mixed feelings about culling. On the one hand, they support culling for a number of reasons. Culling allows for what is, in effect, out-of-season hunting at a time when hunting is subject to a range of restrictions. Indeed, one of the attractions for the hunter of culling crop-raiding wild boars in the autumn is that they have been nicely fattened up by the farmer's crops. For some men culling is an important source of supplemental income (through bounty payments), while for others culling payments help to offset the increasing expense of recreational hunting (licence fees, gear, dogs, etc.). Culling also helps to legitimize hunting in the wider rural society. At a time when hunting is subject to much public criticism, the act of culling the wild boar, widely considered to be the foremost farm pest, serves to affirm the larger importance of hunting to the livelihood security of upland settlements. On the other hand, hunters have their reservations about culling. Summer culling is often an unpleasant activity because of the heat, the forest ticks, and the threat posed (to men and to dogs) by poisonous snakes. Some hunters believe that the summer culling of wild boar depletes the animals available for winter hunting and therefore diminishes the enjoyment of the hunting season. A further objection to out-of-season culling is that it does not present the same kind of challenge as winter hunting. Crop-raiding boars are said to be relatively easy to track, usually to a lair located in the nearby forest within convenient raiding range for the animal. Summer and autumn boars are said to be far less wary and elusive than mid-winter boars that have become fully alerted to the threat posed by hunters and hounds. For this reason, it is generally agreed that the easiest boars to catch are those encountered at the beginning of the winter hunting season, and that hunting becomes progressively more difficult as the season goes on. Culling a boar in the summer is not the same achievement as hunting a boar in the winter.

If the conflict with the wild boar divides farmers and hunters, this farmer–hunter division in turn tends to cause division among hunters themselves—between (pursuit) hunters and trappers. Remote municipalities increasingly rely on trapping to deal with wild boar pests, viewing it as both safer (because there is no risk of accidents through strayfire or hound attacks) and more effective (see Wada 1995: 76). But this trend is opposed by hunters through the local *ryōyūkai*. Hunters claim that trapping is dangerous and indiscriminate (sometimes catching and crippling their hounds, and not just boars). Some hunters believe that trapping is unfair, as trappers are able to catch wild boar with a minimum of effort, compared with the exertions of the pursuit hunter. In addition to being unfair to themselves, some hunters consider trapping to be unfair to the wild boar. The boar is admired by hunters for its great honesty of spirit, and it is because of this that there is a view that the animal should be engaged in a direct hunting contest. From this perspective, the trapping of a wild boar appears to some hunters as *hazubeki goi* or 'shameful conduct' because the animal is denied the chance to fight back (see Sutō 1991: 213). If summer culling is a lesser contest than winter hunting, trapping appears to be no contest at all (needless to say, trappers see things rather differently). A further indication that the hunter's war with the wild boar is different from the farmer's war is to be found in the hunters' attempts to restock the wild boar population. In parts of Wakayama Prefecture, hunters release boar-pig hybrids, known as *inobuta* ('wild boar-pigs'), into local forests in an effort to increase the game population for the coming season.[15] Far from being simple

---

[15] The *inobuta* is larger than the wild boar and easier to hunt. (According to one Hongū hunter, in the northern part of Wakayama Prefecture, where *inobuta* hybrids have become plentiful, boar-

eradicators of the wild boar, hunters (through the *ryōyūkai*) appear to be main-taining and even boosting boar numbers over the longer term.

In this chapter, we have looked at two different, if overlapping, dimensions of the wild boar problem in Japan: first, human conflict *with* the wild boar (both crop-raiding and hunting), and second, human conflict between farmers and hunters *over* the wild boar. Under the conditions of rural depopulation, the wild boar seems to be winning its 'battle' with the farmer. But as this human–animal conflict intensifies, it inevitably exacerbates existing tensions within human society in relation to the wild boar. If many farmers would like to be rid of the wild boar altogether, for hunters the wild boar is a valued hunting resource that should not be depleted. Although hunters naturally tend to represent their hunting in terms of a mutuality of interest with the farmer, farmers know all too well that ulti-mately hunters are concerned with maintaining a population of wild boar as well as catching individual animals. If the Japanese hunter is at 'war' with the wild boar, it is, as Matt Cartmill has remarked for Western hunters who use this same idiom, 'a strange sort of war in which the only side that can win is careful not to do so. Hunting is an end in itself for the hunter, and he wants the beast he kills to be endlessly replaced . . .' (Cartmill 1993: 31). While the upland farmer's 'war' with the wild boar should be a finite conflict that results in the removal, once and for all, of an animal enemy, the hunter's 'war' with the formidable *shishi* should be a renewable contest.

hunting is now 'like shooting rabbits'.) Similar attempts at strategic hybridization of wild boar popu-lations have been reported for hunters in other parts of Japan. Boar-hunters in the southern Ryūkyū Islands have introduced wild boar from the main Japanese islands in order to increase the size of the boars they hunt. In this way, the wild boar population of the Japanese forest is increasingly becoming a managed population.

3
Monkeys

Monkeys are doubly familiar animals to the mountain villagers on the Kii Peninsula. In common with the rest of the country, peninsular villagers know the monkey as an amusing animal celebrity that appears on national television. As one of the most mediagenic wild animals in Japan, monkeys are regularly featured in newspapers and magazines, as well as on television. But unlike city dwellers, villagers also share their living environment with wild monkeys. Monkeys have become a ubiquitous local presence in the forest surrounding peninsular villages and are often to be seen on the roadsides between villages. Of all the animal pests in Hongū, it is the monkey that is most talked about; almost everybody seems to have a monkey story to tell—of monkeys 'stealing' from local shops, cars, and houses, of encounters with monkeys in garden fruit trees, of monkey aggression, and so on. More than other animals, monkeys inspire mixed and varied reactions, from anger and hatred because of the crops they damage, to sympathy and concern at the plight of 'hungry' monkeys. The renowned cleverness of the monkey makes it one of the more persistent wildlife pests, but also makes it an object of local interest and fascination. In Hongū there are people who try to take photographs of raiding monkeys, people who deliberately feed wild monkeys, and people who adopt monkeys as pets. This chapter focuses on people–monkey conflict in the Hongū area. It describes the widespread problem of monkey pestilence faced by mountain villagers, specifically the threat posed to village crops, as well as the local efforts to repel and resist monkeys. Attention is directed to the way in which the monkey problem is represented in the mountain villages of Japan, and in particular the idioms of criminality and war that are applied to it.

The Japanese macaque (*Macaca fuscata*, in Japanese *nihonzaru*) is one of the nineteen species of macaque that make up the genus *Macaca*. Japanese macaques are short-tailed macaques that grow up to one metre in height and weigh up to 15 kilogrammes and that have reddish-brown fur (that becomes bushy in the winter), red faces, and impressive canine teeth. They form troops that average between twenty-five and fifty animals in size. Most of the world's wild primate populations are found in tropical locations, but the distribution of the Japanese macaque extends to the 'snow country' of north-east Honshu, making it the northernmost population of wild primates. Macaque habitat in Japan ranges from subtropical lowland forest to subalpine vegetation, but its typical habitat is elevated primary, mixed primary, and secondary forest (Wolfheim 1983: 485). They feed on the fruit, seeds, leaves, buds, and bark of a range of different trees, but also on insects and small vertebrates. The Japanese macaque used to be hunted in Japan, but it was delisted as a game animal in 1947 in response to overhunting. Japanese primatologists and conservationists have claimed that the monkey is in danger of extinction, and some regional populations of monkeys have become extinct.[1] None the less, in the post-war period monkey numbers overall have recovered from an estimated low of 15,600 animals in 1950 to 100,000 animals in 1999 (*MS* 4 Aug. 1999).

IMAGES OF THE MONKEY

Monkeys have a long-established place in Japanese culture. In Japanese folklore the monkey tends to appear as an inauspicious animal. Bad people are punished by being transformed into monkeys (Higuchi 1991: 118), while in some cases monkeys had the power to possess people walking through the forest (Suzuki 1982: 298). Various forms of monkey behaviour, especially boundary-crossing movements, such as crossing a river or the village–forest boundary, are associated with misfortune and calamity (Hirose 1993: 66; Suzuki 1982: 299). The word for monkey, *saru*, is an inauspicious word, as it is homonymous with the word for 'to go away' or 'to leave' which can refer to the loss of wealth or valuables or even the loss of human life. For this reason foresters and hunters in Hongū avoid saying the word *saru* lest it adversely affect their safety or well-being in the forest. In Japanese folk religion the monkey was associated with the *yama no kami* or 'mountain spirit' (Ohnuki-Tierney 1991: 163). There are Shinto shrines that have monkeys as their *otsukai* or messenger animal, a mediator between *kami* spirits and human beings (Ishizaki 1991*a*: 240). In Japan monkeys have long been trained for public performances—a traditional occupation known as *sarumawashi* (literally, 'monkey-turners') or *saruhiki* ('monkey-pullers') (see Hirose 1984: ch. 6; Ohnuki-Tierney 1987: ch. 5). Monkeys frequently appear on Japanese television (including as amusing characters in commercials) and monkeys are the major indigenous wildlife tourist attraction in Japan in the form of monkey parks (generally known as *saruyama*) found across the country.

A large number of vernacular names for the monkey have been documented across the regions of Japan—up to fifty-five, according to one survey (Kishida 1953: 3). Many of the terms applied to monkeys are anthropomorphic: *aniki* ('elder brother'), *yama no anii* or *yama no nii-chan* ('mountain elder brother'), *danna* ('master'), *wakaishu* ('young man'), *kare* ('he'), *yamabito* ('mountain people') and *mori no kobito* ('forest dwarves') (Chiba 1975: 139; Togawa 1956: 92). It is customary in Japanese to refer to the monkey with the suffix '*san*' that is normally applied to

---

[1] For example, T. Iwano, in Wolfheim (1983: 485), Sprague (1993: 90), and *AS* (19 Sept. 1996). On regional extinction, see Higashi (1992: 38–47).

F ig. 3.1. A troop of Japanese macaques (in the Iwatayama monkey park in Arashiyama, Kyoto)

people—i.e. *Osaru-san*, 'Mr Monkey'. Japanese folk tales and legends attribute to monkeys human capacities, actions, and desires. Examples include monkeys that protect themselves from the hunter's bullets by coating their fur with a kind of natural varnish (Ōta 1997: 193); monkeys that heal sick members of the troop using wild herbs (Mōri and Tadano 1997: 113); monkeys that heal themselves by 'bathing' in mountain hot-springs (Ishizaki 1977); monkeys that invade the huts of charcoal-burners or foresters and cook rice there (Ishizaki 1979*b*: 32–3); monkeys that steal and drink alcohol (a graveyard offering) or make alcohol (by fermenting berries) (Tabuchi 1992: 53); and monkeys that cause mischief by stealing the tools of foresters and farmers and by throwing things at people (Matsuyama 1977*b*: 30). Anthropomorphism is also evident in *sarumawashi* performances in the way that monkeys are dressed in human clothes and made to perform human actions such as walking, dancing, and bowing. As we shall see, anthropomorphism is also pervasive in the way in which monkey pestilence is represented by upland dwellers.

The association also works the other way around: if monkeys are frequently viewed as human-like, people are sometimes likened to monkeys. The monkey figures prominently in Japanese verbal abuse. Among the monkey expressions applied to people are *sarukanja* ('monkey face'), *sarume* ('monkey eyes'), *saruude* ('monkey arms'), *sarugoshi* ('monkey hips'), *sarurikō* ('monkey cleverness'), *sarujie* ('monkey wisdom'), and *sarumane* ('monkey imitation') (Ohnuki-Tierney 1987: 66). In Japan the term *yamazaru* or 'mountain monkey' was conventionally applied to coarse and uncultured people from the countryside, while in rural areas themselves it was applied to people from remoter, upstream villages, including foresters and hunters, who spent much time in the forest. (A similar term is applied to inhabitants of the southern Kii Pennsula: *Kumanozaru* or 'Kumano monkeys' [e.g. Omosu 1997: 24]). The word *en* (an alternative reading of the character for monkey) is one of a number of derogatory animal terms applied to policemen by criminals in Japan (Constantine 1994: 51). Less negatively, the monkey (like the wild boar) is one of the twelve animals of the Oriental zodiac, and people born in the year of the monkey (1944, 1956, 1968, and so on) are said to have monkey-like characteristics such as selfishness and intelligence. There are also examples of the positive self-attribution of a monkey-like identity, usually in connection with physical prowess. A seventeenth-century hunter in northern Japan renowned for his speed and mobility in the mountains was known as *Ōsaru* or 'Great Monkey' (Mōri and Tadano 1997: ch. 3). *Ninja* assassins too identified with monkeys: such as the famous *ninja* known as Sarutobi or 'Monkey Jump' who was able to 'perform feats of running, jumping, and climbing normally possible only by monkeys' (Draeger 1989: 92). Japanese burglars are said to liken themselves to monkeys through the use of the monkey term *ete* that is applied to superior burglars famed for their ability to scale walls and climb up to balconies (Constantine 1994: 35).

MONKEY WARS

Engai

Since the 1970s monkey crop-raiding, generally known as *engai* or 'monkey damage', has emerged as a serious problem in the main islands of Honshu, Shikoku, and Kyushu. In general, *engai* refers to damage to farm crops; other kinds of monkey damage do occur, but tend to be small in scale and relatively minor in their impact.[2] In Japan as a whole in 1997 the area of farmland damaged by monkeys was 6,400 hectares—a fivefold increase on the 1982 figure of 1,300 hectares (*MS* 4 Aug. 1999). This figure refers only to reported damage; the real scale

---

[2] Livestock farmers complain that monkeys deplete the pasture on which their cattle rely (see *NNSC* 2 Mar. 1998). However, there are no reports of attacks on livestock as such, as is the case with populations of wild primates elsewhere, such as baboons in East Africa which reportedly prey on chickens and goats (Else 1991: 158). There are also reports of monkey pestilence in connection with forestry—the eating of the bark of certain commercial tree species (*NNS* 11 Sept. 1998). The monkey can also be a conservation pest: for example, in Yakushima swelling monkey populations are said to endanger the local species of bat (known as *erabuōkomori*) by depleting the wild forage on which the bats depend (*MNSC* 4 June 1998). But such reports of monkey pestilence in relation to livestock farming, to forestry, and to conservation remain exceptional.

of damage is likely to be higher because minor damage tends to go unreported. Monkeys damage almost every kind of crop, including mushrooms, rice, persimmons, chestnuts, loquats, citrus fruits, apples, potatoes, radishes, soya beans, and horseradishes. In one part of Aomori Prefecture in 1993, '74 monkeys in 3 troops caused about ¥7 million worth of damage (about US$70,000) to 190 of the 460 farm households in the village' (*JPN* 1994: 6). In the area of Nikkō, the estimated cost of monkey damage has increased from less than ¥1 million ($4,200) in 1977 to more than ¥20 million ($154,000) in 1997 (*NS* 16 July 1998). Farmers in Kumamoto Prefecture report that 'in one night a field of ten ares [one thousand square metres] can be completely destroyed [by monkeys]' (*NNSC* 2 Mar. 1998), while mushroom-growers in Shizuoka Prefecture complain that a whole *shiitake* crop can disappear in a five or ten minute monkey raid (*SS* 10 Mar. 2000). In the 1990s many orchards in Nagano Prefecture were abandoned as farmers gave up apple farming in exasperation at repeated monkey raids (*AS* 29 Nov. 1995; Wada 1998: 82). Monkeys raid the orchards in the spring to eat the fresh buds and in the autumn to eat the fruit itself. In climbing the apple trees and gnawing the branches, monkeys do considerable damage to the trees themselves, adversely affecting harvests in future years (Wada 1998: 80–2).

The Kii Peninsula is one of the areas most seriously affected by *engai* (*JPN* 1995: 5). A survey of four prefectures, including Wakayama, listed 29 varieties of crops damaged by monkeys (Idani *et al.* 1995: 115). Table 1.1 (in Chapter 1) mentioned 46 incidents of monkey damage in the period 1995–2000, affecting mostly vegetables. But this data would appear to understate greatly the scale of the monkey problem. A more accurate set of figures is available on monkey damage, as Hongū Town Hall carried out a specific survey of municipal households on the subject in 1998. Table 3.1 shows the results of this survey, listing the 33 varieties of cultivated produce mentioned in the responses. The table indicates that the main targets of monkey raiding in Hongū are persimmons, chestnuts, potatoes, rice, and mushrooms.

Kakiyama Kōhei cultivates 50 ares of farmland (consisting of both ricefields and dryfields). After thirty years in the city working for the giant telecommunications company NTT, he took early retirement at 54, returned to Hongū in 1988, and has devoted himself to farming ever since. He cultivates a wide range of produce, including rare varieties of fruit and vegetables, producing a large surplus that he gives away to friends, neighbours, and relatives. He grows a special variety of rice, *hatsushimo* or 'first frost' (so named for the lateness of its harvest in the autumn), which he chose after discovering its delicious taste in a city sushi bar years ago; 40 of his 50 ares of farmland are devoted to rice-growing, and are divided into seven ricefields (in two separate locations). But in recent years he has suffered much crop-raiding by monkeys.

They come in a group, around thirty-strong, though I've heard that in other villages it can vary from just two of them to three hundred . . . Two or three days before [the raid], a

TABLE 3.1. *Monkey farm damage in Hongū-chō*

Category of produce	Item	Number of reports of damage
Fruit	Persimmons	32
	Chestnuts	29
	Oranges	4
	Water-melons	1
	Kiwi-fruit	1
Vegetables	Potatoes (3 varieties)	32
	Pumpkins	12
	Radishes	9
	Cabbage	6
	Onions	5
	Scallion	3
	Tomatoes	2
	Aubergines	2
	Leaf mustard	2
	Other (10 varieties)	13
Grains and pulses	Rice	16
	Soya beans	2
	Peas	2
	Corn	1
Forest products	*Shiitake* mushrooms	17
	Bamboo-shoots	2
TOTAL		193

Source: Adapted from Hongū-chō 1999.

vanguard of one or two monkeys comes to look around, like they are carrying out a reconnaissance mission, to investigate things and to see if there is something to eat. If there is food to eat, then they [the whole group] raid a number of times that week . . . They're very clever—after all, people talk about 'monkey wisdom' [*sarujie*], and I think that monkeys are more clever [than us] . . . They come for the rice just before it ripens, when there's white, milky sap and before the grain has really formed. They suck this juice and spit out the remains in the ricefield . . . They're clever. Just when you start to think they won't come they appear . . . They know just when a food source comes to maturity, because they move around in the forest—they know that in the autumn it is the time for pasania nuts, acorns and so on.

In the summer of 2000 Kakiyama-san lost half of his rice crop due to monkey damage. As he was not insured, he incurred great losses, which he estimates at up to ¥300,000 (calculated on the basis of market prices) or $2,500.

Further down the river, the Hongū village of Takayama is also badly affected by *engai*. Three monkey troops are said to raid three different parts of village farmland on a regular basis, as though they have divided up the village between them. The monkeys raid the vegetable plots near the forest-edge, the village fruit trees, and (in the summer) the ricefields in the lower part of the village. One victim of the monkeys is the mushroom-grower, Asari Tetsuichi, but in his case the vulnerable crop is located in the nearby forest rather than the village as such. Asari-san's *shiitake* mushrooms used to be one of Hongū's leading local specialities that were sold to other parts of the country by mail order. As is common, Asari-san grew some of his mushrooms in the dark conditions of the nearby forest, but this forest location made it difficult to protect the crop from monkeys. From 1993 onwards, monkeys have been raiding the mushroom logs, damaging the logs themselves and spoiling the mushrooms grown on them.

The monkeys would come down in a group, early in the morning . . . About thirty monkeys would come, first a big one who looks around and then the others. They don't actually eat many of the mushrooms. What they do is to pull the cap off the stem, it's a kind of game they play . . . It's the same with people, when we see something like that standing upright it's interesting to us . . . They can't pull them out by the roots because it's quite hard, so they just take off the cap. They find it amusing. So they pull off the caps and throw them around and the place gets all messed up . . . And while they are doing this, they scratch the logs with their nails or they just peel the bark off. After that, water enters the log and it starts to rot . . . It [scratching the log stem] seems to be fun for them, a way of testing their fingernails . . . I mainly grew my mushrooms indoors, but the ones I grew outdoors were all ruined.

Asari-san found that he was losing one-tenth of his mushrooms through monkey damage. He cites persistent monkey damage as one of the reasons why he recently gave up mushroom-growing (the other reason was competition from *shiitake* growers in China). He now runs a coffee bar instead.

   The monkey problem in Japan is not confined to damage to farms and forest products. Monkeys that get accustomed to visiting villages can become a more general nuisance. Monkeys cause damage to houses by dislodging roof tiles, by breaking windows, and by getting into food storerooms. They also enter houses. In Hongū it is said that monkeys get into houses by skilfully opening or unlocking windows and doors. Once inside, they feed on the food they find in the kitchen, and even, in some cases, reportedly open refrigerators. In Tamaigawa (to the north of Hongū) I heard the story of a woman who returned home one afternoon to discover a monkey sitting on the rice-cooker in the kitchen, much to her disgust. In the Hongū village of Shimoyukawa monkeys are known to steal food from houses, as in the following incident recalled by one local housewife in her fifties.

There were oranges placed [on the table] above the *kotatsu* [the central seating area in the room] We always keep that sliding door over there closed, but on that day for some reason it was left open . . . It was around lunchtime and I was in the kitchen thinking about lunch when I heard a noise or something that made me come back into this room. It was then that I saw a monkey eating an orange on the tatami mat, making a mess everywhere! [When it saw me] it took some more oranges and escaped.

Monkeys also feed on the edible offerings (fruit, candies, cakes, etc.) made to family ancestors in the *butsudan* altar.

Even where monkeys do not enter houses, they remain a serious nuisance. Monkeys fiddle with outside television antennae, often loosening or bending them (affecting television pictures), and interfere with telephone cables, occasionally causing village telephone lines to go down. Itani Kosaburō of the coastal village of Tsubaki recalls that visitors to his house found that, when they went to use the outside toilet, curious monkeys would follow them and observe them using the latrine from above the door—much to the shock of the visitors. The monkeys would also interfere with the postman when he called to the house to make a delivery. Another peninsular village where monkeys are a regular nuisance is the Hongū village of Kaki. The housewife Nishide Tachie recounts an everyday incident.

We see a lot of monkeys around here. They come down on to the roof just here at the back, probably from the mountains, to eat the persimmons on the tree outside . . . One day I heard this noise, '*don! don!*', as they jumped on to the roof. When I went outside I saw a monkey's face in the persimmon tree and I was startled. I threw stones at it and it escaped back up the mountainside. It was very frightening as I thought it would come for me. It can be very serious when an animal attacks you . . . This place is now like a zoo. Human beings are being defeated by monkeys.

Another site of monkey pestilence is the village shop. The Sakitani shop, run by an elderly couple in their seventies, has to contend with regular monkey visits. Located at the entrance to the Hongū village of Minasegawa, the shop faces a large mountain to the north across the river, which is connected by a bridge. It is from this northern mountain that a troop of monkeys appears, descending down to the road and crossing the bridge, to snatch the fruit and vegetables displayed outside the shop front, as well as the candies, cakes, and potato chips inside. The Sakitanis complain that, as soon as their backs are turned, the monkeys take their chance to 'steal' from the shop. Monkey shop-raiding is reported in many other parts of Japan too. One shopkeeper in Hyōgo Prefecture, for example, is reported to have found a one metre tall monkey inside his shop eating chocolate bars (*AS* 13 Nov. 1996). Some shop-raiding monkeys are said to be quite discerning in their tastes when it comes to potato chips, taking only the barbecue-flavoured ones and ignoring the rest. Another rural building vulnerable to monkey intrusion is the tourist guesthouse, and in some regions there are reports of monkeys entering *ryokan* inns in search of food (Wada 1994: 173). Monkeys also 'steal' food from parked cars, especially in the summer when the car windows are wound down. In the Hongū village of Bujū, for example, monkeys have been seen to take snacks (such as *kashipan*, a bread confection) and sweets left on the dashboard.

Monkeys snatch not just the food of the living, but also the food of the dead. Food offerings have a central place in the Japanese tradition of ancestor veneration, and represent a symbolic means by which the living care for the ancestral dead. Food is offered both to the *butsudan* in the house and to the graves in the village cemetery. In addition to feeding on the *butsudan* offerings (as noted above), monkeys feed on the edible offerings in the cemetery. These offerings include uncooked rice grains (in contrast to the cooked rice offered at the *butsudan*), fruit (especially *mikan* oranges), and candies (as there are children among the village dead)—all of which are highly appealing foods to monkeys. Monkeys knock over graveside flower vases, pick up the vases and drink the water from them (scattering the flowers in the process), move vases from one plot to neighbouring plots, snatch the foods laid out as offerings, and even drink from the small jars of sake ('One Cup') that are offered to deceased fathers and grandfathers. One of the purposes of the graveyard visit is to clean up the grave—seen as the final resting-place of the village ancestors—by wiping down the stone, weeding the plot, removing old flowers, and so on. But the effect of a monkey visit is to leave the graveyard in a mess that has to be cleaned up all over again. There are reports of gravestones tilting over to one side and even of gravestones knocked over due to monkeys sitting on them or jumping from one stone to another. This can discourage villagers from visiting the cemetery. In the Hongū village of Kotsuga, a 76-year-old widow, Suzuki Shizue, told me that she no longer visits the village cemetery up on the hillside (at the edge of the forest) because of an unpleasant earlier experience when she was threatened by a large group of monkeys sitting on the gravestones and feeding on the offerings. Instead, she now confines her offerings of food to her late husband and the other family ancestors to the *butsudan* and the village temple.

Dangerous Monkeys

When villagers think of dangerous animals in the forest, it will tend to be the bear and perhaps the wild boar that come to mind. The monkey does not readily fall into this category. But monkeys too are sometimes seen as a source of physical danger. Japanese folklore contains references to dangerous monkey-like monsters in the mountains. In Miyazaki Prefecture, for example, folk tales feature a monkey-like goblin known as Sarunoshishi ('Monkey Beast') that threatens the lives of hunters (Nagamatsu 1993: 15–18). A particularly common folk tale is the *sarugami taiji* (Monkey Spirit Conquest) tale that appears in the twelfth-century *Konjaku monogatari*, but is also widely diffused as regional folk legend. This tale tells of frightening monkey-like figures that terrorize villages until they are eventually vanquished by a heroic outsider (variously a passing priest, hunter, or samurai) with or without the aid of a dog (Nakamura 1989: 54–5; Nagano 1991: 115–16). This theme sometimes emerges in connection with monkey crop-raiding. In the 1940s (in the wake of the popularity of the famous Hollywood movie in Japan) there were reports of crop-raiding *Kingu Kongu* (King Kong) figures stalking the forest of the Kii Peninsula and elsewhere in Japan (Tabuchi 1992: 48). In the past, charcoal-burners working alone in the forest are said to have been menaced (and even injured) by wild monkey troops, to the point where they had to flee for their lives to the safety of the village (Matsuyama 1977*b*: 16).

In Hongū there are many tales of monkey mischief, malevolence, and violence towards people. Nishide Toshikazu, the much-liked newspaper deliveryman, claims that on a certain part of his daily round there is a place where rocks tumble down the mountainside on to the road near to where his scooter passes. This, he believes, is the mischief of a group of monkeys that live on the mountain and wait for him each morning (it cannot be children, he adds, because it takes place at 6 o'clock). Many tales of monkey misdemeanours are related to the theme of *shikaeshi* or 'revenge'. Japanese folklore suggests that monkeys recognize the principle of reciprocity in their dealings with people and return any kindness shown to them—for example, by rewarding compassionate people who help them when they are in trouble (Inada 1994: 395; Seki 1966: 66). But by the same token, monkeys become vengeful towards people who harm or offend them. One example of this is the farmer who chases monkeys away from his field with stones and rocks, but discovers the next day that monkeys afterwards returned in greater numbers to ravage the field. In the Hongū village of Kawayu, Kobuchi Masataka told me about the time when he threw stones at monkeys he saw near his flowerboxes to drive them away, and how the following days the monkeys came back and overturned the flowerboxes as a kind of *shikaeshi*. Another common monkey story is where villagers throw stones at monkeys feeding in their chestnut trees, but find that the monkeys react by throwing chestnuts back at them. A similar story involves construction workers who discover that when they throw stones at a group of monkeys on a nearby hillside, the monkeys respond by throwing stones back at them.

In an interview, Suzuki Tokuhei of Kotsuga recalled some of his past encounters with aggressive monkeys.

When they see human beings they make threatening gestures, like they are saying to you, 'Come on, I'll take you on now!' . . . They also shake trees, like they are showing you their strength. So you have a person over here and over there you have a tree, and they shake the tree as hard as they can to show you their strength . . .

When this happens in the village, it is nothing to be concerned about, because the monkeys are wary of people there. But encounters with monkeys in the forest are different.

If you enter the deep forest, if you go there alone, and a big group [of monkeys] comes along, then that's really scary . . . But even then, if you have some bladed object with you things will be fine . . . But if you don't have anything with you, then they will do something to you. If there is only a human being who doesn't have anything with him, no tools or anything, just a weakling like a human being, well . . . A human being is strong when he has a weapon but when he doesn't have anything, then it is possible for just three or four monkeys to kill him . . . If you are alone in the deep forest and you see tens of monkeys coming along, then that's very frightening. Nowadays nobody goes to the forest [alone]. If you did go there by yourself, it would just make other people [back in the village] worry about you.

In one widely told story in Hongū, a forest labourer (a single man in his forties) is said to have been chased through a village by a group of aggressive monkeys. A neighbour and friend of this man (who was also in the same class at school), recounted the story as follows:

In Minasegawa, near the mountains, he was chased by monkeys . . . Apparently, he found a young monkey that had just been born, which was caught up in something and couldn't move. So he picked it up to bring back with him, but then the parent monkeys and other monkeys came after him, baring their teeth, and it was really frightening. He reacted by releasing the baby monkey at once and got on his bicycle and raced away through the village, but the monkeys still chased after him. When he got to the Sakitani shop [at the end of the village] he jumped off his bicycle and ran inside the shop to escape from them. The monkeys were really angry with him and it was very frightening.

The incident (said to have occurred in 1996) is often referred to in Hongū as evidence of the danger of monkeys.[3] Although some people are sceptical about the story (even suggesting that he made it up just to get attention), the neighbour believes it to be true because she herself has experienced first hand how intimidating and frightening monkeys can be—when they look her in the eyes without flinching as she tries to drive them away from her garden. For some people at least, the story illustrates the physical danger posed by monkeys, a theme that is reinforced by media reports of violent monkey behaviour.

Many of the monkey stories told in Hongū and other parts of the Kii Peninsula are exaggerated and are likely to be greeted with a certain amount of local incredulity. They are perhaps better understood as tall stories that serve as sources of entertainment rather than serious reports of actual incidents. But there are documented cases of monkey attacks on people across Japan. Newspaper reports tell of monkeys stealing the shopping baskets of the elderly or stealing sweets from children (*AS* 13 Apr. 1994). In Kyōto Prefecture in 1991 a single monkey is reported to have injured no fewer than 262 people, including children on their way to school and housewives hanging out washing on verandas, in a total of 218 incidents (*JPN* 1993: 5). Between March 1992 and February 1993, around fifty people were attacked by monkeys in Kumamoto Prefecture—all the attacks involved stray single monkeys and not troops (ibid.). Tourists too have been attacked by monkeys (e.g. *AS* 21 May 1992). In villages where monkeys regularly enter houses, the safety of young children is of particular concern. In Owase on the northern part of the Kii

---

[3] According to some versions, the man jumped into a parked car on the roadside (rather than the shop at the end of the village) to seek refuge from the monkey, at which point the irate monkeys following him started to bang loudly on the roof of the car as he cowered inside. Some accounts hold that it was a single monkey rather than a group of monkeys, and that the single monkey was an *oyazaru* ('parent monkey') or a *bosuzaru* ('boss monkey'). According to some of his neighbours, this man was no innocent victim but had provoked the monkey by stealing its baby, and this was why the monkey acted so aggressively towards him. The incident recalls monkey attacks recorded in wild monkey parks, such as in Minō when monkey troops set upon a man who tried to steal a baby monkey (see Mainichi Shinbunsha 1965: 152–3).

Peninsula, monkeys 'open windows and enter houses, causing danger when there are small children present in the house' (*CNS* 22 May 1997). These fears are exacerbated by occasional reports of monkeys biting infants (*NKS* 3 May 1998). These reports tend to suggest that it is certain categories of people that are at risk from monkey attacks.

In Japan there is a widespread belief that women are especially vulnerable to monkeys. On the Kii Peninsula it is said that monkeys are much less afraid of women than of men. Villagers invariably claim that monkeys distinguish between men and women and that 'they make light of women' (*onna no hito o nameru*) when they encounter them—by refusing to flee back to the forest (as they would in the presence of men), by continuing to feed in the field, or by threatening women with aggressive gestures. Old women are said to be particularly ineffectual at dispersing monkeys; it is said that old women who attempt to chase monkeys away from their fields or fruit trees sometimes end up being chased away themselves by the monkeys! But there are bold women who show little fear of monkeys. One example is Fukumoto Yasuko, an old widow in the village of Tamaigawa, whose remote homestead is regularly visited by monkeys. Despite the crop losses she suffers and the large numbers of monkeys that descend to her farm, Fukumoto-san remains defiant—when I interviewed her, she repeatedly used the phrase *makete inai*, 'I am not defeated'. When the monkeys appear, she reacts by running outside and throwing firecrackers in their direction, startling them and sending them back to the forest in a panic. Her boldness has earned her something of a reputation among other villagers. One of her neighbours told me that the monkeys may as well give up on the Fukumoto fields because *that* old woman will never give in to them. The neighbour went on to recall an incident a couple of years earlier during the rice harvest when villagers were working together in a ricefield: as the harvesters rested by the side of the field a rat appeared in front of them, and in a fraction of a second Fukumoto Yasuko sprang to her feet and pinned the rat down with one foot, before slowly crushing it to death.

It is in the forest, even more than the village, where women see themselves as vulnerable to monkey attacks. Some women who work as forestry labourers or plant collectors express their fear of being surrounded by a monkey troop in the forest. Fukumoto Yasuko herself told me that when she and other village women go to the forest to gather plants such as *shikibi* (star anise) and *sakaki* (*Cleyera japonica*)—an important source of seasonal income—they always take sheets of newspaper and a lighter with them for protection against monkeys. She explained that, were she suddenly to find herself surrounded by monkeys in the forest, she would light the newspaper to make a torch with which to frighten the monkeys away (as monkeys are terrified of fire). Other means of protection are also employed. One of Fukumoto-san's neighbours, who also gathers wild plants in the forest, told me that she keeps away monkeys (and other wild animals) by carrying with her a set of Buddhist rosary beads and, whenever she senses danger, by reciting the sacred

words *namumyōhōrengekyō* ('Praise to Holy Law of the Lotus Sutra') to invoke
the protective power of the Lotus Sutra (one of the most important sutras in
Mahayana Buddhism). It should be stressed that this local belief in the particular
vulnerability of women to monkeys does not stop them either from collecting in
the forest or from guarding fields.

Talk of the monkey threat to women sometimes carries a sexual connotation.
During an interview with Suzuki Ryōichi and his wife, who take turns guarding
their ricefields, the wife, after describing how monkeys carry away sheaves of rice,
quipped that '[next time] they'll even take me away with them! They'll carry me
off!' When women's underwear disappeared from a washing line outside a house in
the same village, the incident was attributed to monkeys.[4] In some regions of Japan
there are rumours of monkeys sexually molesting women out herb-picking in the
forest (recalling similar claims involving macaques in other parts of Asia).[5] In fact,
this theme of forest monkeys coveting village women is found in Japanese folklore.
It is evident in the *sarugami taiji* tale mentioned above in which the threatening
monkey-like figures demand from the village an annual *hitomigokū* or 'human
offering' in the form of one of its daughters.[6] The theme appears in *Tōno monogatari* (*Tales of Tōno*) where Yanagita Kunio documents tales of *saru no futtachi*, a
scary human-like monkey in the mountains that 'likes women and steals village
housewives' (Yanagita 1992: 37). In *Yama no jinsei* (*Mountain Lives*) Yanagita suggests that a similar motif is behind the well-known *saru no mukoiri* or 'Monkey
Bridegroom' folk tale, in which a daughter is taken away by a monkey and forced
to become his wife (but in the end manages to trick the monkey and escape)
(Yanagita 1961: 114–15). On the southern island of Yakushima there are legends of
young women abducted by monkeys in the forest, never to return to the village
(Nakashima 1998: 141–7). Such folklore would appear to give expression to the
King Kong theme of a simian sexual 'overreach' to human beings (Haraway 1989:
161).[7]

Another aspect of this perceived monkey threat to human safety emerged in the
interview with Kakiyama Kōhei.

The Japanese monkey has a short tail, but then there is also the Taiwanese monkey that's
been in the news a lot lately which has a long tail. The ones that come and bother us have
long tails—they are groups of Taiwanese monkeys . . . Those monkeys are ferocious [*dōmō*]
and have an aggressive temperament [*kisei ga arai*], much more than the Japanese monkeys.

---

[4] Other interpretations of the incident were also offered—notably, the mischievous suggestion that
the underwear was taken by human, rather than monkey, hands! The underwear incident became an
amusing story that circulated widely.
[5] Eric Laurent, personal communication. Cf *JPN* (1993: 5); see also McNeely and Sochaczewski
(1994: 238–9).
[6] See Ishizaki (1979*a*), Saitō (1983: 98), Unō (1987), Matsunami (1994: 389–90), and Abe (1994:
205–6).
[7] For additional reports of monkey-like monster figures in the Japanese forest, see Jones (1926: 48),
Suzuki (1986: 275–80), and Chiba (1995*b*: 45).

If an old person were to go up and shout at them, they would attack. The same thing happens if a woman shouts at them . . . Where you have an old person or a woman, the whole group can just attack them'.

Since the 1980s there have been reports of feral populations of Formosan rock macaques (*Macaca cyclopis*)—known in Japanese as *Taiwanzaru* or 'Taiwan monkeys'—in various other parts of Japan, such as the Shimokita Peninsula in northern Japan and the island of Izu-Ōshima (Mori 1989; K. Watanabe 1989). In the Shimokita case, the foreign macaques are deemed to pose a serious threat to the indigenous Japanese macaque population through 'gene pollution' (Azuma and Mori 1991). At the time of the above interview in December 2000, the problem of Formosan rock macaques in Wakayama Prefecture had been in the news.[8] But, despite the farmer's claim above, there had been no substantiated reports of these alien monkeys reaching the south of the prefecture where Hongū is located. None the less, all the talk of 'Taiwanese monkeys', said to be so much more aggressive than their Japanese counterparts, only reinforced that sense that monkeys were a threat to human safety as well as to village crops.

THE WAR IDIOM

Monkey crop damage is commonly represented in the language of criminality. Newspapers refer to wild monkeys as *hannin* or 'criminals', *manbiki* or 'shop-lifters', and *gyangudan* or '[criminal] gangs', to rogue male monkeys (believed to be inordinately responsible for crop raids) as *shuhan* or 'main offenders', to monkey crop raids as *jiken* or '[criminal] incidents', and to the damaged fields as the *hankō genba* or 'scene of the crime'.[9] In Hongū this perception is shared to a large extent. Monkeys that enter village farms are *dorobō* or 'thieves' who *nusumu* or 'steal' from people. Hayashi Taiji, the Hongū policeman, told me that local people sometimes come to the police station to complain about monkeys, as though they expected the police to go out and arrest the monkeys for 'stealing' their potatoes! In response, the bemused policeman has even coined a new word for this form of local disor-der—*enzai* or 'monkey crimes' (a playful variation on the word *engai*, 'monkey damage', normally applied to monkey pestilence). This perception of monkeys as criminals is supported by the manner of their crop raids. Unlike wild boar and deer, which tend to affect the fields some distance away from the house, monkeys, attracted by the fruit trees, come right into the garden next to the house.

---

[8]   As was the case elsewhere, the Formosan rock macaques on the Kii Peninsula appear to have orig-inally been zoo animals (belonging to the Wakayama Shizen Dōbutsuen or 'Wakayama Natural Zoo') that became feral when the zoo closed down in the late 1970s. According to some reports, some of the foreign monkeys are said to have escaped from the zoo into the forest even before its closure—by using a workman's ladder to climb over the wall of their pen (Saitō 2001: 119).

[9]   See *AS* (16 Dec. 1993), *NS* (16 July 1998), *KS* (13 May 1998), *AS* (13 Nov. 1996) (cf. *AS* 29 Nov. 1995), *KS* (30 Apr. 1996), and *AS* (12 June 1996).

Crop-raiding monkeys are said to *carry away* potatoes or radishes in their hands or bundles of rice stalks over their shoulders as they make their escapes. In other areas, monkeys have been observed to twist off the watermelon from the calyx and carry it away tucked into their groin with two hands, showing in these actions an uncanny resemblance to human beings (Sakusa 1995: 110). In the Hongū village of Fushiogami I was told that during their raids monkeys practise *tewatashi* or 'passing-by-hand'—i.e. one monkey gets into a field protected by netting and then passes the vegetables through the net mesh to other monkeys outside. There are even tales of monkeys making use of plastic bags for their raids.

The monkey is a particular kind of 'thief'. Monkeys are known to waste much of the crop they ruin. Only a small part of the apple, sweet potato, or radish is eaten before it is discarded for the next one, behaviour which villagers liken to that of children who only eat the tastiest part of a piece of fruit or a vegetable. One villager explained the recurrence of farm damage by stating that monkeys are *namakemono* or 'idlers' who opt for the easiest source of food. The attribution of laziness to monkeys also points to the morally repugnant behaviour of living off the labour of others. This image of the monkey as a lazy harvest-stealer is clearly present in Japanese folklore. In the well-known *sarugani gassen* or 'Monkey–Crab Battle' tale, the monkey tries to cheat the crab out of food they have grown together and to claim the whole of the harvest for itself, but fails and ends up much worse off (Ozaki 1970: 203–13; Seki 1966: 32–4). A similar image of the monkey appears in the eighteenth-century political fable, *Hosei monogatari*, where 'people who greedily consume without cultivating' (such as priests) are branded as 'monkeys' (Hunter 1992: 54). It is also evident in recent press reports on crop damage that refer to *gurume na saru* or 'gourmet monkeys' (*AS* 25 Mar. 1993), a term that suggests that the crop-raiders are spoilt, fastidious creatures which are no longer interested in the fruit-bearing trees of the forest and prefer to dine in luxury on the tasty farm food painstakingly grown by others.

In addition to the idiom of criminality, the monkey problem in Japan attracts the language of all-out confrontation and war. Monkeys appear not just as 'criminals' stealing human crops, but also as war 'enemies' threatening to take over human territory. The Japanese mass media often represents *engai* in sensationalist, zero-sum terms—for example, as a question of 'Monkey or Man?' (Watanabe 1995: 51). Newspapers refer to a *saru gundan* ('monkey army') or *teki* ('enemy') that 'invades' remote villages, and refer to the raided villages as desperately preparing *jiei taisaku* ('self-defence measures') or *sakusen* ('[military] strategies') in response, including *jinkai senjutsu* ('human-wave tactics'), but also depict the villages as on the verge of *oteage* ('surrender') to the 'monkey army'.[10] The tone of some of these reports is one of playful exaggeration and mock terror more than genuine alarm; in

---

[10] See *AS* (15 Feb. 1989), *AS* (3 Mar. 1990), *AS* (13 Apr. 1994), *AS* (20 Dec. 1994), *KS* (8 Apr. 1997), *KS* (23 Oct. 1998), *TYS* (24 Nov. 1999), and *MS* (14 July 1999).

Japan the notion of a 'monkey army' is not without its comical side (the term *saru gundan* is in fact the name of a popular monkey performance troupe based in Nikkō). Yet the cumulative impact of the repeated use of the war analogy is to suggest that Japanese mountain villagers (and by extension human society in general) are engaged in an elemental struggle over territory and livelihood. The idiom of war is also found among local people in the remote areas actually affected by *engai*. Farmers in Hongū characterize the monkeys that come to their fields as *teki* or 'enemies' and *aite* or 'opponents', and refer to *saru to no sensō* or 'the war with monkeys'. There are a number of reasons why villagers consider the war analogy to be particularly apt for monkeys.

First of all, monkeys are viewed as forming stable, tight-knit groups. In the 1950s and 1960s Japanese primatologists tended to portray monkey troops as closed, mutually exclusive societies. In the language and imagery it employed, early Japanese primatology bore a striking resemblance to the then widely accepted sociological view of Japan as a closed, orderly, and hierarchical society (see Dale 1986: 197). Japanese primatology has since moved beyond this closed society model to recognize the existence of contact between different monkey troops. In particular, the discovery of recurrent intertroop movement of males has shown that macaque society is far more open, fluid, and dynamic than the old model suggested. But in Hongū the earlier model of monkeys as living in a closed society is still widely found. Monkey troops continue to be seen as *heisateki* or 'insular', while lone monkeys are characterized as wretched, lonely outcastes that have been rejected and expelled by the group. According to Matsumoto Yukiyasu of the Hongū village of Hoshinbo, the lone monkeys that appear in his fields from time to time are in a state of *murahachibu*—a term, meaning literally 'eight parts of the village', that refers to the traditional ostracism suffered by anti-social individuals or families in rural Japan. This popular perception of monkeys as group animals underpins the association of *engai* with war.

Second, monkeys are known to behave in an organized way. They strike in dawn raids when much of the village is asleep. The farm raid is preceded by a *teisatsu* or 'reconnaissance' mission by a single monkey, variously described as a *mihari* or *mihariyaku* ('lookout'), a *sekkōhei* ('scout soldier'), and a *sentōbutai* ('vanguard'). This monkey will then send *aizu* or 'signals' to inform the rest of the troop that it is safe to come and raid the field. Later, when the time comes for the monkey raiders to escape with the eventual appearance of an irate farmer, the monkey lookout alerts the others with loud cries. Suzuki Tokuhei of Kotsuga described to me the role of the 'lookout':

When the group enters the ricefield or the dryfield, one of them plays the role of lookout who signals to the others. If a human being comes along, the monkey will make a signal to the others and they will all suddenly scatter and escape. And then, when it thinks the human being has gone away, like when he comes over here [away from the fields], it will go '*kokokokoko*' and emerge again into the ricefield to play around . . .

A farmer in Yamagata Prefecture recalls his experience of such co-ordination among crop-raiding monkeys as follows: 'When a person approaches, they shake the tree in anger, and if you go still closer they make a "*kii kii*" cry in a loud voice, probably to warn the others. When they do this, their monkey friends disappear all at once' (*KS* 30 Apr. 1996). This impressive simian division of labour is further expressed in reports of fruit tree raiding in which some monkeys climb the tree to shake off fruit for the others on the ground to eat (Nomoto 1994: 138).

   Monkeys are known to be hierarchical in their organization, and to have an overall leader. A variety of anthropomorphic terms are applied to the leading monkey. One traditional term used in some areas was *ō* or 'King' (Matsuyama 1977*b*: 1–2). Among farmers in Hongū the term used is *bosu* or 'boss' (English loanword), the usual word applied to the leading monkey in Japan (including, until recently, by primatologists). Another, similar term used is *oyabun*, a term conventionally applied to the paternalistic chief in the workplace (the word includes the Chinese character for parent). The Japanese and English words for 'leader'— *shidōsha* and *rīdā*, respectively—are also used. In Japan there is a considerable fascination with the figure of the leading monkey; the 'boss' tends to be the focus of the frequent popular speculations on, and academic analyses of, monkey society that feature in the mass media. The perceived status of the 'boss' as an absolute ruler or militaristic leader is evident in references to him as a *taishō* (general), *daimyō* (feudal lord), or *shōgun* (supreme general).[11] The 'boss' appears as a key figure in monkey crop raids. The other monkeys seem to be under his command and are referred to as the *buka* or 'subordinates' of the boss. As Suzuki Ryōichi of Kotsuga put it, 'he [the boss] is really clever—after all, he brings [to the fields] all those subordinates with him'. The pre-eminent status of the 'boss' is suggested by the claim that for the farmer to so much as glance at him is to risk physical attack by the whole troop (Nomoto 1994: 135). Some farmers in Hongū claim that large-scale monkey raids suddenly end when the boss gets shot (though I have yet to meet a farmer who has actually experienced this first hand).[12]

   This perception of the boss as a kind of absolute ruler is widely found in Hongū. Suzuki Tokuhei explained to me what the monkey boss was like by recalling an experience he had had some years before.

They have something like a boss. I was in Totsukawa once on a job . . . There's a place where you can clearly see the fields on the mountainside [below] . . . There were lots of monkeys running along the stone walls [at the edge of the fields]. I stopped and watched from my car. They were each holding a radish or a potato [as they ran away]—every one of them. There

---

[11]   In an interview Suzuki Tokuhei of Kotsuga, for example, likened the monkey boss to a *daimyō*. The militaristic character of the boss is also reflected in the nicknames given to leading monkeys in monkey parks—such as 'Hideyoshi' (the name of a famous historical warlord) and even 'Fuseyin' (Hussein, i.e. Saddam Hussein)!

[12]   It should be noted that accounts of monkey crop-raiding are somewhat contradictory on this point, as other farmers identify the boss with the monkey playing the 'lookout' role from a nearby tree, which does not come to the field itself.

was not one which was just running. They all had something, as they ran along the walls next to the fields. It was really interesting . . . Then there was a man nearby, the man who owned the land, and I got talking to him. 'Hey, down below there are lots of monkeys! They're all holding radishes and potatoes from the fields, and they are all carrying something!' . . . Then the landowner says to me, 'yes, because if they go back without anything they'll be set upon and even killed by the boss. If they go back without anything, he'll be angry'. That's what the man said . . . So, you see, in their world there is the boss [*bosu*], the patron [*oyabun*], and if you don't take him anything you'll have a hard time and it could even be a matter of life or death . . . From their gestures you can tell that there are definitely patron–client relations [*oyabun kobun*] among them. In their world you have that sort of thing . . . It's like how it was in Japan long ago—they take the 'rice' [*hanmai*] to him as he is like the feudal lord [*daimyō*]. They offer him a tribute [*nengu*]—it's like that.

Third, monkey troops are often very large, like *butai* or 'legions' (Matsuyama 1994: 15, 33). There are local claims of crop-raiding troops of fifty, eighty, and even one hundred monkeys that cause great damage during their visits. A old woman in Kotsuga described the sight of crop-raiding monkeys in the following way: 'there were fifty or sixty of them and the ricefield was full of them and completely black [*makkuro*]'. On the western side of the Kii Peninsula, a retired schoolteacher claims that there now exist unusually large monkey troops which are devastating farmland in remote settlements: 'When eighty or a hundred of them descend on a mountain village, they take all the fruit [from the trees]. The same with the potatoes—they take the lot.' In addition to this perception of enlarged troops, there is a local belief that monkeys are proliferating in number, as expressed in somewhat apocalyptic terms by Taniguchi Sōichi, a 74-year-old man in the village of Kirihata:

You have one of them [monkeys] which after they have mated goes on to become seven or so . . . Where this happens they will come to take over the whole of this area . . . It's incredible the way their numbers just keep growing . . . It's like multiplication, every year they increase. There will be ten of them one year, and this then becomes twenty of them the next year, and then that twenty becomes forty and so on . . . When their numbers keep on increasing like this, in the end there will be nothing left for them to eat [in the forest] and they will come out [to the villages].

Such claims of monkey mega-troops and rapid rates of breeding are, at the very least, questionable and probably exaggerated (farmers scarcely have time to count invading monkeys). But it is possible that monkey troops are getting bigger, and this may be due to the very success of their farm-raiding. Primatologists suggest that an increase in monkey troop size could be accounted for by regular feeding on nutritious crops that increases fertility and reduces mortality in the troop.[13]

[13] See Watanabe (1995: 49); cf. Strum (1994: 300). This would also be supported by the experience of monkey provisioning in the monkey parks, where the feeding regimen appears to have led to the proliferation of monkey populations—see Itani (1975: 117–18), Huffman (1991: 41), Sprague *et al.* (1996: 454), and Asquith (1989: 149).

The threat to farms and villages is not confined to large monkey 'legions', but also comes from lone monkeys. A recognized feature of the 'matrilineal' Japanese macaques is intertroop mobility of young males, behaviour that appears to be related to enhancing their mating prospects and rank status (Itani 1975: 109–12; Sprague 1992). These aggressive young males are known to raid farms over a wide area.[14] Although the scale of damage caused by the visit of a troop will obviously be that much greater, lone monkeys too can prove a serious nuisance, as the following report from Mie Prefecture suggests.

Lone monkeys are a really difficult problem. They live in one place, and regularly feed on farm crops, but also threaten and attack the weaker people [in the village]—the old people and the children . . . The monkey troops in the forest cause their damage all in one go, but the lone monkeys cause damage day after day . . . (Ishikawa 1995: 57)

Lone monkeys are sometimes associated with *ninja*, the trained secret agents-cum-assassins from the feudal era. This is evident in the claim by Fuchi Hiromi of the Hongū village of Ukegawa that lone monkeys approach the vegetable garden next to her house with *shinobiashi* ('on tiptoe'), a term recalling the *ninja*. This association is given an added resonance by the fact that (as noted above) *ninja* were themselves likened to monkeys in their ability to overcome the defences of their enemy (Draeger 1989: 92). The monkey-like nature of the *ninja* thus forms the background to the *ninja*-like character of the monkey. But lone monkeys can also attract the modern language of guerrilla warfare, as when the English loanword *gerira* ('guerrilla') is applied to crop-raiding monkeys (*KS* 30 Apr. 1996; *Asian Primates* 1992: 2).

Fourth, monkeys seem to be colonizing the village and its surroundings. In some cases, monkey chattering in the nearby forest is so loud and noisy that it keeps villagers awake at night. As depopulation progresses and the number of abandoned houses in Japan's upland villages grows, these old buildings may well attract monkeys. Monkeys have been known to occupy empty houses or to sleep under the eaves of houses. An old woman in a village in Yamagata Prefecture, who has suffered many monkey raids on her own house, complains that 'it's just like the monkey area of a zoo around my house. There are monkeys which play on the roof of the empty house next door, treating it as a slide' (*KS* 30 Apr. 1996). Similar complaints are voiced by Taniguchi Sōichi (a retired carpenter), who described to me the way monkeys have taken over a nearby outhouse.

That building over there is my carpentry hut. The monkeys all gather on that roof and form a line along it, and as they eat and play about among themselves they look out towards us. They're clever—they're not worried about us anymore. They sit up there and just groom each other . . . They defecate up there on the roof and it gets all dirty. When things reach this stage it really is the end—when human beings and their houses become

[14]   See Koganezawa (1991: 137), Mori Akio in *AS* (13 Nov. 1996), AS (5 June 1994), and IHSHS (1995: 67).

surrounded like this, and you reach the point where you are desperate to try and escape from the monkeys.

This spatial convergence between humans and monkeys is stigmatizing for the communities affected. For example, the presence of monkeys (in the fields, on the roads, and on the roofs of houses) in Wakinosawa in Aomori Prefecture is so frequent that the place has come to be referred to as *saru no sumu mura* or 'the village where monkeys live' (Isoyama 1999). The same point was made by 80-year-old Naka Kumiko in the Hongū village of Bujū, which has endured serious monkey pestilence: 'Everybody [around here] will become monkeys. We'll all become monkeys.'

There is a further association between *engai* and war that should be mentioned—with the Second World War and its aftermath. Among older villagers in Hongū, *engai* is not just analogically linked to war, but also aetiologically traceable to war. This arises where the apparently excessive numbers of monkeys are attributed to the American Occupation of Japan following the Second World War. In my interview with him, 83-year-old Ōjino Tōru of Bujū, reflecting on the large numbers of monkeys in the forest surrounding his village, explained to me that, 'when General MacArthur came along, we were told not to catch monkeys and so we could not hunt them after that. But today we have to catch them because of the pestilence.' The reference here is to the ban on monkey-hunting introduced in 1947 during the Occupation, which (as this man sees it) has finally had to be reversed half a century later (although, in fact, the ban on hunting monkeys never did prevent culling). These comments suggest that the present-day *engai* problem is due to outside interference that prevented Japanese mountain villagers from controlling monkeys in their own way, through hunting, as they had done until that point. From this perspective, the present-day 'war' with monkeys in the Japanese mountains has its origins in the earlier war between nations.

Responses

Village responses to monkey damage reinforce the impression of a people–monkey 'war'. Frightening imagery is one kind of deterrent employed. *Kakashi* or scarecrows, in the form of simple sticks covered with old clothing, are a common sight in fields, especially vulnerable forest-edge fields, and are directed against monkeys as well as other kinds of animals. Some farmers, believing that monkeys only take notice of *kakashi* that actually look like human beings, create special, customized *kakashi* by placing on the standard *kakashi* frame a doll's head, a noh mask, or a forest labourer's helmet (see Fig. 3.2). *Kakashi* are often dressed in human clothes; I have heard that colourful *kimono* clothing is effective, but more commonly old work clothes are used. In the village of Hoshinbo, the home-made *kakashi* protecting the ricefields of Nojima Kinuko is made from plastic bags filled with sawdust, clothed with her old cast-offs and covered with her old white

Fɪɢ. 3.2. A scarecrow used to protect mushrooms (grown in the forest) from monkeys (Hongū-chō)

smock, and tied to a metal frame (see Fig. 3.3). The moving imagery of television is also used to keep crops safe from monkeys. The electrician Tsuro Kōhei, of the village of Takenomoto, is hired by local farmers to repair old television sets (and radios) and provide long cables to allow them to be placed near their fields to keep monkeys and other animals away. Television is said to be an effective deterrent because of the irregularity of its imagery and sounds (especially the raised voices of films, dramas, and commercials).

Imagery other than human imagery is also employed in this forest-edge 'war'. A farmer in Hoshinbo is known to use the corpse of a trapped monkey, hung upside down near the field, to keep monkeys away from his crops—he describes it as a *miseshime* or 'warning to others' (he was inspired to do this after successfully using dead crows to stop crow damage to his fruit trees). The use of monkey skulls to protect fields is reported for other regions of Japan (Watanabe 1995: 52). These practices recall the widespread belief that wild animals dislike the smell of death where it involves their own kind. But reports from across Japan suggest that a wide variety of other imagery is deployed. In an echo of the macaque crop-raider's association with King Kong noted above, in some areas huge billboards of Godzilla, the conqueror of King Kong in the famous 1962 film *King Kong versus Godzilla* (*Kingu Kongu tai Gojira*), are erected at the edge of the village facing the

FIG. 3.3. A scarecrow used to keep monkeys away from the ricefield (Hongū-chō)

forest in order to protect farms (Nomoto 1994: 136). Home-made life-size models of orang-utans have also been used to protect fields in the belief that Japanese monkeys would be frightened and deterred by the presence of 'monkeys' so much bigger than themselves (*NNSC* 28 Sept. 1998). Meanwhile, farmers in Kyōto Prefecture erect field-side billboards bearing the image of a large red crab to deter persistent crop-raiding by monkeys—a reference to the Japanese folk tale, mentioned earlier, in which the crab outwits and drives away a food-stealing monkey (*AS* 10 Aug. 1994). But frightening images are not the only means of keeping monkeys away from human territory.

Noise is another weapon in the village war with the monkey. A common sight in Hongū villages is the *odoshi*, a home-made clanging device that is also used to frighten away other animals (such as wild boar, as we saw in Chapter 2). The *odoshi* consists of a collection of metal cans (typically of different sizes) which are suspended together from a tree next to fields, and often on the border of village and forest, which works by rattling together when blown by the wind or by being manually activated by the villagers by means of a long wire connecting it to a point close to, or even inside, the house (see Fig. 3.4). Another noise deterrent is the firecracker (that simulates the sound of gunfire) which is thrown at crop-raiding monkeys to startle them into returning to the forest. Physical fortifications form another element in village defences. Fences are erected around individual fields,

FIG. 3.4. A *naruko* noisemaker in the village of Kirihata. The *naruko* is connected by a wire to the house below, and when monkeys are heard or sighted it is tugged to set the cans clanging in order to drive the monkeys away

around a wider area of farmland, or around the village as a whole. In the coastal village of Tsubaki soft-mesh fences have been put up around houses (and around graveyards) in an attempt to stop monkey intrusions. Hard-mesh fences are also used, sometimes extending at the top horizontally to form a roof above the field—a structure routinely referred to as a 'cage' (*ori*). Electric fencing has become widespread, in some cases involving voltages of up to 10,000 volts. In the village of Kotsuga an anti-monkey electric fence, 1.6 metres high and 720 metres in length, runs along the boundary between ricefields and forest. But fences tend to be less effective against the agile monkey than against other animals, as monkeys are able to climb over electric fences by deftly avoiding contact with the live parts of the fence. This resort to 'cages' as a means of defending farmland from monkeys occasions sardonic comments from farmers themselves. As one man in Owase in Mie Prefecture put it, 'for human beings to cultivate inside cages is a bizarre state of affairs, but as protection against damage this is the only method that works' (*CNS* 22 May 1997).

As these examples show, Japanese farmers deploy a wide variety of protective measures to keep monkeys away from their fields. But none of these measures are wholly effective, and monkeys are renowned for their ability to bypass such defences—by seeing through the scarecrows, by losing their fear of firecrackers, by learning how to negotiate fences, and so on. It is for this reason that some Hongū farmers believe that the most reliable way to protect a crop from monkeys is the *sarunoban* or 'monkey watch'—that is, the physical guarding of the fields. The practice of farmers guarding fields from monkeys (and other wildlife pests) has long been carried out in Japan. It is well documented for the Tokugawa period. In his study of documents from the late eighteenth century and the early nineteenth century, the primatologist Mito Yukihisa found many references to the practice of *sarunoban* (Mito 1989). The theme of guarding fields from monkeys is incorporated into Japanese folk culture in the form of annual festivals, such as the *saruoi matsuri* or 'monkey chasing festival' in Hanasaku in Gunma Prefecture (Hirose 1977; Moon 1989: 156–62). *Sarunoban* is carried out to protect vulnerable fields close to the forest. As the macaque is a diurnal animal (like Man, but unlike most other large forest animals), the monkey watch is in principle a day-long, dawn-to-dusk routine, one that tends to be followed more and more strictly as harvest time approaches. The guard is usually protected from the hot midday sun by a small hut or canopy (sometimes just a large umbrella) next to the field that affords a view of the forest. In earlier times, when remote farmers had to protect their fields from monkeys during the day and from wild boar during the night, a division of labour sometimes operated whereby women undertook the daytime monkey watch, while men carried out the night-time duty (Mito 1987: 31). In present-day Hongu, however, such round-the-clock field-guarding is rare, and the *sarunoban* tends to be performed by men and women.

Few people are affected by the *engai* problem as much as Suzuki Tokuhei and his wife Kazue, who give up much of their summer to guard their ricefields from monkeys. The Suzukis are one of the three families in the village of Kotsuga that carry out the arduous task of *sarunoban*. This older couple—aged 73 and 65, respectively—grow 50 ares of riceland, consisting of ten different fields that vary in size from 1.3 ares to 9.9 ares. They farm with the help of their son and daughter (both married with children) who reside in regional cities but return for rice-transplanting in the late spring and again for harvesting in the late summer. Like so many Hongū families today, the Suzuki family has been dispersed by outmigration. Farming provides one of the main occasions when the family gathers together. The Suzukis harvest around 25 bales of rice, and sell around a fifth of this. The bulk of the harvest, 20 bales of rice, is divided between their own household and the households of their two children, while the rest is given away to friends and relatives. As one of the older families of the village (Tokuhei is the 9th generation head of the family), the Suzukis are especially preoccupied with the question of family succession and express the hope that either their son or their daughter will one day return to live in the village with them, so that in the future, long after they themselves have gone, there will be descendants who will continue to cultivate the sizeable family landholding. But along with family succession, their other major concern is with monkeys which threaten to undermine the family farm. In the recent past the Suzukis have lost nearly 10 per cent of their rice harvest (3 bales of rice, at a total cost of around ¥72,000 [$630]) to the monkeys. They believe that they would have lost much more were it not for their regular field-guarding.

The Suzukis carry out *sarunoban* from a *bangoya* (a small lookout hut) at the intersection of their fields. During the months of July and August, they guard the ricefields from 4 o'clock in the morning to 7 o'clock at night. When monkeys do appear in the fields, they must be dispersed, and the Suzukis use a variety of 'weapons' to this end, including firecrackers, catapults (using small metal balls normally used for the popular pachinko game), or just stones and rocks. It is mostly the husband who performs *sarunoban*, but when he cannot do it due to some other commitment, the wife takes over. They do not ask other villagers to help them out, as some farmers do; in the past they have asked a neighbour to help them, but monkeys raided their ricefields without this man noticing. 'Other people are just unreliable, so you have to do your own guarding.' Nor do they risk leaving their fields unattended during daylight, believing that monkeys are all too likely to take their chance to raid at that time. They know this from past experience when they have tried to deceive the monkeys: on one occasion, they left music on inside the *bangoya* to disguise their absence, but this did not stop the monkeys from raiding—it was as though the monkeys somehow knew that there was nobody there. This, alongside other episodes, has led the Suzukis to suspect that much of the time the monkeys are watching them from the forest.

One major problem with field-guarding is the summer heat. Although the *bangoya* allows the guard to monitor the fields while seated in the shade and protected from the hot summer sun, the little hut, with its corrugated iron roof, becomes extremely hot inside. What the Suzukis do to counter this is to place brushwood and vegetation from the nearby forest on top of the roof. As they are constantly sweating during the midday hours, they take along large quantities of water and iced tea to drink. Other sources of discomfort for the field-guard are snakes and insects; the profusion of summer insects in the ricefield represents a serious nuisance, as they can bother and bite throughout the day, and even become a potential hazard (one local field-guard was recently hospitalized after an insect bite). But in addition to physical discomfort, the other major problem for the field-guard is boredom. There is of course work to be done in the fields, such as weeding, and much of the time spent guarding the fields is taken up doing this. Some field-guarding farmers are, in fact, quite proud of the *kirei* or 'clean' appearance of their fields; one of Suzuki Tokuhei's neighbours, Suzuki Ryōichi, for example, described his ricefields to me as 'like the inside of a house that has been scrubbed clean'. Field-guards also carry out other jobs and chores, such as knife and sickle sharpening in the case of men, and sewing (darning, patchwork, etc.) in the case of women. Field-guards also use music, reading-matter, and alcohol to pass the time. Suzuki Tokuhei brings a large battery-operated radio-cassette player to the hut from which he plays his favourite music (nostalgic ballads), alternated with the radio. As well as helping him pass the time, the music helps to keep the monkeys away. He is also in the habit of bringing a bottle of sake with him to the *bangoya*, despite his wife's protests that after drinking he is unable to keep watch properly!

In addition to the heat, insects, and the long hours, the reason that guarding fields from monkeys is so tiring is because it is a battle of wits with the monkeys. The term often used is *saru to no chiekurabe*, 'challenging your wits with those of the monkey'. The guard can only win this battle if he or she stays wide awake and vigilant the whole time. Suzuki Tokuhei again:

Other people have given up monkey guarding because it's so hard . . . If you knew what time they were coming, that would be one thing, but you don't know, so you just go on guarding with no idea. It wouldn't be so bad if, say, you knew that they were definitely coming during the day ahead . . . But you have to be ready to act at any time . . . You sit there, holding on to the firecrackers [to throw at the monkeys], and you have to play the radio and the music throughout . . . You just don't know when they will come. Just when you think they are not going to come, then they will suddenly come . . . It's just like a tug of war . . . It's really hard to compete with wild beasts in this way . . . It's just at this sort of time [early evening] when the sun has set and it has turned dark and there is no longer a human presence [in the fields] that they'll [finally] come. [They come] in the evening [at dusk], at dawn, or they come during the day just when you leave the fields for a while . . .

Some farmers delegate the task of *sarunoban* to dogs, just as the job of guarding fields from wild boar at night is assigned to dogs. In Japan, dogs are known as the fiercest enemy of the monkey, an antagonism captured in the proverb, *yome to shūtome inu to saru*, 'like wife and mother-in-law, so dog and monkey'. Japanese breeds are often used for field-guarding against monkeys, but in some areas of Japan imported breeds may be deployed (for example, Shetland sheepdogs in Nagano Prefecture). However, the efficacy of posted guard-dogs is said to be limited because the clever monkeys soon realize that the dogs are confined and cannot harm them, and proceed to raid the fields with impunity. This view is held by Suzuki Tokuhei who recalls the experience of a friend of his who farms in a nearby village.

The monkeys are clever. They get used to the dogs and realize that the dogs are tied down by the leash. So even if there is a dog it's no use, no use at all . . . Kamidaira-san in Ōtsuga left a dog next to his ricefield, tied with a leash. The monkeys came along and entered the ricefield and the dogs tried to go after them but they couldn't [reach them], so in the end they just sat and watched [the monkeys raiding the field]. I witnessed it with my own eyes . . . The dog just gave up, as it couldn't chase them. So the monkeys, knowing that even though there was a dog it was tied by a leash, just casually entered the ricefield and starting eating the rice-grains. Even though it barked at them, '*wanwanwanwan*' . . . They're really clever.[15]

KILLING MONKEYS

Monkeys have long been hunted in Japan. Although the monkey is generally not considered an edible animal, monkey meat has been consumed in upland areas in the past. In Hongū, when the subject of monkey meat is raised, a typical reaction from old hunters or foresters is *anna umai koto wa nai*, 'there is nothing else so good' (cf. Hirose 1993: 56). Similarly, there is the following saying in mountain villages in Nagano Prefecture: *akizaru o yome ni kuwasu na* or 'don't feed your wife autumn monkey'—to do so would be to waste a fine-tasting delicacy (Matsuyama 1994: 26; Hirose 1993: 56). Monkeys were also hunted to obtain body parts for medicinal or curative uses. Monkey meat and intestines were used for meningitis, heart disease, digestive disorders, blood circulation, chronic catarrh, uterine diseases, and cold constitutions (Hirose 1993: 82; Chiba 1977: 138). The monkey's gall bladder was a common folk medicine, used for a wide range of disorders, including eye diseases, stomach complaints, and even a child's tantrums (Nishiura 1989: 177; Mito 1995: 95–6).[16] Monkey intestines were used to secure an easy childbirth, while monkey meat was given to revive the strength of women who had just given birth (Hirose 1993: 84–5; Suzuki 1982: 301). An especially valuable medicinal part of the monkey was the brain which (in charred form) was used to treat child bedwetting, headaches, dizziness, brain or nervous disorders, sickness at pregnancy, blood circulation, and even backward children (Hirose 1993: 78, 85; Suzuki 1982: 300–1). Salted monkey meat is known as a *geridome* or 'diarrhoea-stopper'. Old forest workers say that if a man with an upset stomach takes it at lunchtime, it will have begun to work by the time he goes to bed. Monkey meat was also used in earlier times by those suffering from cholera (Nishiura 1989: 177; Suzuki 1982: 302).[17]

---

[15]   One option, of course, might be for the farmer to release the dog so that it can chase the monkeys back into the forest. But the problem here is that dogs that chase monkeys may well become so involved in the pursuit they end up getting lost in the forest (cf. Iguchi 1990*a*: 18).

[16]   'Before the bear's gall bladder was widely known about, as is the case today, the monkey's gall bladder was used as medicine' (Chiba 1977: 373). Even today, when there is a general preference for bear gall (see Chapter 5), some people argue for the superiority of monkey gall. The point was made by a Hongū forest landowner who was also a keen hunter. The monkey's gall bladder was, in his opinion, better than the bear's because monkeys are, after all, closer to human beings. He even went on to suggest that the human gall bladder was probably the best of all.

[17]   There have also been more recent demands for the curative power of monkey meat, such as in the outbreak of E. coli food poisoning in Japan in the summer of 1996. This serious outbreak of food poisoning affected some 10,000 people (mostly children) and claimed 11 lives. The outbreak led to a

As previously noted, monkeys ceased to be game animals in 1947, and today hunters can only cull, and not hunt, monkeys. Many rural municipalities have *kujotai* or 'culling squads' to deal with monkeys. In 1996 more than 9,000 monkeys were captured or killed as *yūgai dōbutsu* or 'noxious animals' through trapping or shooting. Since 1985 the average annual figure has been 5–6,000, before nearly doubling in 1996. Compared with 1966, when only 305 monkeys were captured or culled as pests, the 1996 figure represents a thirty-fold increase in thirty years (Anon. 2000*a*; *MS* 4 Aug. 1999). In the ten-year period 1983–92, the reported total capture or cull of wild monkeys exceeded 50,000 (*JPN* 1995: 4)—although Japanese primatologists tend to believe the actual figure to be much higher (Watanabe 1995: 53). Two of the three prefectures on the Kii Peninsula, Wakayama and Mie, are among the top five monkey-catching prefectures in Japan (*JPN* 1995: 5). The job of killing monkeys is generally delegated to hunters. After a monkey crop raid has been reported to the Town Hall, the local *ryōyūkai* is contacted and one or more hunters are nominated (often those who live nearby and know the village involved) to cull the monkeys responsible. The hunter(s) will visit the village in question, talk to the farmers affected (to obtain information—how many monkeys, how often they are seen, which part of the forest they emerged from, and so on), before going on to track and kill the monkeys in the nearby forest. The hunter must submit a part of the monkey (such as the tail or the ears) to the Town Hall as evidence of the kill and as a condition of receiving his bounty.[18] The hunter is free to do what he wants with the rest of the monkey; some men sell or give away monkey parts as medicine (often to the elderly, who tend to be more aware of their curative applications), while others just bury the dead monkey in the forest.

There is none the less a widespread reluctance to use violence against monkeys in Japan. Despite the damage done to their fields, villagers are often unwilling to throw stones and rocks at crop-raiding monkeys, let alone kill them. In Hongū there are occasional instances where villagers take it upon themselves to kill captured monkeys. In one village, for example, a monkey that was recently caught in an enclosure trap (provided by the Town Hall) was drowned by villagers in the local river. However, for some of the villagers involved, the incident proved to be

nationwide panic. Sales of bacteria-killing bleaches and cleaners doubled, while a frantic public debate raged over which digestive medicines could combat the deadly bacteria. One response in Hongū to this fear of food poisoning was for local households to acquire monkey meat in the belief that it had the power to prevent or combat food poisoning. In some cases, villagers sent the salt-dried monkey meat to a son or daughter's family in the city, for the benefit of school-aged grandchildren.

[18] In two adjacent municipalities on the Kii Peninsula the price fetched by monkeys varies by a factor of three: ¥10,000 in Hongū, ¥30,000 in Totsukawa (in 1994). The two municipalities ask for different parts of the monkey's anatomy for proof: Hongū asks for the tail, while Totsukawa asks for the ears. It is said that some enterprising hunters obtain two bounties for one animal by taking the different parts to the two town halls—handing in the tail to Hongū Town Hall and having an acquaintance in Totsukawa hand in the ears to the Town Hall there. That the hunter only needs to hand in to the Town Hall the ears or tail of the monkey (which are photographed and then disposed of) to claim his bounty leads to quips that there are now ear-less and tail-less monkeys running around the forest!

extremely upsetting because of the monkey's obvious state of fear and panic as it was being drowned, and as a result these villagers now oppose the use of the trap in the future. The general unease about harming or killing monkeys is found among hunters too. The *ryōyūkai* sometimes has trouble finding men willing to undertake a monkey cull. While hunters are generally prepared at least to consider culling wild boar and deer, these same hunters are often reluctant to have anything to do with monkeys. Fifteen out of the seventy registered hunters in Hongū have explicitly informed the *ryōyūkai* that they do not want to be considered for monkey culling, while many more simply avoid the duty when it comes up. The high bounty for monkeys paid by the authorities is intended to overcome the hunter's reluctance to shooting monkeys (Wada 1998: 103). Aware of this reluctance, farmers may simply ask a hunter to bring his gun to the fields to scare monkeys away or to fire used cartridges at the monkeys, in order to disperse them without killing them.

One of the reasons that most hunters turn down the opportunity of earning money through culling is that dead monkeys have a strong human resemblance. I have often heard it said that hunters do not like to catch a monkey because *jibun no kao ni nitteiru*, 'its face is just like yours'. The killing of monkeys also appears to be cruel. If the wild boar resists defiantly to the end and even tries to kill the hunter and his hounds, the monkey, by contrast, seems to plead for its life. A monkey about to be shot is said to put its hands together, in a gesture known as *inochigoi* or 'begging-for-life', as though it were pleading with the hunter to be spared. Suzuki Tokuhei of Kotsuga referred to this behaviour as follows:

They are just the same as human beings. I'll tell you something. I don't really know if it's a lie or the truth, but I've heard that when you point a gun at them and are about to shoot, they go like this [putting his hands together] . . . They put their hands together, like they are saying 'pardon me' [*koraete kurete*] . . .

The gesture also resembles the act of Buddhist prayer that is associated with a priest or a Buddha, and is even referred to as *saru no gasshō* or 'the monkey's prayer' (Matsuyama 1977*b*: 59). In a folk tale (from the area of Niigata), a monkey begging the hunter not to shoot is saved when an old man gets in the hunter's way—as a result of which, the old man becomes rich (Inada 1994: 395).

If the hunter does go through with it and shoot, he is likely to witness a scene of great misery. Villagers in Kōchi Prefecture give the following reasons for not killing monkeys.

If you shoot and don't hit them in the right place, there is a big commotion among them and its awful because they appear just like human beings.

Before they die, they look you straight in the eye and then they fall from the tree.

As they were dying, they put their hands to their eyes as though they were crying. I just can't shoot them [anymore]. (in Katsuki 1995: 334–5)

The point is often made by hunters that the monkey's *shinigao* or 'death face' (its facial appearance upon death) is horrible to look at, as it recalls the pale face of a dead child. Taniguchi Sōichi of Kirihata, a former hunter himself, made this point when explaining to me why in his youth he could never shoot monkeys himself.

I used to have a gun a long time ago and at that time I seriously thought about shooting them [the monkeys] . . . But I always felt that it would be wrong to do that because they are so much like humans. Usually, they have red faces don't they, because they are always angry or something, but apparently when you shoot them they [their faces] turn all white as they stop breathing . . . It would just feel wrong to me.

Another reason why killing monkeys is distressing, in addition to the human-like way that monkeys die, has to do with the family ties that are broken as a result. Despite their pest status, monkeys are respected, even admired, for their social ties. As monkeys give birth in the early summer, the sight of female monkeys carrying their young around with them during the summer months is a common one, and even farmers who otherwise complain bitterly about *engai* refer to the sight of monkey mothers and their young with a certain admiration. Taniguchi Sōichi of Kirihata, who believes that monkey numbers need to be controlled by large-scale culling, none the less made the following comments.

They are really careful with their young and look after them. Their love [for their young] is probably deeper than that found among we humans . . . As we all know, there are cases where people stab their parents to death, aren't there? But with them [monkeys] you don't find things like that . . . They are truly richer in love than humans are. There are of course lots of times when they argue among themselves, with their friends, but then on warm days they will take turns to groom each other, I've often observed them doing it . . . There's an atmosphere of tranquility when they do that.

It is these intimate relations between monkeys that culling destroys. There are many reports of the awful scenes that result from the act of shooting monkeys. Wounded monkeys sob like children, dying monkeys groan and scream, orphaned monkeys refuse to accept their loss and cling on to their dead mother, and bereaved mothers carry their dead young around with them for days afterwards![19] Although the monkey-culler may claim to be removing threatening pests, he risks appearing to others as a killer of loving mothers and a destroyer of families.

Killing monkeys can encounter opposition from other villagers. Sometimes monkey cullers arrive at a village to dispatch a problem monkey, in response to local complaints, only to find themselves being urged by other villagers not to kill it.

When it comes to the culling of monkeys, there are few hunters who come out to take part in it, and in many cases they [the cullers] end up shooting in the air or not shooting at all.

---

[19] See Chiba (1975: 151), Tabuchi (1992: 50), and Matsuyama (1994: 40, 44–7).

Consequently, the leader of the culling party has to take responsibility himself for shooting the monkeys . . . Trapping monkeys alive in cages has been successful, but then there is the difficult problem of disposing of the monkeys afterwards . . . [When called out to a village suffering monkey damage], it is of course possible to go and shoot them [monkey pests], but then, when you get there, the local people who haven't had any problem will say, 'Stop! Don't kill them!' . . . (Ishikawa 1995: 57)

Therefore, monkey culling is not simply an issue pitting village proponents against city opponents (as it is sometimes presented), but one that can lead to polarization within rural areas. Monkey culling does not seem to command general support in rural areas, nor among a significant proportion of farmers. In one survey from a rural area of Aichi Prefecture, only 29 per cent of respondents expressed support for culling, and of those engaged in farming this figure did not exceed 50 per cent (Watanabe and Ogura 1996: 10).

Another reason for not killing monkeys has to do with the fears of *tatari* or spirit vengeance that the killing of monkeys tends to raise. Newspaper reports on the *engai* problem sometimes mention that hunters are reluctant to kill monkeys because of their fear of *tatari*.[20] Although this fear also arises in relation to the wild boar (as we saw in the last chapter), the sensitivity towards monkeys appears to be far greater. It will be recalled that tales of boar curses typically have to do with *excess* killing, but the Japanese lore on monkey curses suggests that what is at issue with monkeys is killing *per se* rather than excess killing. Taking even a single monkey life is dangerous. In Japan monkey killers are believed to be especially vulnerable to spirit revenge in the form of assorted misfortunes (death, injury, illness, birth of a monkey-like child, financial ruin, and so on) affecting the killer himself or his family for two, three, or even seven generations.[21] In 1994 I heard a story about a monkey-catcher on the Kii Peninsula whose wife gave birth to a monkey-like child that made animal noises and climbed around the house! If a monkey killer does incur the monkey's curse in the form of some family calamity, this may well be viewed by his neighbours as not without an element of poetic justice. But the slaughter of a monkey can have consequences for the whole community, as is indicated by reports of monkey killers bringing disaster to the rest of the village in the form of great fires that run through the settlement, failed harvests, or (ironically) intensified monkey crop-raiding.[22] This theme, of the spirit retribution visited on people who kill monkeys, is one that appears in Japanese literature and in film.[23] A further indication of the fear of the monkey's *tatari* is the ritual activity that is

[20] See, for example, *AS* (12 June 1996) and *AS* (29 Aug. 1996).
[21] See, for example, Itani (1971: 6); Suzuki (1982: 297); Hayashi (1991); Chiba (1995*b*: 128).
[22] See Chiba (1975: 142), Tabuchi (1992: 50), and Togawa (1956: 119).
[23] The theme appears in Kikuchi Kan's play 'The Madman on the Roof' (*Okujō no kyōjin*) where the cause of the madness of an eldest son (and normative family heir) is attributed to his father having shot all the monkeys in the area. Another example is the film *Himatsuri* or Fire Festival (1985) by Yanagimachi Mitsuo (screenplay by Nakagami Kenji) about a monkey hunter who ends up using the same shotgun to massacre his family in the village.

undertaken to pacify the spirits of the dead monkeys. For example, in Inami-chō to the west of Hongū a special rite is carried out each year at the Raikōji temple for the spirits of culled monkeys, in which the monkey spirits are transferred into a batch of living carp that are then released into a small pond in the temple grounds, in a Buddhist ceremony known as a *hōjōe*.[24]

There are also doubts over the effectiveness of monkey culling and even suggestions that it may be counter-productive. One interpretation of the present-day scale of farm damage by lone crop-raiders is that, on top of normal intertroop transfer of adult males, it is the result of the social fragmentation of macaque populations brought about by the high level of culling. In other words, culling can help to *create* crop-raiding rogue monkeys by destroying the social cohesion of monkey troops (*AS* 5 June 1994; IHSHS 1995: 67). 'Shooting destroys the stability of the troop. If the troop is broken up, countermeasures [against monkey damage] become hopeless' (*KS* 2 Sept. 1997). This perception is supported, to some extent, by the local view of monkeys as hierarchical group animals referred to above. If monkeys are 'ruled' by a boss figure, then the elimination of the boss, as arch-leader, would seem to invite chaos in the troop. Yet the worse that monkey damage gets, the greater the sense of siege on the part of weakened, depopulated villages and the more important do local hunters become as armed defenders of the village. The 'war' idiom therefore seems to have a self-fulfilling character. Some critics, in challenging the effectiveness of monkey culling, see it rather as a symbolic act. The primatologist Koganezawa Masaaki characterizes the culling of monkeys in rural Japan as a *gisei* ('sacrifice') or *korashime* ('punishment') of the animals that serves only to make victim farmers feel better (Koganezawa 1991: 150). The rural sociologist Maita Akio similarly attributes to monkey culling a logic other than utilitarian pest control: *engai* monkeys play *warumono no yaku* or 'the role of scapegoats' for present-day decline in remote areas (Maita 1989: 148–9). Villagers are encouraged to direct their anger and frustrations on to the monkey as the cause of *mura kuzushi* or 'village breakdown', the effect of which is to obscure the failure of state-sponsored rural development efforts (ibid.).

FEEDING MONKEYS

In the sections above, we have examined the farmer–monkey relationship and the hunter–monkey relationship. In the former, monkeys are viewed as illicitly taking human food. In the latter, monkeys were captured for food or medicine, or were killed to prevent crop-raiding. There is, however, a third local relation to monkeys to consider. This involves people giving food to monkeys. On the one hand, there is a degree of acceptance of monkey crop-feeding in rural Japan. A recent rural survey from Aichi Prefecture found that a quarter of farmers believed that monkey

[24] Similar 'animal release' rites, involving the ceremonial release of captured animals (usually birds or fish), are found throughout Buddhist Asia—in China, Thailand, Vietnam, and Korea.

damage had to be tolerated to some extent (Watanabe and Ogura 1996: 10). Given the large scale of farm damage in the area surveyed, it is likely that some of these tolerant responses came from affected farmers. Similarly, in many Hongū villages this or that persimmon or chestnut tree near the forest is known as *saru no ki* or 'the monkey's tree' or its fruit referred to as *saru no bun* or 'the monkey's share'. No one complains about monkeys raiding the fruit of such trees. Even in areas seriously affected by monkey damage to orchards, fruit growers are prepared to accept a degree of damage on the grounds that 'the monkeys have to live too' (Wada 1998: 92). There are reports of similar expressions of sympathy for the plight of wild monkeys on the part of shopkeepers whose goods have been stolen by monkeys (Emoto 1993: 31).

On the other hand, a certain amount of voluntary feeding of monkeys takes place. Charcoal-burners and foresters in Japan have long befriended monkeys (Togawa 1956: 85–126). There is a widespread habit of feeding wild animals in Japan, and informal small-scale feeding of wild monkeys appears to have occurred in many villages. Hungry monkeys readily attract human sympathy and pity. Referring to villagers in Aomori Prefecture, who have long suffered from monkey damage, the zoologist Ochiai Keiji comments that 'no matter how bad the damage done during the summer, when winter comes, and people see the monkeys out there in the falling snow, they cannot help but give them apples' (Ochiai 1991: 213). An observer in the coastal village of Wakinosawa in the same prefecture makes a similar point: although monkeys raid village farms and are a general nuisance, 'when winter comes, and they appear outside the window, an apple will be handed to them without thinking' (Isoyama 1999). In the Hongū village of Minachi, a kindly old woman called Shiba Hiroko scatters oranges in the nearby forest for the wild monkeys to feed on. This devout follower of the Buddhist sect Sōka Gakkai professes a love for all living things and believes that villagers should extend *jihi* or 'compassion' to the animals of the forest. Recognizing this tendency among some villagers to feed and befriend monkeys, public authorities in Japan have now started to carry out campaigns to discourage the practice. Nara Prefecture, for example, distributes leaflets in remote areas that instruct people not to feed monkeys (Inoue 2002: 93). A similar campaign in Mie Prefecture attempts to stop local people feeding monkeys by means of the slogan, 'Monkeys live in the forest and eat the food of the forest' (Shimizu 1987: 16).

One step beyond the informal feeding of wild monkeys is the adoption of monkeys as pets. In the past, some forest workers, who actually lived in the forest (in forest huts) for weeks and months at a time, adopted monkeys (as well as other animals) as pets as a source of entertainment and companionship. Hunters and foresters on the Kii Peninsula have long brought home young monkeys as pets for themselves or for their children. Across Japan, there are many tales of individual monkeys being adopted and nurtured by villagers. There are even rare reports of infant monkeys suckled by village women (Ōta 1997: 196–7). Shiba Hiroko, as well as feeding wild monkeys, is the proud keeper of two pet monkeys (Jirō and Hana). The first monkey was obtained when, as an infant, it was discovered lying injured on the forest floor and brought back to the village where the Shibas offered to look after him and brought him back to health. The monkey was eventually given the name Jirō, a human name usually given to the second son. Jirō is famous in Hongū for eating rice gruel for breakfast, for drinking beer, for watching television, for taking a nightly bath, and for sleeping on a futon inside the house next to the Shibas (as a forest worker, Shiba Takayoshi, Hiroko's husband, sleeps early in the evening and wakes up early in the morning—sleeping hours similar to those of the diurnal forest monkey). The Shibas' pet monkeys attract a lot of media interest, and have often featured in newspaper and magazine articles and appeared on television. There are also reports of lone monkeys that become, in effect, village pets or mascots (Hirose 1982: 43).

Fɪɢ. 3.5. An advertisement for the Nikkō Saru Gundan ('Nikkō Monkey Army') monkey show

Fɪɢ. 3.6. Wrapping paper (for *manjū* cakes) from the Nikkō Saru Gundan visitor attraction. The paper design features the named monkeys of the monkey show

The background to the voluntary feeding of monkeys is the perception of monkeys as cute, childlike animals. The affectionate view of the monkey is one that tends to be associated with the city. Monkeys have become a popular tourist attraction in Japan, and serve as a valuable resource in some rural areas. For tourists, the sight of monkeys is a thrilling one. I recall a party of young women tourists travelling on a bus across the Kii Peninsula who all cooed and shouted *Osaru-san* ('honorable Mr Monkey') as a band of monkeys ran across the road in front of the bus. Sometimes Shiba Hiroko is asked by tourist guesthouses in Hongū to bring a monkey over to show to a group of guests. Some of the guesthouses sell wooden coasters in the shape of a monkey's face and small china monkey figurines. Although associated with urbanites, this cute image of the monkey is familiar to mountain villagers, both through the mass media, through visits to monkey parks, as well as through contact with urban dwellers, both tourists and their own relatives who have outmigrated to the cities. This emerged in my interview with Suzuki Tokuhei. After describing to me all the hardships he endures through guarding his fields from monkeys, he mentioned matter of factly that when his young grandchildren come to the village to stay in the summer they demand to see '*Osaru-san*' and so he takes them with him to the fields to view the monkeys (but, of course, at these times, when he wants the monkeys to appear, they rarely do). On these occasions his normal anxiety, as a farmer, about *pest* monkeys gives way to a desire, as a grandfather, to show off *cute* monkeys. It is this image of the monkey as a cute figure that disposes some villagers to feed them (especially when baby monkeys are present).

Another influence on the voluntary feeding of monkeys are the monkey parks. There exists one such monkey park on the Kii Peninsula: in Tsubaki on the south-west coast, about two hours drive from Hongū. The monkey parks regularly provide food for their monkeys in clearings to ensure their visibility to paying tourists. In many of the parks tourists are also allowed to feed monkeys directly. The parks can have the effect of habituating their visitors to give food to monkeys, behaviour which the visitors are all too likely to reproduce when they encounter monkeys outside the park. In recent years, the impromptu feeding of monkeys along mountain roads in remote areas has become a serious problem in Japan. For example, tourists in Yakushima and Nikkō feed monkeys they spot on the large artificial embankments created when a road passes through a mountainous area (*JPN* 1994: 3; Koganezawa and Imaki 1999). However, mountain villagers too are familiar with the monkey parks, either directly through visits or indirectly through television. One suspects that some of the local people feeding monkeys in Hongū are replicating the recreational feeding behaviour associated with the parks. But there may well be other motivations underpinning the local feeding of monkeys. A man in Hongū who runs a small restaurant is said to have seriously considered planting persimmon and chestnut trees on the facing mountainside in order to attract monkeys. His reasoning was that if monkeys gathered on the mountainside, tourists would gather below to watch and photograph them, and his restaurant would get extra business by providing refreshments and meals to these people.

A further factor in the voluntary feeding of monkeys by villagers has to do with the perception of forest monkeys as hungry animals that come to feed on village crops because they cannot feed in the forest. Although, as seen above, *engai* is commonly attributed to increasing monkey numbers, it is also readily linked to the declining natural food supply available in the mountains as a result of post-war forestry. When talking about monkey damage to their crops, many people in Hongū mention the monkey's lack of food in the forest. Asari Tetsuichi was one of the many Hongū informants who made this point.

Gradually, the food in the interior has disappeared, to the point where they [the monkeys] come out in the open [like this] . . . In the past there was the mixed forest, with lots of deciduous trees . . . When you have deciduous trees, you get buds. And that's what they eat. At that time, they didn't appear in the open [like now]. But then they [the foresters] cut all the trees down and made it [the forest] into [timber] plantations.

Kakiyama Kōhei too directly expressed the idea of an equivalence between the wild foods of the forest and the cultivated foods of the village when he referred to nuts and berries as the monkey's *sakumotsu* or 'crops'. 'It's because there is no more natural forest left that the monkeys come down to where people live, to eat the persimmons and other things. This is because in the forest there are no more trees that grow nuts and berries, the foods that are like their crops.'

  The head of one household in the Hongū village of Kirihata, Sugiyama Eiichi, has come to accept monkeys feeding from his chestnut trees, even though his old father is furious about it. Wild monkeys only run the risk of coming to feed in the village, he believes, because they cannot feed in the forest any more due to the spread of commercial timber trees. The Sugiyamas are a forestry family that has its share of responsibility for the replacement of the surrounding forest by timber plantations. But (to the dismay of his father) the son has become a harsh critic of post-war forestry, believing that families like his own, which cut down the trees on which monkeys used to feed, cannot really complain of farm damage by hungry monkeys now. Sugiyama-san is somewhat exceptional in his tolerance of monkeys and in his forthright view that the forestry villages of Hongū only have themselves to blame for *engai*. Most of his neighbours outwardly show little such tolerance and even less contrition. Yet many of them have laboured in the forests of the peninsula, felled the old stands of horse chestnut, zelkova, and beech and replaced them with timber conifers, and therefore have a similar first-hand experience of the ecological background to *engai*. This is perhaps one of the reasons why foresters have become disproportionately involved in efforts to restore fruit-bearing 'monkey trees' to the forest.[25] From this perspective, *engai* appears not as a war of aggression waged by an enemy, but as a *reaction* on the part of wild monkeys to the human destruction of their forest home. Monkeys feed on the fruit trees of the village because people cut down the fruit-bearing trees of the forest.

As was the case with the wild boar, we have seen that the views of the farmer and the hunter in relation to the monkey both overlap and diverge. Farmers depend on hunters to act as cullers to contain the monkey threat to farm crops. Doubts are raised, as we have seen, about culling monkeys, on the grounds of its efficacy and its morality. But in general, farmers support—indeed demand—the culling of monkeys. From the hunter's point of view, however, the monkey is a very different

[25] For example, one such civic tree-planting initiative (for bears as well as monkeys) in Wakayama Prefecture, while inspired by the retired schoolteacher Higashiyama Shōzō, attracted much support from foresters (Higashiyama Shōzō, personal communication).

animal from the wild boar. The monkey, unlike the wild boar, is not a game animal, and the dispatch of monkeys lacks the kudos of the conquest of the wild boar. If the dangerous encounter with the boar is savoured as a heroic contest in which a man can demonstrate his courage, the killing of 'childlike' monkeys seems far less heroic, notwithstanding the *sarugami taiji* motif. Moreover, because the monkey is not a game animal there is not the same direct hunter interest in maintaining a sizeable wild population of monkeys. Consequently, hunters do not furtively try to boost the monkey population as they do the boar (or pheasant) population. The delisting of the monkey as a game animal after the war means that the wild monkey population has ceased to be controlled through human *mabiki* in the way the wild boar is; monkey 'thinning' only takes place through ordained culling. As we have seen, some farmers in Hongū directly attribute the *engai* problem to this post-war (Occupation-inspired) hunting ban. The post-war state, through its interference in hunting, is deemed to have destabilized the village relationship with monkeys, and provided the conditions for the monkey problem to arise.

Yet in the present day, monkey culling is controversial. The mounting criticism of culling suggests to villagers that outside forces would like to restrict this too. Therefore, much more than antagonism between farmers and hunters, monkeys are the site of tension between farmers and the forces of monkey protection—both town halls and outside conservationists. The macaque has long been held to have a special place in Japanese culture. Japanese primatologists have claimed a unique cultural affinity for, and insight into, macaque behaviour (see Dale 1986: 191–8), a cultural argument that has often been extended to the area of macaque conservation. Conservationist reports on Japanese macaques typically refer, in their preface, to 'our nation's special mammal' (e.g. IHSHS 1995: p. ii), while regional macaque populations are designated *tennen kinenbutsu* or national 'natural treasures'. This sentiment of a special national responsibility for the macaque can even extend to a claim of leadership in international primate conservation. 'Japan is the only advanced country which has wild monkeys. If Japan, given its wisdom and its money, cannot coexist with the monkey . . . then there is no other country which can' (*AS* 22 Dec. 1994). It also leads conservationists to call for greater national intervention in wildlife management. Japanese primatologists have publicly challenged the right of local authorities to issue culling licences by arguing that the monkey is 'the common property of the Japanese people'.[26]

The opposition between local pest control and national conservation perspectives must not be exaggerated. Urban criticism of monkey culling should not conceal the fact that there is a certain degree of sympathy in urban Japan with remote villagers suffering monkey pestilence, and this sympathy potentially extends to support for these rural communities. A striking illustration of this is the phenomenon of urban volunteers undertaking field-guarding duties in remote

[26] See Watanabe (1996: 55), Wada (1994: 182), and *AS* (29 Nov. 1995).

villages to help besieged farmers protect their crops from monkeys (*KS* 23 Oct. 1998). Conversely, there is also a degree of local concern with monkey welfare and conservation, as is evident in the way villagers make the connection between *engai* and post-war forestry. If Japanese mountain villages are at 'war' with monkeys, they present a disunited front to the animal. Monkey culling does not command general support; there is a degree of tolerance of monkey feeding on village fields; and some people actively feed wild monkeys. Antipathy towards the *engai* monkey in upland Japan coexists with a measure of sympathy for the animal, which the zero-sum language of war obscures.

4

Deer and Serow

Village farmland is not the only site of conflict between human society and forest wildlife. The problem of wildlife pestilence also occurs in the forest itself, which is both a site of industrial forestry and a space of wildlife habitat. Much of the Japanese *yama* has been appropriated by human society as a space of forestry production where commercially valuable timber trees are grown for the market. But when wild herbivores such as deer and serow feed on or damage these trees, they become pests in their own habitat space. As it takes place in the *yama*, this conflict with wildlife over timber trees tends to be far less visible than that between the farmer and wildlife in the village over farm crops, yet the effects of forestry damage can be much more costly. The first part of this chapter describes plantation damage and other forms of pestilence associated with the deer and the serow. The second part of the chapter looks at the hunter's perspective on these wild herbivores and the tradition of deer-hunting in particular. Alongside the perspectives of the forester and the hunter, there are other views of these animals to be taken into account. These two wild herbivores are each, in their different ways, positively represented in Japanese society: the deer rivals the monkey as a 'cute' animal favourite that is familiar to the Japanese public from the world of children's entertainment and from deer parks and other visitor attractions, while the reclusive serow, though less well known, is designated a 'natural treasure' in Japan. The third part of the chapter focuses on the tensions that arise from these discrepant local and national representations of the two animals.

There are two subspecies of Japanese deer: *Cervus nippon* (Temminck) (*nihonjika*) in Honshu and the larger subspecies *Cervus nippon yesoensis* (*ezoshika*) in Hokkaido. The Japanese deer weighs between 30 and 40 kilogrammes, has a speckled chestnut coat (in the case of the hind and the calf) that darkens in the winter, and has a white rump. The Japanese deer (or 'sika deer' as *Cervus nippon* is conventionally known outside Japan) is considered to be an intermediate type within the genus *Cervus*, that falls in between the small deer with simple antlers and large tails of south-east Asia and the large deer with complex antlers and short tails of North Asia and North America (Takatsuki 1991: 201). It is known for its high rate of fertility (compared with the red deer), for its wide vocal range (and the whistling cry of the stag), and for its preference for dense tree cover (Springthorpe and Myhill 1994: 78). Hinds and calves live in small groups, while the stags live apart for most of the year and join the hind groups in the autumn for the rutting period that lasts until the beginning of winter. Deer group size generally ranges from three or four individuals to over twenty, but has been shown to vary markedly according to season and according to habitat, with deer in open woodland and clearings tending to aggregate in larger groups (Borkowski and Furubayashi 1998: 33). Reports from some parts of Japan tell of large deer herds of more than 300 animals (Kinoshita 1994: 100). The total number of deer in Japan is estimated to be over 300,000 (*NKS* 17 Jan. 1994). Deer numbers and densities on the Kii Peninsula have increased dramatically in recent decades: in the Ōdaigahara area the average density of deer was fifteen deer per kilometre in 1981, but doubled to thirty deer per kilometre in 1993, with an annual rate of population increase of 6.7 per cent (Akashi and Nakashizuka 1999: 76).

The Japanese deer is known to be flexible and adaptable in its food habits. It both grazes and browses, but as with other larger deer species it prefers grazing to browsing, and is classified as a grazer rather than a browser (Takatsuki 1991: 200). This means that it consumes 'large amounts of low nutritional value foods such as grasses, and [that] ingested foods are well fermented, thoroughly ruminated and slowly pass their alimentary tracts' (ibid.). Zoologists have noted the variation in the diet of deer across Japan, and tend to distinguish between northern and southern populations (Weerasinghe and Takatsuki 1999; Jayasekara and Takatsuki 2000). In south-western Japan the diet of the deer consists mainly of

FIG. 4.1. A stag

the leaves of woody plants, evergreens and conifers, graminoids (such as dwarf bamboo), and acorns in the autumn (Jayasekara and Takatsuki 2000: 156). Northern deer tend to have poorer diets, especially in the winter, when they rely much more on twigs and bark. It is because of this habit of feeding on twigs and branches that deer cause browsing damage to conifer plantations in the winter (Jayasekara and Takatsuki 2000: 156). According to the zoologist Takatsuki Seiki, in Japan the deer has a preference for forest-edge sites rather than the dense forests or open clearings.

They are neither typical forest nor openland dwellers, but forest-edge dwellers. In fact, habitat use by sika deer becomes more intense at forest edges created by logging. For sika deer, a forest edge is a place that both provides cover against predators and foraging ground. (Takatsuki 1991: 202, references removed)

The serow (*kamoshika*, *Capricornis crispus*) is an antelope-like ungulate. It has short horns, cloven hooves, a thick grey-black coat, and a goat-like appearance. The Japanese serow (*nihonkamoshika*) or *Capricornis crispus crispus* Temminck is one of the two subspecies of serow (the second subspecies is the Formosan serow). The other species of serow is *Capricornis sumatraensis*, the Sumatran serow, which is found in India and parts of mainland China, as well as south-east Asia. In contrast to the gregarious deer and other 'sociable ungulates', the serow is known as an 'unsociable' ungulate that leads a largely solitary existence (Masui 1987: 139). As the serow matures, it comes to lead a more sociable life and 'sometimes forms male–female pair units or family groups with up to four individuals'

FIG. 4.2. The Japanese serow in a zoo in Kyoto

(Kishimoto 1987: 104). Serow offspring tend to remain with their mothers for the first year or two, but are forced to leave once the mother gives birth again, and then gradually move out of the mother's range to establish their own separate ranges (Kishimoto 1987: 106). The serow is a territorial animal, with adult males and females having separate, but overlapping, home ranges (of between 10 and 15 hectares) throughout the year, the effect of which is to limit the population density of adult serows in any given area (Ochiai *et al.* 1993*a*: 16). Another expression of serow territoriality is the animal's homing behaviour, which has been documented by Japanese zoologists who monitored the movements of captured serow that were returned to the forest—the animals invariably attempted to return to their former range to live (Maita 1987: 124). The Japanese serow is usually characterized as an animal of the temperate, montane forest. In 1995 there were estimated to be more than 100,000 serow in Japan, compared with the 1955 figure of 3,000 (*NNS* 20 Sept. 1995).

IMAGES OF DEER AND SEROW

On the Kii Peninsula, as elsewhere in Japan, deer were known as *kanoshishi*, rather than the standard Japanese term *shika* (Nomoto 1990: 59). It is claimed that the literal meaning of the name *kanoshishi* is 'fragrant beast' because of the distinctive smell of venison (Tabuchi 1992: 30). The deer is viewed as a *kawaiirashii* ('cute'), *kihin* ('dignified'), and *kiyoi* ('pure') animal', as well as a symbol of regeneration (Sutō 1991: 119; Tabuchi 1992: 29). It is sometimes represented as a special animal, one that is different from all the other animals of the forest. In the *Shuryōkai* hunting magazine, Atobe Takashi offers the following eulogy:

The bear and the wild boar are fierce and wild. The fox, the raccoon-dog and the monkey are clumsy and inelegant and one does not feel moved by them. If you want a likeable animal that can reach human emotions, that is graceful and elegant, that has sad, pitiful eyes, and that possesses three-pronged antlers towering up into the sky, and that runs and sweeps across the plains, it is the stag, which had such a strong appeal for people in ancient times who composed so many songs and poems about it. (Atobe 1988: 93)

In Japan the deer is a symbol of autumn. The rutting stag's whistle-like cry is one of the distinctive sounds of late autumn in the forest. The stag calling out to females below the autumn maple tree is an image that often features in Japanese art, while the stag cries themselves are reproduced in *shakuhachi* flute compositions (such as *Shika no tōne*, 'Distant Cry of the Deer'). This sentiment is captured in the famous poem by Sarumaru Daiyū:

> The leaves turn in the remote forest
> When you hear the cry of the deer
> The sadness of autumn.[1]

---

[1]   The original Japanese reads: 'Okuyama no momiji fumiwake, Nakushika no koe kiku toki zo, Aki wa kanashiki.'

Atobe Takashi reflects on this haiku as follows: 'When the autumn mating season comes, the [stag's] sad "*hyuun*" cry which calls the female flows out from the trees. For the deer's marriage season comes in the autumn, the time when the leaves turn red' (Atobe 1988: 92). The autumnal associations of the deer are also present on the Kii Peninsula. In his memoirs, the former forest labourer Ue Toshikatsu recalls his reaction to hearing a stag's cry nearby: 'The first cry of the deer clearly announced the arrival of autumn. Living alone in the forest hut, that cry would stir me. It also declared that winter was close, leaving me feeling heavy-hearted' (Ue 1983: 236). In Japan the mating deer in autumn is also a metaphor for human romance, a theme that emerges, for example, in certain regional folk songs (see Yanagita 1992: 88).

Autumn is the time when the stag's antlers (that are cast each spring) have fully regrown and are at their most impressive, as Ue Toshikatsu remarks:

The antlers recover by September to become hard and manly. Just as the mating season nears, the fine antlers bring great confidence to the stag. They are a symbol of its sexuality more than a weapon, which serve to coerce rival males and to display its male beauty to its sweethearts . . . Well-polished antlers glisten in the morning sunlight, and even in the dry late afternoon sun they sometimes reflect back the light. Even though you are far away from them, and they themselves think that they are hidden in the shadow of the [forest] trees, you know they are there. (Ue 1983: 235)

The stag is a symbol of masculinity in Japan, as it is elsewhere. Just as the wild boar tends to be known for its tusks, so the stag is known for its antlers. According to the folklorist Chiba Tokuji, 'the Japanese people saw the antlers, which emerge each year and soon branch out and lengthen, as a symbol of vitality' (Chiba 1975: 96). Antlers are a highly prized trophy that is traditionally claimed by the hunter who hits the stag first and hunters often discuss and compare the shape of the antlers of the stags they kill. *Sandantsuno* or 'three-levelled antlers' and *yondantsuno* or 'four-levelled antlers' are especially admired and the stag trophies that are mounted as wall decorations in private houses tend to be of these types. Antlers have long been a martial symbol in Japan, as shown by the medieval warrior's helmet to which was attached impressive antlers to symbolize military prowess (Chiba 1975: 96). A present-day manifestation of this symbolism occurs in Japanese elections when antlered stag heads are put up in election offices as decorative reminders of the fighting spirit needed to secure election victory (Atobe 1988: 92).

The deer is also associated with nature. It is an animal that seems physically to share the natural rhythms of vegetation growth. The stag's antlers are a symbol of regeneration, cast in the spring only to grow again afterwards. It is this fast, sturdy growth of the stag's antlers that makes deer velvet such a highly prized product, one that is associated with vitality. In his examination of the *Manyōshū*, the famous folklorist Origuchi Shinobu detected an association between the remarkable growth of deer antlers in the late spring and the growth of vegetation (Kaneko *et al.* 1992: 45; see also Nomoto 1994: 127). The association between the deer and rice growth is especially marked, but here the focus is on deer reproductive biology rather than antler growth. In many regions of Japan, including the Kii Peninsula, local sayings link the onset of the deer's mating season in the autumn with visible changes in vegetation such as formation of the ears on the pampas grass, a plant closely related to rice (Nomoto 1994: 123–4). As the folklorist Nomoto Kanichi points out, the gestation period of the deer is seven months, from late autumn to early summer, corresponding closely to the period of time in which the rice seed germinates into a seedling, such that the birth of the calf occurs just when the rice seedling emerges in the early summer (ibid.). The linkage between deer and rice is reinforced by the appearance of the deer: the speckled coat of the newborn deer resembles rice grains, leading to the belief that the coat can foretell the rice harvest (ibid.). This association between deer and rice is further evident in the belief that the rice harvest can be boosted by smearing the rice seeds with deer blood (ibid.). The relationship between deer and crop growth is also suggested by the *shishi odori* or 'deer dance' festivals found in some parts of Japan—'a festival where children wearing deer masks pray for rain and an abundance of crops' (Tamanoi 1998: 202–3).

The deer is an animal *otsukai* or 'messenger' of the *kami* at certain famous shrines—for example, the shrines of Kasuga, Miyajima, and Suwa. Some deer shrines have legends in which the deer appears as *kamisama no norimono* or 'the mount of the spirit' (Chiba 1975: 93; Ashida 1999: 116). Traditionally, the deer has not been hunted in the vicinity of such shrines because of its sacred associations. In some shrines the deer is used for divination, with the charred remains of deer bones serving as an oracle (Tabuchi 1992: 29; Naumann 1994: 37). The theme of deer as omen also appears in a famous episode in Japanese history when in 1572 the famous warrior Takeda Shingen went into battle with the forces of Tokugawa Ieyasu at Mikatagahara: as the army was advancing, its path was crossed by a herd of deer which was taken as an inauspicious sign by Takeda's troops. Although Takeda went on to win the battle, he died shortly thereafter, thereby apparently confirming the early deer omen (Atobe 1988: 93). The deer's status as an omen still emerges in Japan from time to time, such as when a stag with unusually shaped antlers is sighted or killed, or when an albino deer appears. The deer to some extent carries Buddhistic associations in Japan, as the deer was the form taken by the Buddha in one of his previous lives. In a well-known Buddhist tale, the Buddha, in his incarnation as the deer, saves the life of a hunter who has fallen into a lake in the forest, but the ungrateful hunter later betrays the deer for money (Ashida 1999: 115–16).

In Japan the serow does not have a clear identity, and has long been the object of a certain taxonomical confusion. It tends to be assimilated to other, more definite categories of animal, such as the deer. The word for serow in Japanese, *kamoshika*, resembles the word for deer, *shika*, and in the past the Chinese character for deer 鹿 has been used in the written form of the word *kamoshika*. In the present day the belief that the serow is a kind of deer is not uncommon (see Ue 1983: 67–8;

FIG. 4.3. An *ema* from Kasuga Shrine in Nara

Ochiai 1992: 23) and some people even mistake serow for wild boar (Itō 1986: 8)! When the word *kamoshika* (or *kamashishi*) is written with Chinese characters, the characters 羚羊 are conventionally used, giving the meaning of 'antelope sheep'. But over time it has been written with an assortment of different Chinese characters, including those for 'mountain sheep', 'large sheep', 'wild sheep', 'flying sheep', 'stone sheep', 'wool deer', and 'nine tail cow'.[2] The serow has attracted a wide variety of other names in the different regions of Japan, including *odorijishi* ('dancing beast'), *bakajishi* ('foolish beast'), and *ahō* ('idiot'). Many of the names given to the serow are related to the animal's appearance and to the rocky terrain it lives in.[3] Most people are surprised to learn that the serow is related to the cow and forms part of the bovine taxon. One of the terms that have been applied to it is *ushioni* or 'cow demon' because it appears to have the head of a demon and the body of a cow (Kaneko *et al.* 1992: 29; Chiba 1995*a*: 27–32). Tales of *ushioni* sightings and encounters are to be found in the interior settlements of the southern Kii Peninsula (Ue 1994: 177). As to contemporary usage, Hongū hunters refer to the

[2] These characters are 山羊 for 'mountain sheep', 大羊 for 'large sheep', 野羊 for 'wild sheep', 翔羊 for 'flying sheep', 石羊 for 'stone sheep', 氈鹿 for 'wool deer', and 九尾牛 for 'nine tail cow' (Chiba 1991: 119).
[3] The names deriving from its appearance include *aojishi* ('blue beast'), *ao* ('[the] blue [one]'), *kuro* ('[the] black [one]'), *susu* ('sooty'), *tankaku* ('short-horn'), *ipponzuno* ('one horn', in contrast to the branching antlers of the deer), and *kebuka* ('[the] hairy [one]') (see Chiba 1991: 119–20). The names related to the rocky terrain with which it is associated include *kamashishi* ('mountain beast'), *iwashika* (rock deer), *iso* (an area of protruding rocky mountain), *dake* (mountain peak), and *yama* (mountain).

serow variously as *ahō* ('idiot'), *kuro* ('blackie'), and *niku* ('meat'). A not uncommon popular characterization of the serow in Japan is that it is *hen* or *kawatteiru*— that is, a 'weird', 'strange', or 'abnormal' animal (terms I have never heard used in relation to the wild boar, monkey, deer, bear, or wolf).

The serow is an animal known for its curiosity. It is said to observe people at work in the forest, such as forest labourers or plant gatherers, from some elevated vantage-point on the mountainside. In contrast to the gregarious deer (but like the bear), the serow appears a *kodoku na dōbutsu* or 'lonely animal' that spends most of its life by itself. One of the most common characterizations of the serow is that it is a *maboroshi no dōbutsu* or 'phantom animal', evocative of the mystery of the *yama* (Furubayashi 1991: 227). In contrast to the deer, the serow is an animal of the *okuyama* or distant forest.

In the nearby forest you never see the serow make an appearance. It is too wary of human noises such as cars or the noise of dogs, and compared with other animals it stays well clear of human settlements. With the deer, you sometimes see a scene in which it is chased into the village by a dog, but I have never seen this [for the serow]. Rather, the serow, in contrast to the deer, has the habit of gazing out from high locations. (Ue 1983: 68)

It is because of this remote habitat, far from human society and apart from others of its kind, that the serow can appear a *muhōmono* or 'outlaw' (Hida 1967: 7). In the eighteenth-century *Hosei monogatari* the serow is portrayed as the archetypal creature of the forest.

[M]y four legs are strong and I know many kinds of trees. In autumn and winter I eat the bark of those trees and in spring and summer I eat a variety of smaller creatures. I can prance about on rocks and boulders, and even perch on their tips. I know what's good and bad about each tree in each season, and I use that knowledge to eat their bark. (in Hunter 1992: 53)

As one of the names for the serow, *iwashika* ('rock deer'), suggests, it is an animal that is well adapted to mountainous terrain. It has a renowned ability to escape its animal foes by ascending steep rocks. When pursued by dogs high up in the mountains, the serow can jump its way to safety, leaping from cliff to cliff, an ability recognized in the hunter's reference to it as a *ninja* (Hida 1967: 24). As we have seen, the *ninja* metaphor is also applied to the wild boar and the monkey, but while in these two earlier cases the specific emphasis of the metaphor is on the respective animals' capacity for surreptitious intrusion (in connection with their crop-raiding behaviour), with the serow the *ninja* metaphor serves to emphasize a superlative agility and surefootedness.[4] Among hunters the serow is famed for its *shissōryoku* or

---

[4] Recognition of its phenomenal balancing ability is also evident in the existence of *kamoshika no gōkaku kiganfuda* or 'serow exam-passing charms', stamped with the hoof-print of the serow, which can be purchased from the Japan Serow Centre (in Mie Prefecture) by students facing exams. The reasoning behind this is that in Japanese the verb *ochiru* ('to fall') is applied to exam failure (*shiken ni ochiru*, 'to fall at the exam'), while the serow is well known as an animal that 'does not fall, even on the edge of a cliff' (*SS* 28 Jan. 1999).

'sprinting ability' in the vertical space of the *yama* (Matsuyama 1978: 120). In Japanese, the serow is a metaphor applied to people (such as sportsmen) who are swift but graceful in their movements (who are said to move *kamoshika no yō*, 'like a serow') (Ue 1983: 69). Recent expressions of the Japanese appreciation of serow mobility include the 'serow' motorcycle produced by Yamaha and the serow (more precisely, a serow-like creature) that appears in the 1997 animation film *The Mononoke Princess* (as the mount of the hero) that outruns horses and leaps high in the air and across long distances.

Herbivore Pestilence

As we saw in Chapter 1, large-scale reforestation took place in post-war Japan, as a result of which timber plantations have come to occupy over four-tenths of the forest area. Like the farmer, the forester must be concerned with the *protection* and not just the *production* of his crop. Many of the recently established conifer plantations in Japan suffer from pestilence of one kind or another, whether by wild vertebrates such as deer, serow, bears, wild boar, hares, voles, squirrels, mice, and an assortment of birds, or by invertebrates such as bark beetles. It is not uncommon for timber plantations to suffer from the attentions of more than one kind of pest, and there is sometimes uncertainty as to the identity of the animal responsible. Deer and serow have become especially serious forestry pests in recent decades. Deer browse young saplings, barkstrip the stems of older trees, and stags rub their antlers against tree stems and side branches. The effects of browsing, barkstripping, and fraying are to delay or retard tree growth, induce fungal entry, and adversely affect the quality of the timber. In some cases, trees soon recover from animal damage, but some forms of damage (such as that arising from major bouts of barkstripping) can lead to the death of the tree. At the national level, deer damage to forestry in Japan was estimated at between 4,000 and 5,000 hectares in 1999 (*KSY* 13 Mar. 2000). Serow damage to forestry is usually estimated to be around half that of deer damage.

Browsing involves the nibbling of the end buds of young saplings (with the serow targeting cypress trees in particular). Once browsed, saplings are unlikely to continue their normative pattern of growth, but may well develop multiple shoots in response and even become bushlike. End-tip browsing compromises the ideally straight, even growth of the tree and tends to result in inferior crooked trees. Browsing deer incur the anger of foresters on the Kii Peninsula. Murata Yoshio of the Hongū village of Shitsugawa, now 91 years old, worked in the forestry industry until his retirement and has long tended his family conifer plantations. He is a leading figure in the village and in the past has served as a town councillor when he often heard complaints about deer from foresters. He described to me the problem of browsing in the following way.

Their [scrow and deer] range is quite narrow, but there is a lot of damage in that area they depend on . . . Cypresses and so on are planted in their area, and in the winter there is nothing else around that is green for them to feed on, so they eat them . . . It's really terrible. When you plant [conifers in the mountains], you plant saplings of about this size . . . , but then they come along and eat the tips of the saplings. So what happens is that in four or five years' time, the saplings only grow up to about here. They don't stretch upwards, but they become like *bonsai* trees. In the end they just wither.

Another victim of deer pestilence is Mori Eizō, a fifth-generation family head in the Hongū village of Kubonodaira. He owns around 100 hectares of forest land, almost all of which is covered with conifer plantations (40 per cent cedar and 60 per cent cypress). Unlike other forest landowners in Hongū, Mori-san does not practise much forestry himself. Until recently, he ran a timber broker company in which he purchased mature plantations, had them felled, and sold the timber at the market. None the less, he told me that in 1995 he lost 1.5 hectares of young cypress trees due to deer browsing of newly planted saplings, and estimates his financial loss at ¥1.3 million (~$5,600). The mountain had to be replanted, and this time protected by extensive netting to ensure that the damage was not repeated. There is also regular small-scale damage by deer, serow, and hares. Mori-san believes that the kind of browsing damage he has suffered has its origin in deer feeding on farm produce.

Until recently we believed that serow and deer just got their food from the natural forest . . . It was only ten years ago that they started eating cypress and cedar leaves. I have often wondered how it was that they started this. What probably happened was that they came to eat the saplings that were grown in village fields that had had lots of fertilizer put on them. They probably tried them out there and found that they liked them.

Like the deer, the serow is an unwelcome browser on saplings in young plantations. One of the fears of forest labourers when planting saplings is that, after planting over a stretch of mountain during the day, the serow (or other animals) will then come along at night, feed on the saplings, and undo their entire day's work. Ue Toshikatsu makes this point when he recalls a scene in which foresters are planting cypress saplings on the mountainside during the day, as a serow, from the safety of a high cliff-top, calmly watches them working away.

The serow, the so-called 'Mr Director', would watch us planting the saplings [during the day], and then at night it would come down to the plantation. You respond by setting the dog on it to chase it away, but then after a short while another one would come along. (Ue 1980: 176)

The men conclude that the serow, which they refer to as *Kantoku-san* or 'Mr Director' because of its tendency to oversee proceedings in the valley from on high, had all the time been contemplating the feeding opportunity that they were unwittingly providing!

Another form of forestry damage caused by the deer is *tsunokosuri* or 'antler-rubbing' in which stags rub their antlers up and down tree stems, fraying the bark. This occurs during the mating season in the autumn between September and November. Consistent with the association of antlers with masculinity, the stag's antler-rubbing has long been seen as a means of attracting hinds. The verb *migaku*, 'to polish', is normally applied to this activity. Matsuyama Yoshio recounts the following view of antler-rubbing in the Nagano area: 'by making its antlers beautiful through polishing, it can display itself to the hind with great dignity. For the stag, this decoration above its head is a proud symbol that it is a man' (Matsuyama 1977*b*: 142–3). On the Kii Peninsula, antler-rubbing is associated with the vitality of the stag: 'They rub the antlers of which they are so proud on to tree stems and rocks in order to polish them, and in this way they stir up the life-force of their bodies, and then they make that heroic cry, "*buooo*"' (Ue 1983: 235). But antler-rubbing is also interpreted as a means of removing the skin from the antlers or as a means of territorial marking (Kanamori *et al.* 1991: 115). It has been suggested that antler-rubbing is related to social competition among young male deer and that high densities of such deer are the reason for severe outbreaks of it (ibid.). Although antler-rubbing mainly affects very young trees, it can also affect plantation conifers of around ten years old. The removal of the bark exposes the stem xylem which becomes discoloured and, within a few years, starts to decay through fungal infection (ibid.). For the forester, the sight of a row of frayed trees in his plantation is an upsetting one. While *tsunokosuri* may make the stag, with its shiny, 'polished' antlers, an all the more imposing sight to behold, it leaves the plantation trees themselves looking *boroboro* ('ragged'), *kitanai* ('dirty'), and *minikui* ('ugly').

Kurisu Hiromasa of the Hongū village of Hagi has suffered from deer antler damage in both cedar and cypress plantations. One day he took me to one of his timber plantations damaged by deer antler-rubbing. The 64 hectare north-facing plantation site is called Jizōdani or Jizō Valley (so named because the mountain is shaped like a statue of Jizō, the popular bodhisattva widely found in Japanese folk religion) and consists of both cedar and cypress trees. He showed me an area of five-year-old cedar trees at the foot of the mountain, and described the damage to them as follows.

With their antlers the deer remove the bark from the stem. Look over there, the stem has turned white. When that much bark has been removed, the tree ends up dying and the leaves turn brown. The trees will continue to fatten afterwards, but [disease] will enter and they will eventually wither. There are about thirty trees now that have turned brown [i.e. the leaves], but because many trees have been damaged this last summer many more trees will wither . . . There are lots of other, natural trees in the forest, but deer like really straight upright trees like these cedars . . . When I come and see that the majority of trees have withered . . . I think, 'ah, after all the care I've put in . . .', and when I think of the deer that are responsible my reaction is to curse them.

FIG. 4.4. A forester in Hongū showing damage to plantation trees caused by deer

This plantation grows a special variety of wavy-grained cedars, known as *tennen-shibori* ('naturally squeezed'), which requires thorough pruning (to prevent knots in the wood). But such pruning makes these high-value trees highly vulnerable to damage because it allows deer to get close enough to the stem to rub their antlers against it.

In contrast to the frequent complaints about deer, in Hongū there is relatively little mention of serow forestry damage. One reason for this is that the serow is associated with the higher, rockier terrain found in Totsukawa to the north, rather than Hongū where there is relatively little of the kind of elevated mountain forest that qualifies as typical serow habitat. This is why plantation damage in Hongū is conventionally attributed to deer, and why little effort is made to distinguish serow damage from deer damage. In discussion, however, foresters may well suggest that some of the damage attributed to deer is probably caused by serow and that there is much more local serow damage than is generally recognized. Mori Eizō, for example, believes that serow are responsible for much more damage than his fellow foresters tend to believe.

'If you go to Heichigawa or Ōtōzan [in the western part of Hongū] you will definitely see serow in low places as well as high places. Although there are many of them in [high] rocky places, there is lots of damage in low places too. They live their lives mostly in those kind of [rocky] places, but they also come down to the plantations, like they are looking for work.

The Kuriyamas are one family that has suffered from serow forestry damage. The Kuriyama family has produced doctors in the Hongū area for many generations. Kuriyama Takayuki, who claims to be the 38th-generation head of the family, has lived and worked in Tokyo for forty years, first as a hospital doctor and then as a professor of medicine. With a forest landholding of 500 hectares, the Kuriyama family is one of the largest landowners on the southern part of the Kii Peninsula. As the Kuriyamas live in Tokyo, the family forest is managed by a local *yamaban* or forest manager who periodically reports to the family members on their visits to Hongū. The *yamaban* will include in his report instances of herbivore damage on the estate, and this will normally involve deer. But the Kuriyama plantations, because they extend up into the serow-inhabited mountains to the west of the municipality, are also vulnerable to serow pestilence. The head of the family, Kuriyama Takayuki, told me of one particularly bad year when 2 hectares of cypress saplings were destroyed by serow browsing. Later, when a new batch of saplings were planted and a net fence was put up to protect them, ten serow got caught up in the netting and died. This is why the cause of the earlier damage is confidently attributed to the serow.

Claims of serow forestry damage do not, however, go unchallenged. First, it is argued that the serow is unfairly blamed for damage that is caused by other forest animals (Torii 1996*a*: 68). Much of the plantation damage supposedly due to serow browsing is actually caused by hares and fieldmice that feed on young conifer saplings (Itō 1986: 71–80). Similarly, it is claimed that in the 1960s bark-stripping by bears on the Kii Peninsula was misattributed to the serow (Mainichi Shinbunsha 1965: 105). Secondly, some forestry specialists and botanists challenge the simple equation of serow browsing and plantation damage, arguing that the effects of early stage browsing on cypress saplings by serow are not irreversible and that it is still possible for affected trees to grow and mature into saleable cypress timber thereafter (Torii 1996*b*: 98). But even where serow leaf-feeding does affect the tree's longer-term growth, this still does not automatically equate with the scale of damage that is claimed. This is because many cypress plantations have been established in inferior, unsuitable locations with poor growth prospects to begin with. In the case of such poorly sited plantations, the recovery of young trees from serow feeding becomes nearly impossible (Itō 1986: 114–15, 188–9). A further reason for the unreliability of serow (and indeed deer) damage claims has to do with the silvicultural practices of modern timber forestry. Typically, Japanese timber plantations are densely over-planted at first, and then repeatedly thinned over the years, such that a plantation of 3,000 trees is progressively reduced, after a period of thirty or forty years, to one of 500 trees. Tree loss caused by serow feeding on young saplings cannot be calculated on a simple pro rata basis because five out of every six trees are not, in any case, destined to become mature timbers, but will be removed as immature (and low value) thinnings (Torii 1996*b*: 98). On the Kii Peninsula the exaggeration effect is likely to be that much greater because of the Yoshino tradition of dense planting practised by many local foresters which involves an even higher ratio of trees planted to trees harvested—that is, up to 12,000 seedlings per hectare.

Despite such doubts about the damage it causes, the serow tends to arouse a deep antipathy among forest-owning families. In response to repeated losses, foresters in Gifu Prefecture banded together to establish a *kamoshika higaisha no kai* or 'Serow Victims Association'. The serow has come to be viewed as 'a pest which threatens the way of life of mountain village people' (Itō 1986: p. i). Some mountain villagers complain that they have been impoverished by serow damage to their cypresses—that 'tomorrow there may be no money to buy rice' (Itō 1986: 116). Serow damage to plantations may well be experienced as a kind of threat to the family which has cared for the trees over generations. One irate villager in Gifu Prefecture explains that his intense dislike of serow is 'because they eat the cypress trees of my forest which I must pass down to my descendants' (in Hirasawa 1985: 58). The full significance of serow damage to timber trees must be understood in the context of the life courses of the people who grow them, as the following remarks by one victim of serow damage illustrate.

Human beings like to play around and enjoy themselves until they are around twenty-seven or twenty-eight years old, but in this area you really have to pull yourself together after that. I have just cut down the forest [i.e. harvested the timber] left to me by the ancestors, and to grow the forest back again will take forty or fifty years. If I don't do it now [i.e. securely establish the conifer saplings], I won't be able to complete it while my eyes are still black. It is one's duty to the ancestors to leave something for one's children. It is with these sorts of feelings that I plant the cypresses in the mountains. (in Hirasawa 1985: 72)

Another Gifu forester complains that the serow has interfered with the marriage of his daughter. 'When a daughter is born, trees are planted to make a cypress chest of drawers for the day she marries, but these trees are eaten by the serow. Do you people [i.e. city dwellers] understand this misery?' (Itō 1986: 116–17).

The deer and the serow are principally forestry pests. Hongū villagers routinely draw a contrast between, on the one hand, deer and serow as typical forestry pests and, on the other, wild boar and monkeys as typical farm pests. Farmer complaints about wild animals are overwhelmingly directed at these two latter crop-raiders, and only a few farmers I have met readily cited the deer as a problem. None the less, deer and serow are a cause of crop damage in upland areas of Japan. Deer feed on the rice seedlings transplanted to the paddyfield in the early summer, on the rice stalks as the rice ear emerges, and on the tips of the maturing rice stalks. Farmers tend to associate the deer threat to their rice crop with the early part of the summer, in contrast to the wild boar which is most dangerous in the late summer. But deer also damage the maturing rice crop, and newspaper reports of deer damage to rice-fields in the months of August and September are not uncommon (*AS* 9 Sept. 1991). As we saw in Chapter 1, in the reports on damage to farm crops in Hongū in the period 1995–2000, deer damage to vegetables, soya beans, and tea does occur, along with damage to rice. The problem appears especially serious in Hokkaido. One newspaper report from Hokkaido warns that the problem of deer farm pestilence is getting worse because the new pattern of crop feeding is making deer numbers grow: 'Farm produce is without doubt good for the [deer's] body. Since they have started to visit fields, the fertility of the deer has greatly increased. As the damage increases, deer increase. It is a vicious circle' (*AS* 6 Aug. 1995).

In contrast to the more commonly sighted deer, the serow has generally not been considered a threat to farmland in Japan's mountain villages. As an animal of the *okuyama* that lives far away from human settlements, the very idea of serow feeding in or around the village is seen as a contradiction in terms by many people in Hongū. Indeed, when somebody claims to have seen a serow near the village, the claim may well be met with scepticism by other villagers and even suggestions that the animal must have been a deer instead. Yet in some areas of Japan the serow is a farm pest, responsible for damage to crops such as carrots, cucumbers, peas, lettuce, chestnuts, and sweet potatoes (Sutō 1991: 171). In the Shimokita Peninsula of Aomori Prefecture serow are known to cause damage to ginger and other farm crops (Itō 1986: 47–8). In one area of the same peninsula, no fewer than thirty kinds of farm crops, including soya beans, azuki beans, cowpeas, carrots, pumpkins, spring onions, burdock, mulberry, cabbages, and radishes, were affected by serow feeding (Ochiai 1991: 208). Serow damage to gardens and fields has been reported even in less remote areas where serow have traditionally been scarce, if not absent altogether (*AS* 17 Mar. 1995). Another serow feeding site is said to be the village cemetery, which tends to be located at the edge of the village, near the forest. For forest animals, cemeteries represent highly attractive clearings close to the forest that offer a rich herbaceous food supply.

How do mountain villagers respond to this threat? In particular, how do they protect their timber plantations from the attentions of the deer and the serow? Japanese foresters are faced with a difficult problem. Timber plantations are difficult to protect from wildlife damage because of their location outside the village in the *yama*. In the case of the farm crops in the village, wild animals must break cover and leave the forest to make the potentially perilous raid into human residential space. But access to timber trees in the forest requires no such hazardous journey on the part of forest animals. In response to the vulnerability of the timber trees, efforts are made by foresters to create a boundary, whether physical or sensory, within the space of the *yama* between the plantations and the rest of the forest. As with farms in the village, plantations in the forest are protected by means of assorted noises, smells, and physical barriers. Battery-powered 'cannons' are used which simulate the sound of gunshot fire at regular intervals. Olfactory repellents such as human hair (obtained from the barber shop), old clothes, animal hair and hides (burnt or charred to create a pungent smell), and modern repellent odours are placed along the plantation perimeter. In this way, forest ungulates learn that the plantations are human territory that is dangerous to enter. Another means of protecting plantations is through the use of netting and fencing.[5] Fences are also used to protect farmland from forest herbivores.[6]

There are also lethal responses to the problem of deer pestilence. In the recent past, deer caught in villages have been dealt with mercilessly. Ue Toshikatsu writes that the sight of a deer chased by hounds into the village is a common one in the winter, and that when this happens it can cause a great stir among villagers.

People would get excited and scream out to each other, 'there's a deer!', and then they would rush to pick up hoes and other things to chase it with. On one occasion, it ran straight into a ricefield where it lost its footing in the mud, and everyone went over and beat it to death. (Ue 1983: 248)

Similar violent responses to deer have been reported in other regions (Takami 1995: 94). The story of the three-legged deer in Gifu Prefecture also reveals a hostile rural reaction to the appearance of a deer. According to a 1990 newspaper report (*AS* 22 Apr. 1990), on discovering a deer caught up in a roadside drain, a local man reacted by hitting the animal with a rock, breaking one of its hind legs. However, rather than kill deer themselves, farmers normally rely on hunters to do this.

HUNTERS AND HERBIVORES

Deer-hunting

In the medieval period, deer-hunting or *shikagari* was a favourite pursuit of the *samurai* warrior. Indeed, in medieval Japan, the term *kari* or 'hunting' immediately suggested *shikagari* (Chiba 1975: 92; Mōri and Tadano 1997: 72). Deer-hunting was not simply an enjoyable pastime, but a *bugei* or 'military art' in which

[5] Net fencing has proved to be controversial in the past. Deer and serow (and other animals) sometimes get caught up in the nets and perish, dying slowly of starvation. Some years ago a photograph of a deer caught up in plantation netting in Hongū appeared in a regional newspaper, leading to a wave of public criticism of Hongū foresters, and the issue was raised in the Hongū town council by a councillor who called for the use of such nets to be discontinued. Since then, Hongū foresters have largely switched over to netting with a finer mesh in which deer cannot get caught up so easily.

[6] On the southern Kii Peninsula, the term usually translated as 'wild boar fence', *shishigaki*, is sometimes written as 'deer fence' by using the character for deer instead of that for wild boar (KHI 1971: 142; KHI 1989: 27).

horsemanship, archery skills, and battleground tactics could be practised (Kaneko *et al.* 1992: 46). The appeal of the deer-hunt lay in the way it replicated many of the conditions of medieval Japanese warfare and provided a useful organizational and logistical test.

For practice in the warrior's arts of archery and swordfighting on horseback, there was nothing as suitable as the deer hunt. As deer form large groups and run fast, they were an ideal stand-in for an enemy army on horseback. They were also found on grassy plains where this sort of military encounter tended to take place . . . The Tokugawa *shōgun* and the fief lords would carry out such exercises from time to time. Compared with this [the deer], the wild boar lives in the forest and, in addition to not presenting an impressive figure, it could not easily be shot with a bow and arrow and was also dangerous. (Chiba 1975: 91)

The appeal of the deer hunt for the warrior was that it allowed an armed group of men to engage a fast-running collective enemy.

The deer has long been hunted on the Kii Peninsula. For local hunters the appeal of the deer hunt is twofold. First, the deer is the source of a number of valuable products. The deer-hunter obtains venison that he can consume himself (with his family), give away to friends and relatives, or sell for money. The consumption of venison is highly valued as a means of boosting human strength at times of weakness; in particular, it is said to warm up the body and to be good for cold constitutions. Hunters in Hongū complain about the contraction of the deer-hunting season, that now runs from 1 December until the end of January. Mori Yukimitsu of Komori believes that deer-hunting should extend into February because the taste of the venison is better then (whereas at the start of the hunting season, because it is so soon after the rutting period, the taste of the venison is poor). Similarly, deer velvet has long been viewed as a tonic, while the foetus of the deer was believed to help with women's diseases. In the past deer-hunters could make money from selling stag antlers to visiting traders known as *tsunokai* or 'antler-buyers'. In his study of mountain villages in the Aichi-Shizuoka area of central Japan, the folklorist Hayakawa Kōtarō mentions a family which on one occasion sold eighteen sets of antlers to a *tsunokai*, and used the money received to purchase a memorial tablet for the family ancestors (1982: 75). A superior set of stag antlers may still be sold today, although some hunters prefer to keep for themselves a really striking set of antlers. Stag heads are on display in the houses of many a hunter in Hongū, often near the entrance where they are most visible to visitors.

Deer-hunting also serves to protect foresters from plantation damage and farmers from crop damage. Foresters support deer-hunting because it reduces the numbers of harmful deer and thereby helps protect their trees from the kinds of deer damage described above. Indeed, this belief in hunting as a form of *mabiki* for the deer population is one of the main reasons that forest landowners assent to hunting on their land. Farmers too depend on hunters to keep down deer numbers, just as they do with the wild boar. Hayakawa Kōtarō describes how in the

Fɪɢ. 4.5. An advertisement from a specialized hunting store showing mounted stag trophies

Meiji period remote villagers in the Aichi-Shizuoka area would petition a hunter to catch deer in the nearby forest, and how they would show their appreciation by presenting the hunter with a bottle of sake afterwards (Hayakawa 1982: 70–1). An indication of the antipathy of present-day farmers to deer in some parts of Japan is evident in the way they beseech hunters to kill as many deer as they can and to target hinds along with stags (Ono 1994: 100). Farmers in Hokkaido beg deer-hunters to 'please hunt them all, because deer do [such] bad things' (Kikuchi 1995: 87) and inform cullers that 'we would not worry if there were not a single deer left' (Satō 1995: 52). While many a deer-hunter arrives in the hunting area as a recreational hunter out to enjoy himself, some of them soon get the impression that local people expect them to carry out a *shika taiji* or 'deer conquest' as though they were the hunting heroes that appear in old folk tales to save remote villagers from dangerous wild animals (Kikuchi 1995: 87).

Three different methods of deer-hunting in Japan can be distinguished: deer-stalking, deer-chasing with dogs, and circle-hunting involving a large hunting group (Tsujioka 1999: 96–7). Deer-stalking, known as *shinobiryō* (literally 'stealth-hunting'), involves a lone hunter tracking deer and then firing at them when he gets the chance. Deer-stalking is the preferred pursuit of those hunters who are more interested in guns than dogs, and many a deer-stalker will invest in a high-powered rifle, in contrast to the shotgun used by other hunters. Typically, the deer-stalker aims at the lower neck of the deer (whereas boar-hunters tend to target the animal's head), as this both ensures the kill *and* preserves the upper neck and head as a possible trophy. A variation on deer-stalking is *kōruryō* or 'call hunting' where the hunter lures the stag to him by imitating the '*pii pii*' sound of the hind in mating season, using what is known as a *shikabue* or 'deer whistle'.[7] There are various sayings in Japanese which refer to this form of hunting and the fatal attraction on which it depends, including, 'The wife-loving deer is drawn to the whistle' and 'The autumn deer is drawn to the whistle' (Takahashi 1997: 121).[8] These expressions are widely used to refer to men whose downfall is brought about by love or lust. It is perhaps for this reason that the deer whistle was considered by some hunters on the Kii Peninsula as a 'cruel' and 'underhand' method of hunting (Ue 1983: 245). The use of the deer whistle is now outlawed in Japan, but it is still allowed in Hokkaido where hunters use imported American whistles. Hunters claim variously that a stag generally appears within thirty minutes of making the call or that the stag replies to the call with a call of his own (Mawatari 1999: 78).

More commonly, hounds are used in the Japanese deer hunt. The hunter takes his dog to an area where he knows there are deer, releases the dogs to chase the deer, and waits along the likely escape path of the deer to dispatch the fleeing animal. This simple method of hunting, known variously as *oidashi* ('chasing out') or *oimawashi* ('chasing-round') (Matsuyama 1977*b*: 99), works because the deer is an animal that, when chased, moves in a highly predictable way. The hunter knows that the deer chased by a hound in the mountains is likely to descend to the river at some stage. But where hunter and hound are weak, *oimawashi* can degenerate into a farce, with 'the deer making a fool of the dog' by letting it run

---

[7] The use of the 'deer whistle' is reported for the Kii Peninsula (Ue 1983: 244–5; Nomoto 1990: 58–9), as well as other areas of Japan. On the Kii Peninsula the deer whistle used to be made of wood and frog's skin or the skin of a deer foetus (Nomoto 1990: 59). In some parts of Japan there are legends of deer-hunters switching from frog skin (in favour of deer foetus skin) after discovering that their frog skin whistles attracted not stags but snakes (Nomoto 1990: 59; Mōri and Tadano 1997: 81). There are even tales of deer whistles being made from the wood of a prostitute's *geta* clogs, suggesting a degree of identification on the part of the human hunter with the stag (Chiba 1975: 93). For other references to the use of the deer whistle, see Chiba (1975: 93–4), Tabuchi (1992: 24), and Mōri and Tadano (1997: 72–86). The Ainu practised a similar method of deer-hunting (Ölschleger 1999: 209). Batchelor reports that the Ainu used an instrument to simulate the cry of a deer fawn in order to lure adult deer to them (Batchelor 1901: 460).

[8] The respective Japanese expressions are: *tsumakou shika wa fue ni yoru* and *aki no shika wa fue ni yoru*.

round and round to no avail, while the deer itself successfully evades the hunter (Matsuyama 1977*b*: 99). The qualities of the good deerhound is a much discussed topic among deer-hunters. Nowadays there tends to be a preference for Western breeds, which are seen as superior to native dog breeds at deer pursuit. A good *tsuisekiken* or 'pursuit dog' should be able to continue the chase over time. By contrast, as we have seen, in the case of the wild boar the fighting spirit and bravery of the dog is emphasized much more. As the deerhound does not have to confront an aggressive animal, what matters instead are the qualities of patience and endurance. Yet some hunters do emphasize the importance of ferocity in the deerhound, something which can lead them to prefer native dogs to foreign ones. 'The ability of Western hounds to relentlessly pursue a deer is a fine thing, but the ability of the Kishū hound [the native breed of the Kii Peninsula] to unleash its sudden ferocious speed to chase the deer to the river is a truly exhilarating experience' (Furuya 1995: 37).

The usual method of deer-hunting is *makigari* or 'circle-hunting'. This normally involves groups of up to ten hunters. As *makigari* entails covering a large area of mountains and many possible escape routes, it invites collective hunting on a large scale, and some *ryōyūkai* hold New Year deer hunts in which all the deer-hunters in the association can participate. The group circles an area of mountains in which the deer herd is located. As with the boar hunt, the deer hunt involves a division of labour between a *seko* and *machi* shooters. The *seko* drives the deer towards the *machi* shooters who are expected to take the chances that come their way. In the deer hunt, like the boar hunt, the *machi* must show patience and discipline while stationed at his spot. While waiting in the cold for long periods of time (waits of three or four hours are not uncommon), a *machi* is naturally tempted to light a cigarette or even a small fire to keep his feet warm, but the mark of a good *machi* is his ability to resist such thoughts and to stay focused and ready for action. The *machi* in the deer hunt knows that the deer has sensitive hearing that will pick up any human movements. Hunters suspect that the moment they do drop their guard will be when the deer passes and they miss their chance. On the Kii Peninsula there are many hunting tales of *machi* who fail to fulfill their role, and inadvertently alert the escaping deer which consequently manages to evade them. The larger the group, the more important does group co-ordination become, with each man expected to carry out his role—to be in the position he is supposed to be, to keep still and quiet when in position, and to be responsible when firing at his target to minimize the risk of stray fire.

Hongū hunters catch more deer than wild boar. Between 1983 and 1992, hunters in Hongū killed 907 deer and 703 wild boar. The difference in the figures is a reflection of the large numbers of deer in the mountains of the Kii Peninsula relative to the wild boar; deer are much more frequently encountered by large game hunters who will catch one if they can. But deer are generally considered to be inferior to the wild boar as a game animal. The deer offers a stark contrast in temperament. As we saw in Chapter 2, hunters associate the wild boar with courage and fighting spirit, but these are not qualities readily attributed to deer, which are known instead to be *shinkeishitsu* or 'nervous', *ki ga chiisai* or 'timid', and even *okubyōmono* or 'cowards'. Unlike the respected wild boar, which fights back (in some cases, lethally) against the hunter, the deer offers only limited resistance and poses little direct physical danger to those who hunt them. The wild boar is an animal that is renowned for its resilience and strength even when it has been hit by the hunter's fire. As we have seen, when wounded the wild boar can become even more formidable and aggressive than normal, such that the hunter cannot be at all sure he will catch it. But when a deer is wounded it is only a matter of time before it expires. While the wild boar is an animal that can turn around and confront its pursuers, the deer just tries to escape in a predictable way, descending to the riverside in the valley. When the hounds do finally catch up with it, the deer shows little of the boar's fighting spirit. One expression of the defeatism of the deer is that when it is being assailed by hounds it sometimes appears to sit down on the ground—as though accepting its fate (Ōsaki 1994: 147).

The character of the deer, like the character of the wild boar, is reflected in the atmosphere of the hunt and the disposition of the hunters. While the hunter reacts positively to the fighting disposition of the wild boar, he may well react negatively to the deer. As we have seen, in the boar hunt a man can 'boil' (*waku*) with excitement and expectation, but the deer hunt does not seem to stimulate this intensity of feeling. In the boar hunt, because of the danger it involves, a man cannot but focus on the task at hand, but in the deer hunt such concentration may prove more difficult. This is the reason that some men give for failure in the deer hunt while acting as *machi*—that is, for failing to dispatch a deer when a clear shooting chance presents itself. Reflecting on the times he has missed when firing at deer, a hunter from Mie Prefecture made the following remarks:

On those occasions when I have failed in the hunt the main reason was that I was not mentally focused. In relation to the wild boar, you find that you have this intense fighting spirit that boils within you, but when you are faced with a deer you have a casual attitude about things and just keep making mistakes time and again. (Ishikawa 1979: 41)

If the prospect of coming face to face with the wild boar demands that a man stay alert, the deer is a far less compelling figure. Some Hongū hunters explain this difference in human attitudes towards the two animals by resorting to sporting analogies—by, for example, likening the hunter to a sumo wrestler who manages to raise the level of his performance when he faces an *ōzeki* or a *yokozuna* (the two highest ranks of wrestler) but then loses to other wrestlers low down in the rankings.

For many Hongū hunters, who hunt deer as well as wild boar, the boar remains the special animal, to which the deer cannot measure up. As the boar-trapper Nakano Jōji put it to me, deer are unimpressive animals.

I catch wild boar and deer. The boars make up about 70 per cent of what I catch. I will look at the tracks and decide 'ah, these are boar tracks', and then place the trap there, along the boar path. But I don't really set traps along the deer paths, as I don't do trapping in order to catch deer. Sometimes deer will pass along the boar path and get caught in the trap, but what matters to me is the wild boar. In this area, it is said that it is better to catch one wild boar than to catch ten deer . . . In the end, I suppose, it's a matter of one's self-respect. When you run around in your truck it looks more impressive to have just one wild boar loaded in the back of your truck than if you had ten deer loaded on. Anybody that sees it [the wild boar] thinks, 'hey, he did really well!' . . . After all, the boar is difficult to catch.

While the wild boar is 'difficult to catch' in that the hunter and hounds risk their lives in the process, deer offer no such challenge and a successful deer hunt does not give the hunter the same sense of satisfaction as success in the boar hunt. In Hongū the successful boar-hunter or trapper knows that he is likely to be spontaneously congratulated by other people, whether they be neighbours in the village or just people who notice the animal on the back of his truck outside the shop where he buys cigarettes after the hunt, but this will not necessarily be the case for the deer-hunter.

It will be recalled that one of the features of the wild boar was the way it managed to confound hunters and hounds with its 'clever' movements on the run from them. Although exasperating for hunters at the time, the cunning of the fleeing boar commands an obvious respect among them. The frequent characterization of the wild boar as *kashikoi* or 'clever' sometimes suggests that the boar has a human-like ability to anticipate the decisions and movements of others in enacting its escape, and it is this *chiekurabe* or 'battle of wits' that gives the boar hunt its special character. As we saw in the last chapter, farmers attribute a similar intelligence to monkeys that manage to defeat their best efforts to protect their crops. Neither the wild boar nor the monkey can be taken for granted by mountain villagers, for they seem able to detect human strategy and to improvise when necessary. By contrast, this element of *chiekurabe* does not seem to apply to the deer (or the serow). The deer is seldom depicted as a 'clever' animal that is able to outwit the farmer or skil-fully escape from the hunter. The typical flight behaviour of the deer, when chased, makes it relatively easy to hunt, once located, because its movements can be anti-cipated and *machi* shooters suitably placed—towards the river, which is often in the direction of the village. Some hunters are left with the impression that the deer does not really expect to escape at all. According to one Chichibu hunter, the atti-tude of the deer is that 'I'm going to die anyway, so I would like to die facing the village' (in Iino 1989*b*: 64). The meekness and resignation of the deer can seriously limit the sense of challenge felt by the hunter.

The contrast between the boar hunt and the deer hunt is not, however, always quite as stark as this suggests. Although it compares poorly with the wild boar, the deer too can show impressive qualities to the hunter. The deer may be predictable in the chase, but it can at times put up a degree of resistance to its pursuers. Deer-hunters point out that the deer may well prove resilient after being shot and that wounded deer have been known to cover long distances in attempting to escape. Just as Japanese hunting magazines contain many accounts of hunters' *tatakai* or 'battles' with wild boar, so they also carry stories of *tatakai* with deer (see Miyoshi 1979; Ōta 1995). The difference is that with the deer the *tatakai* centres on the chase of the wounded deer and not on the direct physical confrontation that arises with the wild boar. This element of contest between deer-hunter and wounded deer is evident in the following excerpt from a description of a deer hunt that appeared in the *Shuryōkai* magazine in 1979:

We were face to face and it was looking at me. I looked into its eyes. As I looked at the colour of its blood, in my heart, which was unbearably excited, I felt a strange feeling. Its head was down and it was vomiting fresh blood from its mouth. It slowly moved its body in a different direction, it was trying to escape . . . Then it got up and started walking away, swaying from side to side . . . Then it turned its head and looked back in my direction, while I looked at it as I tried to pull out new cartridges . . . I had to put it out of its misery . . . At that time when we looked each other in the eyes for just a moment, I saw in the deer a sadness I have never felt in the boar hunt . . . In that graceful deer I had not expected to find such a life-force [*seimeiryoku*], and it is an experience that remains in my heart. (Miyoshi 1979: 53–4)

The sentiments of excitement, admiration, and even regret are all present in this account of a deer chase.

Serow-Hunting

The serow has long been hunted in Japan. Serow-hunting, along with bear-hunting, is especially associated with the *matagi* hunting villages of northern Japan. But in mountainous regions across Japan the serow appears to have been a highly valued wildlife resource, and was hunted for its meat, hide, horns, and other body parts. On the Kii Peninsula it used to be said that 'with the serow, like the bear, nothing is thrown away' (Ue 1983: 77). Serow meat was highly appreciated for its taste; indeed until recently the animal was actually known as *niku* or 'meat'. One peninsular villager, Ue Toshikatsu, recalling the ubiquity of serow meat in his youth (in the 1940s and 1950s), describes its qualities in the following way:

For mountain people, it was an important source of animal protein. In the past there was a lot of it about and it could be easily obtained. The meat quality was as tasty as venison, and when you ate it your body warmed up—it was because of this that it was used as a medicine for bedwetting children. (Ue 1983: 77)

Serow hide had a valuable waterproof property, and until the 1950s foresters and raftsmen wore backflaps made up of serow hide. Serow horns, on being ground and boiled, were used against beriberi and as an antifebrile, while the small intestines and the gall bladder were used to cure stomach aches.

The serow is regarded as a relatively easy animal to hunt. When hounds are chasing it, the serow escapes in the direction of the high mountains (unlike the deer which heads for the river). But the serow's escape strategy is a flawed one because, by seeking refuge on large protruding rocks, it presents an easy target to the marksman. This may well be the origin of the name *ahō* or 'idiot' commonly applied to the serow by hunters. The serow is an animal fool, which almost offers itself up to be shot. A hunting tactic sometimes employed by the serow-hunter was to wave a red cloth to attract the animal's attention and thereby immobilize it, making it an easy shooting target (Udagawa 1979: 150). In total contrast to the wild boar, when the serow is hit, no matter how lightly, it just gives up and stops moving (Sakuma 1985: 179). The relative ease of serow-hunting underpins the widespread belief that it tends to lead to overhunting (Kobayashi 1989: 149). Up until the 1920s, the serow was seriously overhunted in Japan and disappeared from some regions altogether (Tokida 1991: 171–2; Iino 1989*b*: 72). The rationale for the hunting ban lies in this peculiar vulnerability of the serow. It was as a result of overhunting that in 1925 the serow was delisted as a game animal in Japan. In 1934 the serow was designated a *tennen kinenbutsu* or 'natural treasure' under the Historic, Scenic, and Natural Treasure Preservation Law (Chiba 1982: 268). The protected status of the serow was reinforced in 1955 when the state designated the animal a *tokubetsu tennen kinen-butsu* or 'special natural treasure'.

The protection of the serow has been the source of much friction between hunters and the authorities. The serow continued to be hunted in many areas of Japan after the ban in the 1920s. Hunters in the *matagi* villages of the Tōhoku region, for example, hunted serow as before, while pretending that they were hunting bears (Taguchi 1994: 107; Nebuka 1991: 92). Matsuyama Yoshio reports that one Gifu hunter in the 1950s claimed to have killed 300 serow, most of them, by implication, after the animal supposedly enjoyed official protection (Matsuyama 1994: 94). Ue Toshikatsu points out that villagers on the Kii Peninsula continued to hunt serow without any sense of committing a crime (Ue 1983: 76–7). Hunters took care not to be spotted and caught. Thus while the whole body of a wild boar or a deer might be openly brought back from the mountains, hunters could no longer do this with serow. Instead, they would skin the animal, remove its head, and carefully dispose of its remains while still in the mountains, and only then return to the village where they would pretend the meat was venison (Ue 1988: 97). Another tactic was to treat serow meat simply as anonymous meat—hence the common reference to the animal as *niku* or 'meat' by Japanese hunters (Kobayashi 1989: 147). Hunters further avoided mention of the animal's conventional name by referring to it as the *kuroi yatsu* or 'black one' and *kuro* or 'blackie'. In this way the serow continued to be hunted in mountainous areas, despite its legally protected status. But a turning-point came in 1959 when a large nationwide network of serow-hunters and traders was discovered and broken up by the authorities, with 164 poachers arrested. The investigation of a fur dealer in Okayama Prefecture led to arrests across the country, including on the Kii Peninsula (Ue 1983: 79). This major police operation duly resulted in the judicial punishment of those involved, including in some cases custodial sentences (Chiba 1982: 296).

There is considerable local antipathy towards the serow among mountain villagers on the Kii Peninsula. There is no shortage of disgruntled hunters who believe that the serow-hunting ban is wrong and foolhardy and that the national protection of the animal has brought about a situation where serow are now excessive in number and a serious pest. There is also a residual opposition among hunters to the criminalization of serow-hunting and anger at the possible penal consequences with which hunters who continue to catch serow are faced. Many of the hunters in the *matagi* villages of Tōhoku, which have long hunted the serow, feel that the serow should be reinstated as a game animal (Taguchi 1994: 161, *passim*). The implication of these arguments is that the restoration of serow-hunting would help to stem the decline of the *matagi* hunting tradition, nowadays seen as a pre-eminent regional folk tradition. Some hunters on the Kii Peninsula likewise believe that serow-hunting could help to make hunting more popular and boost recruitment among the younger generation. One of the things that is said to put off younger people is the image of hunting as time wasting, one which is reinforced when on a Sunday (the main day of hunting, which has been keenly anticipated all week) groups of hunters return from the mountains empty-handed. If serow became a recognized game animal once more, the argument runs, then this would improve hunting prospects and the overall rate of success.

NATIONAL ANIMALS

A National Treasure

Like the conflicts with boars and monkeys, human conflict with deer and serow is often couched in the language of war and criminality. In the Japanese mass media, deer damage is presented in the idiom of war: *ningen to shika no sensō* or 'the war between Man and deer' (Kameda 1995: 91) and a war that 'Man has lost to the Deer' (*AS* 25 Feb. 1992). Mountain villagers challenge advocates of deer conservation with the question, 'Deer or Man, which one is important?' (Kameda 1995: 91). Commentators refer to the *kamoshika sōdō* or 'serow troubles' (Itō 1986: *passim*), to the *kamoshika sensō* or 'serow war' (Hirasawa 1985: 61), and even to a state of *kaigenrei* or 'martial law' in areas badly affected by serow damage (ibid.). In the mass media, serow plantation damage is characterized in zero-sum terms as a question of *hito ka kamoshika ka* or 'Man or Serow' (in Ochiai 1996: 79). Military analogies are also indirectly made. Gifu foresters justify their call for serow to be shot by claiming that shooting the animal would not necessarily be fatal, because 'in the [last] war, soldiers did not die when hit in the legs' (Itō 1986: 30). The serow also attracts the idiom of criminality. In the debate about whether cypress damage was causcd by scrow or by hares, the question was posed as to which of the two animals was the *hannin* or 'criminal' (Itō 1986: 73).

The status of the serow as a 'natural treasure' makes it an emblematic animal of Japan. The serow is sometimes characterized as 'the representative animal of our country' (Fujiwara 1982: 381), while its special national character is evident in zoological writings which refer to it as a 'primitive relic species' of the Japanese islands (Soma 1987: p. xi), and 'a living witness to the formation of the Japanese archipelago' (Itō 1986: 58). Official and media references to it as *nihonkamoshika* or 'the *Japanese* serow', in addition to differentiating it from other serow subspecies in Asia, serve to reinforce the national associations of the animal. In 1970 the issue of serow conservation became internationalized when it was recognized as an endangered animal by the IUCN, the World Conservation Union (Chiba 1982: 370–1). The serow has even been acclaimed as a *mori no ikiteiru kokuhō* or 'living national treasure of the forest' (Kudō 1996: p. i) and therefore as Japan's equivalent to the giant panda in China (Ue 1983: 67). The national emblematic status of the Japanese serow—and its panda equivalence—was underlined in 1973 when the Japanese government offered two serow to China as a return gift for a giant panda received by Japan (Ue 1983: 88–9). The national associations of the serow can make it the subject of further local designations, such as in Mie Prefecture on the Kii Peninsula where it has been made a *kenjū* or 'Prefectural Animal' (SMS 1969: 23). Some municipalities in Japan have adopted the serow as as a municipal symbol, such as Ōtō-mura (to the west of Hongū) on the Kii Peninsula, which in 1971 established a serow park, and more recently erected a statue of the serow along the main highway that runs through the town (see Fig. 4.6). Nonetheless, the public image of the serow in Japan remains that of a national animal.

The serow's status as a national emblem in Japan is particularly frustrating for foresters who suffer serow damage to their timber plantations. In the 1980s four hundred Japanese foresters took the government to court over serow damage to their timber plantations in what became known as the *kamoshika soshō* or 'serow lawsuit' (*NKS* 28 Feb. 1983; *AS* 24 Feb. 1985). The foresters argued that 'as a result of serow damage the will to continue with forestry is being lost and abandoned forests are increasing', and demanded compensation from the national government for the financial losses they were suffering due to the pestilence caused by a nationally protected animal (*NKS* 28 Feb. 1983). Through the lawsuit, the foresters were explicitly charging the Japanese state with responsibility for the serow damage to their plantations. In addition to bringing to public attention the anger and bitterness felt in mountainous areas, the lawsuit was an attempt by foresters to establish formally a link between the tree-eating serow and the national state that protects it. However, underlying the action was a profound dissatisfaction with the post-war Japanese state for failing to provide proper support to the forestry industry. The litigation portrayed the Japanese state as indifferent to the wider plight of local communities, and suggested that the ungulate 'war' was really part of a larger conflict between mountain villages and the wider national society.

FIG. 4.6. A statue of a serow in Ōtō-mura on the Kii Peninsula

Foresters challenge the serow's special status in other ways as well. In response to the characterization of the serow as a national emblem, Japanese foresters counter-define the serow as alien to their forests. These are the comments of Mori Shigeru (a forester and a hunter) from the Hongū village of Komori.

Scholars and others in the animal-loving movement are always complaining about something or other. But for farmers [and foresters], of course, it's different. Animals cause damage on the farms, and the serow especially causes great damage to the forests [i.e. plantations]. So the views of people who actually live locally are very different. Those other people, the scholars and the others, are not affected by damage to the forests. I think that it eventually comes down to a problem of whether you support forest protection or animal protection . . . Although serow are a natural treasure, there are now too many of them and this situation causes real trouble. If people insist on preserving them as natural treasures, then let the Forestry Agency put up fences on its land and bring them up there!

Although serow are associated with the distant *okuyama*, which tends to be national (i.e. nationally owned) forest, they increasingly visit privately owned forest near the village. This forester's response is to suggest that the animal be confined to nationally owned land rather than allowed to roam on private land. In this way, the serow is represented as a public intruder on to private land and a national trespasser on local land, rather than a given, constituent part of the forest. The foresters' antipathy to the serow suggests that its national designation as a *tennen kinenbutsu* can have the effect, among some villagers at least, of *erasing* its local character. The 'national' status of the serow means that it ceases to be a local—that is, locally huntable and therefore controllable—animal, and instead becomes, as it were, an *alien* animal.

The forester's comments above indicate a widespread hostility among mountain villagers to those people and institutions that support wildlife protection at the expense of local livelihoods. I have often heard foresters and hunters in Hongū refer disparagingly to the *dōbutsu hogo undō* ('animal protection movement'), to the *dōbutsu aigo no renchū* ('animal-loving brigade'), and to *dōbutsu aigosha* ('animal-lovers'). This hostility is intensified in those upland regions suffering from large-scale serow damage where conservationists tend to appear as indifferent to the problems that serow and other wildlife cause. A common conservationist response to wildlife damage is to call for in-depth investigation of the problem in order to provide a more accurate assessment. But the apparent detachment of the conservationists can cause dismay among foresters. One forester in Gifu Prefecture drew the following analogy: 'A child has fallen down the well—NOW! "How did it fall?" "What should be done to ensure that children do not fall down wells?" These kinds of things can be considered later, at greater length. What matters now is deciding how to help the child' (Itō 1986: 117). In addition to frictions between foresters and conservationists, the 'serow war' can generate social tensions within upland communities themselves. In some cases, journalists have been tipped off by local people about illegal serow killing carried out by foresters—such as in Gifu when the regional newspaper, the *Chūnichi Shinbun*, broke the story of serow poaching in one locality (Hirasawa 1985: 62). The story had a great impact in the villages in question, where a boycott of the newspaper was organized and bitter local recriminations surfaced over who had spoken to the journalist and betrayed the community. As a result of the disclosure, there developed a siege mentality in the locality, with outsiders in particular becoming the object of intense suspicion (ibid.). The serow is blamed for such social discord: 'It is because of the serow that Japanese people are fighting each other' (in Itō 1986: 117).

Animal Numbers

Another source of friction with outsiders is over the issue of animal numbers. It is widely believed in remote areas that the numbers of wild ungulates have greatly increased in recent decades. Forest labourers report frequent sightings of deer during the day, as well as many signs of the deer in the forest—deer scats, deer marks on their trees, and so on. Hongū villagers today report regular deer sightings; when driving at night between villages along forest roads, car headlights often reveal the presence of impressive clusters of deer in the nearby forest. Mori Eizō's comments were typical.

There was deer damage in the past, but it was nothing like it is today . . . There are now great numbers of deer . . . They are increasing. You always see them around . . . If you go to the forest you see them, and even during the daytime you see them . . . Even in a village like this . . . [you see them], but in the earlier days this was unheard of.

In some areas deer are even to be seen casually grazing on field grass near open farmland, a sight which prompts one observer to proclaim that a new 'era' has come to pass in rural Japan (Kinoshita 1994: 100), while there are also reports of deer numbers so large that the animals are actually starving to death in some areas (Sakoda 1994: 101). Similarly, the serow was once the remotest of forest animals, inhabiting the distant forest and avoiding human contact, and was rarely seen by upland residents. But it now appears in broad daylight in the nearby forest and even at the edge of the village (Kamata 1992: 17). Most striking of all are those reports of serow sightings in towns and on the outskirts of cities, suggesting that the animal has proliferated to the point where it is spilling over out of the mountains into the plains (Kishimoto 1994: 29).

The scientific determination of accurate population densities for the serow, however, has proved to be extremely difficult, with different counting methods yielding diverging results (Abe and Kitahara 1987). Government authorities, along with wildlife experts, have been accused of systematically undercounting serow numbers (Hirasawa 1985: 60; Tanaka 1996: 28–9). Foresters in Gifu claim that the Forestry Agency (the government division responsible for the national forest), in the face of pressure from conservation groups, under-reports the scale of serow damage in the national forest in order to protect the animal, at the expense of local interests (Hirasawa 1985: 64). There are, however, certain objections to the foresters' claims. Conservationists point out that it does not necessarily follow from their greater visibility that serow are greater in absolute number. Gotō Shin, a retired schoolteacher in the coastal town of Tanabe (to the south-west of Hongū), is a local conservationist who is highly critical of post-war forestry and its effect on wildlife. He challenges the foresters' claim that the numbers of deer and serow are increasing.

They are not increasing, not the absolute number of them. What is happening is that there are now fewer places where they can live, and they all gather together in those narrow places. So when you see them you think they are increasing, but really, when compared with the numbers there used to be in Japan, they have decreased [in number]. As people establish forest roads there and the forest gets brighter, and people can enter it, it is then that they start to notice them [deer and serow], and it is because they notice them [more] that they say they are increasing. It's a mistake.

Forestry practices are an important factor in ungulate population dynamics. The cycle of industrial forestry, whereby protracted periods of timber-growing are punctuated by clearfelling, creates major discontinuities in environmental conditions. These periodic artificial disturbances of forest vegetation have an important knock-on effect on the animal populations dependent on it. The clearfelling practices of modern forestry create a 'super-optimal environment' for the increase of forest ungulates (Putman 1989: 3). When a timber plantation is clearfelled, it creates sudden clearings or 'inner forest-edges' along which a rapid herbaceous growth takes place, representing a great increase in the food supply for herbivores (Reimoser and Gossow 1996: 110). The carrying capacity of the disturbed area increases as a result, allowing herbivore numbers to multiply. However, in contrast to the outer edge of the forest (i.e. that borders farmland), the inner edges created by forestry clearfelling are only temporary (Reimoser and Gossow 1996: 110–12), and the increased food supply they stimulate will diminish over time until the point (between fifteen to twenty years later) when the plantation canopy closes and the undergrowth below is shaded out altogether. At this time the inflated ungulate populations cease to be able to feed in the plantation territories that generated them.

Post-war Japanese forestry appears to have caused such 'eruptive fluctuations' in the numbers of deer and serow. Japanese forestry harvests timber through the clearfelling of parcels of forest land. The effect of clearfelling is to stimulate a sudden profusion of undergrowth plants and create a prime feeding ground for deer. In a study from northern Honshu, the zoologist Takatsuki Seiki found that, in the wake of clearfelling, the number of plant species increased from fifteen to forty-eight, with shrubs, forbs, and grasses invading the clearcut area, and that this in turn stimulated a concentration of deer in and around this newly created forest edge zone (Takatsuki 1989: 292–3). Takatsuki concludes that the Japanese forestry industry, through its clearfelling activities in the post-war period, created precisely the kind of forest-edge environment in which the deer thrives (Takatsuki 1991: 202). It is further claimed that the practice of clearfelling, by creating large food patches, tends to increase deer group size (Borkowski and Furubayashi 1998: 33). It has been reported for the Ōdaigahara area of the Kii Peninsula that following the clearfelling of parts of the natural forest in the 1950s and 1960s, '[t]he vegetation that developed . . . provided abundant forage for deer' and consequently tended to 'increase the deer population' (Akashi and Nakashizuka 1999: 79). But the increased food supply does not last. Within a few years, the clearfelled area is planted over with conifer saplings, and the growth of the new plantation reduces and eventually extinguishes the herbaceous growth of the clearing. The deer react to this situation by moving elsewhere to feed. Where plantations have been created at different points in time in the same area, the swollen population of deer may be able to move to other forestry clearings nearby, but where plantations have been established simultaneously in an area this is not possible, and instead the enlarged herds of deer feed on the forestry saplings themselves—or on nearby farmland.

In the case of the serow, population density is generally stable when habitat conditions are stable (other things being equal) (Ochiai *et al.* 1993*a*). However, in the post-war decades these conditions became extremely unstable, as the vegetation cover of the Japanese mountains changed in conjunction with forestry practices. As in the case of the deer, the clearfelling of the 1950s and 1960s, along with the subsequent establishment of conifer plantations, created the conditions for violent short- and medium-term fluctuations in serow numbers. Research on serow density in Kyushu found the following pattern: in the first stage, a decrease in serow density after logging, as the animals left the area; in the second stage, an increase in serow numbers in the first six or seven years following reforestation in response to the new availability of green foliage at the cleared site; and in the third stage, from the seventh to the thirteenth year after reforestation, a sharp decrease as the canopy begins to close with the maturation of the plantation (Doi *et al.* 1987: 100–1). When plotted on a graph, this sharp fluctuation in serow density over time takes the form of a Λ-shape, denoting a proliferation followed by a rapid contraction (ibid.). Research from northern Japan, while differing in specifics, confirms this pattern: in Aomori Prefecture, serow population densities increased after a five-to-ten year interval following logging, to a level between three and six times that of the earlier mature forest, and were expected to be maintained at this level for up to twenty years after logging (Ochiai *et al.* 1993*b*: 24). The same research shows that where natural regeneration is allowed to take place following a clearfell, there is not the same sharp decline in serow numbers in the future. This is because in the secondary forest the problem of canopy closure does not arise in the extreme form it does in the plantation forest and there is not therefore such a sudden contraction in food supply (ibid.).

In response to this decline in its former food supply, the serow feed instead in younger cypress plantations (including on the tips of saplings) and on farms (Ochiai *et al.* 1993*b*). If there are excessive serow numbers in the Japanese mountains, Japanese forestry would appear to bear much of the responsibility for this. This is the background to the conservationists' assertion that the 'serow war' in post-war Japan is not all that it seems, and even that the serow has been made a scapegoat for bad forestry practice (Itō 1986: 167–9; Mizoguchi 1992: 114). What is referred to as the *kamoshika mondai* or 'serow problem' might instead be called a *ringyō mondai* or 'forestry problem', the cause of which is the plantations themselves rather than the animals forced to feed in them (Kishimoto 1994: 31). But the overriding focus on the serow in public debate and media coverage has tended to conceal the culpability of the forestry industry (ibid.). Yet there is a growing consensus that the post-war policy of *kakudai zōrin* or 'expanded afforestation' went too far. In fact, this connection between ungulate damage and mistaken forestry practices is recognized by foresters themselves. Men such as Murata Yoshio, Mori Eizō, and Kurisu Hiromasa have come to accept that post-war forestry, and the spread of timber plantations deep into the mountains, has caused many of its own problems. The increasing recognition of the link between forestry practices and wildlife population dynamics has also led to demands for new forestry practices consistent with wildlife management, including the replacement of clearfelling with selective felling practices that reduce the sharp discontinuities in vegetational patterns associated with the forestry industry (Kishimoto 1994: 31–2).

Tourism

Even though foresters suffer from damage caused by ungulates, they are not necessarily completely hostile to these animals. Deer are occasionally kept as pets.[9] In the late 1980s the forester Kurisu Hiromasa kept a fawn as a pet, which he called 'Shika-chan'. One of his forest labourers brought it back from the forest after its mother died in a trap, and Kurisu-san adopted it as a pet. The young deer was cared for by Kurisu-san's elderly mother and it became a popular family pet. The young deer was also popular in the village, especially among children who would run after it playfully every time it emerged from the Kurisu homestead. But male deer do not make good pets because of the antlers they grow which become a hazard to the people around them. Shika-chan's growing antlers were dangerous to family members and to children in the village and it was decided to have the antlers sawn off, but the young deer died in the process (from the shock, it is said). After it died, the Kurisu family buried Shika-chan in a scenic spot in the family mountains (where they have also buried pet dogs) and, incidentally, near to the young timber plantations which the family continues to protect from the attentions of other deer. When burying the deer, the family called in the local Buddhist priest to recite a sutra at the grave to ensure that the spirit of the young deer would rest peacefully. At the end of my interview with him about deer damage to his plantations, Kurisu-san made the following comments.

Deer are cute, especially when they are young. Young deer are just like Bambi, really cute. If the deer [Shika-san, 'Mr Deer'] did not do bad things I think that it would be a truly good animal, yes, a good animal. That's why I do not eat venison myself. If I am given any venison [by a hunter], I just give it away to other people. That's because the deer is cute.

---

[9] There have also been rare instances where young serow are adopted as pets by peninsular villagers. In some cases, pet serows become popular animals in the village as a whole, where they are allowed to freely roam about and are pampered by villagers (for example, Ue 1983: 81–9). However, because of the serow's protected status, keeping a young serow as a pet is illegal.

FIG. 4.7. A pet fawn in the Hongū village of Hagi

The cuteness of the deer also makes the animal a tourist attraction in Japan. Nara has the best-known deer park in Japan, in the vicinity of Kasuga Shrine. The park deer are famous for their *ojiki* or 'bowing' before visitors who feed them with rice crackers, and have been acclaimed as the 'stars' of tourism (Mainichi Shinbunsha 1965: 157, 161). Other parts of the country have attempted to imitate the Kasuga deer park (*AS* 15 Mar. 1996). Tourist feeding of deer is very popular, especially among children; cups of feed (often in granule form) are purchased and then fed to deer by hand. In Japan, as elsewhere, the Disney image of Bambi has become widely diffused, and forms part of the popular appeal of the deer. Many a Japanese newspaper article about deer makes reference to 'Bambi', such as when young deer are born in the summer in local deer parks. When in 1994 a white deer was spotted among the deer herds in the city of Nara, newspapers soon started to refer to it as *Shirojika Banbi* or 'White Deer Bambi' (*MS* 22 Nov. 1994). Visitors to deer parks in Japan routinely refer to the deer as 'Bambi' or 'Bambi-chan', while some deer parks name themselves after Bambi—such as 'Bambi Gardens' in Iwate Prefecture (Mainichi Shinbunsha 1965: 157). Often (out of safety considerations) parks and zoos limit the public feeding of deer to special feeding areas containing only deer without antlers, or even just young fawns, enhancing the 'Bambi' effect. Some rural municipalities combine deer-farming and the selling of venison as a local speciality (and *kanpōyaku* deer medicines) with deer tourism (*AS* 17 Oct. 1991). The response of one municipality to its deer problem was to capture the problem deer and create a tourist deer park with them, thereby hoping to make a resource out of a pest (*AS* 9 Oct. 1991). There have also been instances in which foreign deer have been imported to Japan as a tourist attraction, such as the red deer in a deer park in Iwate Prefecture (Tōyama 1998*b*: 47).

In addition to formally established deer parks, there has emerged what is in effect deer parkland in forestry areas. This occurs with older plantation forests that, having undergone successive thinnings, become light and airy places, with a small number of large trees and green expanses in between. In areas where such advanced-aged plantations predominate, deer congregate to feed on the herbaceous undergrowth, and become a wildlife spectacle for tourists, especially over time as the deer become tame through contact with tourists. On the Kii Peninsula this has occurred in the Ōdaigahara forest, a popular tourist destination renowned for its scenic beauty. The writer Tsujioka Mikio recalls his encounter with the deer of this area.

What I was very surprised about was how tame these deer had become. Near the footpath about twenty or thirty deer feed on the grass, and do not run away even when a person approaches them. If you throw a small stone over towards them, they come to gather nearby. The deer presumably think that food has been thrown to them and that's why they gather together. It seems as though they have become accustomed to doing this because hikers offer them food. But when this sort of thing is allowed to happen, their wild character is likely to completely disappear . . . The sort of tension between that still exists between humans and deer in Nikkō has been completely lost here. (Tsujioka 1999: 125)

If deer are increasingly exploited as a tourist resource, they can also have negative effects on tourism. Deer are reported to have an adverse impact on tourism in some areas through the destruction of scenic vegetation such as flower gardens. For example, in the Nikkō area deer have damaged much of the natural vegetation, including distinctive local flowers, of the of the Nikkō National Park (*AS* 10 Aug. 1994; *AS* 21 Aug. 1994; Koganezawa 1999: 5). In the Ōdaigahara forest, high deer densities are responsible for the death of large numbers of trees due to barkstripping, the suppression of natural regeneration through grazing, and consequently the deterioration of parts of the forest to grassland (Sekine and Satō 1992; Akashi and Nakashizuka 1999). The devastating impact on vegetation that large herds of deer can have has led some critics to denounce them as a *gan* or 'cancer' of the natural forest (*AS* 23 July 1995). Deer can also obstruct efforts at renaturalizing or beautifying the forest. One current concern in Hongū is to make the ubiquitous forest, at present dominated by cedar and cypress plantations, more appealing for the tourists from the city. To this end, in the 1990s 400 cherry saplings were planted in place of a 3 hectare timber plantation at the entrance to the hot-spring village of Kawayu. However, within a year of planting, all the cherry saplings were damaged by deer browsing. But the tourist industry, like the forestry industry (albeit to a much lesser extent), bears a certain responsibility for the herbivore damage it suffers. We saw above that plantation forestry stimulates population increase among these animals by creating grassy expanses of potential food supply. The new recreational land-uses associated with tourist development in the 1990s can have a similar effect. The recent boom in golf-course construction across the country has inadvertently created large herbaceous feeding grounds for the deer, contributing to its population increase (*AS* 9 Dec. 1994, Ochiai 1996: 86).[10]

As was the case in Chapter 2 in relation to the wild boar, the deer is both a game animal and a pest—in this case, principally a forestry pest. There is a similar convergence of interest between forester and hunter in relation to the deer, as there was between farmer and hunter in relation to the wild boar. The deer hunt represents a form of *mabiki* or 'thinning' that can help to contain the numbers of deer. The idiom of *mabiki* is one that is readily recognized by foresters who carry out a form of *mabiki* of their own—on timber trees that must be 'thinned' in order to improve the plantation as a whole. Indeed, there is a sense in which successful timber production in the mountains of Japan depends on both kinds of 'thinning' being carried out: on the timber trees themselves and on the wild herbivores that threaten to damage these trees. The hunter's 'thinning' of wild animals would appear to resemble the forester's 'thinning' of cultivated trees: the hunter too claims to remove individual animals in the interests of the population as a whole. But the two forms of thinning are not, of course, identical and diverge significantly as processes. The forester discards and removes individual trees in the interests of the plantation overall, and while the hunter claims to do something similar, the real meaning of the term *mabiki* in relation to deer has to do with the *containment*, rather than the *improvement*, of the deer herd. Foresters support the deer hunt because it appears to relieve the pressure of the deer population on their trees.

Foresters would naturally like the hunter's 'thinning' to include the serow as well as the deer, but state protection of the serow prevents this. It is because of this legal protection of them that serow become associated with the state among foresters. Foresters tend to see the state ban on serow-hunting to be against their interests, just as some farmers see the post-war ban on monkey-hunting to be at odds with their interests. In both cases, the state appears to prevent a harmful animal from being properly controlled at the local level. The confrontation between forester and serow raises the issue of their respective national importance. In its feeding in conifer plantations, the serow damages what was, in a sense, a *national* crop—i.e.

---

[10] Of course, unlike the earlier plantation clearings, these new recreational clearings are, in principle, permanent and should not therefore lead to the same degree of environmental inconstancy. In practice, however, many of the golf courses created in the bubble economy of the early 1990s have been closed.

trees that were planted as part of a nationwide effort to restore forest to the mountainsides and ensure the recovery of the national timber resource. In this sense, in defending their plantations, foresters are defending the national landscape and the achievement of post-war reforestation. But many Japanese foresters indignantly contrast the state protection of the serow with the state's failure to protect the forestry industry itself. In the national importance it accords to a forestry pest, the Japanese state appears to demean the status of the trees damaged and to undermine the communities dependent on them.

5
Bears

The south-east part of the Kii Peninsula is traditionally known as Kumano or 'Bear Plain' (despite its mountainous character). The name 'Kumano' first appears (as 'Kumanu') in the eighth-century *Kojiki* in a passage that describes the founding ancestor of the Japanese imperial line (Jinmu Tennō) slaying a bear. The Kumano region has long had a reputation as a primitive, unruly place. The very name 'Kumano' evokes an image of a wild frontier territory—a primitive 'bear country'. Sometimes when I mention to a new Japanese acquaintance that I do fieldwork in the Kumano area, my interlocutor jokingly feigns surprise that there are actually *people*—rather than bears—living in Kumano. Yet in the time I have spent on the Kii Peninsula, much of it in and around the forest, I have never seen a wild bear, nor have most local people. Despite this, the bear remains the most impressive animal in the forest, one that is much talked about by villagers. Everyone knows that there are bears out there in the *yama*, that there are occasional encounters with them, and that bear attacks on people can have serious, even lethal consequences. In recent years, there has been an increase in bear encounters and pestilence in the bear-inhabited regions in Japan. Bears are viewed as a forestry pest, a farming pest, and a threat to human safety, and the usual response to the 'bear problem' in Japan is culling. At the same time, there is antagonism between mountain villagers and conservationists who are critical of the high rate of culling and who call for the protection of bears. This chapter describes these various human relationships with bears in Japan, with reference to the regions of Japan where conflict with bears has been especially serious.

Two of the world's eight species of bears are found on the Japanese archipelago. The Japanese black bear (*Ursus thibetanus japonicus*), known in Japanese as *tsuki-nowaguma*, is a subspecies of the Asiatic black bear (*Ursus thibetanus*), and is found in Kyushu, Shikoku, and Honshu. The larger Hokkaido brown bear (*Ursus arctos yezoensis*), known in Japanese as *higuma*, is a subspecies of the brown bear (*Ursus arctos*) and is found on the northern island of Hokkaido. The Japanese black bear has a distinctive V-shaped white mark on its upper chest that recalls a lunar crescent—its Japanese name *tsukinowaguma* means 'crescent bear' (literally 'moon circle bear'). The adult black bear averages 1.4 metres in body length and 80 kilogrammes in weight, while the adult brown bear is 1.8 metres in body length and 200 kilogrammes in weight (Maita 1996*a*: 2–3). The population of wild bears in Japan is estimated to be around 16,000 animals: 13,000 black bears and 3,000

FIG. 5.1. Black bears in a bear park in northern Japan

brown bears (Maita 1998*a*: 29; Hazumi 1999: 209). The present-day distribution of bears across Japan is somewhat patchy and uneven. Black bears are found in greater numbers in the mountains of central and eastern Japan than in the relatively low mountain ranges of western Japan. In some parts of western Japan, such as the islands of Kyushu and Shikoku, the bear has disappeared, while on the Kii Peninsula, one of the few remaining bear ranges in western Japan, there are estimated to be around 150 wild bears (Maita 1999: 121).

The original habitat of the Japanese black bear included high subalpine conifer forests (1,500–2,300 metres), cool temperate forests (500–1,500 metres), and warm temperate forests (below 500 metres), but this range has narrowed and bears are now largely confined to elevated forests of 500 metres and above (Azuma and Torii 1980: 71). Much bear habitat in Japan was lost in the course of the twentieth century. The establishment of monocultural timber plantations, along with the spread of forest roads to service them, has destroyed bear territory and isolated bear subpopulations. The roaming bear is known for its large home range requirements, but as the bear's natural habitat diminishes in quality, its home range may expand in order to compensate. Home ranges of between 30 and 50 square kilometres have been reported for eastern populations of Japanese black bears, while western bear populations living in more fragmented environmental conditions have home ranges twice or even three times as large (Hazumi 1994: 145). The more that the

FIG. 5.2. A telephone card showing the brown bear of Hokkaido

bear's home range expands under conditions of habitat degradation, the more likely is the bear to come into conflict with human populations. The large-scale loss of bear habitat arouses conservationist concern about the future of wild bears in Japan. Many zoologists and conservationists warn that, because there is no effective management of bear populations, the Japanese black bear is facing a 'crisis' (Maita 1998*a*: 49–50; Hazumi 1999: 209–10), and that it may even come to share the Japanese wolf's fate of total extinction.[1]

IMAGES OF THE BEAR

The northern island of Hokkaido is one of the main bear regions of Japan. The brown bear has been depicted as *Hokkaidō no kao* or 'the face of Hokkaido' (*AS* 15 Nov. 1984) and is especially associated with the indigenous Ainu who traditionally hunted bears for meat and furs. A well-known expression of the cultural importance of the bear to the Ainu is the famous bear ceremony, known as the *iyomante* or 'sending', in which a captive bear is ritually killed and its spirit returned to the spirit world in order to regenerate bears for the future (Watanabe 1972: 74–7). For the Ainu, bears are believed to be the disguised form of the mountain spirits (known as *kimun-kamuy*) who visit the human world to 'bestow their fur and meat upon humans as gifts' (Akino 1999: 249). The emblematic place of the bear in Ainu culture is evident today in the carved wooden bears sold as souvenirs in Ainu

---

[1] The prospect of bear extinction is raised by many writers, including Watanabe (1981: 583), Miyao (1989: 207), Yamazaki (1996: 38), and Azumane (1997: 143). The threat particularly applies to regional bear populations, such as that on the Kii Peninsula. The 1991 *Red Data Book*, published by the Environment Agency, warned that there was 'a high danger of extinction' on the part of the peninsular bear population (in Hazumi 1992: 297–8), while other scholars predict that 'the disappearance of bear groups [on the peninsula] is just a question of time' (Hazumi and Kitahara 1994: 15).

tourist villages (and sometimes in other parts of Japan).[2] In Japanese society Ainu people are readily linked with the bear (and may even be referred to as *kuma no hito* or 'bear people'), sometimes in a stigmatizing way that points to their 'uncivilized' status, but sometimes in a positive light, such as when (see below) Japanese hunters openly admire Ainu hunters for their bear-hunting skills or when Japanese conservationists praise the Ainu for their 'traditional coexistence' with bears.

It is not just the Ainu who attribute cultural significance to the bear. Bears also have an important place in Japanese culture. The pre-eminence of the bear in regional Japan is indicated by popular references to it as *chikushō no ō* or 'King of the Beasts' and *mori no ōja* or 'King of the Forest'.[3] The bear is known for its solitary lifestyle and is readily contrasted with gregarious forest animals such as the monkey (Hida 1967: 221). The Chinese character for bear 熊 is found in family and personal names in Japan: examples of family names would be Kumamura ('Bear Village'), Kumada ('Bear Field'), and Kumazawa ('Bear Marsh'). The family name 熊谷 Kumagai ('Bear Valley') is found in Hongū, while in other parts of the peninsula the family name Kumamoto ('Bear Origin') is found. Surnames like these that contain the bear character can occasion teasing and joking, especially among children but also among adults. I came across an instance of this kind of name joking in the course of an enquiry into monkey pestilence in one remote Hongū village: when I asked 56-year-old Kumagai ('Bear Valley') Yoshihito of Matsuhata about monkey damage on his land, he immediately quipped, with a smile, that *kuma ga oru kara saru wa yō konai* or 'monkeys never come around because there are bears present'—before then going on to talk about the monkey problem in Matsuhata more seriously. The bear character is also present in Japanese place names, such as Kumayama ('Bear Mountain'), Kumaoka ('Bear Hill'), Kumagawa ('Bear River'), and, of course, Kumano ('Bear Plain').[4] As with the example of Kumano, bear place names may well carry negative associations. In a footnote to his translation of the *Kojiki*, Basil Hall Chamberlain, referring to the area known as Kumaso ('Bear Attack'), suggests that the use of the word *kuma* (bear) as a prefix 'may be traced to the evil reputation of that part of the country [i.e. Kumaso] for robbers and outlaws' (Chamberlain 1981: 25–6). In other words, the term *kuma* points to the bear-like—predatory—character of (at least parts of) the local human population.

In Japan the bear has religious associations, as is the case in other societies (see, for example, Hallowell 1926; Peyton *et al.* 1999: 188–9). The bear is associated with the *yama no kami* or 'mountain spirit', one of the main deities of folk Shinto

---

[2] The tradition of bear-carving among the Hokkaido Ainu would appear, however, to have emerged only in recent times and in response to external contact (Ohtsuka 1999: 93).

[3] Another term is *yama no ōja* or 'King of the Mountains'. On these references to the bear, see Sakuma (1985: 16), Ogura (1993*b*: 99), Kawazaki (1996: 36), *AS* (17 July 1994), and *AS* (5 Apr. 1995).

[4] In Japan family names and place names are not mutually exclusive, and some of the family names listed here are also place names, while some of the place names are also family names.

(Kawasaki 1993*a*: 161; Ogura 1993*a*: 99–100). The Japanese bear's sacred associations extend to Buddhism, as when bears are likened to bodhisattvas (Yamazaki 1996: 15; cf. Miyao 1989: 64–5). With its 'crescent'-marked upper chest, the black bear is also associated with the moon, which, along with the sun, has an important place in folk religion. The 'crescent bear' acquires a sacred significance in connection with the waxing and waning of the moon (Miyao 1989: 64–6). More generally, the bear is associated with rhythmical change, death and rebirth, through its winter denning behaviour and its sudden re-emergence in the spring. Another facet of the bear's sacred character has to do with its metonymical association with the *yama*. As the hardiest of animals that endures the cold winter in the remote *okuyama*, the bear is strongly linked with the natural elements and with the rugged landscape of the Japanese mountains. This bear's intimate connection with the environment finds expression in the folk belief that the killing of a bear in the *yama* leads to a *kumaare* or 'bear storm', as the bear's spirit or soul has the power to affect the weather (Sakuma 1980: 177; Ogura 1993*b*: 98–9). The bear's link with the landscape is further evident in the claim that some of the mountainous hot-springs that have become popular tourist destinations were discovered by bears (for example, Miyao 1989: 190).

The bear is an object of fear in Japan. Notorious bear attacks in the past have had the effect of establishing a popular image of the bear as an aggressor, a mankiller, and even a man-eater. The bear has been variously characterized as a *kyōfu no oni* or 'fearful demon' (Azumane 1997: 33), a *kuroi majin* or 'black devil' (Maita 1998*a*: 60), and an animal synonym for fear itself (Katō *et al.* 1986: 2). A recent report on attitudes towards bears in Hokkaido concludes that '[i]n regions inhabited by bears, the fear and loathing of them remains strong' (Mano and Moll 1999: 130). When deer-hunters in Hokkaido happen to come across bear tracks, they are said to react with an involuntary shudder (Anon. 1979*b*: 44), while hunters in Akita Prefecture refer to 'the bear's eery tracks' (Satō 1979: 115). An indication of the fear that bears can inspire in Japan came when the image of a bear on a roadside billboard (warning of the possibility of wild animals crossing the road) in Iwate Prefecture had to be replaced by an image of a raccoon-dog because the bear image was deemed to be too shocking to passing drivers and a possible cause of road accidents (Azumane 1997: 32). Real bears encountered on the road are more shocking still, and can elicit extreme human reactions. When (in Hokkaido) a bear appeared before a bus, the driver, encouraged by excited passengers demanding that he 'hit it!' (*buttsukechimae*), put his foot on the accelerator and drove the bus into the bear, knocking the animal off the mountain cliff to its death (Honda 1998: 20–1).

The bear is the object of a wide-ranging anthropomorphism in upland areas of Japan. As an animal that uses its 'hands', that 'stands up' on two feet, that leaves human-like tracks on the ground, that has an omnivorous diet, and that carries out prolonged nurturance of its young, the bear is viewed as similar to Man. Bears, like

FIG. 5.3. A brown bear in a Kyoto zoo

people, appreciate sunshine: they enjoy sunbathing and they are known to establish their winter dens in south-facing sites—*hiatari no ii tokoro* or 'places of good
sunlight'—just as people prefer their houses to be south-facing so that they can rely
on winter sunshine to get through the coldest time of the year. Other humanlike
traits of the bear include its sleeping posture (one 'hand' over its face), its snoring,
and its dying scream (Ue 1983: 328, 344). It is said that the bear that is being beaten
to death by the hunter (reluctant to spoil its coat with shot holes) tries to protect its
head from the blows with its 'arms' (Azumane 1997: 6), while the dead bear, once
it has been skinned, has an uncanny resemblance to a human being. Along with
this folk recognition of a wide-ranging (physical and behavioural) bear resemblance to humans, an assortment of anthropomorphic expressions are applied to
bears, including *yamaotoko* or 'mountain man' (Naumann 1963: 175 ff.), *yama no
ossan* or 'mountain uncle' (Hida 1971: 203), *yama no oyaji* or 'mountain father'

FIG. 5.4. A notice board in the Mitsumine area warning hikers of the dangers in the forest

(Nishiura 1989: 178), *mori no ichiban chikaramochi* or 'the foremost strongman of the forest' (Watanabe 1984: 187), *yatsu* or 'bloke' (Kobayashi 1989: 143), *sabishigariya* or 'lonely person' (Hida 1967: 67), and *hitorigurashi* or 'single-dweller'. Many of these expressions point to a certain sympathy, if not pity, for the bear, as one who must live all alone in the mountains.

Some of these terms suggest that the bear has strong associations with masculinity. As we have seen, the character for bear is found in many Japanese family names, but it is also used in personal names for boys. On the Kii Peninsula I have come across names such as Kumaichi or 'Bear One' (for first-born son), Kumami or 'Bear Three' (for third son), and Kumao or 'Bear Man'. The association between boys and bears is especially evident in the bear-hunting areas of north-eastern Japan. An example of this appears in *Tōno monogatari* where Yanagita Kunio tells of an incident (reported in a local newspaper) involving 'a man named Kuma' from the village of Kamigō who, when out hunting with a friend, was attacked by a bear, but, after a bloody fight in which he was slashed by the bear's claws, managed to survive (Yanagita 1992: 36). North-eastern Japan is known for the custom of *kumanori* or 'bear-riding' in which male children are placed on the back of the hide of a recently killed bear. As the boys are placed on the dead bear, they are offered words of encouragement such as 'go on mount [it], you'll become strong', and villagers state that the purpose of the custom is '[to] make [boys] strong and healthy and give them courage' (Amano 1999: 162–3). Even children terrified of riding the bear, who shed tears in the process, are forced to go through with it. The custom can be seen as a kind of initiation rite in which boys are made to confront and overcome their natural fear of the most dangerous animal in the forest, and thereby to develop the highly valued masculine attribute of courage. Here we can recall the Japanese expression *yūhi no shi* or 'bear man', which is applied to 'men who are intrepid like the bear or the brown bear' (Takahashi 1997: 104).

In Japan the bear is also associated with family ties and, in particular, motherly love and nurturance (Yamazaki 1996: 17). Giving birth deep in the *yama* at the coldest time of year, the bear is admired for its maternal dedication and forbearance (Miyao 1989: 18, 193). Hunters respect the determination shown by the pregnant mother bear when, just before giving birth, she leaves the winter den to drink water from a nearby marsh, which enables her to lactate after the cub is born (Tabuchi 1992: 18). The bear's devotion leads to successful nurturance, as the cub, which at birth is 'smaller than a mouse', rapidly grows to become the strongest animal in the forest (Kaneko 1993: 14). The bear is renowned for its light births, with hunters claiming that pregnant bears have been known suddenly to give birth at the sound of a human voice outside the den (Amano 1999: 168). Japanese mountain villagers have long used body parts of the bear (hide, paw, gut, uterus, etc.) to secure an easy childbirth (Suzuki 1982: 224; Sakuma 1985: 173; Tanigawa 1980: 324), and hunters in some areas would give out parts of the bear to any village households in which there was a pregnant woman (Aoki 1996: 45). In northern Wakayama, Higashiyama Shōzō, a retired schoolteacher, recalls from his childhood that whenever a bear was caught in the village, pregnant women would come and *matagu* or 'step across' the hide in the hope of having an easy delivery. Another reason, he explained, for this bear-crossing custom on the part of pregnant women was to promote the healthy growth of their babies, for the bear is known for its remarkable development, from tiny cub to enormous adult—'becoming one thousand times [*sic*] bigger, from three hundred grammes to one hundred kilogrammes'.

If on the Japanese archipelago bears are models of nurturance for humans, there are also instances of bears being nurtured by humans. The Ainu are well known for the custom of nurturing bears, in connection with the aforementioned *iyomante* rite. A bear cub is captured alive and raised within the settlement until the time of its ceremonial slaughter. The bear cub is allowed (while still young) to roam freely about the house, is given toys to play with, is fed the same food that people eat, and is generally 'raised with love by the people of the village' (Ifukube 1969: 24). This care bestowed on the cub in the village, which may last up to two years, is 'because the Ainu believe that the parent bears, as parent gods, have entrusted them to bring up their cubs' (Akino 1999: 249). The missionary John Batchelor has described the traditional Ainu rearing of the bear cub, based on his observations in the late nineteenth century.

Sometimes very young cubs may be seen living in the huts with the people, where they play with the children, and are cared for with great affection. In fact, some of them are treated even better than the children themselves, and I have known cases when the people have wept greatly when the cub has died. (Batchelor 1901: 483–4)

The full extent of this human care of bear cubs emerges when Batchelor goes on to mention that he observed Ainu women nursing bear cubs from their own breasts (Batchelor 1901: 484; see also Ifukube 1969: 23). No such custom of people suckling bears has been reported for mainstream Japanese culture, although in upland areas there are instances of captured bear cubs being raised as pets by hunters.

The theme of the bear as an object of human nurturance is present in the popular culture of modern Japan in the form of the teddy bears and other furry bears that children and adults surround themselves with. Japanese children live in a world of cuddly, cute bear imagery produced, reproduced, and diffused by the mass media and by commerce. Children on the Kii Peninsula, like children across Japan, eat bear-shaped candies, biscuits, and cakes, have stationery, clothes, hand-towels, bags, and lunchboxes imprinted with images of bears, play with teddy bears and other soft, furry bear toys, watch television cartoons featuring friendly, talking bears, dry themselves after the evening bath with bear-patterned towels, and go to sleep at night in bear-patterned pyjamas, sheets, and duvets. Young children talk to their bears; some bears are specifically marketed as discreet confidants to whom one can safely complain about things. Children address and refer to their bears as 'Kuma-chan', 'Teddy-kun', and so on, thus terminologically placing the bear in the position of a younger sibling or a child that is to be cared for and looked after, as well as played with (above all, with its soft, skin-like 'fur', the bear is a toy to touch and hold). Older children (and adults) can visit special bear websites, such as that of the 'Pink Bear' where they can 'play with' this virtual bear. In this 'cute bear' phenomenon children are able, among other things, to act out the roles of their parents, with the bear assuming the child's own otherwise passive position as the object of adult care.

There is an important gendered dimension to this Japanese love of toy bears, as girls are much more involved in it than boys, often continuing it into female adult-hood. Young Japanese women are avid consumers of bear products, and teddy bears of different colours and sizes are commonly found in the cars of women. In addition, young women make gifts of toy bears to each other on birthdays, at Christmas, and so on. These bear collections can also be understood in terms of the sphere of pre-marital romance, as some of the bears originate as gifts from boyfriends. Although in Japan young men too may claim a fondness for bears, this tends rather to be part of a strategy to attract women to them (Nimiya and Ōtsuka 1993: 30). Young women should discard their bears on marriage, but some take them with them to their marital home, and even continue to accumulate them after marriage—one of the best gifts a husband on an overseas business trip can buy

めんこいBear!!
世界一・のぼりべつ クマ牧場

FIG. 5.5. A telephone card showing a 'cute' bear cub in a tree (and advertizing a bear park visitor attraction)

for his young wife is an expensive, high-quality foreign teddy bear (Nimiya and Ōtsuka 1993: 27). When the young wife becomes a mother, the household bears once again become child-centred objects, serving to mediate parent–child ties, only this time with her as the parent. To some extent, the tourist sector on the Kii Peninsula taps into this national demand for toy bears. There is an assortment of bear-related items among the souvenirs in Hongū guesthouses and shops, including key-rings, badges and furry toys (the latest of which, in January 1999, was the teddy bear—'Teddy'—from the British television show *Mr Bean*). Yet these toy bears on show in the tourist villages would appear to have little connection to the bears inhabiting the forest. Indeed, on the face of it, the sentiments associated respectively with toy bears and with forest bears could hardly be more opposed, with the reassurance offered by the toy bears contrasting starkly with the panic inspired by real bears.

THE PROBLEM OF BEARS

Bear Pestilence

People–bear conflict has long existed in Japan. In bear-inhabited regions of Japan the bear can be a serious farm pest that feeds on a wide range of cultivated crops, including fruits, vegetables, and even rice. Bear damage occurs throughout much of the year: bears feed on cultivated bamboo-shoots in the spring, on plums in June, on peaches, silverberries, and sweetcorn in July, on watermelons and corn in August, on apples, pears, chestnuts, sweet potatoes, and rice in September, and on grapes and persimmons in October (Maita 1998a: 167). As with damage by the wild boar and the monkey, bear damage to farms often seems wasteful and wanton to the farmer who suffers it. When a bear feeds on watermelons or pumpkins, it eats only the seeds in the middle and not the fleshy part of the fruit, and the farmer finds a great many of his melons and pumpkins with holes in one side (Watanabe 1984: 185). Another feature of bear damage is that bears do not just feed on the crop, but seem intent on vandalizing the plant as such. When bears enter apple orchards, they snap branches in the process of feeding, disfigure the tree, and adversely affect future harvests (Maita 1996a: 38). For the orchard farmer, bear damage affects not just a single year's crop, but has a long-term impact. Villagers complain that their chestnut and persimmon trees have been turned into 'bonsai' trees by the bears' past attentions (a term also used by foresters, it will be recalled, in relation to serow browsing in the previous chapter). Some farmers give up growing the more vulnerable of their crops (such as corn), while others decide to abandon arable land altogether because of the high risk of damage (Azumane 1997: 131, 215; Palmer 1983: 332).

Bear attacks on livestock are also reported in Japan, albeit to a much lesser extent than in the livestock economies of Europe where shepherds and reindeer-herders suffer from bear depredations.[5] Most attacks on livestock in Japan occur on the northern island of Hokkaido, the most pastoral part of Japan, as well as home to the larger brown bear. One of the worst years for bear attacks on livestock was 1959 when 638 sheep, 40 horses, 34 cows, 14 goats, and 3 pigs were reportedly killed in Hokkaido, with some officials suggesting that the actual figures may have been almost double those reported (Honda 1998: 17). Another bad year was 1962 when '126 horses, 160 cows, and 459 sheep were wounded or killed by bears' in Hokkaido (Moll 1994: 33). Bear attacks on livestock are sometimes reported for the main island of Honshu, where the targets of the bear have included chickens and fish farms.[6] Beehives are a favourite target of Japanese bears; every year around 3,000 beehives are damaged by black bears that break them open to get at the honey (Maita 1998a: 21). There are also reports from parts of the Kii Peninsula of bears lifting up beehives with their arms and walking away with them (as a result of which some such incidents have been mistaken for human crimes) (Ue 1983: 324–5; Matsuyama 1994: 75, 86–7). Finally, there are occasional reports of bear attacks on village dogs.

---

[5] For southern Europe, see Camarra (1987), Clevenger and Campos (1994), and Cozza *et al.* (1996); for northern Europe, see Nyholm and Nyholm (1999: 67); and for Eastern Europe, see Frackowiak *et al.* (1999: 92).
[6] See Hayashi (1993: 127), Takahashi (1995: 100–1), Maita (1996b: 239), Miyao (1989: 198), and Torii (1996c: 1, 2).

In contrast to the wild boar and the monkey, the black bear is above all a forestry pest. The greatest economic damage caused by Japanese black bears is to the timber grown by the forester rather than the food crops grown by the farmer. This damage mainly takes the form of bear barkstripping, known in Japanese as *kumahagi* (literally 'bear-peeling'), which can lead to defoliation, impaired growth, and the death of the tree. Occurring in the summer rainy season, bear barkstripping affects the main commercial plantation species of cedar, cypress, and larch, as well as assorted conifers of the primary forest (altogether damage to seventeen different conifer tree species has been reported) (Watanabe 1981: 581). Large-scale bear damage to conifer plantations dates from the early 1960s and worsened in the 1970s when the annual area of bear damage ranged from 400 to 1,200 hectares (Watanabe 1980: 67). Bear forestry pestilence is unevenly distributed across the bear-range areas of Honshu. While bear damage in the Japan Sea regions and in the north of Honshu is low, bear damage has been very serious in regions on the Pacific coast, including the Kii Peninsula (Watanabe 1981: 582). Bear damage on the Kii Peninsula was particularly heavy in the 1970s, averaging as much as 350 hectares annually between 1973 and 1978 (Shibata and Kobune 1984: 178). In some areas, there are signs that the problem of bear barkstripping has become even more serious. According to a recent newspaper report, fully mature plantation conifers of up to seventy years old (commanding the highest of market values) have been barkstripped by bears (*NKS* 19 Jan. 1997).

In barkstripping a tree, the bear loosens the bark at the base of the tree by peeling strips of it upwards with its claws and teeth, in some cases extending to a height of two metres or more on the trunk, leaving long strips of the peeled bark dangling from the stem (in some species of conifer the bark is removed altogether from the stem) (Watanabe 1981: 581). After the bark has been stripped, the bear proceeds to gnaw and apparently eat the exposed sapwood, leaving shallow groove-marks on the stem (ibid.). Murata Yoshio, in the Hongū village of Shitsugawa, has worked in the forestry industry for many years and has observed first hand the shocking effects of bear damage to plantation trees. He described the bear's barkstripping actions to me in the following way.

When the bear strips the bark away, it's incredible . . . It takes the whole lot off. Then, it [the tree] dries out, and when the wind blows it gets really noisy, as it [the bark] goes '*karakarakarakara*' [against the tree]. I think that, at first, the bear just thinks of biting [the tree] with its teeth, but then it [the bark] peels off and the bear realizes that it can eat [the stem] . . . It's easy to peel. What happens is that it pulls the bark like this and is able to peel it away up to three metres high and right around the circumference . . . It [the tree] gets completely bare . . . After it has peeled it away, the trunk is full of clawmarks and it starts to lick the stuff that comes out . . .

The forest labourer Ue Toshikatsu points out that it is because of barkstripping that bears are viewed by foresters on the Kii Peninsula as a *kataki* or 'enemy' (Ue 1983: 362). Foresters are especially exasperated when, as is often the case, they find that the bear has stripped maturing, high value trees into which much silvicultural labour has been put (Ue 1983: 362–3). Other reports similarly state that superior plantations are inordinately affected, while within the plantation the best-growing trees are picked out (Torii 1996c: 3–4). The bear usually opts for trees with a diameter of between twenty and forty centimetres, which are aged between fifteen and thirty years old (Watanabe *et al.* 1973: 5). Trees near the ridge of the hill or mountain are more vulnerable to barkstripping than those lower down (Watanabe and Komiyama 1976: 4) and the damage tends to be highly localized, involving clusters of trees in close proximity (Watanabe *et al.* 1973: 5). Most of the trees affected are only stripped on one side, but some trees (especially those on a level site) are completely 'girdled', as a result of which they eventually die (Watanabe 1981: 582). All barkstripped trees are likely to be adversely affected to some extent: 'All types of bear-caused wounds permit infection by stain and decay organisms, and such infections can result in [the] deterioration of wood quality' (Watanabe 1980: 69). A majority of the trees in a plantation (up to 80 per cent) may be affected, leading to great economic loss on the part of the forest landowner (Watanabe *et al.* 1970: 12; Torii 1996c: 3). As indicated above, the bear even appears to feed on the stripped tree stems, leaving teeth marks of up to one or even one-and-a-half metres high (a height approximating to that of a human being). This tree-eating behaviour has led one observer to remark that in Japan 'when the bear has its afternoon snack, it costs money' (Hida 1967: 61–2).

Bear Attacks

The bear is not just an economic threat to rural livelihoods, but also appears a physical threat to rural lives. Every year in Japan there are serious bear incidents involving foresters, hunters, herb-gatherers, mushroom-pickers, nut-collectors, anglers, hikers, and other forest recreationists. Forest labourers, who spend up to 300 days a year working in the forest, are particularly vulnerable to bear encounters. They come across roaming bears in the spring, the summer, and the autumn. Many bear attacks occur through sudden face-to-face encounters on the bends of winding mountain paths when neither bear nor human can take evasive action. Murata Yoshio recalled one encounter when he was working as a forester in Mie Prefecture on the eastern side of the Kii Peninsula.

You hear a lot of stories about people being attacked by bears. What happens is that there will be a mountain road with a bend in it, and each of them [bear and person] are coming along like this [gesturing with 'walking' fingers] . . . and as the bear moves along its course there comes a point when it suddenly finds that it has nowhere to run away to. When that happens, the bear will come at you . . . That happened to me once. It was at the foot of Ōdaigahara . . . It was a place with a bend [in the road] . . . In an instant, I suddenly found the bear in front of me. Neither the bear nor I were looking ahead, until we were right in front of each other. It had nowhere to run away to and so it stood up in front of me. When they stand up like that they are frightening and when they stand up it means that they will definitely come at you. If it swats you with one of those arms you won't survive it. It was about eighteen *kan* [nearly 70 kilogrammes] . . . After I shot it, I looked at its face and it was really cute-looking. It had a good face.

Kakimoto Fumio, from the Hongū village of Kotsuga, has worked as a forest labourer for over forty years. He is one of the few forest labourers who still practise *yamadomari* or 'forest-camping'—staying overnight in a forest hut during a job, rather than return each day to the village. A quiet, shy man, Kakimoto-san says that he prefers being in the forest to being in the village because it is only when alone in the forest that he can truly relax. In general, he feels safe in the *yama* and does not consider the animals there to be a danger. When I first asked him about bears, he repeated a phrase often used by foresters: 'the most frightening thing of all in this world is the human being.'[7] But he went on to admit that when working alone in the forest he does worry about encounters with bears, especially when he hears of incidents nearby. In the past he has had his share of close encounters, but has never actually been attacked by a bear. He none the less has definite ideas on how people should deal with bears when encounters occur.

Bears are frightening . . . If you shout at them in a loud voice, they will definitely come at you. What you should do is just keep quiet when they are around . . . If you try to run away from them, they will only come after you and chase you. But if you just stay quiet yourself, they will be the ones to escape . . . well, usually they will. As long as you don't startle them . . . It's the same with us [human beings], isn't it? If we encounter somebody else in the forest, and one person starts shouting in a loud voice at the other person . . . well, it's just the same as that. If you raise your voice, it'll be the end of you. It [the bear] will stand up and come at you.

The problem of sudden bear encounters on mountain paths is mitigated some-what by the precautions that forest labourers learn to take, such as attaching small bells to their clothing or carrying switched-on radios when in the forest in order to alert bears to their presence in advance and allow the animal to avoid an encounter. But some forest labourers believe that, with the recent decline in forestry, the threat of roaming bears in the forest is increasing, despite all the talk of declining bear numbers. It is said that up until the 1970s the regular presence of forest labourers in the timber plantations tended to keep bears away, but that with the decline in the forestry labour force the bears have lost their old caution and now feel free to roam through plantations without fear of human disturbance. These new circum-stances are said to make life that much more dangerous for the men and women who continue to work in the forest. Even in the winter, when bears hibernate in much of Japan's bear range, forest labourers are not entirely free from the bear threat. There are reports of forest labourers inadvertently disturbing denning bears—for example, by stepping on or falling into a den at the base of a plantation tree (an increasingly common site for denning), or by waking up a denning bear

[7] The Japanese expression is: *kono yo ningen hodo kowai koto ga nai* (literally, 'there is nothing as frightening in this world as a human being').

with the loud noise of their chainsaws (Ōta 1997: 126). Recognizing this danger, one bear expert offers forest labourers the following advice: 'When you are thinking of doing some work in the plantation in the winter, you must first make yourself aware of the possibility of falling into a bear den. There may well be a bear den hole just in front of you' (Maita 1998a: 77).

Recreationists and occasional forest visitors tend to be less well prepared for bear encounters than forest labourers. The recent increase in forest recreation in Japan raises the prospect of more bear encounters (Miyao 1989: 198). The summer is a particularly dangerous season, as many people go to the forest to collect herbs and nuts over the summer months, and this foraging activity may well take the gatherers into bear territory and into contact with bears (which are drawn to these same wild foods). The bear's mating season falls in June and July, and at this time adult male bears are very aggressive. Bears have been known to seize the rucksacks of hikers, assuming that they contain riceballs and other foodstuffs. Attacks also occur when bears forage for human foods in and around forestry stations, tourist camping sites, or garbage dumps. Most bear attacks take place in the forest, but incidents in villages are occasionally reported. In many remote settlements where fields are adjacent to the houses, a night-time visit to the ricefield by a bear will bring it into close proximity to villagers. A report from Hiroshima Prefecture about a bear attack on a 62-year-old man shows how dangerous this situation can be: 'When he went out to check the ricefields, he came across a bear which, from about a distance of eight metres away, came and flew at him. He was pulled around by his right arm and was wounded in his right thigh, from which it took him two weeks to recover' (AS 25 Nov. 1995). Although the victim soon recovered from his physical injuries, the attack left him traumatized: 'Ever since then, I have been frightened to go out and check the ricefields' (ibid.).

In 1988 three human deaths from bear attacks occurred in Tozawa-mura in Yamagata Prefecture. In one of the attacks a housewife gathering chestnuts in the forest was killed by the bear (AS 10 Oct. 1988), and the bear was said to have partly eaten its victim (Umeda Yoshimi, personal communication). The *Asahi Shinbun* newspaper published the following report from the village affected.

On the 6th [of October] a 59-year-old woman out collecting nuts, and then on the 9th a 59-year-old woman out gathering chestnuts, were each suddenly attacked in the forest near the village, and died after losing a lot of blood. In the same village in May, a 61-year-old man out gathering bamboo-shoots was attacked and died. All of these victims knew the forest well, and from experience believed that 'when a bear encounters a human being, it escapes' and that 'in this sort of place there are no bears', and accordingly left for the forest without any fear. But this year, these expectations no longer hold . . . The bear, which appeared to be the 'criminal', was shot on the 9th. But the panic continues, with 'Forest Entry Forbidden' billboard signs being put up around the district by the Town Hall, with many reports of bear-sightings by villagers, and with primary schoolchildren being escorted to school by their parents. (AS 29 Oct. 1988)

In other areas too, bear attacks occasion a state of emergency during which certain procedures come into force such as the mounting of patrols, the distribution of small bells and whistles to the local population, and the reorganization of children's movements between home and school, whereby arrangements are made for them to travel together in groups (Torii 1996*c*: 6; Taguchi 1994: 57). Overall, however, fatal attacks involving the back bear are extremely rare.

The worst bear attacks in Japan have occurred in Hokkaido, involving the larger brown bear. In Hokkaido, '[d]uring the first 57 years of this century, when accurate records began to be kept, 141 people died in bear attacks and another 300 were injured' (Fujiwara 1988: 28). In 1915 a fatal bear attack occurred in a village called Tomamae in Hokkaido, in which seven people died and three people were injured (Maita 1996*b*: 16–17). Accounts of the incident portray scenes of horrific carnage in which women and children are devoured by a giant beast (the bear was weighed at 340 kilogrammes) intent on destroying a whole village (Honda 1998: 11–16). But reports also tell of a spirited, if belated, village response to the beast, with large numbers of hunters mobilized to pursue the bear in the mountains. These armed avengers greeted the bear's demise with spontaneous shouts of '*banzai*' ('Long Live the Emperor', literally 'ten thousand years'), as though celebrating a great military victory (ibid.). A monument and a museum were established in Tomamae to commemorate the terrible attack, but arguably the true legacy left by the Tomamae bear lies less in these material forms than in the popular consciousness of the bear it has helped to generate. This attack, which has come to be known as the *Tomamae jiken* or 'Tomamae Incident', is often referred to in the media reporting of bear issues in Japan (for example, *AS* 2 June 1990). Although there have been other fatal bear attacks since—in 1962 three hunters were killed by a bear in Hokkaido (Moll 1994: 34) and in 1970 a bear killed three student hikers in Hokkaido (Hirasawa 1985: 49–50)—it is the 'Tomamae Incident' which has been largely responsible for establishing the popular perception of the bear as a mankiller (Maita 1996*b*: 15–17; Mano and Moll 1999: 130).

Even where no attacks take place, bear encounters or just bear-sightings can generate considerable disquiet in the locality in question. One bear conservationist who has visited many villages affected by roaming bears characterizes this phenomenon as *seishinteki higai* or 'spiritual damage' (Maita 1998*a*: 27). This is because the effect of bear-sightings is to make familiar spaces seem frightening and to restrict human movement across them. A bear-sighting in one part of the forest deters collectors of herbs or mushrooms from going to the area, thereby depriving them of their favourite picking spots. Similarly, a bear-sighting in a field or a timber plantation can make villagers reluctant to work in those areas (in some cases ruining a farm crop by the delay in harvesting). Bears also visit village graveyards, where they feed on the edible offerings made to the dead (sweet wrappers have been discovered in stomachs of dead bears) (Azumane 1997: 25), and again can make the restplace of village ancestors temporarily off limits to living descendants.

But bears are at their most intrusive when they enter homes. There are reports of bears climbing on to roofs, breaking windows, and invading village houses (Miyao 1989: 199; Maita 1996*a*: 175) and tales of village housewives opening windows and suddenly finding themselves face to face with a bear encamped on the roof outside (Maita 1998*a*: 27)! Bears have been known to enter kitchens to feed (in some cases managing to open refrigerators) and drink (there are reports of bears drinking sake) (Honda 1998: 299). In one story a village housewife enters a room and finds a bear sitting in the front of the television (Maita 1998*a*: 27)! Despite the amusing quality of some of these reports, the sudden appearance of a bear can create a general air of anxiety and insecurity among remote villagers; in the wake of a bear-sighting it is not uncommon for local people to observe a night-time curfew and to be unable to rest peacefully at night.[8]

Local concern over another kind of stigma is sometimes voiced. In the newspaper report above on fatal bear attacks in Tozawa, the fear was expressed that, at a time when there was already a shortage of brides in the area, the incident might make getting married even more difficult for local men (*AS* 29 Oct. 1988). The background to these comments is the so-called *yomebusoku* or 'bride shortage' faced by much of rural Japan (see Knight 1995). This is a problem that is particularly pronounced in mountainous parts of Japan that tend to appear as backward and unappealing places to young women who prefer to marry into families in communities located further downstream. The newspaper reference to the 'bride shortage' in connection with bear attacks suggests that bears affect villagers not just through damage to person and property, but also *by association*. Remote places and the people who live in them become, in effect, tainted by their association with bears. Proximity to bears is a source of stigma for a village and an extra reason for leaving it. This same point—that bears compound the spouse-finding difficulties of village men—is expressed by the bear conservationist Hazumi Toshihiro in a passing reference to the rural prejudice 'that brides are not attracted to the kind of place where bears are found . . .' (Hazumi 1992: 308). Hazumi's comments refer to the bear's association with primitiveness and backwardness. In his discussion of the rural prejudice against upstream dwellers, Sakurai Tokutarō recounts that remote villagers may be characterized by their downstream neighbours as *kuma no yō ni kebukai* or 'hairy like bears' and therefore as *ezokei* or 'primitives', and goes on to suggest that such prejudices are linked to the folk belief that *oni* or 'demons' live in the remote mountains (Sakurai 1990: 599). Similarly, the brown bear has long epitomized the status of the northern island of Hokkaido as a wild, uncivilized frontier region. 'Until the 1960s, the very existence of the brown bear symbolized undevelopment, [and] was viewed as an enemy of civilization . . .' (Mano 1991: 158–9). From this perspective, the eradication of the bear was part of the process of modernizing and civilizing the remote parts of Japan.

[8] See Takahashi (1995: 103), *AS* (16 Oct. 1992), *AS* (12 July 1994), and *AS* (25 Nov. 1995).

Responses

Japanese mountain villagers employ various measures to defend their fields, fruit trees, and timber plantations from the bear. As with wild boars, monkeys, and deer, repellent smells and noises are used to keep bears away. Old tyres, human hair, and rice chaff are all burned to produce obnoxious smells (Maita 1998*a*: 139). Oil lamps placed beside a field have a double deterrent effect—both the smell of burning oil and the light they emit (Maita 1998*a*: 137). Timber plantations are protected from bears by coating individual tree stands with strong-smelling substances such as coal tar. There are also reports of bear fat being used to keep bears away (recalling the similar use of body parts and substances in the case of wild boars and monkeys) (Torii 1996*c*: 5). Bears are known to be especially averse to loud noises; this is recognized in a saying found in remote areas of Japan, *inuyama damare, kumayama sawage*, 'be quiet in the wolf forest, be noisy in the bear forest' (*MS* 16 Apr. 1989). Therefore, just as the key to bear avoidance in the forest is to alert the bear in advance to one's own presence in order to give it the chance to escape, so the strategy of bear repulsion in the village is based on informing the roaming bear of an apparent human presence. To this end, farmers in the bear-inhabited regions of Japan protect themselves from bear visits by placing switched-on radios (along with amplifiers) around the edges of the fields to give the impression of a human presence there (Azumane 1997: 214). Another means of simulating human presence is by siting mannekin dolls in and around the plantations (Torii 1996*c*: 5).

Even more effective in keeping bears away is some sort of physical presence. Some rural municipalities establish armed plantation patrols during the summer months when bears are known to roam around (Torii 1989: 196). But in the case of the bear there are few reports of the kind of human field-guarding vigils that take place to protect crops from the wild boar and the monkey. Rather, mountain villagers tend to rely on dogs to guard their farms and settlements from bears. Farmers in Iwate Prefecture, for example, post dogs at the front and back of their houses: if a bear comes near the house, the dogs start barking, and the farmer rushes out to light firecrackers to scare it away (Azumane 1997: 214). In some areas dog packs are used to chase bears back to the forest. In Fukushima Prefecture, for example, robust Hokkaido dogs (bred to fight the larger brown bear) are used to repel intruding bears. According to the dog-breeder who supplied the dogs, the bear, when confronted by the dog pack, 'feels that "this is intolerable" and escapes. I think the dogs teach the bear that "this is not your territory"' (in Azumane 1997: 216). In many cases, village dogs have died defending the village from bear visits. But the efficacy of dogs as field-guards against bears (as was the case with wild boars and monkeys) is limited because of the obligation that villagers are under to keep the dogs confined. This state of affairs occasions much criticism in areas affected by bear damage, such as the following complaint from a farmer in Iwate Prefecture: 'It would be fine if we were allowed to let the dogs roam free as in the old days, but now we are not allowed to do this because they are worried that they will run away and become stray dogs' (in Azumane 1997: 215).

In previous chapters we have seen how people–wildlife conflicts in Japan occasion the language of war. Human conflict with the bear too is often suggestive of warfare. According to Batchelor, among the Ainu when someone had been killed by a bear, the people would 'make war' on the animal by hunting it down (Batchelor 1901: 477). The post-Meiji colonization of Hokkaido is often characterized as a *tatakai* or 'war' between settler and bear.[9] The idiom of war is also employed in parts of north-east Japan where the bear is known as *yama no taishō* or the 'mountain general' (Amano 1999: 166) and among bear-hunters who characterize winter den-hunting (in which the hunter attacks the bear in its den) as *gerira senpō* or 'guerrilla tactics' (Satō 1979: 111). Upon the killing of a bear (as we saw above with the Tomamae bear), hunters announce their achievement by collectively cheering '*banzai! banzai! banzai!*', as though celebrating a victory in battle (Nebuka 1991: 163; Honda 1998: 16). The conflict with the bear can at times become an almost literal war, in which large numbers of police are deployed against the animal. When in the summer of 1994 a bear entered a residential area in Hiroshima and mauled a number of residents, fourteen police patrol cars and fifty policemen were dispatched to deal with it (*AS* 12 July 1994). In Hokkaido troops have been mobilized to deal with dangerous bears. During the 1960s the Japanese army mounted military-style operations against the brown bear.

As an example of the fervour with which bears were being pursued, in Teshio, northern Hokkaido over the course of 10 days in April of 1966, a literal army of 148 hunters with the support of 260 self defense force members, 50 regular vehicles, 4 snow vehicles and 4 helicopters, killed 39 bears. (Moll 1994: 34, references removed)

The main response to bear incidents in Japan is to shoot the bears involved. According to official figures, 77,564 black bears were killed between 1946 and 1994 (Maita 1998*a*: 49). Since the end of the Second World War, bears have increasingly been killed as pests rather than as game animals. Nationally, over half of the 1,695 bears (black and brown) killed in 1994 were killed as pests, but in some prefectures the figure for pest-kills reaches 80 per cent (Maita 1998*a*: 50). Bounties are offered for bears by local municipalities, and bear-culling squads have been established in some regions. In Shizuoka Prefecture, for example, *kuma bokumetsukai* or 'bear extermination groups' were established in 1952, and involved groups of armed men patrolling timber plantations over the summer months (Torii 1989: 196–7). In Hokkaido there has long been an official bounty system for bears in place, representing an important source of income for hunters (Hokkaido hunters estimate that a single healthy brown bear can fetch as much as $9,000) (Moll 1994: 35). Bear-culling generally takes place outside the winter hunting season, usually in the

---

[9] See Mano (1991: 158), Odajima (1993: 27), Chiba (1995*a*: 93), and Honda (1998: 300).

FIG. 5.6. A black bear trapped in an apple orchard in Iwate Prefecture

autumn before denning and in the spring after denning. Summer and autumn culling takes the form of a pursuit of particular *mondai kuma* or 'problem bears' by a party of armed hunters with dogs, while springtime culling represents the precautionary elimination of bears. On the Kii Peninsula, between 1950 and 1985, the annual scale of bear-culling ranged from ten to thirty bears (Yoneda 1991: 150–1; Maita 1999: 121).

Bear culling includes trapping as well as hunting. Bear-trapping usually occurs by means of honey-baited cages (but bears are occasionally caught in the *kukuri-wana* wire traps used for catching wild boar). In October 1994 I interviewed Torii Mitsuya, an old man in the Hongū village of Hagi with experience of trapping bears. Torii-san is a former forest labourer and long-term hunter who served as a hired bear-trapper for seven years (1976–83) in company-owned forests in Totsukawa-mura, to the north of Hongū. During the early 1970s the company's timber plantations suffered considerable bear barkstripping (the cost of which Torii-san estimates to have been around 100 million yen [$750,000]), and the company responded by drawing up a plan to remove the problem bears, hiring Torii-san to help them. Large steel cages were transported into the forest by helicopter and strategically placed near the plantations. It was Torii-san's job to maintain these cages (to keep them baited with honey), to check them periodically to see if anything had been caught, and to dispatch any trapped bears with his gun. In his seven years working for the company he only ever caught five bears, but remembers each time very clearly. What he was most impressed with was the bear's great power and its refusal to die. He points out that even a trapped bear is frightening when you stand in front of it. In particular, he remembers the unnerving roar of the bear, that was rather like the sound of a forester's chainsaw, as well as how red the dark bear's mouth appeared as it growled at him. Such was the bear's physical strength that there were times when the steel bars of the cage had been pulled inwards at an angle. Although it was trapped and had no chance to escape, the bear was not easily finished off, and Torii-san sometimes had to shoot three or four times to kill it. Torii-san himself appears to have diligently checked his cages at regular intervals, but bear cages have not always been regularly checked and captured bears have died slow, miserable deaths from starvation.[10]

HUNTERS AND BEARS

In addition to bear pestilence, the other main form of human–bear interaction in the mountains of Japan is hunting. There is not a celebrated bear-hunting tradition on the Kii Peninsula. Some Hongū hunters have caught bears and made money from selling bear parts. But bear-hunting is something that tends to be associated with other regions of Japan. The best-known regional tradition of bear-hunting in Japan is that of the *matagi* villages of north-eastern Honshu in which the bear (along with the serow) formed an important element of local livelihoods. Bear-hunting can be divided into 'den-hunting' and 'pursuit-hunting' (Azuma and Torii 1980: 74). Den-hunting involves the search for hibernation restplaces, from which bears are lured before being dispatched (to kill a bear too early, while it is still in the den, gives rise to the problem of extracting the heavy animal from it). This form of hunting therefore relies on a knowledge of the whereabouts of bear dens. Bear-hunters in Gifu Prefecture are said to know the locations of between twenty and thirty trees that serve as winter dens (Wakida 1989: 157). One common type of den site is at the base of a large tree such as beech, *Quercus crispula*, horse chestnut, and other fruiting trees on which bears feed. Other likely den sites are the base of the stem of a fallen tree, the stem of a bent tree growing horizontally on a steep incline, or the crevice of a crag. The bear-hunter is always on the lookout for signs of a bear presence in a given area; barkstripped trees, while a cause of considerable vexation for the forester, are a valuable source of information for the hunter. Hunters also pursue mobile bears. In contrast to den-hunting, pursuit-hunting involves a group of men using dogs to track and chase roaming bears, and occurs in the autumn before denning and again in the spring after denning.

Bears were economically important in remote areas of Japan. Bear hides, bear meat, bear organs, and other body parts and substances have long been used by

[10] References to trapped bear starvation are made by Ue (1983: 364) and Tanba (1993: 82).

mountain villagers and traded for money. Curative value was attributed to the
different parts of the bear's body: the brain (in charred form) was a cure for headaches or sickness during pregnancy; the heart and lungs were used for asthma; the
paws were used for neuralgia and rheumatism; and body fat was used on cuts,
burns, rashes, chapped skin, and chilblains.[11] An indication of the importance of
curative bear parts is the existence (until recently) of what were known as *kuma no
mise* or 'bear shops' in remote areas, such as one found in a village to the west of
Hongū (Ue 1983: 317–22; cf. Chiba 1975: 217–19). Most important of all is the gall
bladder (known as the *i* or *tannō*), the muscular sac close to the liver. Bear gall is the
foremost example of a *myōyaku* or panacea, used for a wide range of sicknesses,
including intestinal, liver, and heart disorders (Kaneko *et al.* 1992: 41; Hazumi and
Yoshii 1994*a*: 31). On the Kii Peninsula many local households still keep a dried
bear gall bladder, which is self-administered for medicinal purposes or taken
regularly as a tonic. When travelling abroad, some peninsular residents take bear
gall with them as a safeguard against upset stomachs caused by foreign food. Bear
gall bladders are also sold for money, representing a lucrative source of extra
income for those who manage to obtain them.[12]

    Bear-hunting, in addition to procuring valuable products, is an important
symbolic activity for those who engage in it. One well-known expression of bear-
hunting symbolism is found among the Ainu. The ability to confront a bear was
the supreme test of an Ainu man because of the daring way the bear-hunter risked
his life in the hunt (Batchelor 1901: 471–8; Hallowell 1926: 38–9). Most spectacu-
larly, the hunter would engage the bear by charging at it with a poisoned spear.
Alternatively, the hunter might invite the charge of an angry bear (ejected from its
winter den) on to his spear. This second method involved the hunter strategically
positioning himself in front of a rock, in which a poisoned spear had been lodged,
and moving aside just as the charging bear is about to reach him, allowing the
animal to impale itself on the spear (Ölschleger 1999: 210). Here one recalls the
Ainu saying recorded by Edward Greey in the nineteenth century: 'He who under-
takes to catch a bear must not cry over his wounds' (Greey 1884: 122). This view of
the bear hunt as the ultimate measure of a man's courage is not limited to the Ainu,
but extends to Japanese bear-hunters. Hunters in northern Honshu maintain that
a man's ability to engage a bear face to face without losing his nerve is the test of
whether or not he is truly a *dokyō no ii hito* or 'man of courage' (Taguchi 1994: 93).

---

[11] See Nebuka (1991: 111–12), Ue (1983: 353), Hida (1972: 75–6), and Hazumi and Yoshii (1994*a*: 31).
[12] So valuable were bear gall bladders that they were sometimes likened to 'gold'—see Iino (1989*a*:
87); cf. Ishida (1993: 85), Maita (1996*a*: 100), and Yamazaki (1996: 20). Indeed, the bear's winter den
was known as a *kinko*, a 'treasury' or 'vault' (Azumane 1997: 9–10). In a well-known folk tale from
northern Japan, a man whose house burns down is rewarded for his virtue when he comes across a large
bear killed in an avalanche—from the sale of which (especially gall bladder) he was sufficiently
enriched to recover the family's status (Suzuki 1986: 207–9). Bear gall bladders continue to 'have the
highest commercial value of all Japanese wildlife products' (Hazumi 1994: 147). In order to inflate the
size of the gall bladder and increase its market value, some bear-trappers club or starve the bear to death
(even though this can take some time), rather than shoot and kill it outright—see Azumane (1997:
6–7), Tanba (1993: 82), and *AS* (29 Oct. 1988).

The true bear-hunter is a man who possesses a certain inner fortitude, as expressed by the term *matagi no konjō* or 'hunter's spirit'. The act of confronting a bear is the foremost testament to a man's courage and success in the bear hunt proof of a man's strength and power.

The point is illustrated by the writer Hida Inosuke in a report from *matagi* hunting villages in Aomori Prefecture (Hida 1972: 71–9). Hida tells the story of the eventful apprenticeship of a young bear-hunter, Uesugi Kōji, under an old bear-hunter. The young man left home when he was 15 years old, but instead of migrating to Tokyo like many of his peers, he travelled in the other direction ('with a spirit like that of a warrior on a mission') into the mountains to learn from the veteran bear-hunter. But the young 'warrior' soon realized that he had the most exacting of masters. What the master was looking for in the youngster, apart from an ability to acquire the techniques of bear-tracking, were signs of whether or not he had within him the all-important *konjō*. To this end, the master hunter put the younger man to the test by tricking him into entering a bear's cave (pretending that there was only a young bear inside) where he suddenly found himself face to face with a large adult bear.

Suddenly, there was a roar, '*ooooah* . . .'. There was a large bear sitting in a hole in the wall. The great roar continued. He felt a cold shiver up and down his back. His legs were shaking but he couldn't move. Full of fear, he blew his torch out without thinking. Once it had gone completely dark, the roars stopped and it became quiet. Although the bear could see in the darkness and could tell from the smell that a human being had invaded, everything had gone quiet. Why was that? He no longer had the feeling that the bear was about to fly at him. He was able to calm down . . . Then he lit the torch again and used the arm holding the torch to support the shotgun [as he took aim]. The bear once again gave out a frightening roar, but once he had sighted the 'third rib' below the white crescent [on the bear's chest] he pulled the trigger'. (Hida 1972: 77)

Through his actions, the young apprentice had shown, both to the veteran and to himself, that he was able to confront a bear face to face and that he did possess the bear-hunter's *konjō*.

Another famous bear-hunter is Fujiwara Chōtarō (who frequently appears in the Japanese mass media as the heir to an otherwise disappearing tradition). This man too sees the bear hunt as requiring courage and the ability to confront danger.

You often say to yourself when you are out hunting, 'if I don't kill this rascal, I'll be killed myself'. The encounter with the bear is always a matter of life and death. By deciding within your heart that 'there are two paths to take and I must choose one of them', this leads to a good outcome . . . If you take it easy, you will completely forget that 'I could be eaten by the bear'. (Fujiwara 1979: 36)

Fujiwara goes on to mention the suffering he has experienced in his long contest with the bear. He has killed many bears in his life, but has also endured a number of bear attacks. All this made him the man he is.

F IG. 5.7. A group of bear-hunters in Nagano Prefecture drag away a dead bear they have caught

Hope, determination, courage, resolution. After shooting and stopping two hundred bears, I have come to know the meaning of these four words. The flowers in the grass and on the trees are wonderful. But tales of suffering are even more wonderful still. In my life as a bear-hunter, many wonderful flowers have bloomed, and long may they continue to help me develop and grow. (Fujiwara 1979: 37)

In Chapter 2 we looked at the views of the hunter Inui Mitsunori about hunting wild boar and the quality of *dokyō* or 'courage' necessary for success in the boar hunt. But Inui-san also has experience in bear-hunting, and emphasizes that 'courage' is no less important in confronting the bear than in confronting the boar.

The bear is the same [as the wild boar]. If it has the chance to escape, it will escape. It tries to avoid people, but then you suddenly encounter it on a bend in the road, or under the shade of a tree when it can't escape, and it will then fly at the human being . . . When an animal comes at you, whether it's a bear or whether it's a wild boar . . . whichever animal it is, if you try to run away in the mountains you will never escape. They [bears and boars] are guys that will come after you. You just have to confront them. If you are somebody who really has courage, then when a bear comes at you it will be the one to suffer . . .

Inui-san believes that today bear-hunters (like boar-hunters) no longer display such courage. The younger generation of hunters, in particular, relies on its high-powered rifles to shoot at bears from a distance rather than risk close encounters. In this, Inui-san contrasts his fellow Japanese hunters unfavourably with the traditional Ainu bear-hunter famous for his valour.

Bears are strong, you know. Apart from the Ainu, a man can never beat a bear [in a direct fight], he will lose. An Ainu will take his dagger, with poison on the tip, and then jump into the bear's chest. If he wounds the bear even a little, then he has won. It will be his victory . . . The bear's body starts shaking and it falls over, if you hit it in the right place. The Ainu uses those kinds of weapons.

There are also reports of Japanese bear-hunters who fight and wrestle with bears (Nebuka 1991: 163; NSSKS 1990: 55). The folklorist Taguchi Hiromi has recorded tales of brave bear-fighters from hunting villages in the Ani area of Akita Prefecture. One informant recalls the exploits of such men as follows:

There are many *matagi* hunters who have fought with bears, and fights with bears tended to occur in the autumn. They would use what was called a *nagasa* [a long knife] to stab the bear during the fight, the bear crying out '*guan guan*' before it fell down into the valley. Matsubashi Saburō was one of these men. He got hurt a lot, but his bear wounds always healed quickly, as they tended to be light ones. One time when Saburō was out gathering mushrooms, he suddenly encountered a bear. As he confronted the bear, he said to it, 'With this knife I shall take your life, so prepare to leave this world with no attachments', and then started to fight the bear. At that time, I was near the power station, and I saw him coming down the mountain [afterwards]. He was covered in blood, his clothes and his towel were deep red, and his head had been mauled by the bear and was cut open with blood pouring out. Back then there existed such people. (in Taguchi 1994: 200)

This same, extraordinary spirit is sometimes expressed in the nicknames given to successful bear-hunters, such as *Raion no Kiyoshi* or 'Kiyoshi the Lion' (Taguchi 1994: 294–5).

Bear-hunting is a special kind of village protection because of the elemental fear that the bear arouses. One phrase that regularly appears in newspaper headlines and other publications in connection with bear culling is *kuma taiji* or 'bear conquest'.[13] One of the classic objects of *taiji* in Japanese folklore is the *oni* or 'demon'

---

[13] See *Asahi Shinbun* (17 Oct. 1993), Kudō (1996: 166), and Watanabe (1984: 211).

(hence *oni taiji* or 'demon conquest') (H. Maruyama 1994). It is perhaps on account of its image as an *oni* that the bear readily attracts the term *taiji*. But it is not only the bear that resonates with mythological imagery in media accounts of bear pestilence. In his analysis of mass media coverage of the bear problem, Maita Kazuhiko identifies the recurrence of a particular kind of narrative, what he calls the *buyūden* or 'martial story', in which the bear appears as an evil figure vanquished by the hunter/culler who is cast as the *eiyū* or 'hero' of the story (Maita 1998*a*: 45). In this media narrative the demonic status of the bear establishes the heroic status of the bear-culler. Bear-killing heroism even extends to illegal killing or poaching. Maita Kazuhiko claims that in many remote localities there are certain men who are informally relied on to come to deal with any bears spotted in the area—what he calls *eiyūteki mitsuryōsha* or 'heroic poachers' (Maita 1998*b*: 2). But the heroism of killing bears also means that many an ordinary hunter would like to take up the challenge if the chance arose. This is the background to reports (from Hokkaido) of hunters deliberately contriving bear-sightings and encounters by luring bears (using honey and strong-smelling dried fish) to roads and other public places, as a result of which the local *ryōyūkai* is called on to cull the bear, thus providing the opportunity for the hunters involved to become heroes in their local communities.[14]

It is because of this emphasis on human spirit and courage that some Japanese bear-hunters object to the practice of winter den-hunting. The true bear-hunter is one who faces the bear out in the open, risking his life in a straight confrontation, rather than killing the bear through the underhand 'guerrilla tactics' of den-stalking (Satō 1979: 111). But at least with den-stalking, the bear is made to leave the den, so that a confrontation of sorts occurs. In the case of bear-trapping, there is no real encounter between man and bear at all, and the hunter is simply called on to shoot the trapped bear, which again leads some hunters to object in principle to this practice (Maita 1998*a*: 13). The element of risk-taking is minimized in the case of both den-stalking and (even more so) trapping; in neither case is human courage central to the killing of the bear. The issue of courage and its absence also arises in relation to those men who shoot bears out in the open. The courageous man is one who allows a bear to come into close range before shooting, but the hunter lacking in courage shoots too early and, at most, only wounds the bear. By opting to shoot at a safe distance, the hunter may well fail to kill the bear outright and instead create a wounded, angry animal all the more disposed to attack people (Maita 1998*a*: 57). From this perspective, Japan's 'problem bears' are, in part at least, the result of human cowardice.

Hunters admire the bear's qualities of strength and power. Hunters know that the bear, like the wild boar, is an animal that is not easily killed, and that to catch a

---

[14] This was mentioned by a dietman during a committee hearing (on the revision of the hunting laws) in the Japanese diet on 20 Apr. 1999 (Ogawa 1999).

bear he will probably have to hit it more than once. There are many reports of bears that manage to escape after being shot (Watanabe 1984: 161). As we saw above, bear-trappers tell of bears trapped in cages that have the strength to bend the steel bars of their cages, while bears caught in wire traps manage to escape this confinement by sacrificing the trapped leg and living thereafter as three-legged bears (Maita 1998*a*: 58). The bear's image as an especially powerful, vital animal is also related to its amazing ability to survive the winter without feeding. Taguchi Hiromi recorded the following comments from a bear-hunter in Akita Prefecture: 'Bears don't drink anything or eat anything during the winter, but just rest in a hole and overcome their hunger by licking their palms. It's incredible. Their life-force [*seimeiryoku*] is tens of times greater than that of people' (Taguchi 1994: 303). People can appropriate this power by consuming the animal. One Hongū hunter told me that the former prime minister Tanaka Kakuei, who hailed from the Niigata area of northern Japan (well known for its bear-hunting tradition), used to consume bear gall regularly, which was why 'Tanaka-sensei' ('Teacher Tanaka')— as the hunter called him—was one of the few post-war Japanese prime ministers who showed 'guts' (*gatsu*, English loanword) when in office. A similar idea is found among other Japanese hunters, such as hunters in Hokkaido who (copying a famous Ainu practice) drink the blood of slain bears or eat raw bear meat, believing that they can thereby capture the bear's power (Abe *et al.* 1986: 91–2, 100). The human appropriation of ursine vitality is further evident in the consumption of other body parts of the animal, such as the bear's paw (an aphrodisiac) and the bear's penis (a remedy for venereal disease) (Ōta 1997: 137). It is ideas such as this that underpin much of the Japanese demand for bear products that today (along with the demand elsewhere in East Asia) places such pressure on wild bear populations around the world.

There is an alternative possibility, however. Instead of appropriating the vital power of the bears he kills, the hunter can be destroyed by the vengeful power of the spirits or souls of dead bears. As is the case with wild boars and monkeys, bears can impose *tatari* curses on their human killers. These curses take the form of the death of the hunter himself, the birth of deformed children in the hunter's family, or misfortune inflicted over many generations of the hunter's family (Miyao 1989: 67–8; Hayakawa 1982: 271–2). In other tales, ungrateful or treacherous humans, who are saved or helped by bears in the *yama* (for example, by being allowed to take refuge in the bear's cave den during a snow storm) but then connive with hunters to have the bear killed, incur the *onnen* or malice of the bear's spirit (Hiraiwa 1983: 97–9). Mindful of the power of the bear's spirit, Japanese bear-hunters take a range of precautions following a bear kill, including not bringing the meat into the house or even into the village, avoiding the use of the word *kuma* (bear), not visiting shrines for a week after the kill (Sakuma 1985: 16–17; 1980), performing a ritual to pacify the bear's spirit (Sakuma 1980: 177), reciting a sutra (Yamazaki 1996: 26), establishing 'bear-graves' (Chiba 1975: 117), and worshipping 'the bones of the killed bear, buried behind the house' (Naumann 1974: 7). These reports of the ritual treatment of the dead bear in the bear-range regions of Japan suggest that the lives of bears and humans were, in some respects, viewed as commensurable and even equivalent (see Nakamura 1987: 79–80).

CONSERVATIONISTS AND BEARS

The representation of the bear as a dangerous, destructive creature underpins the status of the hunter as the defender of the village. But, despite the emergence of the 'bear problem', the fearsome image of the bear as a rampaging 'demon' no longer seems so credible. Instead, the bear increasingly appears a victim of the destruction of the forest environment. Conservationists are highly critical of the modern forestry industry for having caused the deterioration of bear habitat (Hazumi 1992: 298). There is evidence to suggest that, just as modern forestry practices contribute to plantation damage by wild ungulates, so they are one of the contributory factors in bear damage (Azuma and Torii 1980). Dam construction and tourist resort development have also contributed to the decline in bear habitat. It is against this background of large-scale habitat loss that bear specialists and conservationists call for the establishment of special bear refuges or reservations in the mountainous interior large enough to ensure the continuity of self-supporting bear populations (Watanabe 1981: 583; Hazumi 1994: 148). Conservationists further argue that effective bear protection would contribute to the conservation of Japanese forest ecology in general. In the words of one conservationist, 'to protect the bear is to protect the forest' (in *AS* 25 Nov. 1995; cf. *AS* 29 Oct. 1988). The state of bear habitat is held to be a 'barometer' of the beech forest ecology (Takahashi 1995: 117). Japanese conservationists argue that the bear is 'the representative large wild animal of our country' (Takahashi 1995: 117) and the representative mammal of the Japanese forest (Kawasaki 1993*b*: 151). There can be no real *mori* or forest without the bear: 'if the bear disappears, the forest becomes empty' (in *AS* 10 Dec. 1994). These terms recall the idea advanced in wider conservation circles that large predators are 'umbrella species', the conservation requirements of which encompass the requirements of a wide range of other wildlife species sharing the same habitat area (see Noss *et al.* 1996).

In addition to the loss of forest habitat, the other main threat to bear numbers in Japan is the high rate of bear culling. Critics charge that the bear culling carried out in the name of pest control is disproportionate to the actual threat posed by bears, and is the result of an irrational fear of bears rather than a proper reasoned response to the bear problem (Hazumi 1999: 211). Some critics go further and suggest that the scale of bear culling in Japan is due to the commercial value of the bear parts, especially the gall bladder, as much as the economic loss due to bear damage (Mizoguchi 1992: 33; Hazumi 1994: 147). It is the high market value of the bear itself (its parts), rather than the value of the damage it causes, which motivates the culling. In short, much bear culling is disguised bear-hunting.[15] Conservationists point out that human society must assume its share of the responsibility for the bear encounters and attacks that occur (and that lead to culling) and that many of these bear incidents are preventable. Bear specialists call for a programme of public education to change human behaviour towards bears in Japan—such as better management of the garbage that inadvertently creates food-conditioned bears (Mano and Moll 1999: 130). Another aim of public education would be to change popular perceptions of the bear. It is often pointed out that there are two dominant images of bears in Japan: the violent monster that mauls and kills people and the cute, toy-like animal. The first image generates an exaggerated fear of the animal, while the second image encourages an inappropriate familiarity towards it. Neither image accords with reality, and one of the main tasks of bear conservation in Japan is to diffuse a more realistic image of the bear (Hazumi and Yoshii 1994*b*: 44).

Japanese conservationists call for the adoption of non-lethal methods of bear control. The Forestry Agency issues guidelines to prefectural governors which stress that the first course of action should be to chase the bear back into the forest, rather than shoot or trap the animal (Mizoguchi 1992: 32). The relocation of captured bears is an alternative to lethal forms of control, one which has been pioneered by a remote municipality in western Japan (Kurisu 2001). In addition to saving the life of the bear, proponents justify bear relocation in terms of the benefits of widening the sphere of genetic exchange—something that becomes all the more important as bear numbers dwindle and the danger of inbreeding among local bear subpopulations increases (Maita 1996*a*: 182). However, bear relocation is only rarely carried out in Japan. One problem is that victim farmers and foresters fear that the bears in question will simply return to bother them. To allay such fears, the authorities promise that bear relocation will take place far away from the place of capture in order to ensure that the bears do not return. But long-distance bear relocation can become a cause of friction between different localities. This is because the relocation of a destructive bear to the distant forest does not necessarily put an end to the matter, for the bear may well descend to cause problems in villages on the other side of the mountains in a different municipal area. Where this occurs, it can give the impression of one municipality simply 'exporting' its bear problem to another, and provoke responses such as the following: 'If a released bear from your municipality causes damage over here, pay compensation!' (see Maita 1996*a*: 187; cf. Azumane 1997: 40). In this way, non-lethal methods of bear management are hampered by local rivalries within the region.

Many conservationists condemn the intolerance shown towards bears in Japan and call instead for a new era of people–bear *kyōzon* or 'coexistence' (H. Watanabe

---

[15] Villagers have sometimes been allowed to keep the commercially valuable parts (such as the gall bladders) of the culled bear pests as a form of compensation for the damage they have incurred (Hazumi 1994: 147).

1989: 141; Hazumi 1992: 308). In one newspaper article on the problem of brown bears in Hokkaido the words of a university professor are quoted: 'there should be an awareness [in Japan] that wild animals are the precious property of the nation as a whole' (*AS* 2 June 1990). But calls for coexistence with bears or respect for bears can elicit angry responses from the people who actually live in bear country. Harato Shōjirō recorded the following comments in rural Hiroshima.

People talk about 'coexistence, coexistence', but it [our situation] is not a joke. It is crazy to talk about coexistence with bears. You are talking about a savage animal, while we are human beings—mostly old people. This is not the bear's land, this is a place where we have lived since long, long ago. Please give a thought to us! (in Harato 1994: 109)

This rural sense of grievance is only heightened when villagers, in whose own area a moratorium on bear culling is in place, see that whenever a bear emerges in a city it is immediately shot dead. Residents in rural Hiroshima make precisely this point: 'when in the city a bear is spotted they kill it, so why do they pressure us about conservation?' (*AS* 25 Nov. 1995). Even though the likelihood of a bear encounter is far greater in remote areas than in the city, mountain villagers see themselves as receiving less protection from bears. The impression is created that public safety in remote rural areas counts for less than in the city.

   Implicit in the conservationist argument for people–bear 'coexistence' is the idea that the bear, as an integral part of the Japanese forest and of Japan's natural heritage, is an intrinsically valuable animal whose survival is in the national interest and should therefore be made a national priority. But some local residents in bear-range areas do not share this view, as is clear from the following comment directed to one bear conservationist: 'In Kyushu, since the bear became extinct, not one person has suffered as a result. What is the reason that bears should exist?' (in Maita 1996*a*: 190).[16] Other conservationists have found themselves challenged along similar lines: 'Which is important, human life or the bear?' (Watanabe 1984: 215; cf. Maita 1998*a*: 13). Conservationists have also suffered attacks on their property and other threatening behaviour towards them (the smashing of windows, nuisance telephone calls late at night, and even physical threats). These expressions of hostility to bears and to bear conservationists would seem to suggest a deep-seated antipathy to the very existence of bears in remote areas of Japan. Yet the conservationist Maita Kazuhiko offers a somewhat different interpretation of these events. He believes that mountain villagers have become hostile to bear conservation not so much because of the damage they have incurred, but because of what they see as the indifference of wider Japanese society to this damage (Maita 1996*a*: 151–2). Mountain villagers experience bear conservation as a set of urban attitudes that downplay or deny their suffering. The national concern for the well-being of the bear presents all too stark a contrast with the national neglect of remote areas.

[16] For similar comments, see H. Watanabe (1989: 138), Yamazaki (1996: 38), and Azumane (1997: 34, 86).

Not unlike the serow in the last chapter, the bear has become a symbol of national disregard of remote areas in the post-war era.

Bears are not, however, simply the object of rural hostility. There also exist more sympathetic views of bears in upland areas of Japan—among hunters and among other villagers. As the people who hunt and cull bears, hunters are on the front line of the struggle against bears. As we have seen, the killing of bears, as a measure of manly status, carries a great symbolic significance among bear-hunters. But the killing of a bear can generate mixed feelings and even sentiments of regret. A reference to this ambivalence felt by the bear-hunter appears in a famous story by the writer Miyazawa Kenji. A bear-hunter explains to a bear why he had to shoot it:

Don't think I killed you, Bear, because I hated you. I have to make a living, just as you have to be shot. I'd like to do different work, work with no sin attached, but I've got no fields, and they say my trees belong to the authorities, and when I go to the village nobody will have anything to do with me. I'm a hunter because I can't help it. It's fate that made you a bear, and it's fate that made me do this work. Make sure you're not re-born as a bear next time. (Miyazawa 1993: 61)

Similar sentiments are apparent even among modern bear-hunters who otherwise celebrate their conquest over bears. Fujiwara Chōtarō tells of how, when on a culling trip to dispatch problem bears, he caught sight of the animals on a distant mountainside through his binoculars.

When I looked closely, I saw one three month old bear cub sitting contentedly in the spring sunlight, another riding on the back of its mother, and a third clinging to its mother's teat. When I saw this innocent scene of the parents and cubs together, even I, who has made a living by killing bears, lost my hunting desire. My heart was attacked by this all too wonderful scene, which I just stood watching, forgetting myself. (Fujiwara 1979: 36–7)

Hunter concern for bears is further evident in reports suggesting that Japanese hunters traditionally avoided killing mother bears (Tabuchi 1992: 18; Tanigawa 1980: 329) and spared bear cubs (Ichikawa and Saitō 1985: 176) in order to ensure that there were bears to hunt in the future.[17]

In addition to such feelings elicited by living bears, hunters may also feel an obligation to dead bears. Precisely because of its contribution to human livelihoods and well-being in the past, the bear can generate feelings of gratitude. This is indicated by one of Azumane Chimao's informants in Iwate Prefecture who points out that in the past the bear's body substances were of great medicinal importance in the doctorless mountain villages of the region. In particular, the local custom existed where hunters would give the invigorating blood of a recently killed bear to women and children back in the village. In this way, bear blood contributed to the

---

[17] It is sometimes claimed that Japanese bear-hunters traditionally observed restraint in the number of bear lives they took. Higashiyama Shōzō recalls the expression, *yotsuguma o toru na* or 'Don't take [all] four bears', although the more common expression is *mitsuguma o toru na* or 'Don't take [all] three bears'.

well-being of childbearing women and to the nurturance of children, just as other parts of its body cured various maladies and disorders (Azumane 1997: 85–6). On the Kii Peninsula, bear gall was valued for similar reasons, and stories are told of people saved by the curative powers of bear gall—such as the Wakayama villagers drafted to Manchuria in the 1930s who believe that, thanks to the bear gall they took with them, they avoided the dysentery and other sicknesses that debilitated so many of their fellow soldiers (WKRNS 1979: 62). This sense of indebtedness to bears is what inspires some people to express support for bear conservation. As Azumane's informant above puts it, just as in the past village ancestors 'were helped by bears', so the current generation of villagers has an *ongaeshi* or 'obligation' to help the bear in its time of difficulty (Azumane 1997: 85–6). One further expression of the hunter's concern for bears is the voluntary moratorium on hunting bears observed by some prefectural *ryōyūkai* (including Wakayama), along with the active involvement in bear conservation of other *ryōyūkai*. The *ryōyūkai* of Toyama Prefecture, for example, is involved in planting fruit-bearing trees and establishing denning sites in the forest for the bears (*AS* 17 Aug. 1990).

Sympathy for the bear is not confined to hunters, but extends to other mountain villagers. In many remote areas there is a routine familiarity with the bear, such that a sighting does not necessarily generate the kind of panic described earlier in this chapter. The point is made by a villager in Akita Prefecture: 'For us, living in these mountains, bears are a normal part of life, because we are in a place where bears live. If we were so scared of bears that we never went to the mountains, we would not be able to live here' (Taguchi 1994: 57). Maita Kazuhiko describes a scene in Hiroshima Prefecture in which three bears (a mother and two cubs) come to a village to feed on a persimmon tree. As the village dogs bark wildly, people come over to watch the bears feeding, and are soon absorbed by the spectacle. At a time when bears had become a serious problem in such remote areas, Maita was impressed at the lack of fear or hatred of the bears shown by the villagers.

One old woman who was beating a *tatami* mat [nearby] said, 'those are bitter persimmons, the bears won't eat them', but the bears were assiduously eating them . . . Three old women came over . . . Each face had a grin on it, as they murmured, 'it's fascinating, isn't it?' Behind them more people were coming over to watch. The old women seemed to realize that bears do not recklessly attack people, and did not say anything like 'shoot that horrible bear!' . . . Perhaps in this lonely depopulated hamlet, the bear is [seen as] just a neighbour in the forest [*mori ni iru rinjin*]. For these grandmothers, even if their persimmons are being eaten up, the feeling is, 'oh, you're back', like they are waiting for the bears to appear each year. (Maita 1996*a*: 52)

As the bear is an annual visitor, villagers are not unduly alarmed by its appearance. Besides, the autumn visit of the bear is a regular event, an expression of the season not unlike the appearance of the bright orange persimmons that attract it. The bear is a neighbour, not a monster.

One would not expect much sympathy for bears from foresters. Given their damage to timber plantations, bears readily appear the enemy of the forester. Yet foresters' views of bears are not reducible to the feelings of outrage felt at the sight of barkstripped trees or fears about possible bear encounters. Working everyday in the forest, many forest labourers are just as aware of the impact of forestry on the bear as that of the bear on forestry. They are aware that the spatial distribution of bears is now different: that bears are observed less and less in their former locations and are increasingly encountered in new places such as near roads and even in town centres (*AS* 12 July 1994; Azumane 1997: 111–12). They are also aware that bears are increasingly unable to find suitable trees for winter denning, and are forced to den in the most inappropriate places, such as near noisy roads, in abandoned charcoal kilns, in old mine shafts, in draughty caves, or indeed in older timber plantations. Foresters recognize that these changes in bear behaviour are related to the human transformation of the *yama* brought about by the modern forestry industry in which they work. Murata Yoshio attributes the cause of the bear problem to the earlier actions of human society.

What it comes down to is that the trees of the mixed forest and of the shiny-leafed forest that have been there since ancient times have all been cut down and replaced by cedars and cypresses. When that happens, the food of the bear disappears. In the mountains there are nuts that fall from trees, the evergreen oaks and so on, aren't there? Well, that's the only food for the bear and the serow and the others. It is because that has disappeared that they leave nature and come down to the edge of the village. Then they run up against human beings. The bear too wants to live its life, and so it comes down [to the village] . . . That's the way it is. In the end, it all has to do with the way human beings have mistreated nature a bit too much.

The bear population also appears to have atomized. As a result of displacement and falling numbers, individual bears have become isolated and have difficulty finding mates. This situation leads some villagers to draw a parallel between the displaced, mateless bears and the generation of young men who have been subjected to urban outmigration, on the one hand, and rural celibacy, on the other.

For bears and people alike, the place of dwelling has been ruined. Just as the bear must come down from the now bald mountain peak to the plantations, so people must leave the village to work outside. Also, as their numbers have decreased, bears have great difficulty meeting a spouse. For example, in the southern mountains of the peninsula, there are isolated bears that will probably end up as lifelong bachelors. Is this not a rather similar situation to that of those mountain village youth who cannot find brides? . . . The situation today is that, because of the damage to the forest, bears and people have together received a great blow. They are both victims [*higaisha*] who have been robbed [*shudatsu sareta*] by the high-growth economy. (Ue 1983: 366–7)

As animal migrants, driven out of their forest home by the forces of modern development, bears can elicit sympathy among villagers whose siblings and children have been forced to migrate to earn a living or who themselves had to migrate before returning in later life.

In mountainous areas, there is a belief that the *yama*, especially the remoter parts of it, is the bear's *kuni* or 'country'. One costly expression of the bear's claim to the forest is the animal's barkstripping of trees, including the conifers of the timber plantations—in which bears assert their 'right of occupancy' of the area to other bears (Hida 1971: 200). Watanabe Hiroyuki makes a similar point when he recounts how in remote parts of Kyōto Prefecture bears chew and knock over the painted red posts placed in the forest by surveyors. While Watanabe himself attributes such incidents to the bears' partiality to the taste of paint, nearby villagers interpret the bear's behaviour as active defiance of human attempts to survey the forest. 'For the mountain people, it showed that the bears were angry at this brazen attempt, without permission, to place landmarks in the natural forest which they [the bears] think of as their own country' (Watanabe 1984: 203). Yet the bears have lost much of their 'country' to forestry and other forms of development. Planted conifers have replaced much of the fruit-bearing forest vegetation on which bears depend, while golf courses and ski-slopes are also responsible for deforestation and habitat loss. A hunter in Iwate Prefecture characterizes the bear's plight in the following terms.

Whether you look to the right or look to the left, where there used to be chestnut and acorn forest there is [now] nothing but ski-slopes. It's like a ski-slope has been built right through the middle of the bear's fields [*kuma no hatake*]. If you are a bear [in this situation], you start to want to descend to the [village] fields, don't you? (in Azumane 1997: 109)

These comments suggest that human–bear relations in upland Japan are interpreted in terms of a principle of reciprocity. While farmers may complain about bear *gaijū* or 'pests' in their fields, there is none the less a recognition among the local population that bears are reacting to prior human actions that have affected them—that is, that the bear's 'fields' have been invaded and that the bear is the victim of human transgressions. This sentiment was explicitly voiced to me during an interview by the retired schoolteacher Higashiyama Shōzō who inverted the usual terms of pestilence discourse to depict the bear as the victim of *human* 'pests': 'When I hear the word "pest" applied to the bear, I say that "it is humans who are the pests".'[18] Bear farm damage is a consequence of human society denying the bear its means to livelihood. It is because the bear has lost its 'fields' in the forest that it decides to come to feed in the human fields in the village. If the cause of bear crop-raiding lies in a prior human appropriation of bear feeding grounds, it follows that the proper human response should be to return to the bear its 'fields'. To this end, Higashiyama Shōzō has himself been in the forefront of efforts in the late 1990s to plant fruit-bearing trees in the mountains of the Kii Peninsula in order

[18] Similar comments appear in reports from other regions—see Takahashi (1984: 92) and Maita (1998a: 80).

to try to restore bear habitat. Similarly, one rural town in Hiroshima planted 15,000 chestnut trees on six hectares of municipal land, with the catchphrase, 'fruit for the bear, wood for the town' (Maita 1996*a*: 188). In some cases, these human attempts to enhance the bear's wild food supply even extend to the establishment of literal fields in the forest—that is, of cornfields in forest clearings which, as *kuma no hatake* or 'the bear's fields', wild bears are at liberty to 'harvest' (Maita 1998*a*: 164).

Just as farmers look to hunters for protection from the wild boar, and foresters rely on hunters for protection against the deer, so foresters look to hunters to protect them from the bear. Moreover, as bears are deemed a threat to human life, as well as human livelihood, there is a sense in which hunters are the protectors of the whole community against the 'black demon' from the forest. But there is another facet to the forester–hunter relationship, one that is absent in the farmer–hunter relationship. Unlike the farmer, the forester has the power to transform the wildlife habitat of the *yama*—the very space in which the hunt takes place. Hunters are all too well aware of the transformation of the *yama* in the post-war period as a result of the forestry industry, not least in the disappearance of old animal trails and paths in the forest. Much of the traditional hunting knowledge of the whereabouts of animals in the *yama* no longer applies in the plantation-dominated landscape of the present day. Forestry's effect on hunting is at its most serious in relation to the bear, the future existence of which appears in doubt in many areas of Japan. If in the short term the successful hunter protects forestry from the bear, in the long term forestry deprives the hunter of the bear. The plight of the bear has become all too visible in recent times, to the point where the animal readily appears a wretched victim of post-war forestry. In contrast to other categories of wildlife, bear numbers are clearly in decline. While animals such as the wild boar, the monkey, and the deer appear excessive in number to the point where they spill over into human territory, the bear appears simply displaced. But as a traditionally unseen animal of the *okuyama* that has descended to villages and surrounding forests, the bear's is an extreme form of displacement. For upland dwellers, the bear appears to be an animal out of place, to the point where it can become a fitting symbol of displacement in human society. When bears are considered *in relation to the forest*, they can bring into view people *in relation to the village*.

6
Wolves

Negative views of wolves have been widely reported. In Europe and North America the wolf has been variously associated with the devil, evil, and death and widely persecuted.[1] It is against this background of widespread human hatred of wolves that the case of the Japanese wolf is of particular interest. On the one hand, the extinction of the wolf at the beginning of the twentieth century is a testament to the human conflict with, and persecution of, wolves that took place in eighteenth- and nineteenth-century Japan. On the other hand, the wolf occupied an important place in folk Shinto as a messenger of the *kami* spirits. Although wolves inspired fear, there also existed a positive view of relationship with the wolf in Japan, one that appears to have been associated with its status as a predator of wildlife crop-raiders. In upland areas of Japan, in other words, the wolf appeared as a human ally in the wildlife 'wars' described in earlier chapters. This chapter examines these different aspects of people–wolf relations in Japan. The first part outlines two contrasting images of the wolf in Japan: the wolf as a threatening predator and the wolf as a benign protector. The second part looks at the strong association between dogs and wolves in Japan, with specific reference to the hounds used by Japanese hunters. The third part of the chapter examines the proposal to reintroduce wolves to Japan, along with the local reactions to it on the Kii Peninsula, and the fourth part considers the implications of the wolf reintroduction proposal for Japanese hunters.

IMAGES OF THE WOLF

Wolves and Space

The Japanese wolf was a grey-haired animal which stood at a shoulder height of just over 30 centimetres and weighed an estimated 20 kilogrammes. This small animal has been viewed as significantly different from other wolves, and even considered a species of wolf in its own right (Obara 1987: 53) and referred to as *Canis hodophylax* (Ueno 1987: 24).[2] Most Japanese biologists reject this claim and regard the

---

[1] See Harting (1994: 12–13), Kavanagh (1994: 135, 119), Bojović and Colić (1975: 60), Fogleman (1989), Lopez (1995), and Hampton (1996).
[2] This 'separate species' position is particularly associated with the zoologist Imaizumi Yoshinori who, on the basis of a comparative craniological analysis of a wide range of wolf specimens, concluded

Japanese wolf as a subspecies of the grey wolf, a status reflected in the use of the scientific name *Canis lupus hodophylax* instead of *Canis hodophylax.* As we shall see, this disagreement about the taxonomic status of the Japanese wolf, while it may at first seem somewhat arcane, re-emerges as a key point of contention in the present-day debate over wolf reintroduction.[3] The conventional name for the wolf in Japanese is *ōkami*, a name homonymic with the word for 'great spirit' (even though they are written with different characters), leading some writers to suggest that the wolf was originally perceived as a *kami* spirit (Saitō 1983: 22). But the wolf has been given many names, including regional variations of the word *ōkami* (such as *ōkame*, *okame*, and *ohokame*); *yamainu* or 'mountain dog', the name by which the wolf was known in much of Japan, particularly on the Kii Peninsula and elsewhere in western Japan; and other names such as *oinu* ('venerable dog'), and *ōkuchino-makami* ('the true god of the large mouth'). Honorific prefixes (such as '*o*') or suffixes (such as-*tono* or-*sama*) are attached to traditional wolf names, indicating that the wolf was an object of respect. The Chinese character for the wolf 狼 (pronounced as *rō* or *ōkami*) consists of two parts: the radical (for wild animal) 犭 and the character for good 良, that, as we shall see, tends to be interpreted as evidence that the wolf was originally viewed as a benign rather than harmful animal in Japan, in contrast to the traditional view of the wolf in Western cultures.

The last known wolf in Japan was killed by a lumber raftsman on 23 January 1905 in a place called Washikaguchi on the Kii Peninsula. The raftsman later asked the local temple priest to carry out a *kuyō* or memorial rite for the wolf, which has become an annual event that continues to this day. The remains of the last wolf were purchased at the time by an American zoologist on behalf of an English duke and are held by the Natural History Museum in London. In recent years the municipality of Higashi Yoshino-mura, in which Washikaguchi lies, projects itself to the wider world as 'the place of the last Japanese wolf'. To this end, it has erected a bronze statue of a howling wolf to commemorate the Japanese wolf. The statue is located near to where the last wolf is believed to have died and has become a well-known local landmark and a tourist attraction. The municipality has also produced glossy publicity pamphlets that describe to visitors what kind of animal the wolf was (a loyal, co-operative, and family-centred animal), the background to the wolf's demise, and the wolf's importance as a part of Japan's natural heritage. One of the pamphlets carries a photograph of the rolling mountains of the Yoshino region, green and lush with snowy white peaks, below which are written the words *maboroshi no nihonōkami*, 'the phantom Japanese wolf'. As part

that the Japanese wolf was 'a distinct species well differentiated from any other forms of the genus' (Imaizumi 1987: 33).

[3] As a result of its extinction and the small number of specimens available, the Japanese wolf has occupied an uncertain place in general wolf taxonomy and international wolf studies. See, for example, Nowak (1983: 11; 1995: 394). On earlier taxonomic doubts about the Japanese wolf, see Satow and Hawes (1884: 40).

FIG. 6.1. A pre-war postcard of a wolf in a Japanese zoo

of its efforts to revive the memory of the wolf, the municipality has even tried to bring back the stuffed remains of the last wolf from London with a view to putting the wolf on display.[4]

However, not everyone in Japan accepts that wolves are extinct. Over the years there have been many reports of wolf-sightings, wolf-tracks, wolf howls, and even wolf remains, along with claims of the discovery of wolf–dog hybrids, especially on the Kii Peninsula.[5] There are amateur naturalists and wolf enthusiasts in different parts of the country who devote much time and energy to trying to prove that wolves still exist by searching the remote mountains for signs and evidence of wolves. One group of would-be wolf-finders mounts all-night vigils, known as *sasoidashi* or 'luring out', during which they broadcast recorded wolf howls into the mountains in order to elicit real wolf howls in response (an established research technique first devised by North American wolf specialists in the 1950s) and

---

[4] During a trip to the Kii Peninsula in 1994 I learnt that Higashi Yoshino-mura had asked the museum to allow it to display the wolf remains locally, but that this request was apparently refused by the museum authorities.

[5] While such claims arise across Japan, a disproportionate amount of them refer to the Kii Peninsula. Hiraiwa (1992: 250–83) gives details of twenty-six separate claims made between 1908 and 1978: twelve of these claims are distributed evenly across the country (from Aomori in the north-east to Ōita in the south-west), but all of the remaining fourteen claims are from the prefectures of Nara and Wakayama on the Kii Peninsula.

thereby obtain proof of wolf existence—though, to date, without any success.[6] A recent example of such 'wolf mania' appeared in November 2000 when a photograph of a wolf-like animal in the mountains of Kyushu was obtained by the mass media, leading to a profusion of newspaper, magazine, and television stories suggesting that a living Japanese wolf had been found.[7] Neither this nor the many other claimed wolf-sightings in Japan have ever been formally confirmed or officially endorsed. Although events like the *sasoidashi* 'wolf hunts' invariably attract considerable tabloid-style publicity, they are not otherwise taken very seriously and appear, above all, to have a public entertainment value, while reports of wolf-sightings tend to be dismissed by academic zoologists and public authorities. In a forest-covered landscape like Japan, the non-existence of a wild animal cannot be definitely proved. Yet in the absence of a *verified* sighting for nearly a century such anecdotal challenges to the wolf extinction orthodoxy have little credibility (especially when extinction is understood in terms of whether or not a reproductive *population* of animals exists). There is a general, albeit not universal, acceptance in present-day Japan that wolves are extinct.

Although there are no longer wolves in the Japanese mountains, there are many rural place-names that contain the character for wolf 狼. Examples of the wolf's toponymic legacy on the Kii Peninsula include place-names such as Ōkamitaira ('Wolf Plateau'), Ōkamikaidō ('Wolf Highway'), and Ōkamizawa ('Wolf Marsh').[8] Typically, these wolf places were viewed as dangerous and to be avoided, especially at night. In some cases, even where there is no explicit place-name, an area is associated with the wolf because wolves were seen, heard, or encountered there in the past. One such place is the forest around the abandoned village of Heichigawa in Hongū, which was known to have a wolf den within it and was reputed to be a strange, mysterious spot that was cold in the summer and warm in the winter (WKMK 1981: 85). In fact, the wolf continues to mark spaces in present-day Japan, such as through the existence of wolf shrines. A wolf shrine is a Shinto shrine in which the wolf serves as the *otsukai* or messenger of the *kami* (a role that may be performed in other shrines by animals such as the fox and the snake). Wolf shrines offered protection from a variety of dangers, including, as we shall see, from farm pests. There are estimated to have been more than twenty main wolf shrines on the

---

[6] The Nara Prefecture Wildlife Protection Committee carried out *sasoidashi* on the Kii Peninsula in 1994, in Okuchichibu in Saitama Prefecture in 1995, and elsewhere in subsequent years (*YS* 12 Nov. 1994; NYSHI n.d.: 230–50).

[7] The term 'wolf mania' (*ōkamimania*) is used by Maruyama Naoki, the head of the Japan Wolf Association.

[8] Other examples include Ōkamiiwa ('Wolf Rock'), Ōkamidaoshi ('Wolf Prey'), and Kobirōtoge ('Howling Wolf Pass'). Some of these places have been renamed over time in an effort to conceal their wolf association—for example, the area of Kobirōtoge (on the border between the modern municipalities of Hongū-chō and Nakahechi-chō) had its Chinese characters changed from 吼比狼峠 (for 'Howling Wolf Pass') to 小広峠 (for 'Small Wide Pass'). Many people in Hongū remain aware of its old wolf-related name.

FIG. 6.2. An *ema* from Mitsumine Shrine

main Japanese island of Honshu, including nationally famous shrines such as Mitsumine in Chichibu, attesting to the existence of an *ōkami shinkō* or 'wolf religion' among the Japanese people (Maruyama *et al.* 1996: 199; Hiraiwa 1992: 90; *MS* 19 Aug. 1990).[9] There were also many small, local wolf shrines, which tended to be related (through the *ofuda* charms enshrined within them) to the larger wolf shrines. There are a number of wolf shrines on the Kii Peninsula, such as Tamaki Shrine and Takataki Shrine (both in Totsukawa-mura).[10]

Wolf as Threat

Compared with the rural livestock economies in Europe and North America, wolf damage to livestock in Japan was on a small scale. Livestock occupied only a minor place in the peasant economy of early modern Japan; domesticated animals were widely kept, but these were animals used for transport and draught purposes rather then for meat and dairy products. None the less, from the late seventeenth century,

---

[9] Many of the wolf shrines have their own wolf legends. For example, the Yamazumi Shrine in Shizuoka Prefecture is known for the legend whereby during the civil war period in the late sixteenth century, at the time of the battle of Mikatagahara, Tokugawa Ieyasu, on the run from the forces of Takeda Shingen, was saved when he hid in the shrine, and a wolf howl frightened their pursuers away (*MS* 19 Aug. 1990). In this way, wolves saved the life of the man who would go on to unify Japan as the *shōgun*. In the Yamatsumi Shrine of Fukushima Prefecture, the *otsukai* is a white wolf that, according to legend, in the Heian period helped save local people from a notorious villain known as Sumitora or 'Charcoal Tiger' (Anon. 2000*b*).

[10] On wolf shrines, see Nakamori (1940: 32–3), KHI (1980: 31), and *Kii Minpō* (29 Sept. 1972).

there are reports of livestock attacks in Japan. Wolves appear to have been a threat to village horses in many regions (Chiba 1995*a*: 175; Maruyama *et al.* 1996: 199). Between 1644 and 1672, over 270 horses were attacked and killed by wolves in one area of Tōhoku (Hiraiwa 1992: 128). In the late 1880s wolf attacks on grazing horses occurred in the Nagano area (Matsuyama 1977*a*: 178). Wolves are reported to have attacked, killed, and even eaten village dogs on the Kii Peninsula and elsewhere.[11] Wolf attacks on village dogs were especially common in the Nagano region, to the point where, in some areas, it became difficult to raise dogs (Matsuyama 1977*a*: 168–70). Hounds (including those bred to hunt bears and wild boar) could be particularly vulnerable to wolf predation because they tended to respond to the nearby presence of wolves by charging off into the forest where they risked fatal attack by packs of wolves (Matsuyama 1977*a*: 167). These attacks on dogs are believed to have been one source of transmission of the rabies pathogen to wolves (Matsuyama 1977*a*: 169).

There is evidence that the wolf was feared as a potential predator on people. Wolf attacks on people are reported from the second half of the seventeenth century. With the spread of rabies in late seventeenth-century Japan, the image of the wolf as a benign spirit started to change to that of a mortal threat. The first report of rabid wolves (in Kyushu and Shikoku) occurred in 1732, after which the disease spread eastwards (Maruyama *et al.* 1996: 200). So widespread was rabies that in the Tokugawa period the word *yamainu* became synonymous with the rabid dog that attacked people (Chiba 1995*a*: 51). In the Shinshū area, while adults gathered grass near the forest they made their children wait in nearby trees as a safeguard against wolf attacks (*MS* 27 May 1990). In the Yoshino area of the Kii Peninsula there is a Jizō statue in the forest commemorating a child killed by a wolf (*MS* 17 Dec. 1989). In *Hokuetsu seppu* (*Snow Country Tales*), written in the early nineteenth century, a wolf incident from Echigo (present-day Niigata Prefecture) is graphically described in which three wolves attacked a remote household and killed three people (Suzuki 1986: 240). One category of people particularly vulnerable to wolf attacks were field-guards protecting crops from the wild boar and other animals (*MS* 21 Jan. 1990; Matsuyama 1977*a*: 160–8). But this duty could prove particularly hazardous for the field-guard because the forest-edge fields would be visited not just by wild boar and deer intent on feeding on the crops, but also by hungry wolves intent on feeding on these animal crop-raiders. The hapless field-guards found themselves inadvertently caught up in the predator–prey relations of the forest, now transposed to the forest-edge. A second reason why wolves threatened field-guards had to do with the noise emitted from the field-guard's hut—the banging of drums and shouting that was intended to keep crop-raiding animals away. In contrast to other forest animals, wolves were known to be drawn to noise, such that field-guards, in their efforts to deter wild boar and deer, were in effect 'calling the wolf' (Miyamoto *et al.* 1995: 394).

---

[11] See Suzuki (1986: 239), *MS* (14 Jan. 1990), *MS* (28 Apr. 1991), and Hiraiwa (1992: 130).

Whatever the precise scale of wolf predation on livestock or wolf attacks on people in Japan, there is no doubt that the wolf was feared, to some extent at least, as a potential threat to Man. There are many Japanese word compounds containing the Chinese character for wolf that have highly negative meanings, including *rōsei* or 'wolf voice' (a frightening voice), *rōko* or 'wolfish look' (a menacing glance), *rōzeki* or 'wolf mess' (riot), *rōshitsu* or 'wolf sickness' (a terrible sickness), and *nakayama ōkami* or 'mountain wolf' (a savage). Dictionaries explain many of these Japanese wolf terms as metaphors of human greed: *rōko* ('wolves and tigers') is 'an expression applied to people who, because of their greed, harm others'; *rōshin* ('wolf heart') is 'a heart that is greedy like a wolf's'; and *rōtan* ('wolf greed') is applied to people who are 'insatiably covetous like a wolf' (Akatsuka *et al.* 1993: 682). An incorrigibly greedy man is an *ōkamimono* or 'wolf man', while the tyrannical mother-in-law who bullies and mistreats her son's wife is an *ōkamibaba* or 'wolf granny' (Suzuki 1986: 244). This impressive Japanese lexicon of wolf terms led one commentator to conclude that 'without a doubt . . . wolves are the most hated of animals' (Iwase Momoki, in Suzuki 1986: 244). In *Tōno monogatari*, Yanagita Kunio records the local view that 'there is nothing that is so terribly frightening as the growl of the wolf [*oinu*]' (Yanagita 1992: 34), while the scholar Ueno Masumi writes that the Japanese wolf has been 'deeply impressed on the memory of people as a dreadful carnivore . . .' (Ueno 1987: 24). Another indication of the frightening image of the wolf was that, up until the end of the nineteenth century, parents on the Kii Peninsula would deal with the unruly behaviour of their children by warning them that 'if you do that, the wolf will carry you off!' (Nakamori 1940: 33–4). A great many other rural tales and legends likewise suggest that wolves were an object of fear.

A variety of means were employed by mountain villagers to keep wolves away. One anti-wolf measure was the physical guarding of livestock. Up until the late nineteenth century in what is now Nagano Prefecture, *yamainuban* or 'wolf watches' were undertaken to guard horses put out to pasture (Matsuyama 1977*a*: 178). Even more than the field-guarding mentioned above, such livestock-guarding appears to have been a dangerous task because of the possibility of wolf encounters. But ritual means were also used to stop wolf attacks, including *kitō* or prayer (Hiraiwa 1992: 132; *MS* 19 Aug. 1990). It has been suggested that wolf shrines too helped to protect people from wolf attacks, with people visiting these shrines to make requests for protection from wolf damage and obtain charms known as *rōgaiyoke* or 'wolf damage repellents' (*MS* 19 Aug. 1990). Villagers on the Kii Peninsula petitioned their tutelary spirit (known as the *ujigami*), through ritual song and dance, to protect them against wolf attacks.[12] In the Hongū village of Fushiogami, farm households nailed *sarunote* or 'monkey hands' on to their cowsheds to repel wolves—the monkey was traditionally a means of repelling the wolf

[12] See *MS* (15 Jan. 1989); *MS* (19 Mar. 1989); *MS* (14 Oct. 1990).

三峯神社

FIG. 6.3. A *fumi* card (a pre-paid card used for post office purchases) sold at Mitsumine Shrine

in Japan—and the practice is still in evidence in this village today. One example is the house of Matsumoto Sadao, which is located near the top of Fushiogami and has a panoramic view of the Hatenashi mountain range. The Matsumotos protected their cows by placing the 'monkey hands' above the entrance to the cowshed. Although Matsumoto-san is not one of those people who think that there are still wolves in the *yama*, he does believe that the monkey hands offer the family a more general protection against misfortune.

Wolves posed a threat to the dead, as well as the living. Reports of grave-robbing by wolves date back to the late seventeenth century, while reports from the nineteenth century tell of corpses exhumed and eaten by wolves.[13] In Hongū folklorists have documented accounts of wolf pillaging of graves (KMG 1985: 294). Graveyards were protected from the threat of wolf grave-robbing by a variety of means. In the Hongū villages of Ukegawa and Shitsugawa, sickles, hoes, and bows were erected over new graves, to warn off any wolves from interfering with the plot (wolves are said to be repelled by sharp iron objects or other weapons) (Nomoto 1990: 67; *Kii Minpō* 29 Sept. 1972). In these same Hongū villages, large stones (or

---

[13] See Hiraiwa (1992: 135–6), *MS* (18 Nov. 1990), *MS* (22 Dec. 1990), and Ōta (1997: 205).

even a layer of concrete) are to this day placed over fresh graves. Repellent smells were also employed to keep wolves away from graves, such as sprigs of the pungent-smelling *sakaki* (*Cleyera japonica*) or *shikimi* (star anise, a plant used to make incense) (WKMK 1981: 84). Similar measures were taken in other areas, including the use of bamboo spike traps in the plot to injure any grave-robbing wolf (Tabuchi 1992: 77; Hiraiwa 1992: 136; Ōta 1997: 206). In a few extreme instances, family graves were established adjacent to houses in order to protect the dead from the wolf: one homestead in the village of Takada (to the south-east of Hongū), for example, sited ancestral graves immediately next to the house building, with the whole homestead protected by a 2 metre-high stone wall (made entirely with large natural stones), a structure which has been likened to a *toride* or 'fort'.

Wolf hunts known as *inugari* (literally 'dog hunts') took place in different parts of Japan.[14] In the Tōhoku area during the eighteenth and nineteenth centuries, battue-style wolf hunts involving hundreds of people were carried out in response to wolf attacks (Hiraiwa 1992: 133–5; Chiba 1995a: 190). According to a report of one such *ōkami taiji* or 'wolf conquest' in Akita in 1866, large numbers of villagers, beating drums and launching fireworks, systematically drove wolves out of the forest into a clearing where the animals were then surrounded and destroyed (Ōta 1997: 206–7). Wolf-trapping, in the form of poisoned-bait traps, pitfalls, and baited ambushes, was also practised (Hiraiwa 1992: 131–2). A wolf attack might well lead to specialized 'wolf-catchers' (known as *ōkamitori*) being called in to deal with the problem—men such as *Ōkamitori Seijurō* ('Seijurō the Wolf-Catcher') with established reputations as wolf-hunters (Hiraiwa 1992: 129–30). Ordinary hunters too could make a name for themselves by killing wolves. When a local hunter killed a mankilling wolf in Yoshino in the late 1880s, grateful villagers rewarded his bravery by exempting him from communal work duties for the rest of his life (Kishida 1963: 7). In response to the wolf problem, bounty systems were established: from the early eighteenth century, *hōbi* or 'rewards' for dead wolves were offered by the *han* authorities (Hiraiwa 1992: 132–3). As with the other wild animals examined in this book, the idiom of war was sometimes applied to the wolf: Chiba Tokuji refers to the wolf's successful *sentō hōshiki* or 'battle methods' against livestock in Hokkaido (Chiba 1995a: 170), while physical conflicts with wolves are described as *ōkami gassen* or 'wolf battles' and the wolf a *teki* or 'enemy' (Hiraiwa 1992: 110–18). The frequently used term *ōkami taiji* or 'wolf conquest' would seem to have only reinforced the sense that the wolf was a dangerous enemy that had to be vanquished.

Wolf as Protector

The wolf was not simply an 'enemy' of the mountain villager that threatened human well-being or human life. The animal could also appear as an ally in the

---

[14] See Chiba (1993); Matsuyama (1977a: 178–81); Matsuyama (1994: 137–40). Wolf hunts are also reported among the Ainu (Batchelor 1901: 461).

wider wildlife 'war'. As noted above, the benign character of the wolf is directly suggested by the written Chinese character for wolf, which consists of two parts that together give the meaning of 'good animal'. When I asked hunters and other people in Hongū about the wolf (its extinction, the prospects for its reintroduction, and so on), they often responded by referring to or writing down the character 狼—on paper or just on the palm of the hand with a forefinger—to show that in Japan the wolf was traditionally considered an *ii dōbutsu* or 'good animal'. The goodness of the wolf is generally believed to have a concrete meaning to do with farm protection.[15] As we have seen in the preceding chapters, Japanese farmers have long been threatened by a variety of forest animals, including the wild boar, the monkey, and the deer. The wolf, as a predator, was seen as helping to protect fields from these farm pests. The folklorist Chiba Tokuji argues that up until the second half of the seventeenth century the wolf was considered an *ekijū* or 'benign animal' by virtue of its predation (Chiba 1995a: 183). In particular, the wolf performed the valuable role of catching wild boar. 'The wolf, by catching the wild boar, a harmful animal that destroys crops, becomes a benign animal for human beings. It is this on which the wolf worship found in the different regions of Japan is based' (Nomoto 1990: 66). This protective function appears to be further in evidence in the wolf's association with the *yama no kami* or 'mountain spirit' in Japanese folk religion (Kaneko *et al.* 1992: 22; Satō 1990: 153–5; Naumann 1994: 34–5). 'The wolf was the protector who conquered the wild boar and deer that ravaged farmland and disturbed the peasants. For the peasants the wolf was a saviour-god [*sukui no kami*]' (Hiraiwa 1992: 88).

The power of the wolf as a guardian of the fields could be invoked through *ofuda* charms obtained from wolf shrines, which were placed at the edge of the field as a *shishiyoke* or 'boar deterrent' (Hayakawa 1982: 41–2; Miyamoto *et al.* 1995: 400–1). The *ofuda* of the most famous wolf shrine, Mitsumine Shrine in Saitama Prefecture, were used throughout Japan to establish the Mitsumine *kami* in local Shinto shrines as a ritual means of defending fields against the wild boar (Chiba 1995a: 217–19). One such wolf shrine in Hongū (in the now abandoned village of Heichigawa) contains 'Mitsuminesama', the *ofuda* of the famous Mitsumine Shrine.[16] In Totsukawa-mura, there is a local belief that farmers in the villages next to the Takataki Shrine suffer little farm damage because they enjoy the protection of the wolf spirit of the shrine, while elsewhere in Totsukawa-mura, following farm damage by wild boars, villagers seek to prevent further boar raids by placing in their fields wooden *gohei* (a sacred Shinto staff used in purifications) obtained from a wolf shrine (*MS* 7 May 1989). In the Hongū area a wolf-petitioning festival used to

[15] Sometimes more specific qualities are read into the written wolf character, as in the following article from a municipal publication: 'as the character 狼 suggests, in reality the wolf is an extremely loving animal . . .' (HYMKI 1987: 5).
[16] This shrine also contains the spirit Wakamiyasama which 'as the peasant's *kami*, is said to take the form of a large wolf, and is worshipped by people who hunt' (WKMK 1981: 189).

Fig. 6.4. The *ofuda* of the Mitsumine Shrine

be held in the late summer in the run-up to the rice harvest to protect the crop (WKMK 1981: 118–19). But the protective power of the wolf could be tapped in other ways. According to Minakata Kumagusu, mountain villagers on the Kii Peninsula used the bark of a particular local cypress tree associated with the wolf—known as the 'dog-howl cypress' (see below)—as a wolf repellent by placing strips of bark in their fields in order to protect their crops (in *MS* 26 Aug. 1990). An alternative means of invoking the presence of the wolf near the fields to create a deterrent effect was to exploit the wolf's scent. Mito Yukihisa cites a seventeenth-century farming manual from the Mikawa area of central Japan which mentions the practice of using wolf's faeces as a repellent to protect fields from monkeys, deer, and other wild animals (Mito 1989: 38). The intention here was to impart the scent of the wild predator to the fields in order to deter visits from its prey animals.[17]

[17] In recent years Japanese researchers into forestry pestilence have been investigating the potential of predator scent as a means of protecting plantation trees from the increasing numbers of deer—and have carried out trials in some areas using the faeces of predators such as lions and tigers obtained from local zoos (*TS* 4 Mar. 2002).

The wolf offered protection not just from crop pests but from other kinds of danger too. The theme of the wolf as protector appears most prominently in the widely recorded tale of the *okuriōkami* or 'escort wolf'.[18] 'Sometimes when someone is walking along forest roads at night a wolf follows without doing anything [bad], but on nearing the house the wolf disappears' (*MS* 8 Apr. 1990). The wolf follows the traveller through the forest until he or she arrives back home; once at home, the traveller should express appreciation to the escort wolf for its protection by offering it something in return, such as salt or water (perhaps the water with which the traveller washes his or her feet on returning home, as this will tend to be salty) (Ōfuji 1968: 368; WKMK 1987: 60).[19] Although *okuriōkami* tales are generally about protection, the motif of predation is not entirely absent. Some versions of the tale emphasize the danger of falling over while being followed by a wolf, something that may well invite the wolf to attack (*MS* 8 Apr. 1990). In fact, this same motif—of an apparently benign protector turning into a threatening predator—comes to the fore in the popular meaning of the term *okuriōkami* in contemporary Japan: the seemingly well-intentioned young man who escorts his girlfriend back to her flat, but then pounces on her on arrival. Here man-eating predation on the part of a literal wolf in the forest becomes sexual predation on the part of a metaphorical 'wolf' in the city, but in both cases the calculating predator waits to seize the opportunity when the victim (forest traveller or single woman) is most vulnerable.

The threat posed by wolves to children was noted above, but wolves can also play the role of protector of children. There are well-known European tales of human children suckled by wolves, including the Romulus and Remus legend in which the founders of Rome are suckled and raised by a she-wolf. This nurturant wolf motif is not widely found in Japanese folklore; indeed, in *Yama no jinsei* the great folklorist Yanagita Kunio, while mentioning reports of 'Romulus' children raised by wolves in India, specifically denies their existence in Japan (Yanagita 1961: 167). Yet there are Japanese echoes of the Romulus and Remus legend. One such tale is that of an infant (of the court noble Fujiwara Hidehara) abandoned in the forests of the Kii Peninsula and brought up by wolves.[20] The nurturant wolf motif is also evident in the custom (in the Kantō area of eastern Japan) of giving the milk of captured pregnant wolves to children: 'if a child is fed with wolf's milk, it grows up strong' (Yanai 1993: 137). In his book on Japanese wolf-lore, Yanai Kenji includes a photograph of Ishikawa Teijiro, a famous hunter, who was said to have been fed wolf's milk as an infant and, as a result, had exceptional eyesight and lived to the ripe old age of 93 (Yanai 1993: 136).[21] In addition to nurturing living children,

[18] The scientific name of the Japanese wolf, *hodophylax*, conferred by C. J. Temminck, is related to this legend (Hiraiwa 1992: 201; Sakamoto 1983). *Hodo* derives from the Greek for 'a way' or 'a path', and *phylax* from the Greek for 'a guard', together giving the meaning of 'guardian of the way'.

[19] See also KMG (1985: 294) and Hiraiwa (1992: 183–9).

[20] See Nakamura (1987: 67), Tabuchi (1992: 84–5), and KHI (1980: 63).

[21] The theme finds a recent expression in Japanese popular culture. One example is the 1964 animated television series *Ōkami shōnen Ken*, 'Ken the Wolf Boy', recalling the story of Mowgli in

the wolf could protect the spirits of dead foetuses or infants. In the Hongū area there is said to be an *ōkami Jizō* or 'Wolf Jizō' in the forest. Jizō, the compassionate bodhisattva, is viewed as a protector of children, and is ubiquitous in present-day Japan in the many temples dedicated to *mizuko kuyō* or memorials for aborted foetuses (see LaFleur 1992). One possible interpretation of the Wolf Jizō in Hongū is that it was petitioned by mothers to care for the spirits of miscarried or aborted foetuses or dead infants buried in the area—that is, to protect them from the attentions of other forest animals (cf. Chiba 1977: 143).

The wolf protects people from other destructive natural forces. One way it does this is through its powers of prophecy *vis-à-vis* the natural world. In the high Tamaki mountains north of Hongū the aforementioned 'dog-howl cypress' is said to be the place where wolves howled continuously on the eve of the great flood of 1889 that killed many people in Hongū and nearby areas (Nakamori 1941: 35–7). The folklorist Nomoto Kanichi interprets the cypress legend as an example of the wolf 'warning Man of abnormalities in the natural world' and thus performing a *banken* or 'watchdog' role in the *yama*, equivalent to that of the canine watchdog in the village (Nomoto 1990: 66). In the mountainous Chichibu area near Tokyo there are claims that wolves howled in the hours before the great earthquake of 1923 (that devastated Tokyo and injured or killed over 150,000 people), even though wolves had already officially become extinct by that time (Yanai 1993: 158). Another example of the wolf informing human society about the unknown world of the *yama* is where wolves tell villagers of human fatalities that occur there. Kubō Terumi of the Hongū village of Fushiogami recalls a story told by her grandfather which she refers to as the *ōkami no shirase* or 'wolf's notification'. A villager gets lost in the forest, and some days later a wolf comes up to the house of the lost person and makes 'a sad howl' (*sabishisō na nakigoe*) outside. The family realize that the presence of the howling wolf means that the missing person is dead and thank the wolf for its troubles. The next day they duly find the body of their loved one in the forest.[22]

The wolf was also a source of protection from harmful spirits. Wolf fangs, wolf hide, and wolf hair were believed to have the power to ward off evil and were used as protective charms by forest workers and other people travelling through the forest (Hiraiwa 1992: 195; Naora 1968: 243–8). In some houses a wolf skull was placed in the household *kamidana* (the shelf that serves as a miniature domestic shrine) to keep away misfortune (Hiraiwa 1992: 195). Wolf skulls and other wolf charms were used in folk religion to expel animal spirits (for example, those of

The Jungle Book. A second example is the popular 1997 animation film *Mononoke hime* (*The Mononoke Princess*), an eco-fable directed by Miyazaki Hayao, in which the leading character 'San' is a wild girl who was abandoned as an infant in the forest and raised by wolves.

[22] Interestingly, in recounting the story, Kubō-san makes no mention of the possibility of wolf predation on the missing person, and instead states that the wolf is acting in a benign way because 'in Japan the wolf is a *kamisama*'.

dogs, foxes, and snakes) and other harmful spirits that possessed human beings (Komatsu 1988: 37; Matsutani 1994: 161, 163). People suffering from fox possession on the Kii Peninsula were brought to the Tamaki Shrine where the wolf spirit was called on to drive out the fox from the possessed person. Another request that was sometimes made of the wolf was protection from illness, especially at times of life-threatening epidemics such as smallpox (Inoue 1998: 8). But the wolf also offered protection from other kinds of threat, including theft and housefires, in urban areas as well as rural ones (*MS* 28 May 1989; Hiraiwa 1992: 89). The wolf was known as the enemy of the thief. Following a theft, the victim would go to the shrine and petition the wolf spirit to identify the culprit (*MS* 21 May 1989). There was a belief in some areas that wolf hides protected those who slept on them from thieves (Yanai 1993: 134). Wolf fangs and jawbones are still kept as family heirlooms on the Kii Peninsula. One example of this is Yabunaka Mamoru from the Hongū village of Kuki who has a wolf's jawbone attached to a purse which has been passed down the Yabunaka family line from distant ancestors—the family members believe it to be a kind of *mamori* (protective charm) used by past generations of the family to protect them from thieves.

On the Kii Peninsula there are even more striking examples of the connection between wolves and specific families that they are believed to protect. The Okazaki family in Takada consider the grave next to their house to be a kind of protective deity associated with the wolf, and carry out a daily worship there. The elderly head of the family recounted the protection received by family members as follows.

It protects us. Whether it is because we worship at it or whatever, there have been no calamities [*wazawai*] . . . I am now 71 years old. I went [overseas] as a soldier, and my elder brothers were soldiers too [in the war]. Around here almost every family had its war dead. But not one of us five brothers died. I think that this is a great mystery—I was in the Special Attack Units [*tokkōtai*] . . .

This old man believes that the house plot grave associated with the wolf protected him and his brothers during the war, ensuring their eventual safe return to the village at a time when many of their village peers perished on foreign soil. He himself was in the suicide-bombing *tokkōtai*, and was waiting his turn to fly to his death when the war ended. It is thanks to the wolf spirit that he has lived to see old age.

In line with the view of the wolf as a protector of farmland, Japanese farmers welcomed any increase in wolf numbers. This is most strikingly illustrated by the custom of offering a gift of food to the wolf when wolf cubs are born—the *inu no ubumimai* or 'wolf's birth gift'.[23] Usually, *sekihan* (azuki bean rice) is offered—

[23] Also known, in other regions, as *ōkami no bokomi* or *ubuyashinai*. For Yamanashi, see Ōfuji (1968: 368); for Gifu, see Terada (1994: 3); and for Nagano, see Matsuyama (1977*a*: 187–9). See also Hayakawa (1982: 398).

sekihan is a ceremonial food traditionally served to celebrate a human birth and on other felicitous occasions such as New Year or festivals for the village deity. This Japanese celebration of wolf increase presents a striking contrast with the institutionalized celebration of wolf reduction that is reported for parts of Europe (Behar 1986: 211, 368; Cátedra 1992: 271–6). But the *ubumimai* also contrasts with those examples of institutionalized wolf-killing in Japan mentioned above. The *ubumimai* custom is often interpreted as illustrating the importance of the principle of reciprocity in human–wolf relations in Japan. In Japanese folklore on the wolf, the wolf appears a *girigatai* or 'dutiful' animal that reciprocates any human kindness it receives (A. Maruyama 1994: 139). The wolf that is helped by human beings is extremely grateful: in some tales the wolf is said to bow repeatedly to its human benefactors before disappearing into the forest (Yanai 1993: 163–4). The wolf may offer some kind of animal prey to the village in return for the earlier help it received. In some regions the *ubumimai* practice was associated with the belief that the wolf would, in return, make a congratulatory offering on the occasion of a human birth in the village (Ishizaki 1991*b*: 236). One story from the Hongū village of Hiba tells of a wolf trapped in a pitfall that is set free by villagers and allowed to return to the forest. A few days later, villagers hear a wolf howl from the vicinity of the pit, and discover a large deer in it—and realize that the wolf has made its return gift (known variously as *ongaeshi* or *oreigaeshi*) (Hongū-chō 1969: 12–13). Similar examples of the wolf's sense of reciprocity, involving offerings of other animals or their parts (a wild boar, a pheasant, a bear's paw, and so on), can be found elsewhere in the region and beyond.[24]

The principle of reciprocity should also work the other way around. Just as wolves reciprocate kindness shown by people, people should act faithfully in their relations with wolves. One situation in which such considerations arose would be when villagers came across abandoned wolf-kill (known variously as *inuotoshi* or *inutaoshi*) in the forest; where the meat was still fresh, it was customary for the finder to claim it and take it back home. However, the villager in question should be sure to leave something behind for the wolf in return, whether this be a limb of the animal or a pile of salt; just to take everything for himself would be to risk incurring the wolf's anger (Nomoto 1990: 65–6; Tabuchi 1992: 79–80). In contrast to views of the wolf in Europe, in Japan the wolf appears not to be attributed an essential or fixed evil character. Rather like a person, a wolf can be good or bad, helpful or dangerous, depending on how the relationship with it is conducted. Provided that the relationship is properly maintained, the wolf will be a benign beast, and it is only when the principle of reciprocity is not observed by Man (when, for example, all the wolf-kill is taken and nothing is left for the wolf or when something is promised to the wolf but not given) that the positive relationship with the animal breaks down and it develops an *ada* or 'enmity' towards humans. In Japan,

[24] For regional examples, see Nakamori (1941: 30–1), Inada (1975: 131–2), Tokuyama (1975: 142–3), Wada (1978: 265), WKMK (1987: 62), HYMKI (1992: 247–9), TMKI (1988: 208–11), and Yanai (1993: 162–6). See also Morita (1994: 141–2) and Sakai (1986) on the motif more generally.

whether the relationship is with other people, with the spirits of the dead, or with animal spirits, great stress is placed on preventing such an outcome. The disposition of the wolf to Man—benign or malign—is an expression of the state of this moral relationship with it. Dangerous wolves are a sign of a human infidelity, or at the least human failure, rather than the animal's bad nature.

Japanese folk tales and legends tell of the disastrous consequences of breaching the principle of reciprocity. One example of this is the *ippontatara* tale, found in the folklore of the Kii Peninsula (WKMK 1981: 84; Wada 1978: 264–5).[25] A man is saved by wolves from a one-legged monster (the *ippontatara*) in the forest, and, indebted to the wolf, promises the wolf his body when he dies, along with the bodies of his descendants. But after his death his family reneges on the promise by building a fortified grave that the wolf cannot enter, and as a result of this broken promise the family is henceforth cursed by the spirit of the wolf. On the Kii Peninsula, this is no abstract legend but one which is associated with particular named local families that are said to have incurred the *tatari* or 'curse' of the wolf in the form of a succession of terrible illnesses, premature deaths, and other calamities among family members over the generations. In 1987 one such family in Takada even arranged for a local *reinōsha* or spiritualist to carry out a *kuyō* memorial in order to pacify the aggrieved spirit of the wolf.[26] Tales of wolf curses also arise in relation to the human killing of wolves. One example of this from the Kitayama area of the Kii Peninsula was the belief that, as a result of their actions, wolf-killers would go on to experience family misfortune of one kind or another, including sudden deaths in the family and the dissipation of family wealth and property (Kishida 1963: 10; see also *MS* 23 Sept. 1990).[27] To stop the curse of the wolf, one must pacify its spirit by carrying out a memorial, as in the Takada case. As noted above, the death of the last recorded wolf in the Yoshino area in 1905 is annually remembered in the form of a *kuyō* ceremony carried out in a local temple (called Hōsenji) at the time of the *bon* midsummer festival. It has even been suggested that the problem of large-scale wildlife pestilence that is afflicting present-day Japan is itself a manifestation of the curse of the wolf on the society that brought about its extinction (*SS* 15 Apr. 1995).

FROM WOLVES TO DOGS

There is another major strand to the human–wolf relationship of reciprocity. As we have seen, hunters play an important role in the various people–wildlife conflicts in Japan. Japanese hunters claim that hunting benefits local society in general

[25] This tale is also found in other regions of Japan—see, for example, Tabuchi (1992: 73–4).
[26] In 1994 I spoke to the *reinōsha* about the 1987 *kuyō*. I did not witness this *kuyō* myself, but I have been shown photographs of it by the *reinōsha* who carried it out (who meticulously keeps a photographic record of his ritual activities).
[27] Thomas Jones reports another example of a wolf curse in his study in the south-central area of Kyushu in the 1920s. Jones wrote that '[n]ot long ago a man wounded a wolf which afterwards died. The suffering provoked his [the wolf's] spirit so that he returned to torment the man' (Jones 1926: 48).

because, by keeping down animal numbers, it protects villagers from the worst consequences of animal damage to farmland and forest plantations. Hunters also contribute to the defence of mountain villages through their culling of wild boar, monkeys, and deer. Hunters may well be lauded for their courage and even accorded a heroic status by the wider village society. But hunting in Japan is only partly a human activity because Japanese hunters hunt with hounds to which they attribute great importance. 'The dog is number one, your legs are number two, and the gun is number three', is a much-repeated saying about hunting priorities.[28] Japanese hunters devote much time and effort into breeding and training hounds, and are prepared to pay large sums of money to buy a good hound that will bring them hunting success. But Japanese hunters also associate their hounds with wolves. There is a widespread assumption in Japan that the *waken* or native dog breeds are descended from the native wolf—that the Japanese wolf is the *senzo* or 'ancestor' of the *waken*—even though the 'ancestors' of Japanese dogs appear to have been continental dogs rather than Japanese wolves.[29] This association with the wolf is also evident in hunting terminology. One of the ways in which Japanese hunters hunt wild boar is actually known as *ōkamiryō* or 'wolf-hunting' (alternatively, *ōkamioi* or 'wolf-chasing') in which the hunting group fans out to surround the boar, while the dogs head off the boar's escape—an operation that is believed to resemble the hunting mode of the wolf pack (Fukushima 1999: 72).

This association with the wolf is especially strong in the case of the Kishū hound. The Kishū hound is the famous local breed of the southern part of the Kii Peninsula and one of the eight recognized regional variants of *waken*.[30] According to a myth on the Kii Peninsula, the first ever hound was obtained by a hunter as a gift from a wolf of one of its cubs. The hunter encounters an ailing wolf in the forest, discovers that it has a bone lodged in its throat and bravely puts his hand in the wolf's mouth and removes the bone. The grateful wolf then reciprocates by giving the hunter one of its cubs and this cub goes on to become a superlative boarhound that brings great fame to the hunter.[31] Even present-day hunters claim that Kishū hounds have wolf's blood. Kishū hounds are known for their distinctive

[28] The saying in Japanese is: *inu ichiban, ashi niban, teppō sanban.*
[29] The accepted view among scholars is that dog populations were brought to Japan from the Asian continent in ancient times, and that the wolves from which they are descended were not Japanese wolves but wolves inhabiting the Arabian Peninsula and South Asia (Okumura *et al.* 1996: 403–4).
[30] Kishū is the name for the southern area of the peninsula, and the Kishū hound is an animal emblem of the region (two municipalities on the peninsula make rival claims to be the home of the *Kishū* breed). Nowadays found throughout Japan, the Kishū breed is also something of a national symbol, and for many fanciers of the breed the dog stands for a Japan of the past. It is characterized as a living relic of the Jōmon era (Ue and Tanba 1987: 43–5), praised as *Nihon no takara* or a 'treasure of Japan' (Kawada 1971: 27), and officially designated as a *tennen kinenbutsu* or 'natural treasure' of the nation.
[31] On this legend, see Seko (1988: ch. 1), Taira (1982: 190), Ishizaki (1991*b*: 236), and Matsutani (1994: 68–71). There are other regional variants of this tale in which it is a charcoal-burner who raises the wolf cub to become a superlative hound—see Murakami (1992: 15–16), Katsuki (1995: 334), and Togawa (1995).

appearance—white coat, narrow eyes, pointed ears, curved upright tails, robust physique, agility and mobility in mountainous terrain, and, more generally, their *subarashii yaseimi* or 'wonderful wildness' (Furuya 1995: 35). Among the physical signs of the wolfish character of the Kishū hound that are mentioned are their feet (*mizukaki* or web-feet) and their fangs (Iwahashi 1989: 21–2).

> The strongest teeth, the fangs, come out at right angles and when they bite into the animal they do not let go . . . It is because of cross-breeding with wolves since ancient times that they [wolf-like fangs] have lasted. These fangs are firmly rooted in the jaws and do not break or come out in a fight [with the boar]. (Furuya 1999*a*: 43)

Kishū hounds are commonly named after the wolf: individual dogs are given names that include the character for wolf (*rō*) in them, for example Tetsurō ('Iron Wolf'), Hakurō ('White Wolf'), and Shirō ('Warrior Wolf').[32]

The theme of the wolfish origins of hounds emerges in the claims by some hunters to have obtained superior hounds from the forest. Mori Eizō is well known among peninsular hunters for having owned one of the most remarkable local hounds of recent times. One day back in the early 1970s a dog emerged from the forest near the Mori homestead. The dog had a strange appearance: its right ear was hanging off, its hair was very long, and its feet were unusually large. Mori-san adopted the dog, which his young daughter named 'John'. John went on to kill ninety-seven wild boars in a five-year hunting career, proving to be by far the best of the ten boarhounds that Mori-san had hunted with. John, the dog from the mountains, earned a huge reputation among hunters across the peninsula, some of whom offered large amounts of money to buy it, but were always turned down. Eventually the dog died a brave death in the course of a hunt when a large boar gored it. Mori-san believes that John was a special dog and claims that he was a *yamainu* which had *ōkami no chi* or 'wolf's blood' flowing through his body.[33] Similar stories are found among hunters in other parts of Japan. In the *Shuryōkai* hunting magazine, a hunter in Kyōto Prefecture tells of how, after he helped release a feral dog that was caught in a trap, he found a white puppy in the forest which he went on to raise to become a superior deerhound. The hunter believes that the puppy was the *yamainu no ongaeshi* or 'return-gift of the mountain dog [wolf]' (recalling the origin myth of the Kishū hound above) (Takami 1995: 94–5). That the hunter associated the *yamainu* with the wolf is confirmed by the fact that he named the puppy Shirō—a name written with the characters for 'samurai' (*shi*) and 'wolf' (*rō*).

There are many tales of wolf–dog hybrids in Japan. It is said that hunters used deliberately to try to mate their hounds with wolves by leaving bitches on heat in

[32] The Chinese characters are 鉄狼 for Tetsurō, 白狼 for Hakurō, and 士狼 for Shirō. Other examples I have come across of Kishū hounds with wolf characters in their names include Korō 古狼 ('Old Wolf'), Toyoichirō 豊一狼 ('Excellent First Wolf'), and Tenrō 天狼 ('Heavenly Wolf').

[33] Mori-san even arranged for 'a professor from Waseda University' to come and examine the skull of the dog, and the professor concluded that it was indeed 'a *yamainu* with wolf's blood mixed in it'.

wolf-inhabited areas of the forest (Iwahashi 1989: 22). Similar claims have been made for the Kii Peninsula. The retired schoolteacher Murakami Kazukiyo, drawing on many decades of private research on the subject, reports as follows:

In the remote forest of the Kii Peninsula, in the period after the war, isolated charcoal-burners would mate their bitches with wolves and, as a result of this, dogs mixed with wolf were born . . . These wolf-crossed dogs were raised by the charcoal-burner and got used to the charcoal-burner's family. They would feed on wild boar and deer in the forest and they had excellent hunting skills. These wolf-crossed dogs did not bite people or do anything like that, but they were extremely scared of people they did not know, and if they were touched by somebody they did not know they would start shaking and would defecate. They would never get used to anyone except the people who first raised them, and even when they were adult dogs, if they were taken to some other place and released, no matter how far away it was (in Nagoya or on the way to Tokyo), they would return to the house of the charcoal-burner in the remote mountains where they were raised. (Murakami 1992: 15–16)[34]

Even among hunters who accept that wolves are extinct, there are claims of wolf–dog crossbreeds—but now involving imported, rather than native, wolves. There are reports of hunters on the Kii Peninsula obtaining male Korean wolves to mate with their *waken* bitches in order to produce superlative boarhounds (Seko 1988: 61). In an interview in 1995 the boar-hunter Hayashi Shigeru from Kamitonda-chō (to the south-west of Hongū) told me that one of his ambitions was to have a *waken* boarhound crossed with a wolf (his preference was for a North American timber wolf) in order to produce a hound that really hunted like a wolf. From time to time, there have even been private attempts on the Kii Peninsula to *recover* wolves through breeding—that is, to cross dogs considered to have wolfish features in order to produce dogs with an enhanced wolfish character, and eventually dogs which have had all the salient wolfish features restored to them. On the Kii Peninsula Murakami Kazukiyo is known to have attempted to produce such *modoriōkami* or 'restored wolves' and thereby bring about *nihonōkami no fukkatsu* or 'the restoration of the Japanese wolf' (Murakami 1992; Seko 1988: 66). Some wolf fanciers have taken this one stage further by actually releasing such wolf-dogs into the wild in order to re-create a free-roaming population of wolves (or, at least, of wolfish feral dogs). For example, in 1988 Seko Tsutomu is said to have released into the forest of the Kii Peninsula the offspring of a cross between a Kishū hound and a Siberian wolf (Hiraiwa 1998: 19). But there are said to be many instances where other wolf-dog owners, no longer able to keep them (for instance, after a biting incident), decide to rid themselves of their troublesome 'pets' by simply abandoning them in some remote part of the mountains (Hiraiwa 1998: 19; 1999: 14).

---

[34] The obvious objection to Murakami's claim above and to similar claims is that, at the time charcoal-burners were supposedly crossing their dogs with wolves, wolves had already been officially extinct for decades (something which Murakami disputes).

The protective role of wolves was noted above. But dogs too have a protective function in rural Japan. Dogs act as a kind of living sensor of movement about the village. Unwelcome strangers do sometimes come to the village—including travelling salesmen, proselytizers for new religions, or politicians at election time. Especially at night-time, when visibility beyond the house is minimal (as many mountain villages have no street lighting), dogs in effect monitor movement outside, providing an extra barrier between domestic and public space. Dogs also protect village fields from crop-raiding wildlife, as we have seen in previous chapters. Dogs posted near fields are used to deter wild boar, monkeys, and bears from approaching. In the past dogs were allowed to roam freely, but nowadays they are generally tethered to a post or fence near the field. This protective role of the dog can even extend to dead dogs whose spirits are petitioned to defend village crops from harmful forest wildlife. Mori Eizō informed me that his fellow Kubonodaira villagers used to protect their fields by burying in them *ofuda* charms on which were written the words *Yuwazō no inu* or 'Yuwazō's dog'—the name of a famous hound owned by one of his ancestors (a great-grandfather on his mother's side) which was known for being a scourge of the wild boar. This practice again points to the parallel between hound and wolf, for in nearby villages *ofuda* from the famous wolf shrine Mitsumine were used in the same way and for the same purpose.[35]

However, as in the case of wolves, dogs are also viewed as a pest and a potential threat. There are many complaints about hounds in Japanese mountain villages. They attract other stray dogs into the village, they fight with these dogs, they are a nuisance to drivers, they foul village paths and roads, they bark continuously, and so on. Of particular concern is the predatory pestilence of dogs. Sometimes hounds, in pursuit of a wild animal on the edge of the forest, catch the scent of livestock animals in the village, with predictable consequences. But hounds can pose a threat to people as well. Hunters themselves recognize that some dogs are *hitokui-inu* or 'man-eating dogs', which may or may not have tell-tale signs such as whitish eyes and hair that stands on end on their upper back (Matsuyama 1977a: 206–7). *Waken* boarhounds have been known to attack owners who try to separate them from the prey. This danger is, in fact, indicated by some of the versions of the legend of the hound's origin mentioned above, in which, before its thousandth kill, the wolf-turned-hound abandons the hunter and returns to the *yama*—lest its next victim be the hunter himself (Sutō 1991: 251–3). Hounds are a particular hazard to other people who use the forest, such as forestry labourers, herb-gatherers, and hikers. The elderly and the young are known to be especially vulnerable to hound

---

[35] The presence of dogs can be simulated in order to protect fields: in Okinawa dog effigies made of pampas grass were placed along boar paths in the forest to stop the wild boar approaching village fields (Suzuki 1982: 64). However, these grass dogs were more than simple canine scarecrows because they had special spells recited over them—and therefore a supernatural power attached to them—in advance.

attacks. In one recent incident in Shimane Prefecture, a 94-year-old woman tending her vegetable patch was attacked and killed by a hound (*MS* 18 Dec. 1995). Free-roaming hounds arouse particular concern among the parents of young children, just as wolves did in the past. Boarhounds have attacked children, sometimes with fatal consequences, in a number of incidents.[36] One recent hound attack in the news (in Kagoshima Prefecture) involved a 9-year-old boy who incurred serious injuries for which he had to have 130 stitches. Media reports carried the angry comments of the headmaster of the boy's school: 'Why do we have to live in fear of gunshots and hounds?' (*MNSC* 10 Feb. 1998).

The category of dogs that would seem most closely to approximate to the wolf is the feral dog. As the story of John shows, in remote areas there is a common belief that feral dog populations have 'wolf's blood'. It has been claimed that Japanese wolves interbred with (feral) dogs from the mid-eighteenth century onwards (Chiba 1995*a*: 191–4). It is sometimes argued that the last wolves in existence at the beginning of the twentieth century were absorbed into the feral dog population, and that therefore, while there are no longer any pure wolves left in Japan, wolves still indirectly exist in the form of the feral dogs that roam the forest (Sakamoto 1983: 255; Hiraiwa 1992: 283), a claim only reinforced by the practice of abandoning wolf-dog pets in the forest in recent decades (as mentioned above). More generally, there is said to be a large feral dog population in the forest, including the forest on the Kii Peninsula, due to the tendency of hunters to abandon the hounds they no longer need rather than have them destroyed or dispatch them themselves.[37] Feral dogs are sometimes attributed a protective role on account of their predation on wild animals that threaten farm crops. It is argued, for example, that in the past the presence of feral dogs kept down monkey numbers and confined the monkey population to the distant mountains far from the village, but that with the decline in the feral dog population (through culling and trapping) this pressure on wild monkeys has been lifted and the monkeys have consequently become that much bolder.[38] This is, of course, the same kind of argument that is made in relation to wolves in the past and, as we shall see, that is invoked to justify wolf reintroduction in the future. Indeed, the argument here is that feral dogs in effect carried out the predatory function of the wolf in the decades following wolf extinction.

However, feral dogs are more likely to be seen as harmful animals. Stray and feral dogs become hunting pests when they prey on the game animals of the hunter. Forming packs of five to ten dogs, they are able to catch pheasants, deer, and wild boar (Sugimoto 1999). Trappers suffer from feral dog predations on their trapped

---

[36] See Kurita (1999: 87), *AS* (13 Dec. 1985), and *MS* (18 Nov. 1997).

[37] See *YS* (22 June 1993), *YS* (22 Aug. 1994), and *AS* (23 Feb. 1995). This practice may well be related to concerns in Japan about dog curses. In Japan there are many tales of dog curses incurred by people who kill dogs—see, for example, Iwasaka and Toelken (1994: 91) and Nishiura (1989: 179). There are stories of dog vengeance in the Hongū area too—see WKMK (1981: 54, 100).

[38] See Watanabe (1995: 50), Maruyama (1995: 4–5), and Mizuno (1995: 15).

animals, and are especially vocal in their demand for these dogs to be culled. Feral dogs are sometimes said to pose a threat to human safety, and there are reports of people being killed by feral dog packs. In February 1988 the dead body of an old man was found in the forest of Kumanogawa-chō (the neighbouring municipality to the east of Hongū) much of the flesh of which had been eaten, an incident that was attributed to feral dogs.[39] The rural fear of feral dogs emerges clearly in newspaper references to *yaken sōdō* or 'feral dog furores' in some areas, where local people complain about the threat to public safety posed by high numbers of aggressive feral dogs that, according to one complainant, can be 'more dangerous than wolves' (*KS* 21 May 1996). Another complaint is that large feral dog populations can spoil the image of remote areas as tourist destinations by annoying and frightening visitors or by openly feeding on the carrion of animals such as deer or serow (ibid.).

Attempts are made to control dogs in response to these problems. There is a clampdown on the movements of hounds. The practice of allowing dogs to roam free, known as *hanashigai*, has been made illegal, and there are recurring public campaigns targeted at free-roaming dogs. Rural town halls regularly remind local dog-owners of the ban on *hanashigai* through public broadcasts over their loudspeaker systems, through warnings in municipal newsletters, and through notices on the *kairanban* clipboards that circulate among village households. In practice, *hanashigai* may well be tacitly accepted by local policemen, aware of the importance of dogs as field-guards. But when a serious biting incident occurs, the authorities are obliged to clamp down, and families that allow their dogs to roam free may well find themselves visited by a policeman or a municipal official. Dog control extends to the feral dog populations in the forest. Special measures are taken against stray and feral dogs, including the use of poisoned bait and the trapping and shooting of feral dog packs. But these programmes are hampered by the opposition of hunters who complain that their hounds sometimes eat the poisoned bait or get caught in the feral dog traps (see Seko 1988: 137–9).

In these various ways, the wolf continues to have an indirect existence in the form of the dog population in the remote areas of Japan. But dogs, while they may evoke the predatory power of the wolf, do not really fill the gap left by wolves. At a time of large-scale rural depopulation, when the number of hunters is declining along with the overall number of villagers, the impact of hunting on forest wildlife diminishes. If hunters and their hounds took the place of wolves for much of the twentieth century, today they are no longer able to do so. This is the background to the proposal to reintroduce wolves to Japan, which holds out the prospect of reversing the twentieth-century substitution of wolves by hunters and hounds.

[39] There were other theories too, such as a bear attack, a wolf attack, or an attack by an escaped wild cat from the Adventure World safari park on the coast.

THE WOLF REINTRODUCTION PROPOSAL

The Proposal

In 1993 the Japan Wolf Association (*Nihon ōkami kyōkai*, hereafter JWA) issued a public call for wolf reintroduction to be carried out in Japan. The JWA proposes that wolves from Chinese Inner Mongolia be used to establish grey wolf colonies (of up to thirty animals) in a number of areas across Japan. Ten (national park) areas have been identified as possible candidate sites for wolf reintroduction, including the Yoshino–Kumano National Park area on the interior of the Kii Peninsula (Takahashi and Maruyama n.d.: 15–16).[40] Interestingly, the wolves that would be relocated to Japan are seen as pests in their native Inner Mongolia: around a thousand of these wolves are destroyed each year as threats to livestock. Japan would therefore obtain its supply of wolves from these unwanted wolves of Inner Mongolia. But the reintroduction of wolves to Japan is a long-term goal rather than an immediate ambition. The first objective of the campaign is to stimulate a national debate by getting the issue of wolf reintroduction on to the public agenda in Japan. Largely through the efforts of the leader of the JWA, the zoologist Maruyama Naoki, an articulate and forceful spokesman, the issue has attracted extensive media coverage and become a topic of public debate in Japan. In the short and medium terms, the JWA aims to build up public support for wolf reintroduction, and to lobby the Japanese government to establish effective wildlife management institutions staffed by suitably trained personnel. Once these foundations of public support and state approval have been laid, detailed plans will be drawn up for the practical implementation of the reintroduction proposal, but the time-frame for reintroduction would appear to be in terms of decades rather than years.

The JWA has a membership of more than six hundred people, drawn largely from the professional classes, including university professors, schoolteachers, writers, journalists, doctors, and artists. The association has a regular newsletter that carries specialized articles as well as contributions from ordinary members. There is a dedicated e-mail message board on the JWA home page where members communicate with each other on wolf-related matters, and exchange information on a variety of topics—wolf literature, wolf memorabilia, and other wolf websites; opposition to wolf culling overseas; wolf-watching opportunities around the world; environmental and wildlife issues in general and so on. Many of the JWA members express a strong identification with the wolf. At a JWA gathering in 1995 that I attended some members wore t-shirts and sweaters bearing images of the wolf (imported from America). E-mail correspondents include the student

---

[40] The other proposed candidate sites are Shiretoko National Park, Akan National Park, Hidaka Mountains Quasi-National Park, Mount Daisetsu National Park, Nikkō National Park, Chichibu-Tama Quasi-National Park, Southern Alps National Park, Kōya-Ryūjin Quasi-National Park, and Kyūshū Central Mountains Quasi-National Park.

who claims to be 'infatuated with wolves'; the elderly man who signs off as 'a black wolf . . . with a white head'; the doctor who named his newborn son after the wolf (Itsuki or 'Brave Moon', written with the characters 'brave' and 'moon'); and the man who confesses that he has always been obsessed with wolves, to the extent that his nickname at school was 'Ōkami' ('Wolf'). Members refer to themselves and address each other as *ōkami fan* or 'wolf fans', *ōkami ningen* or 'wolf people', and even *ōkami furīku* or 'wolf freaks', and when a JWA member was elected as a prefectural governor she was hailed as *hajimete no ōkami chiji* or 'the first wolf governor'. The e-mail addresses of JWA members may well contain references to the wolf (Werewolf@, Wolfpack@, Wolfsong@ etc.). This sentiment is formally reflected by the association, which designates its three categories of members as 'alphas', 'pack wolves', and 'wolf friends', and divides its branches into the 'west pack' and the 'east pack'.

The JWA links wolf extinction with the post-Meiji Westernization of Japan.

It was a highly regrettable episode. Following the Meiji Restoration, Japanese society, in the name of modernization, introduced a great deal of Western culture. Included in this Western culture were 'anti-wolf sentiments'. Without knowing much about the real ecology of the wolf, we Japanese were easily influenced by the Western anti-wolf campaign which was centred on folk tales . . . (Maruyama 1998*c*: 1)

Japanese scholars have long debated the pros and cons of the Meiji Restoration in terms of social progress and cultural continuity with the past. The impact of the Meiji Restoration has been one of the dominant intellectual issues of modern Japan, and the history of Meiji Japan has often been seen as a stark example of uncritical Westernization that destroyed much of the traditional culture of Japan. During the twentieth century there have been countless intellectual backlashes and reactions against Meiji Westernization in the name of reviving the native traditions of pre-Meiji Japan (Havens 1974: 203–11; Gluck 1998: 271–2). Wolf reintroduction can be seen as yet another expression of this critical, anti-Meiji sentiment of twentieth-century Japan, only this time the argument is that, in turning to the West, the Meiji state laid the way for the destruction of the *natural* (and not just cultural) heritage of Japan. The extinction of the wolf in the Meiji period provides a stark expression of the excesses of Westernized modernity. Consequently, the 'nature' to be restored would appear to be that of the Tokugawa period. Indeed, Maruyama Naoki is explicit on this point: when challenged about *which* 'nature' he wants to restore (i.e. from which period of Japanese history), he mentions the nature of the Tokugawa period.[41]

The JWA argues that the legacy of the Meiji-era anti-wolf propaganda continues in present-day Japan. Despite the wolf's sacred associations in traditional Japanese

---

[41] Maruyama made this remark in an exchange of e-mail correspondence in the autumn of 2000 with Tsutsui Toshinari of the *Dōbutsu no inochi no songen o mamoru kai* (Society for the Protection of the Dignity of the Lives of Animals)—see Maruyama (2000).

culture, in modern Japan negative views of the wolf are widespread. 'Since the Meiji period a large part of the Japanese people has been thoroughly dyed in a Christian view of nature, in which nature, along with the wolf, is seen as subordinate to God and to Man, one which derives from the pastoralist view of the wolf as a harmful animal' (Maruyama 1999: 17). Maruyama Naoki refers to lingering popular views of the wolf as a mankiller and man-eater as the *Akazukinchan shōkōgun* or 'Little Red Riding Hood syndrome' (see *KSY* 13 Mar. 2000). Most of the post-war generation of Japanese people have learnt the stories of Little Red Riding Hood and The Three Little Pigs at primary school (often in the first year) by reading the picture books and even enacting the stories in school dramas. The theme also emerges in the exchanges among JWA members who reflect on how as children they absorbed negative images of the wolf that it has taken much time and effort to overcome. Contributors to the home page message board recall reading the Little Red Riding Hood tale as a child or even performing it in a puppet show at school, along with the difficulties they have had dispelling these unfavourable images of the wolf from their minds (Kamata 2000; Matsuo 2000). This is the background to the strong emphasis on knowledge in the JWA campaign, with the task of public education heading its list of formal objectives. To this end, the JWA actively disseminates its message through public lectures, symposia, and meetings; through the writings of its members for newspapers, magazines, and the internet; and through its own media such as the *Forest Call* newsletter and the JWA website.

The JWA puts forward a number of reasons for wolf reintroduction. First of all, it argues that wolf reintroduction is a moral imperative. The fact of wolf extinction demands a process of *seishintekina hansei* or 'spiritual reflection' on the part of the Japanese people and imposes on them an *rinritekina sekinin* or 'ethical responsibility' and *gimu* or 'duty' to do something about it (Maruyama 1998*a*: 5; Maruyama 1999: 15). The reintroduction of the wolf (and other disappearing species) is characterized as *watashitachi no shimei* or 'our mission' for the twenty-first century (Maruyama 1998*b*: 2). JWA discourse invokes the idiom of atonement, with the act of wolf reintroduction represented as a means of 'atoning' for past 'sins' (Maruyama 1999: 15–16) and a kind of 'apology' (the verb *wabiru*, 'to apologize') for the mistakes of the recent past (Maruyama 2001*a*). Implicitly, this apology would seem to be directed to the earlier generations whose legacy modern Japan has destroyed and which should be restored. Wolf extinction is depicted as a wrongful and irresponsible collective act on the part of modern (post-Meiji) Japan. The verb used in this context is *okasu*, variously translated as 'violate', 'sin against', and 'commit [a crime]', the character for which (containing the beast radical 犭) is used in word compounds such as *hanzai* ('crime') and *hansoku* ('transgression') to denote criminal-like behaviour (see Hama 2000). Wolf extinction, in other words, is represented by the JWA as a 'crime' on the part of modern Japan for which today's generation must make amends by restoring what has been destroyed.

Fɪɢ. 6.5. The JWA logo, showing wolves chasing deer in the forest

Modern Japan is therefore characterized as a kind of repenting criminal charged with the duty of rectifying past transgressions.

A second reason for wolf reintroduction is that it would restore Japan's forest. The term *mori*, which nostalgically evokes the traditional forest, is often used in this regard (as opposed to *shinrin* or *hayashi*, words that suggest a modern, productive forest). In some of the JWA literature the word *mori* appears almost as much as the word *ōkami*, and the wolf is seldom mentioned other than in connection with the forest. The title of the JWA newsletter is 'Forest Call' (English loanwords used), the front cover of each issue bears the slogan, *mori-ōkami-hito no yoi kankei o kangaeru* or 'Towards a good relationship between forest, wolves, and people', while a circular JWA logo has been created that shows wolves chasing deer against a backdrop of forest trees (see Fig. 6.5). A common image featured in JWA publications is that of the *hinshi no mori* or 'dying forest' of skeletal trees sticking out of the ground—the result of overgrazing by deer. The wolf is sometimes referred to in the newsletter as *mori o sukuu ōkami* or 'the wolf that will save the forest'. Indeed, there is a strong sense that with the extinction of the wolf the *mori* too has ceased to exist in Japan: 'a forest without the wolf is not a real forest' (Maruyama 2001c: 39). But it follows that Japan's moribund forest can be revived with the restoration of the wolf, its missing core. Wolf reintroduction is represented as the means by which the Japanese people can recover and reunite with their *mori*.

In conjunction with this emphasis on the *mori* is an emphasis on the *shinrin seitaikei* or 'forest ecosystem'. The idea of nature as a *seitaikei* or 'ecosystem' is a central theme in JWA discourse, and the wolf is accorded a special place in the Japanese ecosystem. Based on a key notion of modern ecology, the JWA defines the 'forest ecosystem' in terms of the existence of top-line wild predators such as wolves that, through their carnivory, keep in check the numbers of wild herbivores. This ecological reasoning has a prominent place in the justification of the wolf reintroduction proposal, as the following excerpt from the JWA newsletter makes clear.

As medium and large herbivores increase, they destroy the forest ecosystem. These herbivores, by ruining their own habitat, will in the end bring about their own destruction. This kind of argument is well known, but in Japan there are now dangerous signs of this happening. A Japanese forest without the wolf is one where monkeys, serow and deer lead dull, tedious lives and lose their state of alertness and where they start to ruin the land. For the forest ecosystem and for the prey animals within it, the wolf, as predator, is an indispensable presence. (JWA 1994: 2)

The extinction of the Japanese wolf at the beginning of the twentieth century left Japan with a *hakaishita shizen* or 'broken nature' (Maruyama 2000) and a *yugamerareta seitaikei* or 'distorted ecosystem' (Koganezawa 1999: 5) in which forest herbivores could no longer be kept in check. In order to restabilize the natural ecosystem, the extinction of the wolf must be reversed. The reintroduction of wolves to Japan would 'restore broken nature' (Maruyama 2000) and 'revive the healthy ecosystem' (Koganezawa 1999: 5).

This argument tends to be specifically directed at the deer population. One of the main arguments advanced for wolf reintroduction is *shika taiji* or 'deer conquest', whereby wolves would serve to control the excessive numbers of deer. Many of the discussions of deer in Japan refer to the absence of the deer's *tenteki* or 'natural predator', the wolf. In his book on the deer problem, the writer Tsujioka Mikio makes the following comments.

No animal exists in Japan today that can be called a predator of the deer. As the deer is a herbivore, in the original ecosystem there also existed at the top of the food chain a carnivore that preyed on the deer. In Japan the predator of the deer is the now extinct Japanese wolf. The wolf relied on the deer as a main food source but it did not deplete the numbers of deer because the deer has the reproductive power to increase its numbers beyond those that are preyed upon. When the deer declined in numbers, wolves too declined, as their food supply was reduced. According to the ecological pyramid, the higher up the food chain an animal is, the less prolific is its reproductive ability. On the other hand, the lower down the food chain an animal is, the greater is its reproductive ability. Predator animals and prey animals keep in balance to maintain the natural world . . . With the extinction of the wolf, one of the main means of controlling deer numbers disappeared. We are still coming to terms with the difficult task of controlling an incomplete nature from which the animal at the top of the ecosystem has been lost. (Tsujioka 1999: 49, 56)

The problem of the deer thus appears as a problem of a forest ecosystem that has lost its 'balance'. The JWA goes one step further than this author by calling for the wolf to be reintroduced and the system to be returned to 'balance'.

A third reason advanced for wolf reintroduction, one that follows on from the ecological argument, is that wolves would relieve the problem of wildlife pestilence. The traditional role of the wolf as a protector of farmland from forest wildlife was noted above, and this earlier status of the wolf helps to justify the reintroduction proposal. The opening paragraph on the JWA's main page on the website reads as follows: 'In Japan, a land of farming people, the wolf was a protective spirit [*shugoshin*] that vanquished the beasts damaging the fields.' The JWA claims that restored colonies of wolves in remote areas of Japan would benefit farmers because the wolves would prey on wild crop-raiders such as the wild boar and the deer.[42] In addition, wolf reintroduction offers a solution to the problem of monkey pestilence that was described in Chapter 3. The background to this claim is the argument that in the past wolves kept down monkey numbers and confined the monkey population to the distant forest far from the village.[43] With the extinction of the wolf, monkeys have increased in number, expanded their territory, and become bolder in their behaviour, to the point where they represent an intolerable nuisance in mountainous areas. One benign effect of a restored wolf population would be to make monkeys a great deal more cautious in their daily foraging behaviour, such that they spend much more time in the safety of the forest trees rather than on dangerous open ground such as the farmland at the edge of remote villages (Koganezawa 1999: 6; Maruyama 1999: 21). By, in effect, returning monkeys to the trees, wolves would make cultivated fields that much less accessible to them, thereby helping to protect the farmer's crops from *engai*. But wolves would also reduce monkey pressure on mountain villages by limiting the numbers of monkeys through predation (Maruyama *et al.* 1995: 24; Maruyama 1995: 4–5). In this way, wolf reintroduction offers the prospect of a relatively uncontroversial (because 'natural') means of lethal monkey control.

Similarly, the JWA claims that foresters, in addition to farmers, would benefit from wolf reintroduction. As we have seen in Chapter 4, the large numbers of forest herbivores are a cause of large-scale damage to timber plantations, as well as to remote farmland. It is a problem that occasions widespread complaint in upland areas, and can even lead to acts of lawbreaking (when the protected serow are hunted or trapped). The JWA argues that wolf reintroduction would be a solution to this problem because the new wolves would restore a balance to the forest by

---

[42] See Maruyama *et al.* (1995: 24), Maruyama (1995: 4–5), and Mizuno (1995: 15–16).
[43] See Watanabe (1995: 50), Maruyama (1995: 4–5), and Mizuno (1995: 15).

preying on deer and serow, the two main forestry pests. In this way, the restored 'forest ecosystem', with wolves once again at its apex, would be in the interests of Japan's timber-growers. In an article written for the forestry magazine *Ringyō gijutsu* (*Forestry Techniques*), Maruyama makes the point that measures such as fencing and repulsion merely redirect herbivore pestilence elsewhere and fail to address its root cause—the large numbers of deer and serow (N. Maruyama 1994: 4). A restored wolf presence, however, would reduce the numbers of these destructive herbivores and relieve the suffering of the nation's beleaguered foresters. In short, the reintroductionists' argument that the new colonies of wolves would act as agents of 'deer conquest' is one that is largely directed to foresters. As Maruyama puts it, the reintroduced wolves would be the *kyūseishu* or 'Saviour' of those people suffering from deer pestilence (*CNS* 7 Mar. 2000). Proponents of reintroduction add that the measure would reduce herbivore damage to primary and secondary forest, as well as to the artificial conifer forest. We saw in Chapter 4 that deer are responsible for damage to trees and other vegetation of the (so-called) natural forest, a cause of some concern both to environmentalists and to the municipal authorities who see the remaining natural forest as a valuable tourist resource. The JWA argument is that, by containing deer numbers, the wolf would help to protect the forest flora threatened by deer overgrazing.[44]

Finally, proponents present wolf reintroduction as an act of cultural restoration. In recent decades there has occurred a resurgence of scholarly and popular interest in the mountain village and the forest as sites of Japanese culture and sources of Japanese identity. It is against the background of this trend that the prospect of wolf reintroduction acquires a special resonance. The existence of wolf shrines, the wolf's role in farm protection, and the benign image of wolves in Japanese folklore are all invoked to support the claim that the wolf is an indispensable part of Japanese culture. As we have seen, in the presentation of the wolf reintroduction campaign the JWA explicitly refers to the wolf's earlier status in Japanese folk religion as a *shugoshin* or 'protective spirit' for farmers, by way of predicating its claim that wolves would once again protect the interests of mountain villagers. Members of the JWA invoke the wolf's status as a *seijū* or 'sacred beast' in ancient Japan, and even suggest that prospective wolf reintroduction would amount to a resurgence of

---

[44] An additional conservation benefit claimed for prospective wolf reintroduction is in relation to the wild bear population. According to this argument, the black bear, as an opportunistic omnivore, would benefit from a restored wolf presence in the forest because it would be able to scavenge from wolf-kill and therefore increase the meat content of its diet (Maruyama 1995: 6). This claim recalls a similar claim made for reintroduced wolves in Yellowstone National Park where grizzly bears (and other scavenging carnivores such as foxes, owls, and eagles) are said to benefit from the predatory presence of wolves because of the increased supply of meat that becomes available (Smith 1996: 90; Robbins 1997). Interestingly, the JWA makes little mention of the phenomenon of bear predation on wild herbivores and its significance in conjunction with wolf predation—an issue that is increasingly receiving attention in North America (Boutin 1992: 125). Even if black bear predation is insignificant in the main Japanese islands, it is likely to have a greater impact in the case of the brown bear in Hokkaido.

'the sentiments of people of ancient times' (*kodaijin no kimochi*) in present-day Japan (Ishibashi 1998: 15). Wolf reintroduction promises to restore not just upland nature (forest ecology) but also upland culture.

Reactions

The wolf reintroduction proposal can be seen as a metropolitan initiative that is inspired by foreign examples. The JWA is a Tokyo-based organization whose membership is clustered in the capital, and JWA opinion surveys suggest that the reintroduction proposal commands a degree of support from the metropolitan population. But what is the response to the proposal in the areas where wolf reintroduction would actually take place? Before offering an answer to this question, the point must be made that there is, as yet, only a limited response to the wolf reintroduction proposal in remote areas, as is perhaps to be expected given that there are no immediate plans actually to carry it out. None the less, on the basis of discussions with informants on the Kii Peninsula, as well as information from secondary sources, a preliminary answer can be offered. The proposal would appear to raise two major areas of concern: first, over the *predatory disposition* of the wolves and the dangers related to this, and second, over the *foreign character* of the wolves.

The primary objection to wolf reintroduction is on the grounds of the danger that wolves would pose. One of the main criticisms of wolf reintroduction in North America and wolf conservation elsewhere has been in terms of the wolf threat to livestock, with ranchers and farmers often vociferous in their opposition. In Japan this concern appears relatively minor, as livestock has traditionally had only a minor place in the Japanese rural economy, even though in the present day there is a livestock industry, including cows, pigs, and chickens, as well as wildlife farms. More than attacks on livestock, it is the prospect of wolf attacks on people that appears to be the major concern. On the Kii Peninsula, one local newspaper article critical of the wolf reintroduction proposal asked its readers: 'Isn't there a worry that when the foreign wolf's stomach is empty it will attack children?' (*Kii Minpō* 12 Mar. 1996). Adverse public reactions have also been reported in the Nikkō region (another candidate site for wolf reintroduction), with some people misinterpreting the JWA proposal as an imminent plan to bring back wolves (Tsujioka 1999: 55).[45] One potentially vulnerable category of people are forest workers, who spend much of the day out in the forest. Forestry is already suffering from a labour shortage, and the fear is that the presence of wolves might become a further obstacle to recruiting forest labourers. The concern is expressed that those villagers (often women) who go to the forest to collect wild mushrooms, herbs, and

---

[45] The JWA proposal to reintroduce wolves to Nikkō even caused a stir as far away as Hokkaido, with Hokkaido residents writing letters to newspapers expressing their concern that future Nikkō wolves might stray far north to the great northern island by sneaking through the newly built tunnel linking Honshu and Hokkaido (Tsujioka 1999: 55)!

grasses might be deterred from doing so by the presence of wolves. Another fear is that old people might be victims of the wolf. One peninsular hunter pointed out to me that, given the tendency of wolves to prey on weak or old animals, the introduced wolves might well target the elderly human inhabitants of remote villages!

Tourism is another consideration. At a time when there is a widely held belief in Japan that the nation's forest has lost its natural character due to the spread of timber plantations, wolf reintroduction might conceivably appeal as a means of re-naturalizing the forest and thereby contribute to the touristic appeal of remote areas. But, alongside such hopes, there is the worry that the presence of free-roaming wolves could add a new, and ultimately unacceptable, level of (at least perceived) danger to forest tourism. At a time when large numbers of tourists spend hours in the forest hiking, gathering herbs and mushrooms, and taking scenic photographs, even minor incidents involving wolves could, because of the likely sensationalist media coverage, have the effect of deterring people from visiting the area thereafter. Another possible site where tourists might encounter wolves would be in tourist villages. Garbage dumps in tourist campsites in Hongū contain much leftover food and other edible scraps, making for a highly attractive foraging ground for a variety of wildlife such as raccoon-dogs and crows. But this raises the possibility that wolves too would exploit these sites, a fear that is to some extent substantiated by reports from Italy that reintroduced wolves in some areas have become dependent on garbage dumps in nearby villages as their prime source of food (Boitani 1992: 127). An indication of the possible public reaction to wolf-sightings near tourist villages and campsites is the furore that arises in Japan whenever a bear is sighted. Bear-sightings and encounters, as we saw in Chapter 5, typically lead to panics and result in the dispatch of the animal in question. Another indication of the near-hysteria that wild predators can arouse in Japan was provided by an incident in the mountainous outskirts of the greater Tokyo area in the summer of 1979 when two pet tigers escaped from captivity. The escaped tigers caused a great panic and a large-scale mobilization of policemen and hunters to track down and destroy them (Mitani 1979*a*; 1979*b*). As these examples show, there is a deep-seated intolerance of wild predators in Japan, at least among the public authorities that attach such overriding importance to the maintenance of public safety.

The second major objection to the wolf reintroduction proposal has to do with the foreign character of the wolves to be reintroduced. Doubts are commonly expressed about whether foreign wolves could adapt to the Japanese forest. For example, the tatami-matmaker in Hongū (a keen amateur biologist) told me that even if Chinese wolves were released in Japan, being so much bigger than Japanese wolves they would be ill-suited to Japan's mountainous environment and would be unable to chase their prey up and down the steep slopes. Japanese wild boar and deer, he predicted, would not let themselves be caught by Chinese wolves. A similar objection was raised by a local journalist, who pointed out that the mountains of Japan 'have many folds' (*hida ga ōi*), a characteristic that makes them quite different from the gentler-sloping mountains found on the Asian continent that the introduced wolves would be used to. A similar objection, to do with the difference between the Mongolian and Japanese landscapes, has been raised by JWA members themselves: 'Would a wolf born and raised on the [Mongolian] plains be able to hunt in the Japanese mountains?' (in Maruyama 1998a: 1).[46] Another criticism of the idea of wolf reintroduction is that it would threaten the natural environment and regional ecology. An example of this kind of sceptical reaction came from a Hongū forester whose timber plantations have suffered from repeated bouts of deer and hare damage, and who might therefore be expected to be sympathetic to a proposal that promises a reduction of such forestry pests. But when I raised the subject, he immediately opposed the idea and made the following objection.

If that happened, if there were wolves here, then the ecology would end up being changed forever. I think that in a place like this, this forest, you should only have trees that are local, and so when people bring in strange garden trees that you have never seen before, well that's unnatural [*fushizen*].

This same concern is evident in an article hostile to wolf reintroduction that appeared in *Kii Minpō* (one of the regional newspapers of the Kii Peninsula) which warned that the plan could lead to *seitai no hakai* or 'ecological destruction'.

The Japanese wolf is different from the foreign breed. The irresponsible plan of *introducing* an animal that was not originally in Japan is an abdication of the scholar's duty and amounts to conduct that is difficult to forgive. There is absolutely no understanding of the Japanese wolf. To simply carry out *introduction* without any scientific research survey whatsoever will make Japanese zoology, and even the Japanese people as a whole, a laughing stock around the world . . . (*Kii Minpō* 12 Mar. 1996, emphasis added)

A couple of weeks later, a reader's letter on the subject appeared in the same newspaper.

If foreign wolves are released into the Kii mountains, I think that, rather than the hoped for reduction of deer numbers, what is more likely is that the animal and plant ecology would be destroyed and that a sharp increase in wolf numbers would lead to damage, to danger, and to disease-causing germs . . . They want to restore the Japanese wolf, don't they? But then why are they bringing in a foreign wolf in place of the Japanese wolf? . . . [D]o the people who live on the Kii Peninsula and who until now have protected nature on the Kii Peninsula . . . want foreign wolves to be set loose? . . . We the [Wakayama] prefectural people, to whom the deep mountains of the west of the peninsula belong, should . . . firmly

[46] Maruyama has attempted to answer this concern by pointing out the similarities in the two landscapes—i.e. that forest as well as prairie is found in the Inner Mongolian wolf-range region—but accepts that the mountainous character of Japan does make for a potentially significant difference that must be taken into account (Maruyama 1998a: 5).

oppose it and continue to protect the nature and the way of life of the Kii mountains. (*Kii Minpō* 30 Mar. 1996)

In these objections, reference is made to *two* wolves—*nihonōkami* or the 'Japanese wolf' and *gaikokusan ōkami* or the 'foreign wolf' (sometimes even *gaikokusan urufu*, using the English word 'wolf')—rather than just the wolf. From this perspective, extinction and reintroduction appear to refer to different wolves. The wolf reintroduction plan is represented not as restoring what was lost but as importing something new and alien.

The belief in the continued existence of wolves in Japan is another reason why wolf reintroduction is opposed on nativistic grounds. As we have seen, in Japan there are small numbers of amateur naturalists who believe that the remnants of a wolf population still roam the remote *yama*. One organization associated with such views, *Nihonōkami kenkyūkai* or the Japanese Wolf Research Society (here-after, JWRS), therefore sees the task of wolf conservation in Japan to be one of pro-tecting wolves that still exist rather than replacing wolves that have disappeared (see NYSHI n.d.). From this perspective, wolf reintroduction would represent the *introduction* of *foreign* wolves and would ensure the extinction of the Japanese wolf rather than reverse it. Japan's wolf debate has tended to polarize between the posi-tions of the JWRS and the JWA: on the one hand, passively waiting for native wolves to reappear in the Japanese forest, and on the other actively inserting foreign wolves into it. The objection to the former is that, after nearly a century in which wolves have disappeared from the Japanese landscape, belief in the con-tinued existence of wolves is based on a huge leap of faith, while the objection to the latter is that it involves bringing in a foreign animal to Japan and therefore amounts to a *displacement* rather than *replacement* of the Japanese wolf. Inter-estingly, a middle way has recently been proposed between these two stark alter-natives, one that would meet nativist objections to wolf reintroduction: that cloned Japanese wolves be reintroduced into the Japanese forest (Tōyama 1998*a*: 55). According to this proposal, DNA recovered from the stuffed Japanese wolf specimens held in Japanese or foreign museums would be inserted into the nuclei of fertilized eggs of other species of wolf in order to produce cloned Japanese wolf cubs. Once a viable population of cloned Japanese wolves has been recovered, the second stage could begin of reintroducing these captive-bred wolves into the Japanese forest. In this way, biotechnological advances permitting, an *indigenous* wolf reintroduction could take place in Japan, rather than the foreign wolf reintro-duction proposed by the JWA.

The main response of the JWA to the indigenist criticism levelled at it has been to emphasize the similarity between Japanese wolves and the Chinese wolves of Inner Mongolia to be brought in. As we have seen, some Japanese zoologists argue that the Japanese wolf was a separate species of wolf, and this uniqueness claim is invoked by opponents to wolf reintroduction to argue that the presence of alien

Fɪɢ. 6.6. 'I had this [New Year's] dream'. The various placards read (from the left): 'Welcome, Mr Wolf—All Japan Gourmet Club'; 'Welcome to Japan, Lord Wolf—National Sports Hunters League'; 'Welcome to Japan—Rare Furs Appreciation Society'

wolves would threaten (rather than bolster) the indigenous ecosystem of Japan (see Hatano 1996: 47). The JWA tends to reject or at least downplay the native/alien distinction, and to reframe the issue of wolf reintroduction in less polar terms. To this end, JWA discourse has come to emphasize the similarity of the wolf sub-species of East Asia. In particular, it asserts that there is a genetic continuity between Japanese and Chinese subspecies of the grey wolf—characterizing the Chinese wolves as 'close relatives of the Japanese wolves' (Takahashi and Maruyama n.d.: 6).[47] The Inner Mongolian subspecies is said to be a cognate

[47] The JWA sees an important precedent in the recent decision of the Japanese Environment Agency to use crested ibises from China in order to re-establish the crested ibis in Japan (Maruyama 1998*b*).

subspecies to the Japanese wolf, consistent with the rule of proximity in restoration ecology circles (Brown 1994: 364–5). On its home page and in its publications, the JWA has started to refer much more to the *haiiroōkami* or 'grey wolf'. As part of this broadening of focus, the JWA even invokes *haiiroōkami no hogo* or 'grey wolf conservation' as one of its objectives, in addition to wolf reintroduction in Japan. Maruyama Naoki argues that JWA members should take an interest in wolf conservation in other parts of the East Asian region, as it is from these places that Japan's new wolves would be recruited (Maruyama 1998*c*: 1). The JWA organizes trips to Inner Mongolia in which members of the association have the chance to observe wolves in the wild and acquaint themselves with the wolves of the wider region.[48] The new emphasis on the grey wolf blurs the distinction between new foreign wolves and old Japanese wolves and allows the JWA to talk about *the same animal in different places* and thereby circumvent nativistic objections to reintroduction. The 'Japanese wolf' disappears from the wolf reintroduction argument, becoming simply one of many regional grey wolf populations in East Asia. As a result of this reformulation, the earlier extinction of the wolf in Japan, in effect, comes to be redefined as a *regional* (subspecies) extinction rather than a total (species) extinction.

A third objection to the idea of wolf reintroduction in Japan is on the grounds that there is no longer any space left for wolves (see Kanzaki *et al.* 1995: 1). The argument is that the scale of the human population in present-day Japan precludes the re-establishment of a wolf population. This objection is informed by a deep-seated popular perception in Japan that the country is overcrowded, with too many people and not enough land. The JWA response to this kind of objection is to point to future population trends, and in particular to the projected decline of the Japanese population in the twenty-first century to fewer than 80 million by 2050. This is a change that would make the restoration of a wolf population much more feasible (Maruyama n.d.: 5). The argument is that just as the original extinction of wolves in Japan at the beginning of the twentieth century was related to a rapidly increasing human population, so conversely a necessary condition of wolf reintroduction is for there to be fewer human beings on the archipelago. In practice, this point about human numbers has less to do with national than with regional space. The JWA argues that the depopulation of remote rural areas of Japan in the late twentieth century improves the prospects for wolf reintroduction. As we have seen,

---

[48] This is an experience that can leave a strong impression on those involved, not least because of its power to evoke the now extinct Japanese wolf. These are the comments of one such wolf-watcher, Takatori Kiyoshi, to his fellow wolf enthusiasts in an article on the JWA website:

> In Inner Mongolia I went out three times and I met the wolf three times. Each time it was for just an instant and I can say no more than that 'I saw it', as I was unable to calmly observe it or photograph it. But even now I can clearly remember it. Each of the three times there was only a single wolf. This wolf, which was small in stature with graceful, long legs, was far from the fierce image of a savage beast portrayed by westerners. I had the impression that the Japanese wolf in the past had this kind of [unthreatening] appearance. (Takatori 2000)

between 1955 and 1995 the municipalities of the Kii Peninsula lost over half their population through urban outmigration, and within these municipalities the remoter settlements have been disproportionately affected, leading in many cases to total abandonment. Vacated by human beings, these mountainous areas become available for a restored wolf population (Maruyama n.d.: 5). It is precisely on the basis of estimates of their residential population densities that a list of candidate areas for wolf reintroduction has been drawn up.

Although appearing skilfully to rebut the arguments of its critics, in fact the JWA comes close to adopting some of their reasoning. For in response to objections to wolf reintroduction that are based on the size of the contemporary human population, the JWA refers to projected trends towards a lower population, nationally and regionally, in the future. The problem with this line of argument is twofold. First, it relies on an implicit zero-sum logic according to which fewer people becomes the condition of wolf restoration, something that seems to be potentially at odds with the notion, otherwise stressed by the reintroductionists, of human–wolf coexistence. Secondly, to invoke rural depopulation as an enabling condition of wolf reintroduction risks offending local sensibilities. Great efforts are being made (by the municipal state as well as local groups) in remote areas to stop and even reverse depopulation. Certainly, many upland settlements have been abandoned and are unlikely ever to be resettled, and to this extent, rural depopulation does tend to appear irreversible; it may well be that in the long run the JWA is right and that remote areas in Japan are being vacated by their erstwhile human inhabitants and consequently become available, in theory, for occupation by wolves. But as rural depopulation is not a prospect greeted with any enthusiasm locally, arguments for reintroduction based on it are unlikely to commend themselves to mountain villagers.

Rural depopulation also makes possible the creation of connections between the urban-based JWA and the regions in which wolf reintroduction is to take place. In a remarkable new initiative, the JWA leaders have set up a volunteer organization in which urban members can assist remote villagers in resisting the depredations of wild animals. This is Maruyama Naoki's description of the project to JWA members:

THE 'ANIMAL PATROL PROJECT' APPEAL—DEFENDING FARMING
IN THE MOUNTAINS

Recently, across the nation, with the increase in deer, monkeys and wild boar, the problem of wildlife pestilence affecting farm products in different mountainous regions has been getting more serious. In these regions with poor natural conditions, farming is weak anyway regardless of wildlife pestilence, and people in the past gave up farming, but with the recent outbreak of pestilence it has received a further blow. In these farming villages, ageing is advancing, and the earlier forms of resistance to wildlife pestilence do not suffice . . . It is clear that one way of dealing with this situation would be to stop the farm damage caused by deer, monkeys and wild boar by intercepting these animals and driving them away. But because of ageing, outmigration and so on, the local farming population no longer has the manpower to do this. On the other hand, nature is in demand among urban residents and recently the number of urbanites enraptured by the thought of retiring and living in the countryside has increased. But many of these people do not know how to realize this dream. Now these people can go to the sparsely populated villages that suffer from wildlife pestilence and participate in animal patrols. The 'Animal Patrol Project' will allow these people both to realize their dream of country life and to contribute to mountain farming. (Maruyama 2001*b*)

The idea would seem to have an obvious logic to it: while wolf reintroduction is proclaimed as a solution to the wildlife problem in the future, it offers no relief to remote farmers in the present day. Hence in the meantime Japan's forest-edge communities would be protected by wolf supporters, in the absence of actual wolves. In the process, the wolf supporters will establish longer-term relationships with the villages they assist.

Despite the claim that the wolf reintroduction proposal holds a strong potential appeal among the existing mountain village population, doubts remain about whether wolf reintroduction would be acceptable in the areas where it would actually be carried out. One JWA member expresses such doubts by suggesting that wolf reintroduction may have to be accompanied by *ningen no saidōnyū* or 'human reintroduction' in the areas in question. In other words, one answer to local opposition to the reintroduction proposal would be to change the composition of the local population by encouraging favourably disposed urban dwellers to settle in the areas in question (Fujiwara 2000). The 'Animal Patrol Project' is ostensibly a form of urban support for beleaguered remote areas. But in giving up their spare time to defend forest-edge farms, the urban volunteers will not only establish connections with remote areas, but also introductions to possible rural retirement destinations. To the extent that JWA members do move to remote villages, the JWA would in effect establish a pro-wolf constituency in the regions where wolves are to be reintroduced. At the same time, the publicity that such volunteerism attracts can also help to highlight both the problem of wildlife pestilence and the need for a natural solution to it—that is, wolf reintroduction. Just how appealing the new initiative will be, both among would-be urbanites and the rural areas to receive them, remains to be seen, but it does show creative thinking on the part of the JWA and a way of allowing its members to be active in the interim period while the organization builds support for wolf reintroduction.

HUNTERS AND WOLVES

It has long been a basic tenet of Western wildlife management that human hunters perform the wild predator's 'ecosystem function' of containing herbivore numbers (Gilbert 1995: 16) and that in the absence of wild predators human hunting may become a biological necessity (Sinclair 1997: 387; Terborgh 1992*b*: 289). Indeed, in many cases (for example, in relation to deer), the term 'hunting' is used synonymously with terms such as 'control' and 'management' (Rutberg 1997: 40). In Japan too the argument is often made that, for much of the twentieth century, the true ecological significance of the extinction of the Japanese wolf was concealed by the actions of hunters, who in effect carried out the wolf's role of regulating herbivore numbers.

With the extinction of the wolf, located at the top of the ecosystem, there ceased to be an animal that could catch and eat deer. As a result, deer numbers, which had earlier been stable, started to increase. However, hunters, who took the place of wolves, themselves caught large numbers of deer . . . The reason that nature [without the wolf] has not been completely transformed is because of the deer that are caught by [human] hunting. (Tsujioka 1999: 85)

With the decline in hunting in recent decades, this compensatory effect has diminished and the full impact of wolf extinction has become apparent. This line of reasoning, that is shared by the JWA, suggests not only that hunters and wolves are similar kinds of predator with respect to the forest ecosystem, but also that, because of this common predatory status, there is likely to be competition between them.

Japanese hunters have an ambivalent view of wolves. On the one hand, hunters admire and even identify with wolves. Japanese hunting magazines carry images of wolves (sometimes on the front cover) and there are occasional special features on how wolves and other wild predators hunt their prey. As we have seen, Japanese hunters liken their hounds to wolves, giving them wolf-related names and attributing to them wolf's blood or wolf ancestry. Japanese hunters even hunt like wolves when they simulate the actions of the wolf pack in surrounding the wild boar in the forest, explicitly recognizing this in the use of terms such as 'wolf-hunting' and 'wolf-chasing'. Solo hunters sometimes characterize themselves as *ippiki ōkami* or 'lone wolves' (Umezu 1979: 62). It is not uncommon for Japanese hunters, when discussing the larger significance of the hunt, explicitly to equate it with wolf predation. The following comments, made by a hunter in connection with deer-hunting (and reported in a hunting magazine), are not unusual: 'Damage [by deer] to farm crops and forest trees has become a major problem, but, unlike the earlier era when it was the wolf that maintained the balance, today we are the ones who must maintain the balance' (Itō 1994: 98). Moreover, the national *ryōyūkai* projects hunting as a form of *dōbutsu kanri* or 'animal management' that protects 'nature' and the 'ecosystem', portraying the hunter as a kind of ecological maintenance man, helping to keep in balance what would otherwise be an incomplete and unstable forest ecosystem (*AS* 7 July 1992). This representation of the hunter is formally identical to that of the wolf in the reintroduction proposal.

On the other hand, many Japanese hunters would oppose wolf reintroduction. One of the major objections to wolf reintroduction in Yellowstone National Park came from hunters who were concerned that wolves would compete with them for game animals in areas surrounding the park (Boyce 1992: 134–5). Japanese hunters too have an obvious interest in maintaining exclusive predatory access to the game animals of the forest. The rivalry that tends to exist among hunters (and between different hunting groups) readily extends to a sense of rivalry between hunters and wild predators. Japanese hunters are highly conscious of wild predators such as foxes and raccoon-dogs that prey on game such as pheasants and rabbits, and in the autumn plentiful numbers of these predators are interpreted as a sure sign that there will be diminished numbers of small game in the coming winter season. Hunters matter of factly make a similar connection between wolves and large game animals, seeing reintroduced wolves as likely to diminish the numbers of wild boar and deer in the forest and therefore to spoil their own hunting prospects. As noted above, hunters complain that feral dog populations diminish the game available in the forest by hunting down animals themselves or by scavenging human catches (that is, trapped animals). Given the great concern among hunters over the issue of game animal stocks, and sensitivity to any possible threat to their numbers, it is hardly surprising that similar objections are raised to wolves. It follows that if the farmer sees the wolf as a helpful pest controller in the mountains, the hunter will tend to see the wolf as a harmful rival hunter. JWA members even express the fear that Japanese hunters might decide to hunt the reintroduced wolves.[49] Some Japanese hunters already hunt large predators: Japanese hunting magazines advertise overseas 'big game hunting' trips in which wild predators can be hunted (lions in South Africa, mountain lions in America, leopards in Nepal, and so on). Even though reintroduced wolves would probably be given protected status, legal protection would not necessarily prevent some hunters targeting wolves (as the incidence of serow poaching shows).[50]

[49] This fear of hunters targeting wolves is directly voiced by a JWA member who, in the course of a discussion of the potential problem of feral dogs, argues that the elimination of these dogs is necessary because their existence would give hunters a pretext for hunting wolves. He suspects that some hunters would publicly justify their actions by claiming that they thought the animal was a dog, while privately bragging among themselves about their wolf-killing feat (Hatano 1996: 52).

[50] A qualification should be added to this depiction of the hunter as the enemy of the wolf. The website discussions of JWA members occasionally mention the Ainu. One contributor raised the question of why the wolf was sacred among the Ainu, even though they were a hunting people, while another member responded by arguing that Ainu hunters practised hunting in moderation and did not therefore see the wolf as a rival. 'Like carnivorous animals, indigenous people such as the Ainu people practise hunting only for their own food, becoming a part of the ecosystem' (Kamata 2001). Like wolves themselves, Ainu hunters appear moderate in their predation and therefore a part of nature. By contrast, the excessive predation on the part of modern (post-Meiji) Japanese hunters makes them a threat to the ecosystem and places them outside of nature. In this way, the discussion of wolves and the prospect of wolf reintroduction readily leads to a contrast between traditional Ainu hunting and modern Japanese hunting. The Ainu become exemplars of past coexistence with wolves, just as they are sometimes invoked as examples of traditional coexistence with bears. Ainu society

The other point, as already touched on, is that Japanese hunters claim that they regulate the forest themselves. Here we can recall one of the arguments made by local opponents of wolf reintroduction in the American West. In response to the reintroductionists' claim that the wolf would restore balance to the ecosystem, residents of Montana and adjacent states argue that nature is already controlled and regulated by human actions, including hunting and culling. In this way, they oppose the call for a restoration of the 'natural ecosystem' by asserting that there already exists a human-regulated ecosystem that ensures sound, orderly management of the natural world (Paystrup 1993: 148–9). Similarly, Japanese hunters argue that hunting and trapping, which they characterize as *mabiki* or 'thinning', acts to control the wildlife populations of the forest. In response to the JWA position that, in the absence of the wolf, the forest ecosystem is unbalanced and unstable, the hunters argue that the system can be controlled by human activity. Where game animals are obviously excessive, the hunter's view is that the problem lies in the existing hunting laws in Japan which constrain hunters from catching more animals—particularly the restrictions on hunting deer hinds and on hunting serow. If these laws were to be eased, hunters would be able to carry out their function of *mabiki* much more effectively. In short, from the hunter's perspective the Japanese forest is already subject to a regime of control, one that, while it may be imperfect at present, can be tightened and improved.

The response of the JWA is to point out that, while hunting may once have performed this role of containing wild herbivore populations, with the decline in the number of registered hunters in recent decades it can no longer do so and that responsibility for the ecosystem must be passed over to wolves. If, in the twentieth century, (extinct) wolves were replaced by hunters, in the twenty-first century (reintroduced) wolves should replace (or at least supplement the diminishing numbers of) hunters. There also appears to be an implicit assumption in the JWA proposal that wolves would be superior to hunters. This is because wild predators are believed to have a beneficial selection effect on their prey: by catching old, weak animals, they improve the remaining population. By contrast, human hunting does not select for an improved overall quality of the wildlife population, and may well have the reverse effect of diminishing overall population quality because of the way hunters target healthy animals (Rodriguez de la Fuente 1975: 107–8). This is why human hunters are inferior stand-ins for wild predators. It would follow that the hunters' prime justification of their hunting as *mabiki* becomes questionable. The term *mabiki*, when applied to the ricefield, involves the removal of the inferior individual plants to the benefit of the overall crop, and is an exercise in

becomes a ready counterpoint to modern Japanese society, and is held up as a source of traditional wisdom that modern Japan should emulate. Wolves therefore mediate not just the relation between traditional and modern Japan, but also that between indigenous and settler Japan, with Ainu society representing an alternative point of inspiration on wolf matters to JWA members, and a focus for the critique of modern society.

quality improvement. But when the hunter pursues a wild boar or a deer, he is not intent on removing inferior animals—indeed, on the contrary, Japanese hunters typically boast about the size, ferocity, or speed of the animals they catch. The hunter out in the forest is concerned with the quality of the individual animals he hunts rather than the overall quality of the animal population that remains.

In all of the animals looked at in previous chapters there has been an obvious convergence of interests between farmers and foresters on the one side, and hunters on the other. Although this convergence is only partial—as hunters seek to maintain wildlife *populations*, even as they hunt and cull *individual* animals—there remains a clear overlap of interests. But in the case of the wolf, there is a much more obvious conflict of interest between the two sides. This is because the reintroduced wolves, by virtue of their supposed capacity for regulatory predation, would benefit the forester and the farmer, but, by the same token, would in principle replace the hunter. Indeed, the appeal of the wolf reintroduction proposal is that wolves, unlike hunters, would not be constrained in their hunting by the panoply of restrictions (hunting seasons, hunting grounds, huntable species, etc.) to which the human hunter is subject. With the reintroduction of wolves, therefore, wildlife pests such as the wild boar, the monkey, and the deer would become subject to a new, naturalized process of *mabiki*, one that has the potential to operate at a much higher level than that achieved by the declining numbers of human hunters. The wolf reintroduction scenario would, in effect, make obsolete the hunter's role in the wildlife wars of upland Japan.

Conclusion

Rural peripheries in many parts of the world have undergone large-scale depopulation in connection with national trends of urbanization and industrialization.
As a result of urban outmigration, rural areas lose their younger reproductive age
bands and are left with aged residential populations. Demographic decline leads to
changes in local patterns of land-uses, with far-reaching ecological consequences.
As a result of agricultural contraction, there is an increase in fallowlands and wild
vegetation. With the withdrawal of an agrarian human presence, the regime of
human disturbances of plant growth is arrested and natural succession resumes.
Within decades farmland and grassland give way to secondary forest and its fauna.
In this way, the decline in the human population of remote areas comes to be associated with an increase in the populations of wild mammals. Some striking examples of this pattern of change have been reported. Rural depopulation and agrarian
abandonment in parts of Spain and Italy have resulted in an increase in wild ungulate numbers and, in turn, have helped to expedite a recovery in wolf numbers
(Tellería and Sáez-Royuela 1984: 55; Meriggi and Lovari 1996: 1562). Rural depopulation in the Alps, by drastically reducing the numbers of grazing livestock,
has allowed an expansion of woodland and an increase in the number of wild ungulates—a set of environmental changes that makes for an improved habitat for large
carnivores such as wolves, bears, and lynxes which are, as a result, 'now gradually
recolonizing the Alps' (Breitenmoser 1998b: 284).

The ecologist has an obvious interest in this phenomenon. In their discussion of
the changing Mediterranean landscape, Debussche *et al.* write that 'the analysis
of this marked and rapid trend [i.e. depopulation and reduced human land-use]
and the understanding of its ecological and biological mechanisms provide keys to
evaluating the ability of vegetation to re-establish after heavy disturbance'
(Debussche *et al.* 1999: 3). Similarly, at a time when wilderness around the world is
rapidly being eroded, there is a growing conservationist interest in the habitat
potential of the countryside, including abandoned and reforesting parts of it, and
in the ability of wild animals and birds to adapt to such human-altered environments (Western 1989; Green 1989: 195–6; Daily 1997). But this situation can also
offer the anthropologist insights into certain assumptions and self-understandings
on the part of the societies that experience it. Although the *longue durée* studies of
landscape ecologists tend to look at the relationship between rural depopulation
and environmental change as a sequential transformation, in practice rural

depopulation is likely to be a protracted process spanning decades. What this means is that the environmental changes that result from rural depopulation become apparent, to some extent, to contemporary human society, especially the remaining local residents. Given the prominence of the 'civilizational' motif of an original human transformation of wild space in mythology and folklore around the world, this reverse process, in which human space gives way to wild space, becomes of obvious interest to the anthropologist.

The reforestation of national peripheries arouses divergent human reactions. At the national level this environmental change may be favourably viewed as evidence of a resurgence of nature that challenges modern perceptions of civilization's remorseless erosion of nature. The reforested peripheries of urban-industrial societies become popular leisure and recreational destinations, valued sites of landscape improvement and restored natural heritage, and even national carbon sinks that help to reduce global warming (Bell and Evans 1997; Romano 1995). The return of large 'charismatic' wildlife associated with the trend of forest revival can occasion much public enthusiasm, while the acceptance of wild carnivores is held up as a measure of the civilized or progressive status of a society (Lienert 1998: 133; Breitenmoser 1998*a*: 135–6; Steinhart 1989). But there tends to be a rather different perspective among the local populations directly affected by these changes. As a transformation of the physical and perceptual environment, reforestation is often negatively viewed by local people, as has been reported for Switzerland (Hunziker 1995: 405–7), Finland (Karjalainan and Komulainan 1998: 89), and Spain (Gómez-Limón and Fernández 1999: 170–1). Where it involves the areal expansion of forest and woodland at the expense of clearings and vistas, reforestation may well be experienced by local residents as the loss of land more than the return of forest. The disappearance of arable land and the contraction of open space that occurs with forest expansion become disturbing signs of community decline. Similarly, the increase in wildlife populations can appear a threatening development that points to the retrenchment of human society rather than a benign revival of nature.

This book has examined the way in which this process of environmental transformation is locally experienced in Japan, with specific reference to people–wildlife relations. The decline in the human population brings about a new context for people–wildlife interactions. The rural exodus transforms the landscape, which comes to be marked by a proliferation of empty houses, abandoned farm plots, and neglected timber plantations, as well as an increase in forest cover. Under these conditions, villagers can no longer rely on their erstwhile level of environmental control. Villages become easier for wild animals to raid both because of the decrease in the number of people and because of the increase in wild vegetation. The remaining elderly villagers are unable to maintain field defences (which become porous and ineffective) or to put in the long hours of field-guarding. The decline in cultivation in depopulated villages leads to overgrown fields and the disappearance of the clearing between the fields and the forest-edge, conditions that help to conceal the intrusions of wild boar, monkeys, and deer on to village farmland. As the *satoyama* forest floor is no longer cleared by human hands, the process of forest succession resumes, the effect of which is to hasten the replacement of pine forest with deciduous oak forest, a change in forest vegetation that is advantageous to forest wildlife. As a result of the neglect of timber plantations, the amount of edible undergrowth within them increases, and they become more attractive feeding sites for wild animals. In short, the human withdrawal from upland areas of Japan allows animals to enter, feed in, and occupy human spaces with impunity.

If depopulation contributes to the wildlife problem, the wildlife problem in turn exacerbates depopulation. Rural depopulation in Japan must be understood, first and foremost, in terms of the larger economic forces associated with a national labour market that draws away village youth to live and work in the cities. But in addition to this 'pull' factor, there are various 'push' factors within the rural periphery itself that can contribute to urban outmigration and rural depopulation, including the low appeal of employment opportunities in the rural economy, the relative absence of public amenities, and the logistical inconvenience of everyday life in mountain settlements. Wildlife damage is another potential 'push' factor. The new scale of wildlife pestilence makes everyday life that much harder in remote villages and can render some of them virtually uninhabitable. Repeated damage by wild boar, monkeys, and deer can make villagers give up farming or forestry and even leave the village altogether. Yet the nature of this wildlife threat in upland Japan must be kept in perspective. It should be stressed that the stakes involved in farming failure today are not nearly as high as they were in earlier times, when animal damage to the harvest had the potential to inflict hunger, debt, and poverty on its victims. Present-day mountain villagers are *not* threatened in *this* way. The present-day wildlife problem in Japan is sometimes referred to as though it were a threat to human life—for example, as a *shikatsu no mondai* or 'a matter of life and death'. But this expression should be understood as referring to the prospects for the village more than the lives of the villagers, because of the way the wildlife problem calls into doubt the very future of upland settlement in an era of large-scale depopulation. In other words, the impact of the wildlife pest is not confined to the material damage it causes to individual farmers and foresters, but extends to its negative symbolism *vis-à-vis* the community as a whole.

THE SYMBOLISM OF THE PEST

Enemy or Victim?

To account for people–wildlife relations in the Japanese mountains, consideration must be given to this symbolic dimension of the wildlife problem. Wild boar, monkeys, and bears feed on human crops and adversely affect human livelihoods, but in their forays into villages they also breach important human boundaries. When wild animals from the forest invade farms, graveyards, and houses in the village, they threaten the spatial order of remote rural areas. The status of forest animals as signs of an elemental disorder is expressed in the following comments of villagers in the Okutama region, as reported by Iguchi Matoi.

With a worried look on her face, the grandmother said, 'It's frightening when the things from the forest come down to the village. I hope that something bad is not about to happen' . . . Animals now commonly appear in the village, whereas before they could not be seen even if one tried to see them . . . For the grandmothers and grandfathers who live on this land, as well as for a city dweller like myself, when the wild beasts that are supposed to live in the forest start to appear in the village to such an extent, it suggests that 'something bad' [*warui koto*] is happening . . . (Iguchi 1990*b*: 14)

Iguchi is struck by the old woman's suggestion that the unprecedented presence of forest animals in the village is a bad omen that presages impending disaster. He takes these comments as evidence that, in addition to the material damage they incur from crop-raiding, remote villagers suffer from what he calls *shinritekina appaku* or 'psychological oppression' because of the invasion of their everyday living space by forest animals (ibid.).

There is a perception among Japanese mountain villagers that the wild animals of the forest are taking over their land. In his book *Kaso shakai* ('Depopulated Society'), the cultural anthropologist Yoneyama Toshinao recalls the words of an elderly resident in a depopulated area of Gifu Prefecture on the impending abandonment of his village: 'soon this place will become land that belongs only to the snakes' (Yoneyama 1969: 9). For many remote rural dwellers the present-day animal encroachment on to farmland and timber plantations, in conjunction with continuing depopulation, occasions a similar pessimism. The rural sociologist Hasegawa Akihiko offers the following interpretation of the despairing comments he has heard from farmers in mountainous regions.

They mean that territory is being lost which has been established as a place of human dwelling over hundreds and even thousands of years of human history during which Man did battle with nature. Man has become weary and tired in the war with nature, he has abandoned the war, and he has conceded defeat. Depopulation can be understood in terms of the people who live on the frontier with nature having to withdraw, as a result of this defeat, back to the [human] base in the cities. (A. Hasegawa 1996: 25)

Here we can recall the idiom of warfare that has recurred throughout the previous chapters. The wild boar, the monkey, the deer, the serow, and the bear are all likened to enemies that seem to be waging a kind of elemental warfare on upland settlements, prompting mountain villagers to defend themselves and resist this apparent animal takeover of their land. But under the conditions of large-scale depopulation, villagers can no longer effectively defend themselves from the animal adversary. From this perspective, the depopulation of the mountain communities of Japan represents a retreat from the wild frontier and a kind of loss of national territory. It is as though Japan is undergoing an historical regression in its mountainous interior. This sense that the wildlife problem represents a territorial takeover is informed by a particular 'folk demography' in which the wild animals of the forest are understood to be a rival population—what we might call a *zoodemography*. The already existing sense of human–animal rivalry is only exacerbated by the trend of rural depopulation. While the wildlife population appears prone to proliferation, in modern times the human population of the village has sharply declined. When upland space becomes depopulated, it loses its capacity to resist the rival (animal) claimants to it. The perception of wild animals as a rival population makes the wildlife pest a powerful symbol among the remaining residents in depopulated areas.

One might expect such zero-sum representations to promote social unity in upland areas. The war idiom ought to encourage a united front among mountain villagers in opposition to the threat of the 'four-legs' from the forest. This is, to some extent, borne out in practice. When a farm in the village has been raided by wild boar, village neighbours share the victim's sense of outrage, and when a bear is sighted in the nearby forest everybody in the village takes notice and able-bodied villagers may be mobilized to patrol the area. Villagers pool their labour to protect the human settlement from wildlife intrusions, such as by establishing and maintaining physical barriers and other defences and by taking turns in field-guarding. The wildlife problem can also engender a sense of social solidarity over time and across generations. Despite repeated damage to a field, many a farmer will defiantly continue to cultivate it rather than abandon land that has been farmed for generations. Long-standing village defences against wildlife such as the old stone 'boar walls' are a visible reminder that ancestors too had to struggle with animal raids but persisted in order to pass down farmland to the present generation. However, there are clearly limits to the solidarity of the village in the face of the wildlife threat from the forest. For instead of uniting human society against it, the wildlife pest can become a source of tension and division among people. In short, along with human conflict *with* wildlife, there is human conflict *over* wildlife.

First of all, this human conflict over wildlife has to do with divergent human interests. In this book we have seen that forest wildlife becomes a source of division among different categories of stakeholder. The farmer sees the wild boar as a serious farm pest, but the hunter sees the wild boar as a valuable game animal. As those who cull the problem animals that cause farm damage, hunters support the interests of farmers, but, as we saw in Chapter 2, hunters also have misgivings about culling. This farmer–hunter tension over the wild boar tends to lead to division within the *ryōyūkai* between those hunters who cull and those who do not, and between (pursuit) hunters and trappers. The human conflict with monkeys described in Chapter 3 was also informed, to some extent, by divisions on the human side over the monkey's status. While most villagers complain that monkeys are a farm pest, as well as an all round nuisance, municipal officials and guesthouse owners see these animals as a potentially important tourist attraction (hence the strategic provisioning of wild monkeys in some areas). Along with the farmer, the hunter, and the tourist promoter, another party to the conflict over wildlife in Japan is the conservationist. As we saw in Chapters 4 and 5, the forester sees the serow and the bear as plantation pests, but the conservationist sees these animals as a valuable part of Japan's natural heritage that should be protected. Typically, in these various stakeholder conflicts, one party complains that there are too many animals and that they need to be controlled, while the other party complains that they are too few or endangered and that they need to be protected.

Social division also arises from differential exposure to wildlife damage. Upstream villages tend to be more seriously affected by wildlife pestilence than downstream villages. Upstream villagers sometimes complain that, because of the small populations in their settlements, local government does not take the wildlife problem as seriously as it should. Similarly, within villages the households that suffer the greatest damage tend to be those with fields nearest to the forest, while more central households, with fields closer in, are relatively unaffected. This unequal impact may well limit the degree of concerted village action in response to it; in some villages wildlife pestilence is seen as a problem for forest-edge households rather than a problem for the village as such. A further source of resentment in the village is where households protect their own fields and plantations from wildlife damage, but in the process appear to deflect the problem on to their neighbours. Another kind of neighbourly dispute that arises is where a household is deemed to be encouraging the problem by not taking appropriate or responsible countermeasures, leading irate neighbours to link damage to their crops to such irresponsible conduct. This sort of complaint has been directed at organic farming incomers who sometimes appear less than robust in their response to wildlife damage.

Divergent interests are not the sole basis of social division over wildlife in upland Japan. Another constraint on the emergence of the kind of social unity implied by the war idiom has to do with the existence of local sympathy for wildlife pests. It is clear from the examples of human–animal relations examined in this book that the wild animals of the forest are not always viewed as dangerous enemies, but may appear instead as victims. Although mountain villagers highlight the threat posed by animals, there is also a degree of recognition that the animals are, in a sense, under threat themselves. There is a widespread awareness in Hongū that the larger situation of the Japanese mountains is one of double encroachment: that, in addition to wildlife encroachment on the village, there has taken place a developmental encroachment (principally in the form of the forestry industry) on the forest. Viewed against this background, the recent wave of wildlife pestilence points not so much to immoral wildlife behaviour as to morally questionable *human* conduct—that is, to the prior human destruction of the forest. This sentiment is captured in a common local expression that is sometimes applied to the wildlife problem: 'When you do something bad, it returns to you.'[1] This puts a different complexion on present-day wildlife damage, which, while undesirable and to be resisted, appears as the price that human society pays for destroying the animals' own feeding grounds in the forest. Wildlife crop-raiding in human settlements can, in this way, be viewed as an act of desperation rather than belligerence, while the animals themselves become an object of pity more than hatred. If animals now bother people, it is because people first bothered animals. Wild animals breach the boundaries of the village because people earlier breached the boundaries of the forest.

Another reason why wildlife pests may be viewed by villagers as victims rather than enemies is because of the way the new trend in animal mobility resonates with the new order of human mobility. Urban outmigration has become a way of life for rural-born Japanese. Nowadays, those people born in villages naturally expect to leave them when they grow up. One indication that modern Japan has become, in effect, a society of migration is the diffusion of the word *furusato* in public discourse and popular culture. Often translated as 'hometown', *furusato* refers to one's place of birth and upbringing which one has left to live elsewhere. Containing the characters for 'old' and for 'village', the word *furusato* also has the meaning of ancestral or family village, the place where one's father was born and raised and where the family graves are located. It is this latter sense of *furusato* as a rural place that still tends to predominate, to the point where those people born and raised in the fast-changing urban spaces of Japan are said not really to have a *furusato* any longer. At the same time, national modernization has transformed and standardized much of the rural periphery of Japan, such that many villages have lost their former rustic character to become regional extensions of the metropolitan centres. This is the background to a recurring theme in the cultural self-commentary of post-war Japan: that, as a result of the remorseless trend of urban development, modern Japanese society is afflicted by a demoralizing sense of homelessness known as *furusato sōshitsu* or 'hometown loss' (Yasui 1997: 215). A measure of the importance of this issue in Japan is the national government's response to it in the form of community revival initiatives aimed at restoring the sense of belonging associated with the *furusato*, such as the *furusato sōsei* ('Re-creating the Hometown') policy.[2]

This condition of *furusato* loss is not confined to the human inhabitants of the Japanese archipelago, but can extend to the animal inhabitants of the *yama*. In the Japanese mass media the forest is sometimes characterized as the *furusato* of wild

---

[1] The Japanese expression is: *warui koto shitara, yappari nanka kaette kuru.*

[2] In 1988 the then prime minister Takeshita Noboru launched a government initiative known as *Furusato sōsei* or the Hometown Revival Programme in which each of Japan's 3,255 municipalities would receive a one-off grant of 100 million yen ($750,000) to be used to promote local revitalization in a manner of their own choosing.

animals (*AS* 22 Apr. 1990; *IT* 4 July 1999). The analogy implies that, just as every person should have a *furusato*, a place where he or she can feel at home and at ease, so too should the animals of the forest be allowed to keep their home. The analogy is further evident in the characterization of *engai* monkeys as 'homeless' (*homuresu*, English loanword used) in which they are likened to the growing human population living on the streets of large cities (Emoto 1993: 31). The use of such terms in relation to the wildlife problem suggests that in modern Japan wild animals and human beings have somehow undergone symmetrical dislocations and face a similar predicament. The idiom of *furusato* evokes sympathy for the plight of the nation's forest animals by recalling the all-too-familiar human experience of migration, displacement, and homelessness. For wildlife conservationists in Japan, the representation of forest animals as being in a state of displacement akin to that of the urban migrant is a rhetorically powerful means of alerting the general public to the threat of wildlife habitat destruction. This is clear from a newspaper article on the establishment of a wildlife protection area in Kanagawa Prefecture that carried the headline, *Yasei dōbutsu ni furusato* or 'Hometown for Wild Animals' (*AS* 6 Mar. 1991).[3] This conservationist call for the revival of the *furusato* home (forest habitat) of wild animals carries an obvious resonance with the *furusato sōsei* policy. The wildlife problem in Japan, when considered as a *double encroachment* of village and forest, can engender a sense of *shared displacement* with the animals of the forest.

Animate Symbols

How can we square this apparent human identification with forest animals with the anthropological tradition of natural symbolism studies? The discipline of anthropology has tended to emphasize human–animal difference and discontinuity. By according a special or unique status to humanity *vis-à-vis* animals, anthropology has played its part in 'policing' the human–animal boundary in Western society (Cartmill 1993: 177; Roebroeks 1995: 177). But this analytical preoccupation with separation and discontinuity can have the effect of neglecting or at least understating the human interest in nature–culture continuity and human–animal commonality and thereby obscuring the real complexity of animal symbolism in human societies (Willis 1990: 18). Wendy James has made this point in relation to anthropological accounts of human–animal relations in Africa.

In ethnographic description and anthropological analysis, we have tended in the past to impose rigid structures of dichotomy, of separation and classifying distinctions, and even of confrontation, on the animal world as supposedly understood by African peoples. Man transcending nature and imposing control through formal principles of separation and

---

[3] Cf. *AS* (16 June 1989), *AS* (22 Apr. 1990), and *AS* (11 Apr. 1992). The word *furusato* is widely used in Japanese environmentalism: for example, the terms *shizen hakai* ('nature destruction') and *kankyō hakai* ('environmental destruction') can readily be transposed to become *furusato hakai* or 'home destruction' (see Kurahashi 1994: 106; Funaki 1994: 46).

classification tends to be the dominant theme . . . As a tool for ethnographic analysis it may miss indigenous themes of continuity, of integration, and of interaction between the various species of the living world, including ourselves. (James 1990: 198, references removed)

This book's focus on people–wildlife relations in Japan provides an interesting challenge to anthropological studies of animal symbolism and their dualistic assumptions. On the one hand, Japan is often represented as an example of a culture that, through its Shinto and Buddhist traditions, denies any essential distinction between humans and animals in favour of an emphasis on human–animal continuity (Ohnuki-Tierney 1990: 90–1; Kitahara-Frisch 1991: 74–5). We might well expect that the absence of a direct Cartesian heritage would make Japanese dispositions to animals less dualistic and more inclusive. In fact, precisely this argument has been made in relation to Japanese zoology, and to Japanese primatology in particular. Thus Japanese primatology 'may well reflect the traditional Japanese way of looking at nature, that is to say, an affinity and sympathy with all living things' (Watanabe 1974: 281). According to Umesao Tadao, 'the development of primatology in Japan is due to the intimacy which subsists here [in Japan] between man and monkey. For Europeans, of course, there is an unbridgeable gap between man and the animal kingdom . . .' (in Dale 1986: 193). In the course of this book we have seen evidence of human identification with the wild mammals of the forest. For Japanese mountain villagers, the actions and behaviour of forest animals can often seem human like—the cunning and the courage of the wild boar, the cleverness and the teamwork of the monkey, the dignity of the deer, and so on. The wild boar, the monkey, and the serow are all admired, in their different ways, for their mobility in the mountains, while the wild boar, the stag, and the bear express the desirable qualities of strength, power, and fighting spirit.

On the other hand, the reality of people–wildlife conflict in the Japanese mountains provides a ready check on the more romantic claims that are made for human–animal relations in non-Western cultures. This book has examined a range of examples of wildlife pestilence and pest control measures, including lethal ones, that clearly show antagonism and hostility to be central to people–wildlife relations along the Japanese forest-edge. Japanese pestilence discourse would seem to be a prime example of anthropocentric and dualistic pragmatism, whereby wild animals are relegated to the status of 'harmful beasts' to be removed in the interests of human society. The question arises as to how this situation of people–wildlife conflict in Japan can be squared with Japanese culture's supposed emphasis on human–animal continuity. The discourse of wildlife pestilence would seem to be a hierarchical one, whereby the animal in question is relegated to the inferior status of a 'pest' to be repelled or erased in the interests of human beings. The label 'pest' or 'vermin' has the effect of distancing and depersonalizing an animal, removing it from the sphere of moral considerations. 'No consideration at all is given to the interests of the "pests"—the very word "pest" seems to exclude any concern for the animals themselves' (Singer 1990: 233). When animals are objectified as pests or vermin, they become eradicable. 'The category of vermin implies that certain animals or plants (weeds are plant vermin) can or must be exterminated' (Katcher and Wilkins 1993: 189). However, we should beware of undue simplification. Pestilence discourse should not be reduced to its effects, but understood in the round. Although it may consign this or that animal to the diminished status of pest, it could be argued that the starting-point of pestilence discourse, when applied to wildlife crop-raiders, is that of a problematic human–animal equivalence or parity.

Crop-raiding wild mammals behave in rather familiar ways that recall human behaviour. They live in similar ecological spaces, they covet similar foods, they display 'intelligent' behaviour in their crop raids, and so on. Wildlife pests must be killed or otherwise controlled because, with respect to their harmful behaviour, they occupy the same trophic level as Man himself—that is, they seek to eat the crops that humans grow (or, in the case of predators, the animals that humans raise for food). As pests, wild animals do not, in the first instance, form part of human productive strategies; rather, human beings are part of *their* productive strategies. It is because these animals are, in their material and ecological conditions of existence, continuous with human beings that they threaten human livelihoods. It is in this respect that a zero-sum or oppositional view of animals can be understood as premised on assumptions of human–animal continuity rather than discontinuity. The anthropologist Brian Morris has made this same point in relation to farmers in Malawi.

As subsistence agriculturists experiencing continual depredation of their crops by wild mammals, there is a pervasive sense that animals are in 'opposition' to human concerns and wellbeing . . . This opposition, however, must not be construed as involving an attitude of control or domination, still less one of technological mastery over nature. It implies that humans and animals are essentially equals but in competition . . . (Morris 1998: 120)

Similarly, the human 'war' with wildlife in the Japanese mountains is founded on an *opposition of interests* rather than an *opposition of kinds*. Human–animal continuity may well take the form of a human recognition of animals as *equivalents* or *rivals* with opposed interests.

This understanding of the human–animal relationship in terms of equivalence and competition has important implications for animal symbolism. Viewed dualistically, in terms of the existence of separate domains of 'nature' and 'culture', the wildlife pest can appear to be a boundary-crosser and even an 'anomalous' animal in the structuralist tradition of natural symbolism studies. But this does not really account for the sense of symbolic threat posed by the wildlife pest to Japanese mountain villagers. This threat can only be fully appreciated when the status of wildlife pests as ontological equivalents or rivals is recognized. Here we can recall the zoodemographic self-understandings of Japanese mountain villagers in which forest animals are represented as rivals that do not simply breach the village boundary, but threaten to *cross over* and reclaim the land of the village. Another way of expressing this point is to say that the new mobility of wild animals is symbolically reckoned not simply in terms of the village–forest *boundary*, but also in terms of the relationship between *domains* on either side of this boundary. Indeed, there is even a sense in which these wildlife pests threaten to nullify the village boundary altogether and reclaim the village as a space of wildlife habitat.

One of the main critiques of anthropological symbolism in recent years has been directed at the analytical privileging of metaphorical association. Critics have called for a new approach that 'avoids the reductionist and idealist tendencies of much symbolic and metaphor theory' by analysing symbols as 'constituents of contextually and historically situated social interaction' (Turner 1991: 122, 123). This historicization of symbolic association is to be realized by means of a dynamic understanding of symbolic processes in general, and of the changes in domain 'geography' in particular. A central feature of this approach is the idea of the constitutive character of metaphor and the emergent character of domains. There is an increasing recognition that metaphor is generative of metonymy because it can 'draw the world together' by joining up what were separate domains (Durham and Fernandez 1991: 197–8; Turner 1991: 127–8). This approach can be applied to the field of animal symbolism to challenge the status accorded to 'nature' and 'society' as key domain distinctions.

Anthropological analyses of natural symbolism are typically predicated on an a priori nature–culture or nature–society opposition, one that is then mediated by certain resemblances symbolically picked out. It is in this sense that animals are said to be natural 'metaphors' or 'mirrors' of human society (Douglas 1990; Mullin 1999). Given the similarities between human and animal mobilities noted above, could not the wildlife pest be said to be a natural 'mirror' or 'metaphor' of the migrant society that mountain villages have become? Metaphor implies a distinction between different sides or domains, such as a 'natural' (source) domain and a 'social' (target) domain, across which symbolic association takes place in the form of the recognition of resemblance. But in present-day Japan, as a result of what I have called double encroachment, wild animals and mountain villagers cannot be neatly placed into separate 'natural' and 'social' domains with the former representing a 'mirror' to change in the latter. On account of the transformation of the Japanese mountains in the modern era, the village boundary no longer effectively serves as a definite frontier with a wild forest. It is in terms of this transformation of remote rural space in the modern era that contemporary movements, human and non-human, within it can be understood.

Human movement has a transformative effect on space. Roads for motorized traffic profoundly redefine village and forest space. The recently established network of forest roads creates a new infrastructure for human mobility in the *yama*, potentially opening up the forest to human presence, even if the reality of rural depopulation means that these roads are barely used. The new roads, many of which have been carved out of the mountainous landscape, also have the effect of interfering with animal movements, fragmenting animal habitats, and isolating animal subpopulations. But it is not only human mobility that redefines the character of upland space. Animal movements too have the power, cumulatively, to inscribe a new spatial sensibility among mountain villagers. Although the human developmental impact on the mountains (forestry, forest roads, and so on, that redefine animal territories) obstructs animal movements, it also leads to the emergence of new patterns of animal movement, including transversal movements that pass through the *satoyama* and *okuyama* zones and cross the boundary between village and forest. Viewed in this way, the depredations of wildlife pests become so many physical expressions of the newly merged spatial order of the *yama* in modern Japan. Forest wildlife is not a 'mirror' of the village because it is no longer routinely confined to a separate forest domain, but has instead become a mobile sign—an animate symbol—of the transformation of upland space.

For Japanese mountain villagers familiar with the forest around them (through forestry labour, gathering, hunting, etc.), the new order of animal mobility appears unnatural and points to a larger historical change. Something is wrong when monkeys enter houses, when serow are spotted in graveyards, and when bears den in charcoal kilns or in timber plantations. When the animals of the forest appear in and around the village, they are conspicuously out of place. What stands out is not just the boundary-crossing *per se*, but the contrast between this present-day boundary-crossing and the past when it occurred much more rarely, if at all. The impression of spatial anomaly combines with a perception of temporal discrepancy. Because of the way this animal movement in space suggests a contrast in time, the behaviour of forest wildlife comes to be experienced as *historical*. This discrepancy between past and present animal mobility in turn invites associations with the changing pattern of human mobility in rural Japan. Animal migrants driven out of their forest home by the forces of modern development readily elicit sympathy among villagers whose siblings and children have been forced to migrate to earn a living or who themselves had to migrate before returning in later life. But because of the reality of spatial convergence in the Japanese mountains, the animal pest is not a natural metaphor of the migrant village, but a coeval presence that shares the new era of upland modernity.

Having looked at the symbolism of the wildlife pest, we can now turn to the symbolism of wildlife pest control, specifically the animal that holds out the promise of a new era of *natural* pest control—the wolf.

THE SYMBOLISM OF THE WOLF

Japan's wildlife problem, as we have seen, has a dual character, whereby animal pests appear both as *enemies* besieging mountain villagers and as *victims* of the forces of human development. The peculiar appeal of the JWA wolf reintroduction proposal should be understood in this context. It follows from the two-sided character of Japan's wildlife problem—animal intrusion into the village and developmental erosion of the forest—that an effective solution should offer a double protection: the protection of village livelihoods from forest animals and the protection of wildlife habitat from human development. There is a tendency in Japan, as elsewhere, for the issues of wildlife pestilence and wildlife conservation to be seen as distinct and even opposed. Lethal pest control measures attract outside criticism on conservationist (and animal welfare) grounds, while outside conservationist efforts to protect wild animals encounter hostility on the part of local producers who view these animals as a harmful threat. The wolf reintroduction proposal promises a solution to *both* pestilence and conservation concerns. The JWA assigns the wolf a twofold protective function: to protect the forest through predator restoration (ecosystem 'repair') and to protect the village from wildlife pests. The rhetorical force of the reintroduction proposal derives from the way it condenses the two poles of the wildlife problem—the local concern with pestilence and the wider concern with conservation—to appear as a complete remedy for human–animal relations in the Japanese mountains.

Recalling the anthropological tradition of animal symbolism studies, one obvious interpretation of the Japanese wolf reintroduction proposal might be that, notwithstanding its overt utilitarian appeal as a means of pest control, it is also a cultural discourse of boundary maintenance. If wild boar, monkey, and deer 'pests' are symbolically interpreted as breachers of important human boundaries, it follows that the reintroduced wolf might itself be viewed as a kind of boundary guard. Here we can recall the folklorist Nomoto Kanichi's characterization of the traditional role of the Japanese wolf as a *banken* or 'watchdog' in the forest (in Chapter 6). The JWA proposal might accordingly be read as a call for the return of nature's 'watchdog' to regulate wild herbivore numbers in the forest and contain their transgressions into the village. By, in effect, redividing the village from the forest, wolf predation would facilitate the recovery of the erstwhile order of the Japanese mountains. In addition to being a functional solution to pestilence with respect to forest ecology, the wolf would therefore become a symbolic corrective to the pest in relation to upland culture. The new wolf would not simply be an ecological regulator of the Japanese forest, but would also serve as a symbolic regulator of upland space. Interpreted in this way, the notion of regulatory predation would become a double process, both ecological and symbolic. The full appeal of the reintroduced wolf would lie in its promise to restore the *boundary* as well as the *balance* of nature in the Japanese mountains.

The status of the wolf as a potential human ally in Japan's wildlife wars is not, however, as clear-cut as this suggests. As we saw in Chapter 6, in Japan the wolf's status as a protector of people was not an unambiguous one. The Japanese wolf clearly did appear as a protector of human interests in some contexts, most notably that of farming where it helped to protect vulnerable fields from crop-raiding animals. As the predator of such harmful animals, the wolf was an *ekijū* or 'benign beast'. But the wolf was also viewed as a potential source of harm to the village in its own right. It too could breach village boundaries and harm human livelihoods—albeit through attacks on livestock rather than damage to crops. The wolf was additionally a threat to human safety, including night-time field-guards who, in defending fields from wild boar and deer, became vulnerable to the wolves pursuing these animals. The same tension was evident in the 'escort wolf' tales, in which wolves protect human travellers in the forest, but retain the potential to attack those they are supposedly guarding. Even in the case of the dog—the wolf's 'gift' to the village—the motif of protection of village interests is not wholly disconnected from the potential for predation on villagers (a danger most explicitly recognized in references to 'man-eating dogs'). Thus Japanese folk tradition does not provide the straightforward endorsement of the wolf's status as a 'benign beast' that wolf supporters claim. But it is not only Japanese folk culture that raises doubts about the wolf's status as a benign predator.

The scientific basis of the JWA claim that reintroduced wolves would restore order to the ecosystem also appears uncertain. Ecologists have become increasingly sceptical about the ecosystem concept and the mechanistic assumptions on which it is based (O'Neill 2001). More specifically, the one-time orthodoxy of predator regulation of prey numbers has been widely called into question by zoologists and ecologists. There is a fundamental disagreement over the predatory impact of wolves—whether wolves are 'compensatory' predators that simply prey on weak or old animals (that are likely to die anyway) or 'additive' predators that also feed on healthy members of the prey population and therefore represent an additional source of mortality that affects reproduction and total numbers (Steinhart 1995: 61–77). The once-celebrated Isle Royale example of regulatory wolf predation has called into doubt in recent years with the decline of the wolf population and its failure to recover in response to rising numbers of moose (as predator–prey theory would predict) (Mlot 1993; Peterson *et al.* 1998). Revised models have emerged in which the predatory impact of wolves is said to vary in relation to a number of other factors, including prey population size, predator population size, the presence or absence of other categories of prey, the presence or absence of other categories of predator (including human hunters), and the degree of human alteration of the natural environment (Mech 1966: 168; Talbot 1978: 312–14). For example, it is argued that wolves have a high impact when ungulate densities are low, but a low impact when ungulate densities high (Bergerud *et al.* 1983: 987; Messier and Crête 1985; Quigley and Hornocker 1992: 1092). In some situations wild predators can even have the effect of destabilizing, rather than stabilizing, the numbers of prey animals (Talbot 1978: 315–16; Budiansky 1995: 214–16).

These doubts over the ecological impact of wolves have not been dispelled by the actual experience of wolf reintroduction, such as the recent example of

Yellowstone National Park. Since the 1970s the Yellowstone authorities have practised a 'hands-off' form of park management, known variously as 'natural regulation' or 'natural control', whereby wild herbivore populations were allowed to increase unchecked in the belief that they would eventually reach a natural equilibrium with the vegetation (Boyce 1998; Huff and Varley 1999). This orthodoxy of bottom-up regulation accounts for the relative absence of the (top-down) argument of predatory control of herbivores in the park's justification of its policy of wolf reintroduction. But the idea of regulatory predation has not been wholly absent from the Yellowstone debate. One report on the likely impact of the reintroduced wolves predicted that they would 'reduce prey abundance in the park by 10–30 per cent, with elk as the principal prey species. Predation by wolves should dampen the substantial fluctuations that park ungulates undergo due to variations in climate' (Boyce 1992: 123). Wolf reintroduction might even remove the need for human culling of the elk herd in the Yellowstone area in the form of the annual elk hunt, a practice that has become mired in controversy (Boyce 1995: 205). Although it is too soon to make reliable assessments about the actual impact of the Yellowstone wolves, the experience to date provides no clear evidence of regulatory predation. There are claims that reintroduced wolves are responsible for beneficial 'ecological changes' in the park (Clark and Gillesberg 2001: 149), but the impact on ungulates does not seem to support the regulatory predation thesis. Wolf specialists at a recent conference on the Yellowstone wolves reported that 'available data indicates wolves having a minimal effect on their prey: taking virtually no prime females' (Anon. 2001).

The impression given by JWA rhetoric is that the reintroduced wolf in Japan would be a strong or 'additive' predator, which has the ability to control wild herbivores in a way that present-day human society in upland Japan cannot. The JWA position is that the new wolves would be a solution to the problem of ungulate pestilence because of the likely impact of wolf predation on the level of prey numbers. But the critique of wolf predation in the North American wildlife ecology literature calls into question the wolf's efficacy as a predator able to control the numbers of herbivores and stabilize the wider ecosystem. The principal JWA rationale for wolf reintroduction—the argument that wolves would serve as natural pest controllers in the Japanese forest—is therefore thrown into doubt. This raises certain questions. If the wolf is not the dominant apex of the forest ecosystem, what is it? If the ecological function of the wolf does not account for its supreme status, what does? If wolf predation is not functionally necessary for the forest ecosystems of the Northern hemisphere, why are wolves being reintroduced? One answer to this might be that wolves are being reintroduced because they are *culturally*, rather than *ecologically*, special. This kind of cultural interpretation has, in fact, been applied to the wolf reintroduction movement in America.

A broad distinction within American ecology can be drawn between scientific ecology which is consistent with modernism and directed to the goal of resource management, and romantic ecology which challenges modernism over its destructive impact on the natural world and emphasizes the importance of human contact with wild nature (Worster 1977). Although underpinned by modernistic scientific arguments, wolf reintroduction in America can readily be viewed in terms of the latter tradition of romantic ecology. It has been argued that the wolf reintroduction campaigns in Yellowstone and elsewhere are informed by powerful cultural narratives of loss and recovery that have long characterized nature writing in America (Dizard 2001: 75). This recalls the tradition of 'wilderness thinkers' such as Thoreau, Muir, and Leopold for whom wilderness represented a source of moral or spiritual renewal (see Oelschlaeger 1991). In late twentieth-century America the wolf came to stand for the wilderness. Thus one of the leaders of the Yellowstone project cites wolf restoration as 'a dramatic expression of the goodness and power of the human spirit' (Phillips 1996*a*: 120). The human morality figured by the wolf is at times expressed in a quasi-religious (and, specifically, Christian) idiom, as when wolf restoration is justified in terms of a human 'need to redeem our own species' for 'the ultimate sin' that was wolf extermination (DeBoer 2000: 98–100). American newspaper editorials likewise hail wolf reintroduction as 'atonement', 'corrective repentance', and a 'declaration of the redemptive decency of the human spirit' (Primm and Clark 1996: 1038). Proponents argue that the new tolerance shown to the wolf in the form of the reintroduction initiative makes the animal a potent symbol of democracy in America (Phillips 1996*b*: 30), while government politicians declare wolf reintroduction to be 'an important statement about who we are as Americans' (Bruce Babbitt, in Brick and Cawley 1996: 2).

   In Japan too the language of contrition and redemption is used in connection with wolf reintroduction, as we saw in Chapter 6, with JWA leaders invoking twenty-first-century Japan's duty to 'atone' for past 'sins' and 'apologize' for past 'mistakes'. Here we can clearly see the influence of the American reintroduction campaign on the Japanese debate, which suggests that the Japanese reintroductionists have borrowed twice over from their American counterparts. Although the JWA accords pride of place to the American tradition of scientific ecology (to support the claim that the wolf would be a regulatory predator), it also draws on American romantic ecology. This was illustrated in a recent issue of the JWA newsletter which carried an article on Aldo Leopold's land ethic, where the author discussed Leopold's famous dictum, 'Thinking like a mountain', and described Leopold's own personal transformation from wolf-killer to wolf-supporter (Sekine 2001). Despite the dominant emphasis on scientific ecology among the JWA leadership, there is therefore clear evidence of anti-materialist sentiments among the JWA membership. Support for wolf reintroduction in Japan is not, therefore, reducible to utilitarian considerations or necessarily inspired by a belief in scientific progress in the field of restoration ecology. The wolf also appears a symbol of renovation in a modern Japan that is finally coming to terms with its own unbalanced history of industrialization and exploitation of the natural world. In short, the call for wolf reintroduction in Japan may well be more an expression of redemptive politics than a credible technical response to the wildlife 'wars' looked at in this book. The reintroduced wolf in Japan, like its counterpart in America, is a powerful anti-modernist symbol.

Despite these common elements, important differences between the two campaigns remain. In particular, to return to the motif of redemption, one crucial difference centres on the status of the 'sin' of past wolf eradication. In the American context, responsibility for the disappearance of the wolf is firmly located in the tradition of frontier conquest whereby the wilderness was made safe for farming and other forms of exploitation. Americans attribute responsibility for wolf eradication to the intolerance shown towards wild predators on the part of earlier settlers colonizing the frontier. Consequently, the present-day generation of Americans becomes duty bound to reverse the mistakes of its settler forebears. The task of wolf reintroduction assumes a pronounced moral character as a kind of (intergenerational) atonement for past sins. But in Japan, as we have seen, responsibility for wolf extinction is attributed to the post-Meiji contact with the wider world and the phase of uncritical westernization of the nation that ensued. Wolf extinction in Japan is associated with the unstable interface with the outside world that characterized Meiji Japan, rather than with *traditional* Japan *per se*, which tends to be located in pre-Meiji times. Therefore, while JWA discourse refers to wolf extinction as a past 'sin' for which the Japanese people must atone, this should be understood as a sin caused by the *deviation from* Japanese tradition rather than any sin arising from that tradition itself. The effect of absolving traditional Japan from responsibility for wolf extinction in this way is to leave Japanese folk tradition discursively available to serve as a rhetorical focus for wolf reintroductionism in a way in which American settler tradition cannot. In Japan proponents are therefore able to present wolf reintroduction as a *revival* rather than a *reversal* of the traditional disposition to the natural world.

In this respect, the wolf reintroductionism of the JWA recalls the larger motif of modernist nostalgia in Japan. Commentators on modern Japanese society refer to 'a redemptive impulse' in Japan (Ivy 1995: 20), depict the Japanese countryside as a 'landscape of nostalgia' (Robertson 1998: 121), and identify a Japanese preoccupation with 'resurrecting "lost" traditions' (Harootunian 1989: 66). Japan in the late twentieth century was marked by a chronic sense of 'loss and the desire to recover that loss' (Ivy 1995: 57). The ubiquitous motif of cultural rediscovery and recovery in present day Japan is evident in visitor attractions such as folk museums and reconstructed period-style villages ('Heian Village', 'Edo Village', 'Meiji Village', and so on); in trends in domestic travel and tourism to folklore-rich regions that present themselves as repositories of tradition; and in television programmes that focus on arts, crafts, and other surviving local customs that provide a window on to earlier times. In these various ways, Japan's disappearing past is captured and preserved, represented and re-created, and passed on to new generations as national tradition in an effort to redress the imbalances of Japanese modernity. But this modern concern with overcoming 'loss' or 'rupture' is not confined to Japanese *culture*. Japanese *nature* is another important site of nostalgic reconnection with the traditional past. One prominent expression of this trend is the national designation of special parts of Japanese nature (including some of the animals featured in this book) as *tennen kinenbutsu* or 'natural treasures'. Another would be the rise of tourism in mountainous regions since the 1960s that offers visitors the opportunity for renewed 'contact with nature'. A third example would be the current fascination with the indigenous *mori* or forest and with the secondary pine forest, both of which are prized as important sites of natural heritage. Along with the cultural heritage movement, the preservation of natural heritage forms an integral part of the effort to re-enchant Japanese modernity.

It is tempting to view the wolf reintroduction proposal—coming as it did at the end of the twentieth century or, according to the *gengō* system, the beginning of the Heisei era—as yet another manifestation of this preservationist or restorationist tendency in modern Japan. There is, however, a crucial difference. The JWA claim is that the reintroduced wolves would be living constituents of Japanese nature and not exhibits or objects of display in a visitor attraction. Although the JWA is active in reviving the memory of the wolf as part of its campaign to raise public awareness, the aim of the reintroduction campaign is to re-establish living wolves rather than celebrate dead ones. Wolf reintroduction is envisaged as the reversal of an earlier loss and not simply the evocation of that loss as is the case with museums and other heritage facilities. Japan's heritage industry aims to be self-reproducing in the sense that it must constantly generate the nostalgia on which it depends. The nostalgia industry is, after all, premissed on the fact of irreversibility; the issue of deleting this loss and making good the deficit in which nostalgia inheres does not arise. The heritage industry is founded on an acceptance that the past cannot, by definition, be brought back, only evoked. But the avowed purpose of the JWA campaign is the restitution of wolves to the Japanese forest rather than a decontextualized representation of them. Although the JWA does promote sentiments of cultural nostalgia, along with awareness of natural function, the aim is to bring about the return of real wolves.

It might be objected that, strictly speaking, the natural past is no less elusive than the cultural past and that reversing wolf extinction is no more possible than travelling back in time to the Heian or Edo eras. Viewed in this way, reintroduced foreign wolves would be little more than stand-ins for the Japanese wolves of the past that are now extinct, in much the same way that the re-created period-style villages of Japanese theme parks are stand-ins for the real villages of the past. In short, wolf reintroduction would be tantamount to a kind of *simulation* of past nature, rather than a genuine recovery of it, and would therefore be vulnerable to the charge of inauthenticity. As we saw in Chapter 6, objections are in fact raised to the wolf reintroduction proposal that centre precisely on the inauthentic, *foreign* character of the wolves to be reintroduced. Wolf reintroduction is portrayed by critics as the *introduction* of an alien animal rather than the *reintroduction* of a missing animal. This negative reaction to the wolf reintroduction proposal recalls other instances of nativistic alarm over alien wildlife in Japan, such as the furore over the Formosan rock macaque (mentioned in Chapter 3) that is deemed to threaten the indigenous Japanese macaque population with 'gene pollution'. It also recalls examples from other parts of the world where wolf conservation arouses nativistic criticism, sometimes in the form of an explicit xenophobia. Examples of this include Norwegian sheep farmers who 'tell the press that Swedish protectionists breed wolves, which are then let loose in Norwegian forest pastures' (Brox 2000: 391) and opponents of wolf reintroduction in rural America who complain that 'it's the New York Jews that are shoving this down our throat' (in McNamee 1994: 17; cf. Capps 1994: 22). Viewed in this way, reintroduced wolves in Japan, instead of being positive symbols of nature's restoration, become negative symbols of foreign encroachment (cf. Moore 1994).

The Japanese situation is not without irony. Proponents justify future wolf reintroduction in Japan as an act of nature restoration that would also provide an answer to the problem of wildlife pests. But the effect of the nativistic critique of the wolf reintroduction proposal is to portray the foreign wolves to be brought in as themselves a threat to Japanese nature. The JWA responds to this nativistic objection by arguing that the extinct wolves of the past and the reintroduced wolves of the future are *not* fundamentally different animals, but are biologically equivalent as grey wolves of a common (East Asian) bioregion. This is the background to the emergence of the grey wolf as the subject of wolf reintroduction and the agent of regulatory predation in JWA rhetoric. As a result of this, the JWA wolf reintroduction proposal comes to appear anything but nativistic, in so far as it effectively redefines a key part—indeed, what is claimed to be *the* key part—of the Japanese forest ecosystem in terms of a *shared* natural heritage with other parts of Asia. It is a measure of the power of the holistic nature discourse underpinning wolf reintroduction that the JWA is prepared to stretch the 'ecosystem' across cultural and national boundaries and thereby risk incurring the very (nativistic) critique that is otherwise associated with wildlife biologists and conservationists themselves. So important, it seems, is the ecological gap left by the disappearance of the top predator that Japanese wolf conservationists are prepared (as opponents would have it) to transgress nature's national frontiers in order to fill it.

The objection to the wolf reintroduction proposal made in this book is a different one from that made by its nativistic critics and has to do with the exaggerated functional claims made for reintroduced wolves rather than their exogenous origins. If this objection stands—if the reintroduced wolves will neither balance the forest nor protect the farmer—the case for wolf reintroduction would seem to be that much weaker. But my criticism has been directed at the reasoning used to support the wolf reintroduction proposal, rather than at the act of wolf reintroduction *per se*, which arguably could be justified on different grounds. An environmental case could be made for wolf reintroduction in Japan without relying on the doctrine of regulatory predation. The current 'wolf boom' raises the possibility that reintroduced wolves might contribute to the conservation of the Japanese *yama* in a different way. If the 'charismatic' presence of wolves can persuade Japanese society to protect wolf habitat by restricting harmful and destructive land-uses, other endangered animal and plant species of the forest would stand to benefit from such a protective 'umbrella' (an argument that was also advanced to justify bear conservation in Chapter 5). The impact of the wolves would therefore be felt less through their predation on animals harmful to human society than through their appeal to a human society otherwise harmful to wildlife. The *environmental* efficacy of the restored wolf would lie not in its predatory control of ungulates, but in its symbolic power—as a 'focal' species within human society—to resist the developmental pressures on the mountains in which the ungulates and other animals live. Although it might not have the status of an ecological keystone, the wolf could become (to use an expression applied to lynx reintroduction in Europe) a 'psychological keystone' (Breitenmoser 1998*a*: 135). The new wolf might, after all, become a protector of the Japanese *yama*, but this would be as an iconic prompt to *human* self-regulation rather than as an ecological tool for the regulation of nature.

BIBLIOGRAPHY

JAPANESE

Books and Articles

ABE H., TAWARA K., HATTORI K., and SAITŌ S. (1986), 'Higuma no hogo' ('Conservation of the brown bear'), in Saitō S. (ed.), *Higuma—sono, ningen to no kakawari* (*Brown Bears: Their Relations with People*) (Tokyo: Shisakusha), 61–114.

ABE T. (1994), *Eto no dōbutsushi* (*A History of the Twelve Animals of the Zodiac*) (Tokyo: Gihodo Shuppan) (Director: Konishi Masayasu).

AKATSUKA T., *et al.* (1993), *Kanwa jiten* (*Chinese Character-Japanese Dictionary*) (Tokyo: Ōbunsha).

AMANO T. (1999), *Kari no minzoku* (*The Folklore of Hunting*) (Tokyo: Iwata Shoin).

ANON. (1995), 'Konna hatsuyume o michatta' ('I had this New Year's dream'), *Oikos File*, 36: 6–7.

ANON. (2000*a*), 'Nihonzaru kujo tōsū' ('Numbers of Japanese monkeys culled'). Available at: *http://www.asahi-net.or.jp/~zb4h-kskr/monkey.html* (accessed 28 Sept. 2000).

ANON. (2000*b*), 'Ōkami ni matsuwaru jinja shōkai' ('Introduction to shrines at which the wolf is worshipped'). Available at: *http://www.jca.apc.org/~kuzunoha/newsletter11-3.html* (accessed 26 Sept. 2000).

AOKI K. (1996), *Mori ni yomigaeru nihon bunka* (*The Revival of Japanese Culture Through the Forest*) (Tokyo: Sanichi Shobō).

ASHIDA S. (1999), *Dōbutsu shinkō jiten* (*Dictionary of Animals in Religion*) (Tokyo: Hokushindō).

AZUMANE C. (1997 [1993]), *SOS tsukinowaguma* (*Bear SOS*) (Morioka: Iwate Nippōsha).

CHIBA H. (1982), 'Kamoshika nikki' ('Serow diary'), in Uchida S., Ōmura H., and Chiba H. (eds.), *Zenshū nihon dōbutsu shi 8* (*Collected Accounts of Japanese Animals*, viii) (Tokyo: Kōdansha), 263–374.

——(1991), 'Hito to no kakawari' ('The connection with people'), in Ōmachi Sangaku Hakubutsukan (ed.), *Kamoshika: hyōgaki o ikita dōbutsu* (*The Serow: An Animal of the Glacial Period*) (Nagano-shi: Shinano Mainichi Shinbunsha), 119–36.

CHIBA T. (1975), *Shuryō denchō* (*Hunting Legends*) (Tokyo: Hōsei Daigaku Shuppankyoku).

——(1977), *Shuryō denchō kenkyū* (*Research on Hunting Legends*) (Tokyo: Kazama Shobō).

——(1993), 'Kinsei Kanazawa-Hirano chiiki no yajūgai: toku ni nihonōkami ni tsuite' ('Wild animal damage in the Kanazawa-Hirano area in the modern era'), *Rekishi Chirigaku*, 16: 38–47.

——(1995*a*), *Ōkami wa naze kieta ka* (*Why Did the Wolf Disappear?*) (Tokyo: Shinjinbutsu Ōraisha).

——(1995*b*), 'Sanchūikairon josetsu' ('Introductory remarks on the mountain-as-other world theory'), in Kawai M. and Hanihara K. (eds.), *Dōbutsu to bunmei* (*Animals and Civilization*) (Tokyo: Asakura Shoten), 26–51.

Eguchi Y. (2001), 'Inoshishi no kōdō to nōryoku o shiru' ('Knowledge of wild boar behaviour and ability'), in Takahashi S. (ed.), *Inoshishi to ningen—tomo ni ikiru* (*Wild Boars and Man: Living Together*) (Tokyo: Kokon Shoin), 171–99.

Emoto M. (1993), 'Kokuritsu kōen no mori o owareru yasei dōbutsu' ('The wild animals that are driven from National Park forest'), in Rizōto Gorufujō Mondai Zenkoku Renrakkai (eds.) *Yasei seibutsu kara no kokuhatsu* (*Wildlife Indicts Us*) (Tokyo: Recycle Bunkasha), 29–35.

Fujiwara E. (1982), 'Kaisetsu: kamoshika nikki' ('Commentary on serow diary'), in Uchida S., Ōmura H., and Chiba H. (eds.), *Zenshū nihon dōbutsu shi 8* (*Collected Accounts of Japanese Animals*, viii) (Tokyo: Kōdansha), 381–4.

Fujiwara T. (2000), 'Message 426'. Available at: *http://www.egroups.co.jp/messages/wolf-japan/328* (accessed on 1 June 2001).

Fukuda A. (1994), 'Inoshishi mukoiri' ('Wild boar bridegroom'), in Inada K. *et al.* (eds.), *Nihon mukashibanashi jiten* (*Dictionary of Japanese Old Tales*) (Tokyo: Kōbundō), 74–5.

Funaki T. (1994), 'Ikimono no mirai ni me o muketa tachiki torasuto' ('The Standing Tree Trust concerned with the future of living things'), in Yamada K. (ed.), *Satoyama torasuto* (*The Satoyama Trust*) (Tokyo: Hokuto Shuppan), 34–46.

Furubayashi Y. (1991), 'Kamoshika mondai o kangaeru' ('Considering the serow problem'), in NACS-J (ed.), *Yasei dōbutsu hogo—21 seiki e no teigen* (*Wild Animal Protection: A Proposal for the Twenty-first Century*) (Tokyo: Nihon Shizen Hogo Kyōkai), 227–43.

Hagihara S. (1996), 'Kurashi to dōbutsu' ('Living with animals'), in Akada M., Katsuki Y., Komatsu K., Nomoto K., and Fukuda A. (eds.), *Kankyō no minzoku* (*Environmental Folklore*) (Tokyo: Yūzankaku), 195–220.

Hama Kenji (2000), 'Message 364'. Available at: *http://www.egroups.co.jp/messages/wolf-japan/364* (accessed on 1 June 2001).

Hanai T. (1995), 'Kinsei shiryō ni miru gaijū to sono taisaku' ('Pestilence and its countermeasures as viewed through written materials of the early modern period'), in Kawai M. and Hanihara K. (eds.), *Dōbutsu to bunmei* (*Animals and Civilization*) (Tokyo: Asakura Shoten), 52–65.

Harato S. (1994), 'Kōyōju fubatsu no mori kōsō' ('The idea of a forest of unfellable trees'), in Yamada K. (ed.), *Satoyama torasuto* (*The Satoyama Trust*) (Tokyo: Hokuto Shuppan), 107–13.

Hasegawa A. (1996), 'Kasoka no shinkō to kasotaisaku no suii' ('Ongoing depopulation and trends in depopulation countermeasures'), in Hasegawa A., Fujisawa K., Takemoto T., and Arahi Y. (eds.), *Kaso chiiki no keikan to shūdan* (*Landscape and Groups in Depopulated Areas*) (Tokyo: Nihon Keizai Hyōronsha), 19–50.

Hasegawa M. (1996), *Nezumi to nihonjin* (*Mice and the Japanese*) (Tokyo: Sanichi Shobō).

Hatano I. (1996), 'Motto deta o, motto giron o' ('More data, more discussion'), *Forest Call*, 3: 46–53.

Hayakawa K. (1982), *Hayakawa Kōtarō zenshū 4* (*Collected Works of Hayakawa Kōtarō*, iv), ed. Miyamoto T. and Miyata N. (Tokyo: Miraisha).

Hayashi K. (1991), 'Saru no tatari' ('The monkey's curse'), *Monkey*, 35(5): 18–21.

Hayashi N. (1993), 'Nōsakubutsu e no higai' ('Damage to farm crops'), in Gifuken Honyūrui Dōbutsu Chōsa Kenkyūkai (ed.), *Horobiyuku mori no ōja: tsukinowaguma*

(*The Imminent Extinction of the King of the Forest: The Black Bear*) (Gifu: Gifu Shinbunsha), 126–7.

HAZUMI T. (1992), 'Kikiteki jōkyō ni aru tsukinowaguma—chiiki kotaigun no hogo kanri keikaku no teian' ('Current status and management of the Asian Black Bear in Japan'), *WWFJ Science Report*, 1(2): 293–333.

—— and KITAHARA M. (1994), 'Tsukinowaguma no bunpu' ('The distribution of the black bear'), in Toyama-ken (ed.), *Kuma to ningen: tsukinowaguma—mukashi to ima, soshite . . .* (*Bears and Humans: The Black Bear in Early Times, the Present-day, and Hereafter*) (Tateyama: Toyama-ken Tateyama Hakubutsukan), 12–16.

—— and YOSHII R. (1994*a*), 'Tsukinowaguma to hito—sono kakawari no rekishi' ('Bears and people: the history of the relationship'), in Toyama-ken (ed.), *Kuma to ningen: tsukinowaguma—mukashi to ima, soshite . . .* (*Bears and Humans: The Black Bear in Early Times, the Present-day, and Hereafter*) (Tateyama: Toyama-ken Tateyama Hakubutsukan), 28–39.

—— and—— (1994*b*), 'Tsukinowaguma no genzai soshite mirai' ('The present-day situation of the black bear and its future'), in Toyama-ken (ed.), *Kuma to ningen: tsukinowaguma—mukashi to ima, soshite . . .* (*Bears and Humans: The Black Bear in Early Times, the Present-day, and Hereafter*) (Tateyama: Toyama-ken Tateyama Hakubutsukan), 40–7.

HIDA I. (1967), *Yamagatari nazo no dōbutsutachi* (*Animals in Mountain Tales*) (Tokyo: Bungei Shunjū).

—— (1971), *Yamagatari—nihon no yasei dōbutsutachi* (*Mountain Tales: The Wild Animals of Japan*) (Tokyo: Bungei Shunjū).

—— (1972), *Yamagatari—daishizen no dōbutsutachi* (*Mountain Tales: Nature's Animals*) (Tokyo: Bungei Shunjū).

HIDAKA K. (1996), *40 sai kara no inakagurashi* (*Country Life after Forty*) (Tokyo: Tōyō Keizai Shinposha).

HIGASHI S. (1992), 'Rikujō shuryōjū no shigenryō' ('The quantity of the terrestrial game animal resource'), in Koyama S. (ed.), *Shuryō to gyorō—Nihon bunka no genryū o saguru* (*Hunting and Fishing Labour: Tracing the Origins of Japanese Culture*) (Tokyo: Yūzankaku), 26–56.

HIGUCHI A. (1991), 'Saru chōja' ('Monkey rich man'), in Nihon Minwa no Kai (ed.), *Gaidobukku nihon no minwa* (*A Guidebook to Japanese Folktales*) (Tokyo: Kōdansha), 117–18.

HIRAIWA Y. (1983), 'Watashi no inu' ('My dogs'), in Hiraiwa Y., Shimomura K., and Miura S. (eds.), *Zenshū nihon dōbutsushi 9* (*Record of Japanese Animals*, ix) (Tokyo: Kōdansha), 5–112.

—— (1992), *Ōkami—sono seitai to rekishi* (*The Wolf: Its Ecology and History*) (Tokyo: Tsukiji Shokan).

—— (1998), 'Nihonōkami to wa nanika—sono sonzai no kanōsei' ('What is the Japanese wolf? On the possibility of its existence'). *Forest Call*, 5: 16–21.

—— (1999), 'Ōkami no roman ni tsukareta hitobito' ('The people who are captivated by the romance of the wolf'), *Forest Call*, 7: 13–14.

HIRASAWA M. (1985), *Kieyuku yasei to shizen* (*Disappearing Wild Nature*) (Tokyo: Sanichi Shobō).

HIROSE S. (1977), 'Saruoi matsuri' ('Monkey chasing festival'), *Monkey*, 21(5): 35.

—— (1982), 'Gifu-ken Nishino ni nihonzaru no minzoku o otte' ('Pursuing monkey folklore in Nishino, Gifu-ken'), *Monkey*, 26(3–4): 38–43.

—— (1984), *Animaru roa no teishō—hito to saru no minzokugaku* (*Advocating Animal Lore: The Folklore of Humans and Monkeys*) (Tokyo: Miraisha).

—— (1993), *Saru* (*Monkeys*) (Tokyo: Hōsei Daigaku Shuppankyoku).

HONDA K. (1998 [1961]), *Kitaguni no dōbutsutachi* (*The Animals of the North*) (Tokyo: Asahi Shinbunsha).

HONGŪ-CHŌ (1969), *Yamabiko* (*Echo*) (Hongū: Town Hall).

—— (1992), *Kōhō Hongū* (*Public Information Hongu*), 1 Nov. 1992 (Hongū: Town Hall).

—— (1996), *Kumano bunka, Hongū kōsō—Hongū-chō dai ni ji chōki sōgō keikaku* (*Kumano Culture, the Hongū Plan: The Second Long Term General Plan for Hongu-cho*) (Hongū: Town Hall).

—— (2000*a*), *Shiryōhen* (*Statistical Survey Data*) (Hongū: Town Hall).

—— (2000*b*), *Hongū -chō shi—kingendaishiryōhen* (*The History of Hongū-chō: The Modern and Contemporary History Edition*) (Hongō: Town Hall).

—— (2000*c*), *Heisei 7–12 nendo jūgai chōsahyō* (*Wildlife Damage Survey Results, 1995–2000*) (Hongū: Town Hall).

HYMKI (Higashi Yoshino Mura Kyoiku Iinkai) (1987) (ed.), 'Nihonōkami' ('The Japanese wolf'), reproduced in Higashi Yoshino Mura (ed.), *Maboroshi no nihonōkami— nihonōkami ni kansuru shiryō* (*The Phantom Japanese Wolf: Materials on the Japanese Wolf*) (Higashi Yoshino: Kyōiku Iinkai), 5.

—— (1992) (ed.), *Higashi Yoshino mura no minwa* (*Folktales of Higashi Yoshino Mura*) (Higashi Yoshino: Education Committee).

IHSHS (Ishikawa-ken Hakusan Shizen Hogo Sentā) (1995), *Yasei chōjū ni yoru nōrinsanbutsu higai bōshitō o mokuteki to shita kotaigun kanri shuhō oyobi bōshi gijutsu ni kansuru kenkyū* (*Research on Management Methods and Technology aimed at Preventing Wildlife Damage to Farm and Forestry Products*) (Yoshinotani-mura, Ishikawa: IHSHS).

IBARAKI A. (1993), *Nihon no minwa—ki no kuni hen* (*Folktales of Japan: Ki Country Edition*) (Osaka: Nenshosha).

ICHIKAWA T., and SAITŌ I. (1985), *Saikō—Nihon no shinrin bunkashi* (*The History of Japanese Forest Culture Reconsidered*) (Tokyo: NHK Books).

IDANI G., IHOBE H., and KAWAI K. (1995), 'Kinki chihō ni okeru engai no jittai' ('The state of monkey crop damage in the Kinki Region'), *Reichōrui Kenkyū* (*Primate Research*), 11: 113–22.

IFUKUBE M. (1969), *Saru Ainu no kumamatsuri* (*The Bear Festival of the Saru Ainu*) (Sapporo: Miyama Shobō).

IGUCHI M. (1990*a*), 'Okutama no nihonzaru tanpōki—1' ('Report from the monkeys of Okutama—no. 1'), *Monkey*, 34(3): 14–18.

—— (1990*b*), 'Okutama no nihonzaru tanpōki—2' ('Report from the monkeys of Okutama—no. 2'), *Monkey*, 34(4): 11–14.

IINO Y. (1989*a*), 'Shishioi to kuma no i' ('Wild boar chasing and bear gall'), in Sanson Minzoku no Kai (ed.), *Shuryō* (*Hunting*) (Tokyo: Enterprise), 78–90.

—— (1989*b*), 'Chichibu no shuryō' ('Hunting in Chichibu'), in Sanson Minzoku no Kai (ed.), *Shuryō* (*Hunting*) (Tokyo: Enterprise), 60–77.

IMAIZUMI Y. (1987 [1970]), 'Nihonōkami no keitōteki chii ni tsuite' ('Concerning the taxonomic status of the Japanese Wolf'), in *Honyūdōbutsugaku zasshi*, 5(2). Reproduced in Higashi Yoshino Mura (ed.), *Maboroshi no nihonōkami—nihonōkami ni kansuru shiryō* (*The Phantom Japanese Wolf: Materials on the Japanese Wolf*) (Higashi Yoshino: Kyōiku Iinkai), 33–7.

INADA K. (1975), *Kiihantō no mukashibanashi* (*Old Tales from the Kii Peninsula*) (Tokyo: Nihon Hōsō Shuppan Kyōkai).

——(1994), 'Saru hōon' ('Monkey gratitude'), in Inada K. *et al.* (eds.), *Nihon mukashibanashi jiten* (*Dictionary of Japanese Old Tales*) (Tokyo: Kōbundō), 395.

INOUE M. (2002), *Yama no hatake o saru kara mamoru* (*Protecting Mountain Fields from Monkeys*) (Tokyo: Nōbunkyō).

INOUE T. (1998), 'Ōkami fukkatsu ni yume nosete' ('Dreaming of wolf revival'), *Forest Call*, 5: 2–8.

——(1999), 'Ōkami saidōnyū e no kitai to kanōsei' ('Wolf reintroduction: prospects and possibilities'), *Forest Call*, 6: 27–9.

ISHIBASHI H. (1998), 'Dōtaku ni kakareta nazo no dōbutsu wa ōkami ka' ('Is the mystery animal drawn on the bronze bell a wolf?'), *Forest Call*, 5: 14–15.

ISHIDA K. (1993), 'Kōka na yūtan' ('Expensive bear gall'), in Gifuken Honyūrui Dōbutsu Chōsa Kenkyūkai (ed.), *Horobiyuku mori no ōja—tsukinowaguma* (*The Imminent Extinction of the King of the Forest: The Black Bear*) (Gifu: Gifu Shinbunsha), 85–6.

ISHIZAKI H. (1991*a*), 'Saru' ('Monkey'), in Nihon Minwa no Kai (ed.), *Gaidobukku nihon no minwa* (*A Guidebook to Japanese Folktales*) (Tokyo: Kōdansha), 240–1.

——(1991*b*), 'Ōkami' ('Wolf'), in Nihon Minwa no Kai (ed.), *Gaidobukku nihon no minwa* (*A Guidebook to Japanese Folktales*) (Tokyo: Kōdansha), 235–6.

ISHIZAKI T. (1977), 'Toyama-ken ni tsutawaru saru no minwa—5' ('Monkey folktales told in Toyama Prefecture—no. 5'), *Monkey*, 21(4): 32–3.

——(1979*a*), 'Hokuriku ni tsutawaru saru no minwa—2' ('Monkey folktales told in the Hokuriku area—no. 2'), *Monkey*, 23(3): 26–7.

——(1979*b*), 'Hokuriku ni tsutawaru saru no minwa—3' ('Monkey folktales told in the Hokuriku area—no. 3'), *Monkey*, 23(5): 32–3.

ISOYAMA T. (1999), 'Saru no sumu mura' ('The village where monkeys live'). Available at: *http://www.hasestudio.com/morinonakade/topic.html* (accessed on 21 Sept. 2000).

ITANI J. (1971), *Takasakiyama no saru* (*The Monkeys of Takasakiyama*), ed. Imanishi Kinji (Tokyo: Shisakusha).

ITŌ Y. (1986), *Kamoshika no sōdōki—tennenkinenbutsu ka gaijū ka* (*Record of the Serow Troubles: National Treasure or Pest?*) (Tokyo: Tsukiji Shokan).

IWAHASHI K. (1989), 'Rekishi' ('History'), in Aiken no Tomo (ed.), *Kishūken* (*The Kishū Dog*) (Tokyo: Seibundō Shinkōsha), 13–22.

JWA (Japan Wolf Association) (1994), 'Nihon no mori ni ōkami o yobimodoshite mimasenka' ('Shouldn't we call the wolf back to the Japanese forest?'), *Forest Call*, 1: 2.

KAMATA C. (2000), 'Message 227'. Available at: *http://www.egroups.co.jp/messages/wolf-japan/227* (accessed on 1 June 2001).

——(2001), 'Message 519'. Available at: *http://www.egroups.co.jp/messages/wolf-japan/519* (accessed on 1 June 2001).

KAMATA K. (1992), 'Kumagera no sumu hayashi o mamoru' ('Protecting forests where the black woodpecker lives'), in Nebuka M. (ed.), *Mori o kangaeru—shirakami bunagenseirin kara no hōkoku* (*Thinking About the Forest: Reports from the Shirakami Primeval Beech Forest*) (Tokyo: Rippū Shobō), 16–21.

KANEKO H., KONISHI M., SASAKI K., and CHIBA T. (1992), *Nihonshi no naka no dōbutsu jiten* (*A Dictionary of Animals in Japanese History*) (Tokyo: Tōkyōdō Shuppan).

KANEKO H. (1993), 'Seichō' ('Growth'), in Gifuken Honyūrui Dōbutsu Chōsa Kenkyūkai (ed.), *Horobiyuku mori no ōja—tsukinowaguma* (*The Imminent Extinction of the King of the Forest: The Black Bear*) (Gifu: Gifu Shinbunsha), 14–16.

KANKYŌ CHŌ (2000*a*), 'Shubetsu shuryō menjō kōfu jōkyō' ('The different categories of hunting licences'). Available at: *http://www.asahi-net.or.jp/~zb4h-kskr/license.html* (accessed on 28 Sept. 2000).

—— (2000*b*), 'Shuryō ni yori hasshōshita jiko kensū' ('The number of accidents caused by hunting'). Available at: *http://www.asahi-net.or.jp/~zb4h-kskr/accident.html* (accessed on 28 Sept. 2000).

KANZAKI N. (2001), 'Inoshishi no shōhinka to kotaigun kanri' ('Wild boar commoditization and the management of wild groups'), in Takahashi S. (ed.), *Inoshishi to ningen—tomo ni ikiru* (*Wild Boars and Man: Living Together*) (Tokyo: Kokon Shoin), 258–88.

—— MARUYAMA N., and INOUE T. (1995), 'Ankēto chōsa—ōkami ni taisuru nihonjin no ishiki' ('Questionnaire survey: Japanese consciousness of wolves'), *Forest Call*, 2: 1–3.

KATŌ T., TSUJII M., YOSHIZAKI M., and SAITŌ S. (1986), 'Imēji no sekai no higuma' ('The world of imagery with regard to the brown bear'), in Saitō S. (ed.), *Higuma—sono, ningen to no kakawari* (*Brown Bears: Their Relations with People*) (Tokyo: Shisakusha), 1–59.

KATSUKI Y. (1995), *Yama ni sumu* (*Inhabiting the Mountains*) (Tokyo: Miraisha).

KAWADA M. (1971), 'Kishūken no seino to tokuchō' ('The skills and characteristics of Kishū hounds'), in Aiken no Tomo (ed.), *Nihonken chūgata* (*Medium-sized Japanese Dogs*) (Tokyo: Seibundōsha), 22–7.

KAWAOKA T. (1994), 'Nōgyō' ('Agriculture'), in Inada K. *et al.* (eds.), *Nihon mukashibanashi jiten* (*Dictionary of Japanese Old Tales*) (Tokyo: Kōbundō), 719–21.

KAWASAKI T. (1993*a*), 'Zetsumetsu e no michi (sono 5)—shuryōjū' ('The road to extinction [no. 5]: game animals'), in Gifuken Honyūrui Dōbutsu Chōsa Kenkyūkai (ed.), *Horobiyuku mori no ōja—tsukinowaguma* (*The Imminent Extinction of the King of the Forest: The Black Bear*) (Gifu: Gifu Shinbunsha), 161–2.

—— (1993*b*), 'Kokusaitekina hogo dōbutsu' ('An internationally protected animal'), in Gifuken Honyūrui Dōbutsu Chōsa Kenkyūkai (ed.), *Horobiyuku mori no ōja: tsukinowaguma* (*The Imminent Extinction of the King of the Forest: The Black Bear*) (Gifu: Gifu Shinbunsha), 151–2.

KHI (Kumanoji Hensan Iinkai) (1971), *Kumano-Nakahechi Saijiki* (*Kumano-Nakahechi Almanac*) (Tanabe: Kumano Nakahechi Kankōkai).

—— (1980), *Kumano nakahechi densetsu* (*Legends of Kumano Nakahechi*) (Tanabe: Kumano Nakahechi Kankōkai).

—— (1989), *Minzoku* (*Folklore*) (Tanabe: Kumano Nakahechi Kankōkai).

KISHIDA H. (1963), *Nihonōkami monogatari* (*Tales of the Japanese Wolf*), Yoshino Fūdoki No. 20 (Ōyodo, Nara: Yoshino Kondankai).

KISHIDA K. (1953), *Daihyōteki rinseihonyūdōbutsu honzaru chōsa hōkoku* (*Report on the Survey of the Japanese Macaque, a Representative Forest Mammal*), Ornithological and Mammalogical Report No. 14 (Tokyo: Ministry of Agriculture and Forestry). Includes English-language summary.

KISHIMOTO R. (1994), 'Kamoshika no shakai kōzō to shokugai mondai' ('The serow's social structure and the pestilence problem'), *Shinrin Kagaku* (*Forest Science*), 11: 26–32.

KKTK (Kasochiiki Kasseika Taisaku Kenkyūkai) (1994), *Kasochiiki kasseika handobukku* (*Handbook on Revitalization of Depopulated Areas*) (Tokyo: Gyosei).

KMG (Kinki Minzoku Gakkai) (1985) (ed.), *Kumano no minzoku—Wakayama-ken Hongū-chō* (*The Folk Customs of Kumano: Hongū Town, Wakayama Prefecture*) (Osaka: Kinki Minzoku Gakkai).

KOBAYASHI M. (1989), 'Minami-Arupusu kitabu no yaseijū' ('The wild beasts of the north part of the southern Alps'), in Sanson Minzoku no Kai (ed.), *Shuryō* (*Hunting*) (Tokyo: Enterprise), 137–50.

KOGANEZAWA M. (1991), 'Nihonzaru no bunpu to hogo no genjō oyobi sono mondaiten—Nikkō o chūshin ni' ('The present state of distribution and protection of the Japanese monkey and related problems: focussing on Nikkō'), in NACS-J (ed.), *Yasei dōbutsu hogo—21 seiki e no teigen* (*Wild Animal Protection: A Proposal for the Twenty-first Century*) (Tokyo: Nihon Shizen Hogo Kyōkai), 124–57.

—— (1999), 'Nikkō ni okeru shika no zōka to shinrin seitaikei no eikyō—soshite ōkami dōnyū no hitsuyōsei' ('The increase of deer in Nikko and its effect on the forest ecosystem: the necessity of the wolf'), *Forest Call*, 6: 4–6.

—— MARUYAMA N., TAKAHASHI M., CHINEN S., and CAITLIN A. (1997), 'Ōkami ni taisuru nihonjin no ishiki' ('Japanese awareness of wolves'), *Forest Call*, 4: 2–6.

KOMATSU K. (1988), *Nihon no noroi* (*Curses in Japan*) (Tokyo: Kōbunsha).

KUDŌ J. (1996), *Kamoshika no mori kara* (*From the Serow's Forest*) (Tokyo: NTT Shuppan).

KURAHASHI N. (1994), 'Toshi jūmin ni totte no torasuto' ('The Trust as seen by urban citizens'), in Yamada Kunihiro (ed.), *Satoyama torasuto* (*The Satoyama Trust*) (Tokyo: Hokuto Shuppan), 103–6.

KURISU K. (2001), *Kuma to mukiau* (*Confronting Bears*) (Tokyo: Sōshinsha).

KUSAKA M. (1965), *Yama no kotowaza* (*Forest Proverbs*) (Tokyo: Zenkoku Ringyō Kairyō Fukyō Kyōkai).

MAINICHI SHINBUNSHA (1965), *Nihon no dōbutsuki* (*Record of the Animals of Japan*) (Tokyo: Mainichi Shinbunsha).

MAITA A. (1989), 'Sengo sanson shakai no "mura kuzushi" to shinrin kanri' (' "village breakdown" in postwar mountain village society in relation to forest management'), in Uchiyama S. (ed.), *Shinrin shakaigaku' sengen* (*Declaration on Forest Sociology*) (Tokyo: Yuikaku Sensho), 130–56.

MAITA K. (1996a), *Yama de kuma ni au hōhō* (*Ways to Encounter Bears in the Mountains*) (Tokyo: Yama to Keikokusha).

—— (1996b), *Kuma o ō* (*Pursuing Bears*) (Tokyo: Dōbutsusha).

—— (1998a), *Ikashite fusegu kuma no gai* (*Preventing Bear Damage*) (Tokyo: Nōbunkyō).

—— (1998b), 'Nihon no kuma no genjō' ('The situation of the Japanese bear'). Available at: *http://www.yasuda.co.jp/environment/98t1_5b.html* (accessed on 18 Sept. 2000).

MAITA K. (1999), *Tsukinowaguma no iru mori e* (*Towards a Forest Where Bears Can Live*) (Tokyo: Adthree).

MANO T. (1991), 'Ezohiguma hogo kanri no mondaiten to kadai' ('Problems and tasks in the conservation management of the Hokkaido brown bear'), in NACS-J (ed.), *Yasei dōbutsu hogo—21 seiki e no teigen* (*Wild Animal Protection: A Proposal for the Twenty-first Century*) (Tokyo: Nihon Shizen Hogo Kyōkai), 158–68.

MARUYAMA A. (1994), 'Ōkami' ('The wolf'), in Inada K. *et al.* (eds.), *Nihon mukashibanashi jiten* (*Dictionary of Japanese Old Tales*) (Tokyo: Kōbundō), 139.

MARUYAMA H. (1994), 'Onitaiji' ('Demon conquest'), in Inada K. *et al.* (eds.), *Nihon mukashibanashi jiten* (*Dictionary of Japanese Old Tales*) (Tokyo: Kōbundō), 165–6.

MARUYAMA N. (1994), 'Dōbutsu ni yoru shinrin higai wa naze okiru no ka' ('Why does animal damage to forests occur?'), *Ringyō Gijutsu*, 633: 2–6.

—— (1995), ' "Nihon no honyūruigaku no mōten o tsuku—ōkami fuzai no ekoroji" o kaisai' (The opening address to the conference on 'Challenging the blindspot of Japanese mammalogy: wolfless ecology'), *Forest Call*, 2: 4–7.

—— (1998*a*), ' "Ōkamifan ni yoru ōkami saidōnyū hantai iken" ' ("Opposition to wolf reintroduction from a wolf fan"), *Internet Forest Call*. Available at: *http://www2s.biglobe.ne.jp/~wolfpage/fan.html* (accessed on 19 Sept. 2000).

—— (1998*b*), 'Chūkokusantoki nihon e dōnyū keikaku kara no tenkai—ōkami e' ('The implications for the wolf of the plan to introduce the crested ibis from China to Japan'), *Internet Forest Call*. Available at: *http://www2s.biglobe.ne.jp/~wolfpage/toki.html* (accessed on 19 Sept. 2000).

—— (1998*c*), 'Ōkami saidōnyū towa nandeshō' ('What is wolf reintroduction?'), *Internet Forest Call*. Available at: *http://www2s.biglobe.ne.jp/~wolfpage/topic.html* (accessed on 19 Sept. 2000).

—— (1999), 'Ōkami no fukkatsu ni mukete' ('Towards the restoration of the wolf'), *Forest Call*, 6: 15–23.

—— (2000), 'Message 353'. Available at: *http://www.egroups.co.jp/messages/wolf-japan/353* (accessed on 1 June 2001).

—— (2001*a*), 'Message 636'. Available at: *http://www.egroups.co.jp/messages/wolf-japan/636* (accessed on 1st June, 2001).

—— (2001*b*), ' "Animal Patrol Project" hassoku appiiru' ('Founding appeal for the "Animal Patrol Project" '), in Message 682. Available at *http://www.egroups.co.jp/messages/wolf-japan/682* (accessed on 27 Sept. 2001).

—— (2001*c*), 'Towards a good relationship between forest, wolves and people (*mori-ōkami-hito no yoi kankei o kangaeru*)', *Forest Call*, 8: 39.

—— WADA K., and KANZAKI N. (1995), 'Dai 38 kai shinpojiumu "ōkami fuzai no ekorojii" ni tsuite no shusaisha sokatsu' ('Review of the 38th symposium of the Mammalogical Society of Japan, "Ecology Without Wolves" '), *Honyūrui Kagaku*, 35(1): 21–7.

MATSUNAMI H. (1994), 'Sarugamitaiji' ('Monkey spirit conquest'), in Inada K. *et al.* (eds.), *Nihon mukashibanashi jiten* (*Dictionary of Japanese Old Tales*) (Tokyo: Kōbundō), 389–90.

MATSUO T. (2000), 'Message 165'. Available at: *http://www.egroups.co.jp/messages/wolf-japan/165* (accessed on 1 June 2001).

MATSUTANI M. (1994), *Ōkami, yamainu, neko* (*Wolves, Mountain Dogs and Cats*) (Tokyo: Rippū Shobō).

MATSUYAMA Y. (1977*a*), *Kari no kataribe—Ina no yamagai yori* (*Hunting Storytellers: From the Ina Gorge*) (Tokyo: Hōsei Daigaku Shuppankyoku).

—— (1977*b*), *Kari no kataribe—Ina no yamagai yori II* (*Hunting Storytellers: From the Ina Gorge. II*) (Tokyo: Hōsei Daigaku Shuppankyoku).

—— (1978), *Kari no kataribe—Ina no yamagai yori III* (*Hunting Storytellers: From the Ina Gorge. III*) (Tokyo: Hōsei Daigaku Shuppankyoku).

—— (1994), *Inadani no dōbutsutachi* (*The Animals of Inadani*) (Tokyo: Dōjidaisha).

MITO Y. (1987), ' "Monkey-watching" to edo jidai—Suzuki Bokushi no baai' ('Monkey-watching in the Tokugawa period: Suzuki Bokushi's perspective'), *Monkey*, 31(1–2): 30–4.

—— (1989), ' "Monkey-watching" to edo jidai—nōmin no baai' ('Monkey-watching in the Tokugawa period: the farmer's perspective'), *Monkey*, 33(3–4): 34–9.

—— (1995), 'Nihonzaru no bunpu hensen ni miru nihonjin no dōbutsukan no henten' ('Transformation of the Japanese view of animals as reflected in the changing distribution of monkeys'), in Kawai M. and Hanihara K. (eds.), *Dōbutsu to bunmei* (*Animals and Civilization*) (Tokyo: Asakura Shoten), 89–105.

MIYAMOTO T. *et al.* (1995) (eds.), *Nihon zankoku monogatari 2—wasurerareta tochi* (*Tales of Cruelty from Japan*, ii. *Forgotten Land*) (Tokyo: Heibonsha).

MIYAO T. (1989), *Tsukinowaguma—owareru mori no jūnin* (*The Black Bear: A Fugitive Forest Dweller*) (Nagano-shi: Shinano Mainichi Shinbunsha).

MIZOGUCHI M. (1992), *Mori no dōbutsu to ikiru gojū no hōhō* (*Fifty Ways of Coexisting with Forest Animals*) (Tokyo: Buronzu Shinsha).

MIZUNO A. (1995), 'Hakusan chiiki no engai to inu' ('Monkey damage in the Hakusan region and the connection with dogs'), *Wildlife Forum*, 1(1): 11–17.

MORI O. (1989), 'Shimokita hantō no Taiwanzaru mondai' ('The Formosan rock macaque problem on the Shimokita Peninsula'), *Monkey*, 33(5–6): 3–7.

MŌRI S., and TADANO A. (1997), *Sendai matagi shikagari no hanashi* (*Sendai Matagi Tales of Deerhunting*) (Tokyo: Keiyūsha).

MORITA M. (1994), 'Ōkami hōon' ('The wolf's obligation to return'), in Inada K. *et al.* (eds.), *Nihon mukashibanashi jiten* (*Dictionary of Japanese Old Tales*) (Tokyo: Kōbundō), 141–2.

MUKŌYAMA M. (1993), 'Shishiyarai' ('Boar-scaring'), in Amino Y., Kinoshita T., and Kamino Y. (eds.), *Umi, kawa, yama no seisan to shinkō* (*The Sea, Rivers and Mountains: Production and Religion*) (Tokyo: Yoshikawa Kōbunkan), 27–34.

MURAKAMI K. (1992), *Nihonōkami* (*The Japanese Wolf*) (Kōza-chō: Self-published).

NAGAMATSU A. (1993), *Shuryō minzoku to shugendō* (*Hunting Folklore and Shugendo*) (Tokyo: Hakusuisha).

NAGANO F. (1991), 'Sarugamitaiji' ('Monkey spirit conquest'), in Nihon Minwa no Kai (ed.), *Gaidobukku nihon no minwa* (*A Guidebook to Japanese Folktales*) (Tokyo: Kōdansha), 115–16.

NAGAOKA I. (1999), 'Moriagaru ōkami būmu e no kitai' ('The promise of the exciting wolf boom'), *Forest Call*, 7: 11–12.

NAKAMORI S. (1940), 'Yoshino no ōkami no hanashi' ('Tales of wolves in Yoshino'), ed. Hiraiwa Y., *Dōbutsu Bungaku*, 68: 26–36.

NAKAMORI S. (1941), 'Yoshino no ōkami no hanashi (II)' ('Tales of wolves in Yoshino II'), ed. Hiraiwa Yonekichi, *Dobutsu Bungaku*, 76: 30 8.

NAKAMURA H. (1981), *Dōbutsumei no yurai* (*The Origin of Animal Names*) (Tokyo: Tōshosensho).

NAKAMURA T. (1987), *Nihon dōbutsu minzokushi* (*Japanese Animal Folklore*) (Tokyo: Kaimeisha).

——(1989), *Dōbutsutachi no reiryoku* (*The Spiritual Powers of Animals*) (Tokyo: Chikuma Shobō).

NAKASHIMA N. (1998), *Yakushima no kankyō minzokugaku* (*The Environmental Folklore of Yakushima*) (Tokyo: Akashi Shoten).

NAKATANI J. (2001), 'Shirarezaru inoshishi no seitai to shakai' ('Wild boar ecology and society'), in Takahashi S. (ed.), *Inoshishi to ningen—tomo ni ikiru* (*Wild Boars and Man: Living Together*) (Tokyo: Kokon Shoin), 200–20.

NAORA N. (1968), *Shuryō* (*Hunting*) (Tokyo: Hōsei Daigaku Shuppankyoku).

NAUMANN N. (1994), *Yama no kami* (*The Mountain Spirit*), trans. from the German by Nomura S. and Hieda Y. (Tokyo: Gensōsha).

NEBUKA M. (1991), *Yama no jinsei—Matagi no mura kara* (*Mountain Life: From the Village of Matagi*) (Tokyo: NHK Books).

NIMIYA K., and ŌTSUKA E. (1993), *Kuma no jidai* (*The Age of the Bear*) (Tokyo: Kōbunsha).

NISHIURA S. (1989), 'Tanba-Miyama shuryō hiwa' ('The secret hunting history of Tamba in Miyama'), in Sanson Minzoku no Kai (ed.), *Shuryō* (*Hunting*) (Tokyo: Enterprise), 165–94.

NOMOTO K. (1990), *Kumano sankai minzokukō* (*A Treatise on the Mountain and Coastal Folk Customs of Kumano*) (Kyoto: Jinbun Shoin).

——(1994), *Kyōsei no fōkuroa—minzoku no kankyō shisō* (*The Folklore of Co-existence: The Environmental Thought of Folklore*) (Tokyo: Seidosha).

——(1996), 'Shini no naka no dōbutsu' ('Animals in folk consciousness'), in Akada M., Katsuki Y., Komatsu K., Nomoto K., and Fukuda A. (eds.), *Kankyō no minzoku* (*Environmental Folklore*) (Tokyo: Yūzankaku), 221–34.

Nōrinsuisanshō. (n.d.), *Nōgyō sensasu* (*Agricultural Census*) (Tokyo: Ministry of Agriculture) Obtained from Hongū Town Hall.

NSSKS (Nōson Seikatsu Sōgō Kenkyū Sentā) (1990), *Sanchison shūraku no seikatsu kōzō* (*The Livelihood Structure of Mountain Villages*), Seikatsu Kenkyū Report No. 31 (Tokyo: NSSKS).

NYSHI (Nara-ken Yasei Seibutsu Hogo Iinkai) (n.d.), *Kii sanchū no nihonōkami* (*The Japanese Wolf in the Kii Mountains*) (Tenri-shi: Self-published).

OBARA I. (1987 [1984]), 'Zetsumetsu shita nihon no ōkami' ('The extinct Japanese wolf'), *Dōbutsu to shizen* (*Animals and Nature*), 14(11). Reproduced in Higashi Yoshino Mura (ed.), *Maboroshi no nihonōkami—nihonōkami ni kansuru shiryō* (*The Phantom Japanese Wolf: Materials on the Japanese Wolf*) (Higashi Yoshino: Kyōiku Iinkai), 53–7.

OCHIAI K. (1991), 'Aomori-ken Wakinosawa-mura ni okeru jirei' ('An example from Wakinosawa village in Aomori Prefecture'), in NACS-J (ed.), *Yasei dōbutsu hogo—21 seiki e no teigen* (*Wild Animal Protection: A Proposal for the Twenty-first Century*) (Tokyo: Nihon Shizen Hogo Kyōkai), 204–14.

——(1992), *Kamoshika no seikatsushi* (*The Life of the Serow*) (Tokyo: Dōbutsusha).

—— (1996), 'Shinrin shigyō ga kamoshika ni ataeru eikyō' ('The influence on the serow of forest management'), *Honyūrui Kagaku* (*Mammalian Science*), 36(1): 79–87.

ODAJIMA M. (1993), 'Idainaru yamanokami "kimun kamui" ' (' "Kimun kamui", the grand mountain spirit'), in Rizōto Gorufujō Mondai Zenkoku Renrakkai (eds.), *Yasei seibutsu kara no kokuhatsu* (*Wildlife Indicts Us*) (Tokyo: Recycle Bunkasha), 22–8.

ŌFUJI T. (1968), 'Ōkami minzoku' ('Wolf folklore'), *Encyclopaedia Japonica*, 18(5:3) (Tokyo: Shogakkan), 368.

OGAWA K. (1999), 'Minshutō Ogawa giin shitsugi' (Question by Representative Ogawa of the Democratic Party). Available at: *http://www.asahi-net.or.jp/~zb4h-kskr/d2-ogawa. html* (accessed 28 Sept. 2000).

OGURA I. (1993a), 'Kuma to yama no kami' ('Bears and the mountain spirit'), in Gifuken Honyūrui Dōbutsu Chōsa Kenkyūkai (ed.), *Horobiyuku mori no ōja—tsukinowaguma* (*The Imminent Extinction of the King of the Forest: The Black Bear*) (Gifu: Gifu Shinbunsha), 99–100.

—— (1993b), 'Kumaare' ('Bear storms'), in Gifuken Honyūrui Dōbutsu Chōsa Kenkyūkai (ed.), *Horobiyuku mori no ōja—tsukinowaguma* (*The Imminent Extinction of the King of the Forest: The Black Bear*) (Gifu: Gifu Shinbunsha), 98–9.

OMOSU T. (1997), *Ki no kuni Kumano kara no hasshin* (*A Message from the Tree Country of Kumano*) (Tokyo: Chūō Kōronsha).

ŌTA Y. (1997), *Matagi—kieyuku yamabito no kiroku* (*Matagi: A Record of a Disappearing Mountain People*) (Tokyo: Keiyūsha).

SAITŌ H. (1983), 'Aiken monogatari' ('Tales of favourite dogs'), in *Zenshū nihon dōbutsushi 12* (*Record of Japanese Animals*, xii) (Tokyo: Kōdansha), 5–102.

SAITŌ K. (2001), 'Nihonzaru ga nihonzaru de wa nakunaru hi' ('The day when Japanese monkeys cease to be Japanese monkeys'), *Outdoor* (Feb.): 118–21.

SAKAI S. (1986), 'Ōkami hōon' ('The return made by the wolf'), in *Nihon denki densetsu daijiten* (*Dictionary of Japanese Romantic Legends*) (Tokyo: Kadokawa Shoten), 175–6.

SAKUMA J. (1980), 'Uzenogunikyo no shuryō girei' ('The hunting rituals of Uzenogunikyo'), in Chiba T. (ed.), *Nihon minzoku fūdoron* (*Japanese Folklore and Climate*) (Tokyo: Kōbundō), 161–81.

—— (1985), *Shuryō no minzoku* (*The Folklore of Hunting*) (Tokyo: Iwasaki Bijutsusha).

SAKURAI T. (1990), *Minkan shinkō no kenkyū—Sakurai Tokutarō chosakushū 4* (*Research on Folk Religion: The Collected Works of Sakurai Tokutarō*, iv) (Tokyo: Yoshikawa Kōbunkan).

SAKUSA K. (1995), *Dōbutsu kotowaza jiten* (*Dictionary of Animal Proverbs*) (Tokyo: Bijinesusha).

SATŌ S. (1990), *Yama no kami no minzoku to shinkō* (*Mountain Spirit Folklore and Religion*) (Tokyo: Chūōkōron Jigyō Shuppan).

SEKINE T., and SATŌ H. (1992), 'Ōdaigaharasan ni okeru nihonjika ni yoru jumoku hakuhi' ('Tree-barking by deer on Mount Ōdaigahara'), *Japanese Journal of Ecology*, 42: 241–8.

SEKINE Y. (2001), 'Yama no mi ni natte kangaeyo' ('Thinking like a mountain'), *Forest Call*, 8: 18–19.

SEKO T. (1988), *Nihonōkami o ō* (*Pursuing the Japanese Wolf*) (Tokyo: Tokyo Shoseki).

SHIBATA E., and KOBUNE T. (1984), 'Kiihantō ni okeru tsukinowaguma ni tsuite' ('On the bears of the Kii Peninsula'), *Shinrin Bōeki* (*Forest Pests*), 10(391): 175–80.

SHIMIZU M. (1987), 'Mie-ken Fujiwara-chō ni okeru engai to sono taiō hōhō ni tsuite' ('On monkey damage in Fujiwara, Mie Prefecture and the forms of response to it'), *Monkey*, 31(1–2): 14–17.

SMS (Shinano Mainichi Shinbunsha) (1969) (eds.), *Shinano dōshokubutsuki* (*Record of Animals and Plants of Shinano*) (Nagano-shi: Shinano Mainichi Shinbunsha).

SUTŌ I. (1991), *Yama no hyōteki—inoshishi to yamabito no seikatsushi* (*The Mountain Landmark: A Record of the Way of Life of Wild Boars and Mountain People*) (Tokyo: Miraisha).

SUZUKI T. (1982), *Nihon zokushin jiten* (*Dictionary of Popular Beliefs*) (Tokyo: Kadokawa Shoten).

TABUCHI T. (1992), 'Chichishiro mizu' ('The teats' white water'), in Tanigawa K. (ed.), *Dōshokubutsu no fōkuroa 1* (*Animal and Plant Folklore*, i) (Tokyo: Sanjūichi Shobō), 9–94.

TAGUCHI H. (1994), *Matagi—mori to kariudo no kiroku* (*Matagi: A Record of the Forest and its Hunters*) (Tokyo: Keiyūsha).

TAIRA Y. (1982), *Shin Kumano fūdoki* (*A New Kumano Record of Local Customs*) (Kumano: Kumano-shi Kyōiku Iinkai).

TAKAHASHI S. (1995), *Yasei dōbutsu to yaseika kachiku* (*Wild Animals and Feral Livestock*) (Tokyo: Taimeidō).

——(1997), *Dōshokubutsu kotowaza jiten* (*Dictionary of Animal and Plant Proverbs and Sayings*) (Tokyo: Tokyōdō Shuppan).

——(2001), 'Chiikizukuri no naka de inoshishi o kangaeru' ('Considering the wild boar in relation to local development'), in Takahashi S. (ed.), *Inoshishi to ningen—tomo ni ikiru* (*Wild Boars and Man: Living Together*) (Tokyo: Kokon Shoin), 355–97.

TAKAHASHI Y. (1984), *Inakagurashi no tankyū* (*Investigating Country Life*) (Tokyo: Sōshisha).

TAKATORI K. (2000), 'Ōkami to deatta toki' ('When I met the wolf'). Available at: *http://www.egroups.co.jp/files/wolf-japan/takatori2.txt* (accessed 29 May 2001).

TANAKA A. (1996), '*Mori o mamore*' *ga mori o korosu* (*To "Save the Forest" is to Kill the Forest*) (Tokyo: Yōsensha).

TANBA A. (1993), 'Yūtan' ('Bear gall'), in Gifuken Honyūrui Dōbutsu Chōsa Kenkyūkai (ed.), *Horobiyuku mori no ōja—tsukinowaguma* (*The Imminent Extinction of the King of the Forest: The Black Bear*) (Gifu: Gifu Shinbunsha), 82–3.

TANIGAWA K. (1980), *Tanigawa Kenichi chosakushū 1* (*Collected Works of Tanigawa Kenichi*, i) (Tokyo: Sanichi Shobō).

TERADA K. (1994), 'Inadani ni ita ōkami no denshō' ('Legends of wolves in Inadani'), *Inadani shizen tomo no kaihō*, 52: 3.

TMKI (Totsukawa Mura Kyōiku Iinkai) (1988), *Totsukawa-gō no mukashibanashi* (*Old Tales of Totsugawa Village*) (Totsukawa: Kyōiku Iinkai).

TOGAWA Y. (1956), *Nihondōbutsushi* (*Record of Japanese Animals*) (Tokyo: Bungei Shunjū).

——(1995), 'Yamainuzuka' ('The mountain dog mound'), in *Inubaka* (*Dogcrazy*) (Tokyo: Shōgakkan).

TOKIDA K. (1991), 'Kamoshika hogo, kanri' ('Serow conservation and management'), in Ōmachi Sangaku Hakubutsukan (ed.), *Kamoshika—hyōgaki o ikita dōbutsu* (*The Serow: An Animal of the Glacial Period*) (Nagano-shi: Shinano Mainichi Shinbunsha), 169–78.

—— (2001), 'Chōjū hogo seido to inoshishi kanri' ('The wildlife conservation system and the management of the wild boar'), in Takahashi S. (ed.), *Inoshishi to ningen— tomo ni ikiru* (*Wild Boars and Man: Living Together*) (Tokyo: Kokon Shoin), 244– 57.

TOKUYAMA S. (1975), *Kishū no minwa* (*The Folktales of Kishū*) (Tokyo: Miraisha).

TORII H. (1989), 'Shizuoka-ken ni okeru tsukinowagumaryō to sono rinboku higai' ('Bear-hunting in Shizuoka Prefecture and bear damage to forest trees'), *Shinrin Bōeki* (*Forest Pests*), 38(11): 195–202.

—— (1996*a*), 'Higai kanri no genkyō' ('The present-day situation of damage management'), in NACS-J (ed.), *Yasei dōbutsu hogo—2* (*Wild Animal Protection*, ii) (Tokyo: Nihon Shizen Hogo Kyōkai), 64–9.

—— (1996*b*), 'Higai kanri ni kansuru chōsa kenkyū' ('Survey research in connection with damage management'), in NACS-J (ed.), *Yasei dōbutsu hogo—2* (*Wild Animal Protection*, ii) (Tokyo: Nihon Shizen Hogo Kyōkai), 98–101.

—— (1996*c*), 'Tsukinowaguma no higai to higai bōji' ('Bear damage and damage prevention'), *Ringyō to Yakuzai* (*Forestry and Drugs*), 135: 1–8.

TSUJIOKA M. (1999), *Shika no shokugai kara Nikkō no mori o mamoreruka* (*Can We Protect the Nikko Forest from Deer Damage?*) (Utsunomiya: Zuisōsha).

UE T. (1980), *Yamabito no ki: ki no kuni, hatenashi sanmyaku* (*Diary of a Mountain Person: The Hatenashi Mountain Range, Tree Country*) (Tokyo: Chūkō Shinsho).

—— (1983), *Yamabito no dōbutsushi* (*A Mountain Villager's Record of Animals*) (Tokyo: Fukuinkan Shoten).

—— (1987), *Seishun o kawa ni ukabete—ki to ningen no uchū II* (*Youth Afloat in the River: The Universe of Trees and Men*, ii) (Tokyo: Fukuinkan Shoten).

—— (1988), *Sumiyaki nikki—Yoshino-Kumano no yama kara* (*A Charcoal-burner's Diary: From the Mountains of Yoshino-Kumano*) (Tokyo: Shinjuku Shobō).

—— (1990), *Kumano sōshi* (*Kumano Storybook*) (Tokyo: Sōshisha).

—— (1994), *Mori no megumi* (*The Blessing of the Forest*) (Tokyo: Iwanami Shoten).

—— and TANBA Y. (1987), 'Kumano ni "Jōmon" o saguru' ('Searching for "Jōmon" in Kumano'), *Kiba*, 2: 41–5.

UNŌ Y. (1987), 'Taiji sareta sarugami' ('The conquered monkey god'), *Monkey*, 31(3): 13–15.

WADA H. (1978), 'Wakayama no minwa, densetsu' ('Folktales and legends of Wakayama'), in Ando S. (ed.), *Wakayama no kenkyū 5* (*Research on Wakayama*, v) (Osaka: Seibundō Shuppan).

WADA K. (1994), *Saru wa dono yō ni fuyu o kosu ka* (*How Do Monkeys Get Through the Winter?*) (Tokyo: Nōbunkyō).

—— (1998), *Saru to tsukiau—ezuke to engai* (*Interacting with Monkeys: Provisioning and Damage*) (Nagano-shi: Shinano Mainichi Shinbunsha).

WAKIDA M. (1989), 'Minōtokuyama-mura no kumagari' ('The bearhunting of Minōtokuyama village'), in Sanson Minzoku no Kai (ed.), *Shuryō* (*Hunting*) (Tokyo: Enterprise), 151–64.

WATANABE H. (1984 [1974]), 'Tsukinowaguma no hanashi' ('Tales of the black bear'), in Mizuhara Y. *et al.* (eds.), *Zenshū nihon dōbutsushi 26* (*Collected Works on Japanese Animals*, xxvi) (Tokyo: Kōdansha), 155–220.

WATANABE H. (1989), 'Tsukinowaguma—sono hogo o megutte' ('The black bear: towards its conservation'), *Dōbutsu to Dōbutsuen* (*Animals and Zoos*), 41(470): 138–41.

—— and KOMIYAMA A. (1976), 'Tsukinowaguma no hogo to shinrin e no higai bōjo (II)' ('Conservation of wild bears and forest damage control II'), *Kyōto daigaku nōgakubu fuzoku enshūrin hōkoku* (*Bulletin of the Kyoto University Forests*), 48: 1–8.

—— NOBORIO J., NIMURA K., and WADA S. (1970), 'Ashū enshūrin no tsukinowaguma—toku ni sugi no ataeru higai ni tsuite' ('Damage to cryptomeria by wild bears in the Ashū Experimental Forest of Kyoto University'), *Kyōto daigaku nōgakubu fuzoku enshūrin hōkoku* (*Bulletin of the Kyoto University Forests*), 41: 1–25.

—— TANIGUCHI N., and SHIDEI T. (1973), 'Tsukinowaguma no hogo to shinrin e no higai bōjo (I)' ('Conservation of wild bears and forest damage control I'), *Kyōto daigaku nōgakubu fuzoku enshūrin hōkoku* (*Bulletin of the Kyoto University Forests*), 45: 1–8.

WATANABE K. (1989), 'Izu-Ōshima no Taiwanzaru' ('The Formosan rock macaques of Izu-Ōshima'), *Monkey*, 33(1): 4–7.

—— (1995), 'Chiiki ni okeru yasei nihonzaru hogo kanri no mondaiten to kongo no kadai' ('The problems of protecting and managing wild Japanese monkeys in the regions and tasks for the future'), *Reichōrui Kenkyū* (*Primate Research*), 11: 47–58.

—— (1996), '"Genkyoken" kara no nihonzaru hogo no tame no seimei' ('Declaration in the name of the conservation of the Japanese macaque from the "Research Group on Present-day Conditions"'), *Reichōrui Kenkyū* (*Primate Research*), 12: 55–6.

WATANABE O., and OGURA S. (1996), 'Nōson chiiki ni okeru yasei dōbutsu no kachi ninshiki to hogo-kanri seisaku e no ikō' ('Relationship between perceptions toward wildlife and opinions about wildlife management policy in rural areas of central Japan'), *Wildlife Conservation Japan*, 2(1): 1–15.

WKMK (Wakayama-ken Minwa no Kai) (1981) (ed.), *Kumano-Hongū no minwa* (*Folktales of Kumano-Hongū*) (Gobō: Wakayama-ken Minwa no Kai).

—— (1987) (ed.), *Kishū-Ryūjin no minwa* (*Folktales of Kishū-Ryūjin*) (Gobō: Wakayama-ken Minwa no Kai).

YAGASAKI T. (2001), 'Shishigaki ni miru inoshishi to no kōbō' ('The struggle with the wild boar viewed in relation to the boar wall'), in Takahashi S. (ed.), *Inoshishi to ningen—tomo ni ikiru* (*Wild Boars and Man: Living Together*) (Tokyo: Kokon Shoin), 122–70.

YAMAZAKI T. (1996), *Fukui no tsukinowaguma to genpatsu* (*The Fukui Bear and Nuclear Power Stations*) (Tokyo: Hachigatsu Shokan).

YANAGITA K. (1961), 'Yama no jinsei' ('Mountain lives'), in *Sekai kyōyō senshū 21* (*Collected Works of World Learning*, xxi) (Tokyo: Heibonsha), 97–209.

—— (1992 [1910]), *Tōno monogatari* (*Tales of Tōno*) (Tokyo: Shinchō Bunko).

YANAI K. (1993), *Maboroshi no nihonōkami* (*The Phantom Japanese Wolf*) (Urawa, Saitama: Sakitama Shuppankai).

YASUI M. (1997), 'Machizukuri, mura okoshi to furusato monogatari' ('Tales of town-building, village revitalization and home villages'), in Komatsu K. (ed.), *Matsuri to ibento* (*Festivals and Events*) (Tokyo: Shōgakkan), 201–26.

YONEYAMA T. (1969), *Kaso shakai* (*Depopulated Society*) (Tokyo: NHK Books).

YOSHINO H. (1989), *Yama no kami* (*The Mountain Spirit*) (Kyoto: Jinbun shoin).

Hunting Magazines

ANON. (1979*a*), 'Tsuribari de inoshishi o tsuru' ('Fishing for wild boar with a fishhook'), *Shuryōkai*, 23(1): 171.

—— (1979*b*), 'Higumagari e no keikoku' ('A warning about hunting brown bears') *Shuryōkai*, 23(9): 43–4.

—— (1998), 'Tochigi Ashikaga de inoshishi no shokugai shinkoku!' ('Serious state of boar damage in Ashikaga, Tochigi!'), *Shuryōkai*, 42(12): 65.

ATOBE T. (1988), 'Rokusei shūshū' ('Imitating the deer's cry'), *Shuryōkai*, 32(7): 92–5.

BEKKI S. (1979), 'Nigeru inoshishi—sono tonsōjutsu' ('The escaping boar—its powers of flight'), *Shuryōkai*, 23(2): 106–8.

FUJIWARA C. (1979), 'Kuma nihyakutō shakaku no waga satori' ('My enlightenment after shooting two hundred bears'), *Shuryōkai*, 23(3): 33–7.

FUJIWARA T. (1999), 'Ōmonoryō e no michi—9' ('The path towards big-game hunting— part 9'), *Zenryō*, 64(2): 52–5.

FUKUSHIMA K. (1999), 'Inoshishiryō no mikiri wa' ('Tracking in boarhunting'), *Shuryōkai*, 43(1): 72–7.

FUKUYA Y. (1979), 'Kizukurai no inoshishi o ou' ('Chasing a wounded wild boar'), *Shuryōkai*, 23(2): 74–9.

FURUYA M. (1995), 'Kishūken no honshitsu to sentaku ikusei' ('The nature of the Kishū hound and rearing options'), *Shuryōkai*, 39(9): 33–7.

—— (1999*a*), 'Kishūken o aishite gojūnen—1' ('Fifty years of loving the Kishū hound—part 1'), *Zenryō*, 64(5): 40–3.

—— (1999*b*), 'Kishūken o aishite gojūnen—2' ('Fifty years of loving the Kishū hound— part 2'), *Zenryō*, 64(6): 80–4.

IMAI T. (1979), 'Waga shi no oshie' ('My master's teachings'), *Shuryōkai*, 23(5): 68–9.

ISHIKAWA T. (1979), 'Inoshishi to shika no yauke jōkyō to shagekijō no mondaiten' ('Situations where wild boar and deer are wounded and problems with shooting'), *Shuryōkai*, 23(3): 38–43.

—— (1995), 'Yugai chōjū kujo no genjō to mondaiten—Mie-ken' ('The state of wildlife pest culling and its problems: Mie Prefecture'), *Shuryōkai*, 39(5): 56–60.

ITŌ K. (1994), 'Ankēto' (Questionnaire [responses]), in *Zenryō*, 59(9): 98.

KAMEDA A. (1995), 'Yugai chōjū kujo no genjō to mondaiten—Yamaguchi-ken' ('The state of wildlife pest culling and its problems: Yamaguchi Prefecture'), *Shuryōkai*, 39(8): 88–91.

KIKUCHI T. (1995), 'Ezoshikaryō' ('Hunting the Ezo deer'), *Shuryōkai*, 39(7): 86–92.

KIMURA K. (1979*a*), 'Yūza no hōkoku' (Users' reports), *Shuryōkai*, 23(2): 64–5.

—— (1979*b*), 'Waga hokoritakaki inoshishiinu to inoshishiryō no jissai' ('A true tale of a boarhunt involving my brave boarhound'), *Shuryōkai*, 23(5): 48–53.

KINOSHITA K. (1994), 'Ankēto' (Questionnaire [responses]), in *Zenryō*, 59(9): 100.

KINOSHITA Y. (1979), 'Satsuma no "doramukan" o taosu' ('Felling the "drumcan" of Satsuma'), *Shuryōkai*, 23(9): 74–7.

KITAGAWA T. (1979), 'Dokuzetsu—inoshishiken seppō' ('Attacking the boarhound orthodoxy'), *Shuryōkai*, 23(8): 54–9.

KURITA H. (1999), 'Inoshishi no wanaryō' ('Wild boar trapping'), *Shuryōkai*, 43(2): 86–90.

MATSUOKA S. (1979), 'Yūza no hōkoku' (Users' reports), *Shuryōkai*, 23(2): 60–2.

MAWATARI M. (1999), 'Shikabue no kōyō' ('The utility of the deer whistle'), *Shuryōkai*, 43(1): 78–9.

MITANI K. (1979*a*), 'Tora sōdō tokuhō daiichidan' ('The tiger furore—the first special report'), *Shuryōkai*, 23(10): 175–82.

—— (1979*b*), 'Tora sōdō tokuhō dainidan' ('The tiger furore—the second special report'), *Shuryōkai*, 23(11): 209–17.

MIYOSHI T. (1979), 'Shika to inoshishi ni dai gēmu ni okeru hidan jōkyō to seimeiryoku no hikaku' ('Comparing wounded states and life force among deer and wild boar, the two main game animals'), *Shuryōkai* 23(3): 52–5.

ONO H. (1994), 'Ankēto' (Questionnaire [responses]), in *Zenryō*, 59(9): 99–100.

ŌSAKI Y. (1994), 'Kita no katte ryōron' ('A personal view of hunting from the north'), *Zenryō*, 59(10): 144–7.

ŌTA K. (1995), 'Hanyajika no yatsuyosa' ('The resilence of the wounded deer'), *Shuryōkai*, 39(4): 46–9.

SAKODA K. (1994), 'Ankēto' (Questionnaire [responses]), in *Zenryō*, 59(9): 101–2.

SATŌ K. (1979), 'Jūryōken to shite no shibainu' ('The shiba dog as a large game hound'), *Shuryōkai*, 23(7): 114–15.

SATŌ Y. (1995), 'Ezoshikaryō no mondaiten' ('Issues in deerhunting'), *Shuryōkai*, 39(10): 52–5.

SATŌ Z. (1979), 'Genba kara no teigen' ('Proposal from the field'), *Shuryōkai*, 23(3): 109–11.

SHIBAHARA K. (1995*a*), 'Inoshishiryō biggu faito 1' ('The boarhunt that became a big fight, part 1'), *Shuryōkai*, 39(6): 36–41.

—— (1995*b*), 'Hanyajishi to no kōbō' ('The struggle with a wounded wild boar'), *Shuryōkai*, 39(10): 68–73.

SHINODA T. (1995), 'Watakushiryū no raifurujū no kaizō' ('My personal method for improving the use of the rifle'), *Shuryōkai*, 39(7): 51–5.

SUGIMOTO H. (1999), 'Tanzawa sankai no noinu' ('Feral dogs of the Tanzawa Mountains'), *Shuryōkai*, 43(2): 49–51.

TAKAMI F. (1995), 'Yamainu no ko "Shiro" no omoide' ('Memories of "Shiro" the child of the mountain dog'), *Shuryōkai*, 39(7): 94–6.

TAKASHITA Y. (1995), 'Waga inoshishiinutachi no nessenfu' ('War record of my boarhounds'), *Shuryōkai*, 39(5): 44–7.

TŌYAMA E. (1998*a*), 'Nihonōkami wa mada ikinokotteiruka' ('Does the Japanese wolf still exist?'), *Shuryōkai*, 42(5): 55.

—— (1998*b*), 'Okuba sanmyaku no hikyō ni akashika no rakuen' ('A red deer paradise in the remote land of the Okuba mountains'), *Shuryōkai*, 42(10): 47.

UDAGAWA T. (1979), 'Tori no me, jū no me' ('Bird's eyes, beasts' eyes'), *Shuryōkai*, 23(12): 148–52.

UMEZU M. (1979), 'Gēmu no bikkuri taikenki—10' ('Recollections of surprising incidents involving game animals—no. 10'), *Shuryōkai*, 23(3): 62–3.

URAYAMA Y. (1995), 'Waga inoshishiken no funshi isshunen tsuitoki—2' ('Memorial on the first anniversary of the death of my boarhound—part 2'), *Shuryōkai*, 39(5): 94–7.

WADA M. (1995), 'Yūgaichōjūkujo no genjō to mondaiten' ('The state of wildlife pest culling and its problems'), *Shuryōkai*, 39(6): 74–9.

WKRNS (Wakayama-ken Ryōyūkai Nishimurō Shibu) (1979), 'Nanbyō ga chōjū no myōyaku de naotta hanashi' ('Tales of wildlife cures for serious illnesses'), *Shuryōkai*, 23(4): 60–2.

YAMAMOTO H. (1995), 'Inoshishi no kukuriwanaryō' ('Wire-trapping wild boar'), *Shuryōkai*, 39(10): 62–5.

Newspapers

Asahi Shinbun (*AS*) (15 Nov. 1984), 'Hokkaidō no kitsune shuryō kaikin, kotoshi mo ichimanpiki shasatsu e' ('Opening of the foxhunting season in Hokkaido—this year a target of ten thousand animals').

—— (24 Feb. 1985), 'Hogo no ato satsugai' ('After protection, murder').

—— (13 Dec. 1985), 'Ryōken ni osowareta shōnen shinu' ('Child dies attacked by hound').

—— (10 Oct. 1988), 'Kuma mata osou' ('Another bear attack').

—— (29 Oct. 1988), 'Mori owareta tsukinowaguma' ('Bear chased through the forest').

—— (15 Feb. 1989), 'Dōbutsu no sakumotsu arashi "yowatta"' ('Animal farm product damage') (Kanagawa).

—— (16 June 1989), 'Dai ni no furusato, yume to kieru!' ('Disappearing with the dream of a second hometown') (Kanagawa).

—— (3 Mar. 1990), 'Saru gundan shiitake arashi' ('Monkey army destroys mushrooms').

—— (22 Apr. 1990), 'Hokaku sareta shika, kata ashi o ushinai furusato no yama e' ('Captured deer with one leg missing to be returned to hometown mountains').

—— (2 June 1990), 'Higuma hogo e ippo' ('One step towards brown bear conservation').

—— (17 Aug. 1990), 'Mori no hantā, kuma ni sukui no te, Toyama no ryōyūkai' ('Forest hunters helping bears—the Hunters' Association of Toyama').

—— (6 Mar. 1991), 'Yasei dōbutsu ni furusato' ('A hometown for wild animals') (Kanagawa).

—— (9 Sept. 1991), 'Shika, suiden mimawarichō no otoshiyori sasshō' ('An old person patrolling the ricefield is killed by a deer') (Ōsaka).

—— (9 Oct. 1991), 'Yūgai hokaku shika, kankō ni hitoyaku' ('Deer captured as pests: a role in tourism').

—— (17 Oct. 1991), 'Yaseijika, shokunikuka no ugoki' ('Wild deer: the trend towards farming for meat').

—— (18 Nov. 1991), 'Tozan no josei o inoshishi osō' ('Woman hiker attacked by wild boar').

—— (25 Feb. 1992), 'Sagasenuka, shika to kyōzon no michi' ('Won't you search for it? A path towards co-existence with the deer') (Hyōgo).

—— (21 May 1992), 'Kankōkyaku ga saru ni osoware, kega' ('A tourist attacked and injured by a monkey').

—— (7 July 1992), 'Hantā o hanto seyō' ('Let's hunt the hunters').

—— (16 Oct. 1992), 'Kuma no shutsubotsu aitsugu Tajima chihō' ('Repeated bear encounters in the Tajima region') (Hyōgo).

—— (22 Nov. 1992), 'Inoshishi—Tanzawa' ('Wild boar in Tanzawa') (Tokyo).

—— (25 Mar. 1993), 'Saru no mure, shizen ni kaesō' ('Let's return the monkeys to nature') (Osaka).

Asahi Shinbun (7 Oct. 1993), 'Aware inoshishi, hito o kande shasatsu' ('A wild boar appears, bites a person, and gets shot') (Kyoto).

—— (17 Oct. 1993), 'Dōbutsutachi no himojii aki' ('The animals' hungry autumn').

—— (16 Dec. 1993), 'Maebara-shi de hokaku no saru o jūmin shūgeki no "hannin" to dantei' ('The monkey caught in Maebara City is adjudged to be the "criminal" responsible for attack on residents').

—— (13 Apr. 1994), 'Nozaru no shinnyū kuitome e shinheiki dōnyū' ('Introducing new weapons for stopping the invasions of monkeys') (Kanagawa).

—— (5 June 1994), 'Engai taisaku shidōin Takagi Naoki' ('Takagi Naoki, an advisor on countermeasures for monkey damage').

—— (12 July 1994), 'Ie ni kuma, hitori kega' ('A bear in a house, one person injured') (Osaka).

—— (17 July 1994), 'Tsukinowaguma no kōdō ō' ('Following the black bear's behaviour') (Okuyama).

—— (10 Aug. 1994), 'Kichō na shokubutsu o tabecha dame' ('You mustn't eat valuable plants!').

—— (21 Aug. 1994), 'Nikkōsuge hobo zetsumetsu' ('Nikkōsuge—almost extinct') (Tochigi).

—— (2 Dec. 1994), 'Shikakanashi' ('Deer sorrow') (Kanagawa).

—— (9 Dec. 1994), 'Fueru shika o heraseruka' ('Should the increasing numbers of deer be reduced?').

—— (10 Dec. 1994), 'Kuma o sukue, hito to no kyōzon hōhō saguru' ('Saving the bear, finding a way of co-existence with people').

—— (22 Dec. 1994), 'Yasei ni manabu' ('Learning from nature').

—— (23 Feb. 1995), ' "Noinu" to "yaken" no kubetsu konnan' ('The difficulty of differentiating "feral dogs" from "stray dogs" ').

—— (17 Mar. 1995), 'Kotoshi mo uraniwa ni kamoshika tōjō' ('Serow appear in back gardens this year too').

—— (5 Apr. 1995), 'Yama no ōja' ('King of the forest').

—— (9 Apr. 1995), 'Naki Leo e no omoi, kokeshi no hyōjō ni' ('Memories of the late Leo, preserved in a wood-carving').

—— (23 July 1995), 'Ōdaigahara, Hakkotsu jurin, Naraken-Kamikitayama-mura, midori o taberu shika' ('Ōdaigahara, Hakkotsu forest, Kamikitayama Village, Nara Prefecture—deer eating greenery').

—— (6 Aug. 1995), 'Kakashi no sato' ('The scarecrow village').

—— (25 Nov. 1995), 'Kyōzon no michi motome hogo mosaku' ('Groping for conservation and the path to coexistence') (Osaka).

—— (29 Nov. 1995), 'Onsensaru ni hinin shochi' ('Sterilizing treatment for spa monkeys').

—— (19 Jan. 1996), 'Nara-Yoshino de taijū 148 kiro no ōinoshishi shitomeru' ('Catching a giant boar of 148 kilogrammes in Yoshino, Nara') (Osaka).

—— (15 Mar. 1996), 'Hageyama taisaku ni sakura no naegi gohyappon' ('Five hundred cherry saplings to revive bare mountain') (Saitama).

—— (12 June 1996), 'Atama itai engai taisaku' ('Headaches over countermeasures for monkey damage') (Tokyo).

—— (29 Aug. 1996), 'Yaseisaru no shasatsu chūshi o' ('Towards a cessation of monkey-shooting').

—— (19 Sept. 1996), 'Saru wa naze sato made oriruka' ('Why do monkeys come down to the village?').

—— (13 Nov. 1996), 'Saruhōrōtabi' ('Monkey wandering') (Osaka).

Chūgoku Shinbun (*CGS*) (9 Jan. 2000), 'Inoshishi to ningen, kutō tsuzuku' ('Wild boars and humans—the struggle continues').

—— (30 Jan. 2000), 'Urayama no jūnin' ('The resident of the rear forest').

Chūnichi Shinbun (*CNS*) (22 May 1997), ' "Engai" ni nōka ga himei—Owase' ('Farmers' cry for help over monkey damage in Owase').

—— (7 Mar. 2000), 'Shokugai no shika—ōkamitsukai taiji' ('The deer pest: overcoming it with the wolf'). Evening edition.

Ehime Shinbun (*ES*) (6 Dec. 1997), 'Gaijū inoshishi naze hanasunoka' ('Why do you release the wild boar pest?').

Ikimono Tsūshin (*IS*) (4 July 1999), 'Tōkyōtoshin saru tōsō' ('The flight of the monkey in central Tokyo'). Available at: *http://www.mars.dti.ne.jp/~takumi-m/ikimono/009.html* (accessed 19 Sept. 2000).

Kahoku Shinpō (*KS*) (30 Apr. 1996), 'Nōsakumotsu no higai shinkoku, saru gundan ni sensenkyōkyō, Yamagata-Yamadera' ('Worsening crop damage—the great fear of the monkey army in Yamadera in Yamagata').

—— (21 May 1996), 'Murenashi kamoshika osō, Aomori-Yakita no noinu shutsubotsu' ('Feral dog outbreak in Yakita Aomori—pack attacks serow').

—— (8 Apr. 1997), 'Saru gundan' ('Monkey army').

—— (2 Sept. 1997), 'Arasareru tabata Akita-ken Hachimori-chō kara no hōkoku' ('Report from Hachimori Town in Akita Prefecture on damaged fields').

—— (13 May 1998), 'Engai shinkoku—Aomori-Wakinozawa-mura, mizukara to o ake jinka shinnyū' ('Worsening monkey damage—opening doors themselves and entering houses in Wakinozawa Village in Aomori').

—— (23 Oct. 1998), ' "Engai" fusege! Borantiatai katsuyaku' ('Defend against monkey damage! Volunteer corps activism').

Kahoku Shinpō Yūkan (*KSY*) (13 Mar. 2000), 'Shika shokugai taisaku ni ōkami yobō' ('Let's call on the wolf as a countermeasure against deer damage').

Kii Minpō (29 Sept. 1972), 'Ōkami wa ikiteiru' ('The wolf still lives!').

—— (12 Mar. 1996), 'Nara yasei i ga hantai mōshiire' ('Nara Wildlife Committee declares opposition').

—— (30 Mar. 1996), 'Koe—dokusha no ran' (Voice: readers' column).

Mainichi Shinbun (*MS*) (15 Jan. 1989), 'Ōtō-mura no Shinohara odori' ('The Shinohara dance of Ōtō-mura').

—— (19 Feb. 1989), 'Jūgai' ('Beast damage').

—— (19 Mar. 1989), 'Denshō' ('Legend').

—— (16 Apr. 1989), 'Yama no ō' ('Kings of the mountains').

—— (7 May 1989), 'Shinshi' ('Sacred messenger').

—— (21 May 1989), 'Oinu' ('Lord Dog').

—— (28 May 1989), 'Komainu' ('Komainu').

—— (17 Dec. 1989), 'Kinse' ('The modern era').

Mainichi Shinbun (14 Jan. 1990), 'Nōsho' ('Farm treatise').

—— (21 Jan. 1990), 'Shugeki' ('Attack').

—— (8 Apr. 1990), 'Oinu kawara' ('Wolf riverbed').

—— (29 July 1990), 'Shōhin sakumotsu' ('Commercial crops').

—— (19 Aug. 1990), 'Shinkō rufu' ('Dissemination of the faith').

—— (26 Aug. 1990), 'Tamaki jinja' ('Tamaki Shrine').

—— (23 Sept. 1990), 'Ōkamemiya' ('Wolf shrines').

—— (14 Oct. 1990), 'Futatabi Shinohara e' ('Visiting Shinohara once more').

—— (18 Nov. 1990), 'Hōrōsha' ('Wanderers').

—— (22 Dec. 1990), 'Yamai' ('Illness').

—— (28 Apr. 1991), 'Inu to ōkami' ('Dogs and wolves').

—— (22 Nov. 1994), 'Nara kōen no shika no mure no naka ni "Shirojika" Banbi' (' "White Deer" Bambi among the deer herd in Nara Park').

—— (18 Dec. 1995), 'Ryōken santō ni osaware. 94 sai no josei shibō' ('A 94-year-old woman dead after she was attacked by three hounds').

—— (18 Nov. 1997), 'Inoshishigari no ryōken santō, gekōchū no ni jidō osou' ('Three hounds from a boarhunt attack two children on their way back from school').

—— (3 June 1999), 'Oware, kieyuku yasei—31, nihonjika' ('The hounded, disappearing wild—no. 31. Japanese deer') (Nagano).

—— (14 July 1999), 'Meiwaku, saru gundan shutsubotsu' ('Appearance of the nuisance monkey army') (Gifu).

—— (4 Aug. 1999), 'Saru to kyōzon' ('Co-existence with monkeys') (Yamamoto Yasuhisa).

Minami Nihon Shinbun Chōkan (*MNSC*) (10 Feb. 1998), 'Ōguchi-shi no tsūgakuro de ryōken ga jidō o shūgeki' ('Assault on child travelling to school by a hound in Ōguchi City').

—— (4 June 1998), 'Tennen kinenbutsu erabuōkomori, engai de zetsumetsu no osore' ('Fear of Erabuōkomori [natural treasure] extinction due to monkey damage').

Nihon Keizai Shinbun (*NKS*) (28 Feb. 1983), 'Kamoshika "hikokuseki" e' ('The serow "in the dock" ').

—— (17 Jan. 1994), 'Shika zōshoku, nōringyō ni kiki' ('Deer multiplication: a crisis for farming and forestry').

—— (19 Jan. 1997), 'Yasei dōbutsu to dō kyōzon?' ('How to coexist with wild animals?').

—— (3 May 1998), 'Kankōkyaku ya sanrin ni higai, saru shika ni Nikkō maitta' ('Harming tourists and forests: Nikkō defeated by monkeys and deer').

Nihon Nōgyō Shinbun (*NNS*) (20 Sept. 1995), 'Chōjū higai, hogo to kujo dō oriauka' ('Wildlife damage—how to reconcile protection with culling?').

—— (11 Sept. 1998), 'Engai kaihisaku gaisoku no edakiri taisetsu' ('The importance of cutting branches at the exterior of monkey fences').

Nikkan Supōtsu (16 July 1998), 'Nōsakumotsu arashi, manbiki—Nikkō no "muhansei" saru 2000 man en settō' ('Crop damage and shoplifting—the "unreformed" monkeys of Nikkō responsible for theft losses of 20 million yen').

Nishi Nihon Shinbun Chōkan (*NNSC*) (2 Mar. 1998), 'Ken wa jū de no kujo kentō' ('Prefecture will examine culling with guns').

—— (28 Sept. 1998), 'Utsushiyo no ushirosugata' ('The rear view of the picture world').

Sankei Shinbun (*SS*) (15 Apr. 1995), 'Asebi—shika no tsukutta fūkei' ('Japanese andromeda—a landscape created by the deer').

—— (27 May 1997), 'Ōkami būmu ga kita' ('The wolf boom is here').

—— (28 Jan. 1999), 'Zeppeki ni tatasaretemo kesshite ochimasen' ('Even on the edge of a cliff it does not fall').

Shizuoka Shinbunsha (10 Mar. 2000), 'Engai—hasshinki de "shūrai" tanchi' ('Monkey damage—"invasion" detection with transmitter').

Shizuoka Shinbun Chōkan (*SSC*) (28 July 1998), 'Inoshishi mura ga keieiken o jōto' ('Management of Wild Boar Village changes').

Tokushima Shinbun (*TS*) (4 Mar. 2002), 'Tora no fun de shika gekitai' ('Repelling deer with tiger faeces').

Tōkyō Yomiuri Shinbun (*TYS*) (24 Nov. 1999), 'Shizen to kyōsei (5)—saru' ('Coexistence with nature [no. 5]—monkeys'). Morning Edition.

Yomiuri Shinbun (*YS*) (22 June 1993), 'Suterareta ryōken' ('Abandoned hounds') (Yokohama).

—— (22 Aug. 1994), 'Tanzawa sanmyaku ryōken poisute' ('Abandonment of hounds in the Tanzawa mountains').

—— (12 Nov. 1994), 'Detekoi ōkami' ('Come out, wolf!'). Evening edition.

ENGLISH

Books and Articles

ABE, M., and KITAHARA, E. (1987), 'Censusing Japanese serow by helicopter in deciduous mountain forests', in Soma H. (ed.), *The Biology and Management of Capricornis and Related Mountain Antelopes* (London: Croom Helm), 110–18.

AKASHI, N., and NAKASHIZUKA, T. (1999), 'Effects of bark-stripping by Sika deer (*Cervus nippon*) on population dynamics of a mixed forest in Japan', *Forest Ecology and Management*, 113(1): 75–82.

AKINO, S. (1999), 'Spirit-sending ceremonies', in W. W. Fitzhugh and C. O. Dubreuil (eds.), *Ainu: Spirit of a Northern People* (Washington: National Museum of Natural History, Smithsonian Institution, in association with the University of Washington Press), 248–55.

ANDERSON, S. S., PRIME, J. H., HARWOOD, J., and BONNER, N. (1989), 'British seals: vermin or scapegoats?', in Putman R. J. (ed.), *Mammals as Pests* (London and New York: Chapman and Hall), 251–60.

ANDRZEJEWSKI, D. D., and JEZIERSKI, W. (1978), 'Management of a wild boar population and its effects on commercial land', *Acta Theriologica*, 23: 309–39.

ANON. (2001), 'Notes from Chico Wolf Conference, 4/3–4/5/01'. Available at: *http://www.yellowstone-bearman/conf-notes.html* (accessed 31 Aug. 2001).

ASQUITH, P. J. (1989), 'Provisioning and the study of free-ranging primates: history, effects, and prospects', *Yearbook of Physical Anthropology*, 32: 129–58.

AZUMA, S., and MORI, O. (1991), 'Hazard of gene pollution in Shimokita Japanese monkeys: management problems concerning hybridization with introduced Formosan monkeys', in N. Maruyama, B. Bobek, Y. Ono, W. Regelin, L. Bartos, and P. R. Ratcliffe (eds.), *Wildlife Conservation: Present Trends and Perspectives for the Twenty-first Century* (Tsukuba: Japan Wildlife Research Center), 196–9.

AZUMA, S., and TORII, H. (1980), 'Impact of human activities on survival of the Japanese black bear', in C. J. Martinka and K. L. McArthur (eds.), *Bears: Their Biology and Management. International Conference of Bear Research and Management* 4, Bear Biology Association Conference Series (Morges, Switzerland: IUCN), 71–9.

BATCHELOR, J. (1901), *The Ainu and their Folklore* (London: The Religious Tract Society).

BEHAR, R. (1986), *The Presence of the Past in a Spanish Village: Santa Maria del Monte* (Princeton: Princeton University Press).

BELL, M., and EVANS, D. M. (1997), 'Greening "the heart of England"—redemptive science, citizenship, and "symbol of hope for the nation"', *Environment and Planning D: Society and Space*, 15: 257–79.

BERGERUD, A. T., WYETT, W., and SNIDER, J. B. (1983), 'The role of wolf predation in limiting a moose population', *Journal of Wildlife Management*, 47(4): 977–88.

BIRD-DAVID, N. (1993), 'Tribal metaphorization of human-nature relatedness: a comparative analysis', in Kay Milton (ed.), *Environmentalism: The View From Anthropology* (London and New York: Routledge), 112–25.

BJERKE, T., REITAN, O., and KELLERT, S. R. (1998), 'Attitudes toward wolves in southeastern Norway', *Society and Natural Resources*, 11: 169–78.

BOITANI, L. (1992), 'Wolf research and conservation in Italy', *Biological Conservation*, 61(2): 125–32.

BOJOVIĆ, D., and COLIĆ, D. (1975), 'Wolves in Yugoslavia: with special reference to the period from 1945 to 1973', in D. H. Pimlott (ed.), *Wolves: Proceedings of the First Working Meeting of Wolf Specialists and of the First International Conference on Conservation of the Wolf* (Morges, Switzerland: IUCN Publications), 53–62.

BORKOWSKI, J., and FURUBAYASHI, K. (1998), 'Seasonal and diel variation in group size among Japanese sika deer in different habitats', *Journal of Zoology*, 245: 29–34.

BOURNE, J. (1995), 'Hyde County's wolf war', *Defenders*, 70(2): 10–17.

BOUTIN, S. (1992), 'Predation and moose population dynamics: a critique', *Journal of Wildlife Management*, 56(1): 116–27.

BOVENG, P. L., HIRUKI, L. M., SCHWARTZ, M. K., and BENGSTON, J. L. (1998), 'Population growth of Antarctic fur seals: limitation by a top predator, the leopard seal?', *Ecology*, 79(8): 2863–77.

BOYCE, M. S. (1992), 'Wolf recovery for Yellowstone National Park: a simulation model', in D. R. McCullough and R. H. Barrett (eds.), *Wildlife 2001: Populations* (London and New York: Elsevier Applied Science), 123–38.

—— (1995), 'Anticipating consequences of wolves in Yellowstone: model validation', in Ludwig N. Carbyn, Steven H. Fritts and Dale R. Seip (eds.), *Ecology and Conservation of Wolves in a Changing World* (Edmonton: Canadian Circumpolar Institute), 199–211.

—— (1998), 'Ecological-process management and ungulates: Yellowstone's conservation paradigm', *Wildlife Society Bulletin*, 26(3): 391–8.

BREITENMOSER, U. (1998a), 'Recovery of the Alpine Lynx population: conclusions from the first SCALP report', in C. Breitenmoser-Würster, C. Rohner, and U. Breitenmoser (eds.), *The Re-introduction of the Lynx into the Alps* (Strasbourg: Council of Europe Publishing), 135–44.

—— (1998b), 'Large predators in the Alps: the fall and rise of Man's competitors', *Biological Conservation*, 83(3): 279–89.

BRICK, P. D., and CAWLEY, R. M. (1996), 'Knowing the wolf, tending the garden', in P. D. Brick and R. M. Cawley (eds.), *A Wolf in the Garden: The Land Rights Movement and the New Environmental Debate* (Lanham, Md.: Rowman and Littlefield), 1–12.

BROCH, H. B. (1998), 'Local resource dependency and utilization on Timpaus', in A. Kalland and G. Persoon (eds.), *Environmental Movements in Asia* (London: Curzon), 205–26.

BROOKS, J. E., AHMAD, E., HUSSAIN, I., and KHAN, M. H. (1989), 'The agricultural importance of the wild boar (*Sus scrofa L.*) in Pakistan', *Tropical Pest Management*, 35(3): 278–81.

BROWN, J. S. (1994), 'Restoration ecology: living with the Prime Directive', in M. L. Bowles and C. J. Whelan (eds.), *Restoration of Endangered Species: Conceptual Issues, Planning and Implementation* (Cambridge: Cambridge University Press), 355–80.

BROX, O. (2000), 'Schismogenesis in the wilderness: the reintroduction of predators in Norwegian forests', *Ethnos*, 65(3): 387–404.

BUDIANSKY, S. (1995), *Nature's Keepers: The New Science of Nature Management* (London: Phoenix).

BULMER, R. (1967), 'Why is the cassowary not a bird? A problem of zoological taxonomy among the Karam of the New Guinea Highlands', *Man*, NS 2: 5–25.

CAMARRA, J. J. (1987), 'Changes in brown bear predation on livestock in the western French Pyrenees from 1968 to 1979', *International Conference of Bear Research and Management*, 6: 183–6.

CAPPS, K. (1994), 'Wolf wars', *Alaska*, 60(6): 20–7.

CARTMILL, M. (1993), *A View to a Death in the Morning: Hunting and Nature through History* (Cambridge, Mass.: Harvard University Press).

CÁTEDRA, M. (1992), *This World, Other Worlds: Sickness, Suicide, Death, and the Afterlife among the Vaqueiros de Alzada of Spain* (Chicago: University of Chicago Press).

CHAMBERLAIN, B. H. (1981), Translator's notes, *The Kojiki: Records of Ancient Matters* (Tokyo: Charles E. Tuttle).

CLAPHAM, Jr. W. B. (1973), *Natural Ecosystems* (New York: Macmillan).

CLARK, T., and GILLESBERG, A.-M. (2001), 'Lessons from wolf restoration in Greater Yellowstone', in V. A. Sharpe, B. G. Norton, and S. Donnelley (eds.), *Wolves and Human Communities: Biology, Politics, and Ethics* (Washington and Covelo, Calif.: Island Press), 135–49.

CLEVENGER, A., and CAMPOS, M. (1994), 'Brown bear *Ursus-Arctos* predation on livestock in the Cantabrian Mountains, Spain', *Acta Theriologica*, 39(3): 267–78.

COLEMAN, J. D. (1993), 'The integration of management of vertebrate pests in New Zealand', *New Zealand Journal of Zoology*, 20: 341–5.

CONSTANTINE, P. (1994), *Japanese Slang Uncensored* (Tokyo: Yen Books).

COZZA, K., FICO, R., BATTISTINI, M., and ROGERS, E. (1996), 'The damage-conservation interface illustrated by predation on domestic livestock in central Italy', *Biological Conservation*, 78(3): 329–36.

CURLEE, A. P., and CLARK, T. W. (1995), 'Nature's movers and shakers', *Defenders*, 70(2): 18–19.

DAILY, G. C. (1997), 'Countryside biogeography and the provision of ecosystem services', in P. Raven (ed.), *Nature and Human Society: The Quest for a Sustainable World* (Washington: National Academy Press), 104–13.

DALE, P. M. (1986), *The Myth of Japanese Uniqueness* (London: Routledge).

DEBOER, K. (2000), 'Dreams of wolves', in J. Elder (ed.), *The Return of the Wolf: Reflections of the Future of Wolves in the Northeast* (Hanover, NH: University Press of New England), 64–107.

DEBUSSCHE, M., LEPART, J., and DERVIEUX, A. (1999), 'Mediterranean landscape changes: evidence from old postcards', *Global Ecology and Biogeography*, 8(1): 3–15.

DESCOLA, P. (1994), *In the Society of Nature: A Native Ecology in Amazonia* (Cambridge: Cambridge University Press).

D'HUART, J.-P. (1993), 'The forest hog (*Hylochoerus meinertzhageni*)', in W. L. R. Oliver (ed.), *Pigs, Peccaries and Hippos* (Gland, Switzerland: IUCN), 84–93.

DISILVESTRO, R. L. (1991), *The Endangered Kingdom: The Struggle to Save America's Wildlife* (New York: John Wiley).

DIZARD, J. E. (2001), 'In wolves' clothing: restoration and the challenge to stewardship', in V. A. Sharpe, B. G. Norton, and S. Donnelley (eds.), *Wolves and Human Communities: Biology, Politics, and Ethics* (Washington and Covelo, Calif.: Island Press), 75–92.

DOI, T., ONO, Y., IWAMOTO, T., and NAKAZONO, T. (1987), 'Distribution of Japanese serow in its southern range, Kyushu', in H. Soma (ed.), *The Biology and Management of Capricornis and Related Mountain Antelopes* (London: Croom Helm), 93–103.

DOUGLAS, M. (1957), 'Animals in Lele religious thought', *Africa*, 27(1): 46–58.

—— (1966), *Purity and Danger* (London: Routledge and Kegan Paul).

—— (1975), *Implicit Meanings: Essays in Anthropology* (London: Routledge).

—— (1990), 'The pangolin revisited: a new approach to animal symbolism', in R. Willis (ed.), *Signifying Animals: Human Meaning in the Natural World* (London and New York: Routledge), 25–36.

DRAEGER, D. F. (1989), *Ninjutsu: The Art of Invisibility* (Rutland and Tokyo: Tuttle).

DUNSTONE, N., and IRELAND, M. (1989), 'The mink menace? A reappraisal', in R. J. Putman (ed.), *Mammals as Pests* (London and New York: Chapman and Hal), 225–41.

DURHAM, D., and FERNANDEZ, J. W. (1991), 'Tropical dominions: the figurative struggle over domains of belonging and apartness in Africa', in J. W. Fernandez (ed.), *Beyond Metaphor: The Theory of Tropes in Anthropology* (Stanford, Calif.: Stanford University Press), 190–210.

EGUCHI, S. (1991), 'Between folk concepts of illness and psychiatric diagnosis: *kitsune-tsuki* (fox possession) in a mountain village of western Japan', *Culture, Medicine and Psychiatry*, 15(4): 421–51.

ELLEN, R. (1993), *The Cultural Relations of Classification: An Analysis of Nuaulu Animal Categories from Central Seram* (Cambridge: Cambridge University Press).

ELSE, J. G. (1991), 'Nonhuman primates as pests', in H. O. Box (ed.), *Primate Responses to Environmental Change* (London and New York: Chapman and Hall), 155–65.

EMBREE, J. F. (1939), *Suye Mura: A Japanese Village* (Chicago: University of Chicago Press).

Environment Agency (1997), *Quality of the Environment in Japan—1995* (Tokyo: Environment Agency, Government of Japan).

ESTES, J. A., RATHBUN, G. B., and VANBLARICOM, G. R. (1993), 'Paradigms for managing carnivores: the case of the sea otter', in N. Dunstone and M. L. Gorman (eds.), *Mammals as Predators* (Oxford: Clarendon Press), 307–20.

FIDDES, N. (1991), *Meat: A Natural Symbol* (London and New York: Routledge).

FISCHER, H. (1991), 'Discord over wolves', *Defenders*, 66(4): 35–9.

—— (1995), *Wolf Wars: The Remarkable Inside Story of the Restoration of Wolves to Yellowstone* (Helena, Mont.: Falcon).

FOGLEMAN, V. M. (1989), 'American attitudes towards wolves: a history of misconception', *Environmental Review*, 13(1): 63–88.

FOX, M. W. (1980), *The Soul of the Wolf: A Meditation on Wolves and Man* (New York: Lyons and Burford).

FRACKOWIAK, W., GULA, R., and PERZANOWSKI, K. (1999), 'Status and management of the brown bear in Poland', in C. Servheen, S. Herrero, and B. Peyton (eds.), *Bears* (Gland, Switzerland: IUCN), 89–93.

FUJISAKA, S., DAPUSALA, A., and JAYSON, E. (1989), 'Hail Mary, kill the cat: a case of traditional upland crop pest control in the Philippines', *Philippine Quarterly of Culture and Society*, 17: 202–11.

FUJIWARA, E. (1988), 'Wildlife in Japan: crisis and recovery', *Japan Quarterly*, 35(1): 26–31.

FURUYASHIKI, K. (1999), *Ivory Tales: Policy and Discourse of Wildlife Conservation in Japan*, OCEES Research Paper No. 17 (Oxford: Oxford Centre for the Environment, Ethics and Society).

GILBERT, F. F. (1995), 'Historical perspectives on wolf management in North America with special reference to humane treatments in capture methods', in L. N. Carbyn, S. H. Fritts, and D. R. Seip (eds.), *Ecology and Conservation of Wolves in a Changing World* (Edmonton: Canadian Circumpolar Institute), 13–17.

GLUCK, C. (1998), 'The invention of Edo', in S. Vlastos (ed.), *Mirror of Modernity: Invented Traditions of Modern Japan* (Berkeley: University of California Press), 262–84.

GÓMEZ-LIMÓN, J., and VICENTE DE LUCÍO FERNÁNDEZ, J. (1999), 'Changes in use and landscape preferences on the agricultural-livestock landscapes of the central Iberian Peninsula (Madrid, Spain)', *Landscape and Urban Planning*, 44: 165–75.

GRAHAM, M. (1973), *A Natural Ecology* (Manchester: Manchester University Press).

GREEN, B. H. (1989), 'Conservation in cultural landscapes', in D. Western and M. Pearl (eds.), *Conservation for the Twenty-first Century* (New York and Oxford: Oxford University Press), 182–98.

GREEY, E. (1884), *The Bear Worshippers of Yezo* (Boston: Lee and Shepard).

GROOMS, S. (1993), *The Return of the Wolf* (Minocqua, Wis.: NorthWord Press).

GUZZETTI, F., and REICHENBACH, P. (1994), 'Towards a definition of topographic divisions for Italy', *Geomorphology*, 11(1): 57–74.

HAIRSTON, N. G., SMITH, F. E., and SLOBODKIN, L. B. (1960), 'Community structure, population control, and competition', *The American Naturalist*, 94: 421–5.

HALLOWELL, A. I. (1926), 'Bear ceremonialism in the northern hemisphere', *American Anthropologist*, 28: 1–175.

HAMPTON, B. (1996), 'Shark of the plains: early western encounters with wolves', *Montana: The Magazine of Western History*, 46(1): 2–13.

HARAWAY, D. (1992 [1989]), *Primate Visions: Gender, Race, and Nature in the World of Modern Science* (London: Verso).

HAROOTUNIAN, H. D. (1989), 'Visible discourses/invisible ideologies', in M. Miyoshi and H. D. Harootunian (eds.), *Postmodernism and Japan* (Durham, NC, and London: Duke University Press), 63–92.

HARTING, J. E. (1994 [1880]), *A Short History of the Wolf in Britain* (Whitstable: Pryor Publications).

HAVENS, T. R. H. (1974), *Farm and Nation in Modern Japan: Agrarian Nationalism, 1870–1940* (Princeton: Princeton University Press).

HAZUMI, T. (1994), 'Status of the black bear', *International Conference of Bear Research and Management*, 9(1): 145–8.

—— (1999), 'Status and management of the Asiatic black bear in Japan', in C. Servheen, S. Herrero, and B. Peyton (eds.), *Bears* (Gland, Switzerland: IUCN), 207–11.

HEINEN, J. T. (1996), 'Human behaviour, incentives, and protected area management', *Conservation Biology*, 10(2): 681–4.

HELL, B. (1996), 'Enraged hunters: the domain of the wild in north-western Europe', in P. Descola and G. Palsson (eds.), *Nature and Society: Anthropological Perspectives* (London and New York: Routledge), 205–18.

HILL, C. M. (1997), 'Crop-raiding by wild vertebrates: the farmer's perspective in an agricultural community in western Uganda', *International Journal of Pest Management*, 43(1): 77–84.

HOLLIMAN, J. (1990), 'Environmentalism with a global scope', *Japan Quarterly*, 37: 284–90.

HONE, J. (1994), *Analysis of Vertebrate Pest Control* (Cambridge: Cambridge University Press).

HOWARD, W. E., and DUTTA, J. J. (1995), 'Animal damage control techniques', in S. H. Berwick and V. B. Saharia (eds.), *The Development of International Principles and Practices of Wildlife Research and Management: Asian and American Approaches* (Delhi: Oxford University Press), 421–33.

HOWE, N. (1995), 'Fabling beasts: traces in memory', *Social Research*, 62(3): 641–59.

HOWELL, S. (1996), 'Nature in culture or culture in nature? Chewong ideas of "humans" and other species', in P. Descola and G. Pálsson (eds.), *Nature and Society: Anthropological Perspectives* (London and New York: Routledge), 127–44.

HOWELLS, O., and EDWARDS-JONES, G. (1997), 'A feasibility study of reintroducing wild boar *Sus scrofa* to Scotland: are existing woodlands large enough to support minimum viable populations?', *Biological Conservation*, 81(1–2): 77–89.

HUFF, D. E., and VARLEY, J. D. (1999), 'Natural regulation in Yellowstone National Park', *Ecological Applications*, 9(1): 17–29.

HUFFAKER, C. B. (1973), 'Predators, parasites and populations', in N. Calder (ed.), *Nature in the Round: A Guide to Environmental Science* (London: Wiedenfeld and Nicolson), 183–92.

HUFFMAN, M. A. (1991), 'History of the Arashiyama Japanese macaques in Kyoto, Japan', in L. M. Fedigan and P. J. Asquith (eds.), *The Monkeys of Arashiyama: Thirty-five Years of Research in Japan and the West* (Albany, NY: SUNY), 21–53.

HUFFORD, M. T. (1992), *Chaseworld: Foxhunting and Storytelling in New Jersey's Pine Barrens* (Philadelphia: University of Pennsylvania Press).

HUNTER, J. (1992), *The Animal Court: A Political Fable from Old Japan* (translated from Ando Shoeki's *Hosei monogatari*) (New York: Weatherhill).

HUNZIKER, M. (1995), 'The spontaneous reafforestation in abandoned agricultural lands: perception and aesthetic assessment by locals and tourists', *Landscape and Urban Planning*, 31: 399–410.

INGOLD, T. (1994), 'From trust to domination: an alternative history of human–animal relations', in A. Manning and J. Serpell (eds.), *Animals and Human Society: Changing Perspectives* (London and New York: Routledge), 1–22.

ITANI, J. (1975), 'Twenty years with Mount Takasaki monkeys', in G. Bermant and D. G. Lindburg (eds.), *Primate Utilization and Conservation* (New York: Wiley), 101–25.

IVY, M. (1995), *Discourses of the Vanishing: Modernity, Phantasm, Japan* (Chicago: University of Chicago Press).

IWASAKA, M., and TOELKEN, B. (1994), *Ghosts and the Japanese: Cultural Experience in Japanese Death Legends* (Logan, Ut.: Utah State University Press).

JAMES, W. (1990), 'Antelope as self-image among the Uduk', in R. Willis (ed.), *Signifying Animals: Human Meaning in the Natural World* (London and New York: Routledge), 196–203.

JAYASEKARA, P., and TAKATSUKI, S. (2000), 'Seasonal food habits of a sika deer population in the warm temperate forest of the westernmost part of Honshu, Japan', *Ecological Research*, 15: 153–7.

JOFCA (Japan Overseas Forestry Consultants Association) (1996), *Forestry in Japan* (Tokyo: JOFCA (Supervised by the Forestry Agency)).

JONES, T. E. (1926), 'Mountain Folk of Japan', Ph.D. diss., Columbia University (abridged version).

JUSSAUME, Jr. R. A. (1991), *Japanese Part-time Farming: Evolution and Impacts* (Ames, Ia.: Iowa State University Press).

KALLAND, A., and MOERAN, B. (1992), *Japanese Whaling: End of an Era?* (London: Curzon).

KAMADA, M., and NAKAGOSHI, N. (1996), 'Landscape structure and the disturbance regime in three rural regions Hiroshima Prefecture, Japan', *Landscape Ecology*, 11(1): 15–25.

KANAMORI, H., INOUE, J., and SATO, Y. (1991), 'Stem bark damage of coniferous trees by antler-rubbing of sika deer', in N. Maruyama, B. Bobek, Y. Ono, W. Regelin, L. Bartos, and P. R. Ratcliffe (eds.), *Wildlife Conservation: Present Trends and Perspectives for the Twenty-first Century* (Tsukuba: Japan Wildlife Research Center), 114–15.

KARJALAINAN, E., and KOMULAINEN, M. (1998), 'Field afforestation preferences: a case study in northeastern Finland', *Landscape and Urban Planning*, 43: 79–90.

KATCHER, A., and WILKINS, G. (1993), 'Dialogue with animals: its nature and culture', in S. R. Kellert and E. O. Wilson (eds.), *The Biophilia Hypothesis* (Washington: Island Press), 173–97.

KAVANAGH, W. (1994), *Villagers of the Sierra de Gredos: Transhumant Cattle-raisers in Central Spain* (Oxford: Berg).

KELLERT, S. R. (1991), 'Japanese perceptions of wildlife', *Conservation Biology*, 5(3): 297–308.

—— (1994), 'Attitudes, knowledge and behaviour toward wildlife among the industrial superpowers: the United States, Japan and Germany', in A. Manning and J. Serpell (eds.), *Animals and Human Society: Changing Perspectives* (London and New York: Routledge), 166–87.

—— BLACK, M., RUSH, C. R., and BATH, A. (1996), 'Human culture and large carnivore conservation in North America', *Conservation Biology*, 10(4): 977–90.

KENT, S. (1989), 'Cross-cultural perceptions of farmers as hunters and the value of meat', in S. Kent (ed.), *Farmers as Hunters: The Implications of Sedentism* (Cambridge: Cambridge University Press), 1–17.

KISHIMOTO, R. (1987), 'Family break-up in Japanese serow, *Capricornis crispus*', in H. Soma (ed.), *The Biology and Management of Capricornis and Related Mountain Antelopes* (London: Croom Helm), 104–9.

KITAHARA-FRISCH, J. (1991), 'Culture and primatology: East and West', in L. M. Fedigan and P. J. Asquith (eds.), *The Monkeys of Arashiyama: Thirty-five Years of Research in Japan and the West* (Albany, NY: SUNY), 74–80.

KNIGHT, J. (1995), 'Municipal matchmaking in rural Japan', *Anthropology Today*, 11(2): 9–17.

KNOBLOCH, F. (1996), *The Culture of Wilderness: Agriculture as Colonization in the American West* (Chapel Hill, NC: University of North Carolina Press).

KOGANEZAWA, M., and IMAKI, H. (1999), 'The effects of food sources on Japanese monkey home range size and location, and population dynamics', *Primates*, 40(1): 177–85.

KUBŌ, H. (1994), 'Japan and rice: a new vision', *Look Japan*, 40(465): 4–8.

LAFLEUR, W. R. (1992), *Liquid Life: Abortion and Buddhism in Japan* (Princeton: Princeton University Press).

LEACH, E. (1964), 'Anthropological aspects of language: animal categories and verbal abuse', in E. H. Lenneberg (ed.), *New Directions in the Study of Language* (Cambridge, Mass.: MIT Press), 23–63.

LEOPOLD, E. B. (1998), 'Why we need the wolf', *Defenders*, 73(4): 41–2.

LÉVI-STRAUSS, C. (1966), *The Savage Mind* (London: Wiedenfeld and Nicolson).

—— (1969 [1963]), *Totemism*, trans. Rodney Needham (Harmondsworth: Penguin).

LIENERT, L. (1998), 'The development of the desire and its consequent undertaking for the resettlement of the lynx in Obwalden', in C. Breitenmoser-Würster, C. Rohner, and U. Breitenmoser (eds.), *The Re-introduction of the Lynx into the Alps* (Strasbourg: Council of Europe Publishing), 131–4.

LINDQUIST, G. (2000), 'The wolf, the Saami and the urban shaman: predator symbolism in Sweden', in J. Knight (ed.), *Natural Enemies: People–Wildlife Conflicts in Anthropological Perspective* (London and New York: Routledge), 170–88.

LOPEZ, B. H. (1995 [1978]), *Of Wolves and Men* (New York: Touchstone).

McLAREN, B. E., and PETERSON, R. O. (1994), 'Wolves, moose, and tree rings on Isle Royale', *Science*, 266: 1555–8.

McNAMEE, T. (1994), 'Warring over wolves', *Defenders*, 70(1): 15–17.

McNEELY, J. A., and SOCHACZEWSKI, PAUL S. (1994), *Soul of the Tiger: Searching for Nature's Answers in Southeast Asia* (Honolulu: University of Hawaii Press).

MAITA, K. (1987), 'Radio-tracking of Japanese serow in Akita Prefecture, Japan', in H. Soma (ed.), *The Biology and Management of Capricornis and Related Mountain Antelopes* (London: Croom Helm), 119–24.

MANO, T., and MOLL, J. (1999), 'Status and management of the Hokkaido brown bear in Japan', in C. Servheen, S. Herrero, and B. Peyton (eds.), *Bears* (Gland, Switzerland: IUCN), 128–31.

MARUYAMA, N. (n.d.), 'Extermination and recovery of wolves in Japan', Manuscript in author's possession.

—— KAJI, K., and KANZAKI, N. (1996), 'Review of the extirpation of wolves in Japan', *Journal of Wildlife Research*, 1(2): 199–201.

MASUI, M. (1987), 'Social behaviour of Japanese serow, *Capricornis crispus crispus*', in H. Soma (ed.), *The Biology and Management of Capricornis and Related Mountain Antelopes* (London: Croom Helm), 134–44.

MECH, L. D. (1966), *The Wolves of Isle Royale*, Fauna of the National Parks of the United States, Fauna Series 7 (Washington: US Government).

—— (1977), 'Wolf-pack buffer zones as prey reservoirs', *Science*, 198: 320–1.

—— (1981 [1970]), *The Wolf: The Ecology and Behavior of an Endangered Species* (Minneapolis: University of Minnesota Press).

—— (2001), 'Wolf restoration to the Adirondacks: the advantages and disadvantages of public participation in the decision', in V. A. Sharpe, B. G. Norton, and S. Donnelley (eds.), *Wolves and Human Communities: Biology, Politics, and Ethics* (Washington and Covelo, Calif.: Island Press), 13–22.

MERIGGI, A., and LOVARI, S. (1996), 'A review of wolf predation in southern Europe: does the wolf prefer wild prey to livestock?', *Journal of Applied Ecology*, 33: 1561–71.

—— and SAACHI, O. (1992), 'Factors affecting damage by wild boars to cereal fields in northern Italy', in F. Spitz, G. Janeau, G. Gonzalez, and S. Aulagnier (eds.), *Ongules/Ungulates 91: Proceedings of the International Symposium* (Paris/Toulouse: SFEPM–IRGM), 192–6.

MESSIER, F. (1995), 'On the functional and numerical responses of wolves to changing prey density', in L. N. Carbyn, S. H. Fritts, and D. R. Seip (eds.), *Ecology and Conservation of Wolves in a Changing World* (Edmonton: Canadian Circumpolar Institute), 187–97.

—— and CRÊTE, M. (1985), 'Moose–wolf dynamics and the natural regulation of moose populations', *Oecologia*, 65: 503–12.

MILLS, L. S., SOULÉ, M. E., and DOAK, D. F. (1993), 'The keystone-species concept in ecology and conservation', *BioScience*, 43(4): 219–24.

MILSTEIN, M. (1995), *Wolf: Return to Yellowstone* (Billings, Mont.: The Billings Gazette).

MILTON, K. (2000), 'Ducks out of water: nature conservation as boundary maintenance', in J. Knight (ed.), *Natural Enemies: People–Wildlife Conflicts in Anthropological Perspective* (London and New York: Routledge), 229–46.

MISHRA, C. (1997), 'Livestock depredation by large carnivores in the Indian trans-Himalaya: conflict perceptions and conservation prospects', *Environmental Conservation*, 24(4): 338–43.

MIYAZAWA, K. (1993), *Once and Forever: The Tales of Kenji Miyazawa*, trans. J. Bester (Tokyo: Kodansha International).

MLOT, C. (1993), 'Isle Royale: end of an era?', *Science*, 261: 1115.

MOLL, J. P. (1994), 'Western Influences on the Management of Brown Bears in Hokkaido, Japan', M. Sc. diss., University of Montana.

MOON, O. (1989), *From Paddyfield to Ski-slope: The Revitalization of Tradition in Japanese Village Life* (Manchester: Manchester University Press).

MOORE, R. S. (1994), 'Metaphors of encroachment: hunting for wolves on a central Greek mountain', *Anthropological Quarterly*, 67(2): 81–8.

MORRIS, B. (1998), *The Power of Animals: An Ethnography* (Oxford: Berg).

MOULTON, M. P., and SANDERSON, J. (1997), *Wildlife Issues in a Changing World* (Delray Beach, Fla.: St Lucie Press).

MULLIN, M. (1999), 'Mirrors and windows: sociocultural studies of human–animal relationships', *Annual Review of Anthropology*, 28: 201–24.

MUNRO, N. G. (1962), *Ainu Creed and Cult*, ed. with a preface by B. Z. Seligman (London: Routledge and Kegan Paul).

NAKAGOSHI, N. (1995), 'Pine forests in East Asia', in E. O. Box (ed.), *Vegetation Science in Forestry: Global Perspective Based on Forest Ecosystems of East and South-East Asia* (Dordrecht: Kluwer Academic Publishers), 85–104.

NAUGHTON-TREVES, L. (1998), 'Predicting patterns of crop damage by wildlife around Kibale National Park, Uganda', *Conservation Biology*, 12(1): 156–68.

NAUMANN, N. (1963), 'Yama no kami', *Asian Folklore Studies*, 22: 133–366 (in German, with English summary 341–9).

—— (1974), 'Whale and fish cult in Japan: a basic feature of Ebisu worship', *Asian Folklore Studies*, 33(1): 1–15.

NEWSOME, A. E. (1991), 'Environmental facilitation of regulatory predation by carnivores on wildlife including vertebrate pests', in N. Maruyama, B. Bobek, Y. Ono, W. Regelin, L. Bartos, and P. R. Ratcliffe (eds.), *Wildlife Conservation: Present Trends and Perspectives for the Twenty-first Century* (Tsukuba: Japan Wildlife Research Center), 42–7.

NIIDE, M. (1994), 'Rice imports and implications', *Japan Quarterly*, 41(1): 16–24.

NOSS, R. F., QUIGLEY, H. B., HORNOCKER, M. G., MERRILL, T., and PAQUET, P. C. (1996), 'Conservation biology and carnivore conservation in the Rocky Mountains', *Conservation Biology*, 10(4): 949–63.

NOWAK, R. M. (1983), 'A perspective on the taxonomy of wolves in North America', in L. N. Carbyn (ed.), *Wolves in Canada and Alaska: Their Status, Biology, and Management* (Ottawa: Canadian Wildlife Service), 10–19.

—— (1995), 'Another look at wolf taxonomy', in L. N. Carbyn, S. H. Fritts, and D. R. Seip (eds.), *Ecology and Conservation of Wolves in a Changing World* (Edmonton: Canadian Circumpolar Institute), 375–97.

NYHOLM, E. S., and NYHOLM, K.-E. (1999), 'Status and management of the brown bear in Finland', in C. Servheen, S. Herrero, and B. Peyton (eds.), *Bears* (Gland, Switzerland: IUCN), 63–7.

OCHIAI, K., NAKAMA, S., HANAWA, S., and AMAGASA, T. (1993a), 'Population dynamics of Japanese serow in relation to social organization and habitat conditions. I. Stability of Japanese serow density in stable habitat conditions', *Ecological Research*, 8: 11–18.

—— (1993b), 'Population dynamics of Japanese serow in relation to social organization and habitat conditions. II. Effects of clear-cutting and planted tree growth on Japanese serow populations', *Ecological Research*, 8: 19–25.

OELSCHLAEGER, M. (1991), *The Idea of Wilderness: From Prehistory to the Age of Ecology* (New Haven and London: Yale University Press).

OGURA, T. (1979), *Can Japanese Agriculture Survive?* (Tokyo: Agricultural Policy Research Center).

OHNUKI-TIERNEY, E. (1987), *The Monkey as Mirror: Symbolic Transformations in Japanese History and Ritual* (Princeton: Princeton University Press).

—— (1990), 'Monkey as metaphor? Transformations of a polytropic symbol in Japanese culture', *Man*, 25(1): 89–107.

—— (1991), 'Embedding and transforming polytrope: the monkey as self in Japanese culture', in J. W. Fernandez (ed.), *Beyond Metaphor: The Theory of Tropes in Anthropology* (Stanford, Calif.: Stanford University Press), 159–89.

—— (1993), *Rice as Self: Japanese Identities through Time* (Princeton: Princeton University Press).

OHTSUKA, K. (1999), 'Tourism, assimilation, and Ainu survival today', in W. W. Fitzhugh and C. Q. Dubreuil (eds.), *Ainu: Spirit of a Northern People* (Washington: National Museum of Natural History, Smithsonian Institution, in association with the University of Washington Press), 92–5.

OKUMURA, N., ISHIGURO, N., NAKANO, M., MATSUI, A., and SAHARA, M. (1996), 'Intra- and interbreed genetic variations of mitochondrial DNA major non-coding regions in Japanese native dog breeds (*Canis familiaris*)', *Animal Genetics*, 27: 397–405.

OLIVER, W. L. R., BRISBIN, JR. I. L., and TAKAHASHI, S. (1993), 'The Eurasian wild pig (*Sus scrofa*)', in W. L. R. Oliver (ed.), *Pigs, Peccaries and Hippos* (Gland, Switzerland: IUCN), 112–21.

ÖLSCHLEGER, H.-D. (1999), 'Technology, settlement, and hunting ritual', in W. Fitzhugh and C. O. Dubreuil (eds.), *Ainu: Spirit of a Northern People* (Washington: National Museum of Natural History, Smithsonian Institution, in association with the University of Washington Press), 208–21.

O'NEILL, R. V. (2001), 'Is it time to bury the ecosystem concept? (With full military honors, of course!)', *Ecology*, 82(12): 3275–84.

OZAKI, Y. T. (1970), *The Japanese Fairy Book* (Tokyo: Charles E. Tuttle).

PALMER, E. (1983), 'Rural Depopulation in Post-war Japan, with Reference to Remote Rural Settlements of the Tajima Region', Ph.D. diss., SOAS, University of London.

PARRISH, A. M. (1995), ' "There were no *sus* in the old days": post-harvest pest management in an Egyptian oasis village', *Human Organization*, 54(2): 195–204.

PAVLIK, S. (1999), 'San Carlos and White Mountain Apache attitudes toward the reintroduction of the Mexican wolf to its historic range in the American Southwest', *Wicazo Sa Review*, 14(1): 129–45.

PAYSTRUP, P. (1993), 'The Wolf at Yellowstone's Door: Extending and Applying the Cultural Approach to Risk Communication to an Endangered Species Recovery Plan Controversy', Ph.D. diss., Purdue University.

PETERSON, R. O. (1995), *The Wolves of Isle Royale: A Broken Balance* (Minocqua, Wis.: Willow Creek Press).

——PAGE, R. E., and DODGE, K. M. (1984), 'Wolves, moose, and the allometry of population cycles', *Science*, 224: 1350–2.

——THOMAS, N. J., THURBER, J. M., VUCETICH, J. A., and WAITE, T. A. (1998), 'Population limitation and the wolves of Isle Royale', *Journal of Mammalogy*, 79(3): 828–41.

PEYTON, B., *et al.* (1999), 'Status and management of the spectacled bear in Peru', in C. Servheen, S. Herrero, and B. Peyton (eds.), *Bears* (Gland, Switzerland: IUCN), 182–93.

PHILLIPS, M. K. (1996*a*), 'Into the future', in M. K. Phillips and D. W. Smith, *The Wolves of Yellowstone* (Stillwater, Minn.: Voyageur Press), 117–23.

——(1996*b*), 'A strategy for restoring wolves', in M. K. Phillips and D. W. Smith, *The Wolves of Yellowstone* (Stillwater, Minn.: Voyageur Press), 25–32.

PRIMM, S. A., and CLARK, T. W. (1996), 'Making sense of the policy process for carnivore conservation', *Conservation Biology*, 10(4): 1036–45.

PUTMAN, R. J. (1989), 'Introduction: mammals as pests', in R. J. Putman (ed.), *Mammals as Pests* (London and New York: Chapman and Hall), 1–20.

QUIGLEY, H. B., and HORNOCKER, M. G. (1992), 'Large carnivore ecology: from where do we come and to where do we go?', in D. R. McCullough and R. H. Barrett (eds.), *Wildlife 2001: Populations* (London and New York: Elsevier Applied Science), 1089–97.

RABINOWITZ, A. (2000), *Jaguar: One Man's Struggle to Establish the World's First Jaguar Preserve* (Washington: Island Press).

RANGARAJAN, M. (1996), *The Politics of Ecology: The Debate on Wildlife and People in India, 1970–95*, Occasional Papers on Perspectives in Indian Development, Number LI (New Delhi: Nehru Memorial Museum and Library).

REIMOSER, F., and GOSSOW, H. (1996), 'Impact of ungulates on forest vegetation and its dependence on the silvicultural system', *Forest Ecology and Management*, 88(1–2): 107–19.

ROBBINS, J. (1997), 'In two years, wolves reshaped Yellowstone', *New York Times*, 30 Dec. 1997, F1–F2.

ROBERTSON, J. (1998), 'It takes a village: internationalization and nostalgia in postwar Japan', in S. Vlastos (ed.), *Mirror of Modernity: Invented Traditions of Modern Japan* (Berkeley: University of California Press), 110–29.

ROBINSON, W. L., and BOLEN, E. G. (1989), *Wildlife Ecology and Management*, 2nd edn. (New York: Macmillan and London: Collier Macmillan).

RODRIGUEZ DE LA FUENTE, F. (1975), 'Protection of the wolf in Spain: notes on a public awareness campaign', in D. H. Pimlott (ed.), *Wolves: Proceedings of the First Working Meeting of Wolf Specialists and of the First International Conference on Conservation of the Wolf* (Morges, Switzerland: IUCN Publications), 103–12.

ROEBROEKS, W. (1995), ' "Policing the Boundary"? Continuity of discussions in nineteenth and twentieth century paleoanthropology', in R. Corbey and B. Theunissen (eds.), *Ape, Man, Apeman: Changing Views since 1600* (Leiden: Dept. of Prehistory, Leiden University), 173–9.

ROMANO, B. (1995), 'National parks policy and mountain depopulation: a case study in the Abruzzo region of the Central Appenines, Italy', *Mountain Research and Development*, 15(2): 121–32.

RUTBERG, A. T. (1997), 'The science of deer management: an animal welfare perspective', in W. J. McShea, H. B. Underwood, and J. H. Rappole (eds.), *The Science of Overabundance: Deer Ecology and Population Management* (Washington and London: Smithsonian Institution Press), 37–54.

RYE, S. (2000), 'Wild pigs, "pig-men" and transmigrants in the rainforest of Sumatra', in J. Knight (ed.), *Natural Enemies: People–Wildlife Conflicts in Anthropological Perspective* (London and New York: Routledge), 104–23.

SAKAMOTO, H. (1983), 'Wolf, Japanese', *Kodansha Encyclopedia of Japan* (Tokyo: Kodansha), 255–6.

SATOW, E. M., and HAWES, A. G. S. (1884), *Murray's Handbook for Japan: A Handbook for Travellers in Central and Northern Japan*, 2nd edn. (London: John Murray).

SCHALLER, G. B. (1972), *The Serengeti Lion: A Study of Predator–Prey Relations* (Chicago and London: University of Chicago Press).

SEIDENSTICKER, J., and MCDOUGAL, C. (1993), 'Tiger predatory behaviour, ecology and conservation', in N. Dunstone and M. L. Gorman (eds.), *Mammals as Predators* (Oxford: Clarendon Press), 105–25.

SEIP, D. R. (1992), 'Wolf predation, wolf control and the management of ungulate populations', in D. R. McCullough and R. H. Barrett (eds.), *Wildlife 2001: Populations* (London and New York: Elsevier Applied Science), 331–40.

SEKHAR, N. U. (1998), 'Crop and livestock depredation caused by wild animals in protected areas: the case of Sariska Tiger Reserve, Rajasthan, India', *Environmental Conservation*, 25(2): 160–71.

SEKI, K. (1966), 'Types of Japanese folktales', *Asian Folklore Studies*, 25(1): 1–211 (special issue).

SERPELL, J. (1996 [1986]), *In the Company of Animals: A Study of Human–Animal Relationships* (Cambridge: Cambridge University Press).

SHANKLIN, E. (1985), 'Sustenance and symbol: anthropological studies of domesticated animals', *Annual Review of Anthropology*, 14: 375–403.

SINCLAIR, A. R. E. (1997), 'Carrying capacity and the overabundance of deer: a framework for management', in W. J. McShea, H. B. Underwood, and J. H. Rappole (eds.), *The Science of Overabundance: Deer Ecology and Population Management* (Washington and London: Smithsonian Institution Press), 380–94.

SINGER, P. (1990), *Animal Liberation*, 2nd edn. (London: Thorsons).

SMITH, D. W. (1996), 'Kills', in M. K. Phillips and D. W. Smith, *The Wolves of Yellowstone* (Stillwater, Minn.: Voyageur Press), 85–91.

SMITH, T. C. (1977), *Nakahara: Family Farming and Population in a Japanese Village, 1717–1830*, with R. Y. Eng and R. T. Lundy (Stanford, Calif.: Stanford University Press).

SOMA, H. (1987), 'Preface', in H. Soma (ed.), *The Biology and Management of Capricornis and Related Mountain Antelopes* (London: Croom Helm), p. xi.

SPRAGUE, D. S. (1992), 'Life history male intertroop mobility among Japanese macaques (*Macaca fuscata*)', *International Journal of Primatology*, 13(4): 437–54.

—— (1993), 'Applying GIS and remote sensing to wildlife management in Japan: assessing habitat quality for the Japanese monkey (Macaca fuscata), *NIAES Chikyū Chiimu Kenkyū Shuroku*, 3: 89–100.

—— SUZUKI, S., and TSUKAHARA, T. (1996), 'Variation in social mechanisms by which males attained the alpha rank among Japanese macaques', in J. E. Fa and D. G. Lindburg (eds.), *Evolution and Ecology of Macaque Societies* (Cambridge: Cambridge University Press), 444–58.

SPRINGTHORPE, G. D., and MYHILL, N. G. (1994), *Wildlife Rangers Handbook* (London: Forestry Commission).

STEINHART, P. (1989), 'Taming our fear of predators', *National Wildlife*, 27(2): 4–13.

—— (1995), *The Company of Wolves* (New York: Vintage Books).

STRUM, S. C. (1994), 'Prospects for management of primate pests', *Revue d'Ecologie*, 49(3): 295–306.

SUNSERI, T. (1997), 'Famine and wild pigs: gender struggles and the outbreak of the Majimaji War in Uzaramo (Tanzania)', *Journal of African History*, 38(2): 235–59.

SUZUKI, B. (1986), *Snow Country Tales: Life in the Other Japan*, trans. J. Hunter with R. Lester (New York and Tokyo: Weatherhill).

TAKAHASHI, N., and MARUYAMA, N. (n.d.), *Is There Room Left for Reintroduced Wolves in Japan?*, paper (in author's possession) presented to the conference *Coexistence of Large Carnivores with Man*, Saitama.

TAKATSUKI, S. (1989), 'Edge effects created by clear-cutting on habitat use by sika deer on Mt. Goyo, northern Honshu, Japan', *Ecological Research*, 4: 287–95.

—— (1991), 'Food habits of sika deer in Japan with reference to dwarf bamboo in northern Japan', in N. Maruyama, B. Bobek, Y. Ono, W. Regelin, L. Bartos, and P. R. Ratcliffe (eds.), *Wildlife Conservation: Present Trends and Perspectives for the Twenty-first Century* (Tsukuba: Japan Wildlife Research Center), 200–4.

TALBOT, L. M. (1978), 'The role of predators in ecosystem management', in M. W. Holdgate and M. J. Woodman (eds.), *The Breakdown and Restoration of Ecosystems* (New York and London: Plenum Press), 307–19.

TAMANOI, M. A. (1998), *Under the Shadow of Nationalism: Politics and Poetics of Rural Japanese Women* (Honolulu: University of Hawaii Press).

TAMBIAH, S. J. (1969), 'Animals are good to think and good to prohibit', *Ethnology*, 8(4): 423–59.

TELLERÍA, J. L., and SÁEZ-ROYUELA, C. (1984), 'The large mammals of Central Spain: an introductory view', *Mammal Review*, 14(2): 51–6.

TERBORGH, J. (1988), 'The big things that run the world—a sequel to E. O. Wilson', *Conservation Biology*, 2: 402–3.

—— (1992*a*), *Diversity and the Tropical Rain Forest* (New York: Scientific American Library).

—— (1992*b*), 'Maintenance of diversity in tropical forests', *Biotropica*, 24: 283–92.

TOTMAN, C. (1989), *The Green Archipelago: Forestry in Preindustrial Japan* (Berkeley: University of California Press).

TURNER, T. (1991), ' "We are parrots", "twins are birds": play of tropes as operational structure', in J. W. Fernandez (ed.), *Beyond Metaphor: The Theory of Tropes in Anthropology* (Stanford, Calif.: Stanford University Press), 121–58.

UENO, M. (1987), 'The last wolf of Japan' (in English), reproduced in Higashi Yoshino Mura (ed.), *Maboroshi no nihonōkami—nihonōkami ni kansuru shiryō* (*The Phantom Japanese Wolf: Materials on the Japanese Wolf*) (Higashi Yoshino: Kyōiku Iinkai), 24.

UMEBAYASHI, M., and OYA, K. (1993), 'Participatory forest development and management: the Japanese experience', *Regional Development Dialogue*, 14(1): 202–18.

VERCAMMEN, P., SEYDACK, A. H. W., and OLIVER, W. L. R. (1993), 'The bush pigs (*Potamochoerus porcus* and *P. larvatus*)', in W. L. R. Oliver (ed.), *Pigs, Peccaries, and Hippos* (Gland, Switzerland: IUCN), 93–101.

WATANABE, H. (1972), *The Ainu Ecosystem: Environment and Group Structure* (Tokyo: University of Tokyo Press).

WATANABE, H. (1980), 'Damage to conifers by the black bear', in C. J. Martinka and K. L. McArthur (eds.), *Bears: Their Biology and Management* (*International Conference of Bear Research and Management* 4), Bear Biology Association Conference Series (Morges, Switzerland: IUCN), 67–70.

—— (1981), 'Black bear damage to artificial regeneration in Japan: conflict between control and preservation', in IUFRO (ed.), *XVII IUFRO World Congress Proceedings* (Kyoto: International Union of Forest Research Organizations), 581–5.

WATANABE, M. (1974), 'The conception of nature in Japanese culture', *Science*, 183: 279–82.

WEERASINGHE, U. R., and TAKATSUKI, S. (1999), 'A record of acorn eating by sika deer in western Japan', *Ecological Research*, 14: 205–9.

WESSING, R. (1986), *The Soul of Ambiguity: The Tiger in Southeast Asia* (Urbana, Ill.: Center for Southeast Asian Studies, Northern Illinois University).

WESTERN, D. (1989), 'Conservation without parks: wildlife in the rural landscape', in D. Western and M. Pearl (eds.), *Conservation for the Twenty-first Century* (New York and Oxford: Oxford University Press), 158–65.

WILLIS, R. (1990), 'Introduction', in R. Willis (ed.), *Signifying Animals: Human Meaning in the Natural World* (London and New York: Routledge), 1–24.

WOLFHEIM, J. H. (1983), *Primates of the World: Distribution, Abundance and Conservation* (Seattle: University of Washington Press).

WORSTER, D. (1977), *Nature's Economy: A History of Ecological Ideas* (Cambridge: Cambridge University Press).

YONEDA, M. (1991), 'The status of the Asian black bear in the western part of Japan', in N. Maruyama, B. Bobek, Y. Ono, W. Regelin, L. Bartos, and P. R. Ratcliffe (eds.), *Wildlife Conservation: Present Trends and Perspectives for the Twenty-first Century* (Tsukuba: Japan Wildlife Research Center), 148–52.

YUIZE, Y. (1978), 'Truth about Japanese agriculture', *Japan Quarterly*, 25(3): 264–97.

Newsletters

Asian Primates (1992), Maruhashi, T., Sprague, D. S., and Matsubayashi, K., 'What future for Japanese monkeys?' Primate Society of Japan. Vol. 2 No. 1.

Japan Primate Newsletter (*JPN*) (July 1993), 'Monkeys attack people'. Primate Society of Japan.

—— (Apr. 1994), 'Protected monkeys may be captured again'. Primate Society of Japan.

—— (Nov. 1995), 'Mass culling of hot spring monkeys in Shiga Heights'. Primate Society of Japan.

INDEX

Bold numbers denote reference to illustrations